Chess Skill in Man and Machine

Chess Skill
in Man
and Machine

Edited by

Peter W. Frey

With 104 Illustrations

Springer-Verlag
New York   Berlin   Heidelberg   Tokyo

Peter W. Frey
Northwestern University
CRESAP Laboratory of Neuroscience
  and Behavior
2021 Sheridan Road
Evanston, Illinois 60201
USA

AMS Subject Classification: 68-02, 68A45
(C.R.) Computing Classification: 3.64

Library of Congress Cataloging in Publication Data
Main entry under title:
Chess skill in man and machine.
  Bibliography: p.
  Includes index.
  1. Chess—Data processing—Addresses, essays, lectures.
  1. Frey, Peter W. (Peter William), 1942–
GV1318.C45 1984 794.1'7   82–19474

Typeset by Maryland Linotype, Baltimore, Maryland.
Printed and bound by Halliday Lithograph, Plympton, Massachusetts.
Printed in the United States of America.

This book is also available in a clothbound edition within
Texts and Monographs in Computer Science, *Chess Skill in
Man and Machine, Second Edition.*

9 8 7 6 5 4 3 2 1

ISBN 0–387–90790–4 Springer-Verlag New York Berlin Heidelberg Tokyo (hardcover)
ISBN 3–540–90790–4 Springer-Verlag Berlin Heidelberg New York Tokyo (hardcover)
ISBN 0–387–90815–3 Springer-Verlag New York Berlin Heidelberg Tokyo (softcover)
ISBN 3–540–90815–3 Springer-Verlag Berlin Heidelberg New York Tokyo (softcover)

This volume is dedicated to my wife, Ruth, and my family, and to my colleagues whose contributions made this volume possible. I am especially indebted to David Slate whose comments and suggestions greatly improved the final version of this book.

Preface

Ten years of intensive effort on computer chess have produced notable progress. Although the background information and technical details that were written in 1975 for the first edition of this book are still valid in most essential points, hardware and software refinements have had a major impact on the effectiveness of these ideas. The current crop of chess machines are performing at unexpectedly high levels. The approach epitomized by the series of programs developed by David Slate and Larry Atkin at Northwestern in the middle 1970s (i.e., a sophisticated search algorithm using very little chess knowledge) was expected to reach an asymptotic level of performance no higher than that of a class A player (USCF rating between 1800 and 2000). This perspective was argued quite vigorously by Eliot Hearst in Chapter 8 of the first edition and was held at that time by many chess experts. Subsequent events have clearly demonstrated that the asymptotic performance level for this type of program it at least as high as the master level (USCF rating between 2200 and 2400). Current discussions now focus upon whether the earlier reservations were wrong in principle or simply underestimated the asymptote. If there is a real barrier which will prevent this type of program from attaining a world championship level of performance, it is not evident from the steady progress which has been observed during the last decade.

The second edition of *Chess Skill in Man and Machine* includes new material highlighting recent developments. A newly added Appendix includes a summary of recent games selected by David Slate which characterize the current level of achievement in machine chess. In addition, the new appendix provides information about the International Computer Chess Association, the establishment of several major prizes for chess programs, and developments in microcomputer chess. The bibliography has also been greatly expanded.

The second edition also keeps pace with the development of new ideas with the addition of two chapters. These chapters extend the debate initiated by their predecessors concerning the relative merits of search-based and knowledge-based programs. In Chapter 9, Ken Thompson and Joe Condon describe the architecture and inner workings of Belle, the current world champion and the most effective example of a search-intensive program. In Chapter 10, David Wilkins provides information about his program, PARADISE, which is currently the most impressive example of a knowledge-intensive chess program. PARADISE solves deep tactical positions by using a highly focused search. The different approach used by these two programs is emphasized by the number of nodes each examines in analyzing a position. PARADISE generates several hundred nodes, while Belle generates more than ten million. The ideas expressed in these new chapters provide two fascinating perspectives on an issue which is crucial to further developments in computer chess. In its general form, this issue has important ramifications for the entire field of artificial intelligence and will be the subject of active debates for many years.

Evanston, Illinois   PETER W. FREY
May, 1982

Contents

Contents

Chess Skill in Man and Machine

A brief history of the computer chess tournaments: 1970–1975

Benjamin Mittman
Northwestern University

Game annotations by Craig Chellstorp

Introduction

At the time of writing this chapter (March 1976), ten major computer chess tournaments have been held, six in the United States (1970–1975) sponsored by the Association for Computing Machinery (ACM), one in Sweden (1974) sponsored by the International Federation for Information Processing (IFIP), two in Canada (1974 and 1975) and one in Germany (1975). These unique events have attracted worldwide attention (and sometimes amused interest) from the chess-playing public and from specialists in computer science and artificial intelligence. These tournaments have also been an arena for many formal and informal discussions among the leading chess programmers in the world and therefore have been a vital stimulus for research and development. Several of the authors in this volume (Harris, Newborn, and Slate and Atkin) have been regular participants in these events.

This chapter reviews the background of these tournaments, presents the results for some of the more noteworthy games, and concludes with a brief discussion of the significance of the tournaments. Monroe Newborn and the author have organized most of the championships. Professor Newborn was the originator of the first tournament in New York in 1970 and has been a prime mover for all of the ACM and the IFIP-sponsored events. In addition, he has served as a fund raiser, a participant, a rule maker, and an arbiter. David Levy has also played a major role, lending his chess skill, wisdom, and wit to his official role as Tournament Director in each of the last five U.S. championships and in the first World championship. But perhaps the most deserving of appreciation are the dozens of inspired chess programmers who brought their creations to compete in New York, Chicago, Boston, Atlanta, Waterloo, Stockholm, San Diego, Edmonton,

Dortmund, and Minneapolis. The history which follows is a record of their tireless efforts to program a machine to play chess as well as a man.

Background

A computer chess tournament matches computer chess programs against each other. The rules of play are almost identical to human tournaments. The U.S. and World tournaments have been run during the annual ACM conferences and at the IFIP Congress in 1974. The tournament sites have been hotel ballrooms which were equipped with computer terminals, telephones, chess clocks, display boards and all the other paraphenalia which accompany any chess tournament (see Figure 1.1). The programs are generally run on computers located at the home institutions of the participants. These computers are connected to the tournament site via time-sharing terminals and/or voice telephone communication. Participants who have developed their programs on minicomputers sometimes bring their small machines with them to the tournament site.

The tournaments have been run according to rules of the Swiss system, with three or more rounds. With this procedure, no team is eliminated. To illustrate how the system works, assume a tournament in which 12 programs have been entered. The programs are ranked initially by the tournament director and organizers from 1 to 12, according to their anticipated strength, with past performances and/or sample games as criteria for this ranking. In the first round, the program ranked 1 is matched against program 7, program 2 against program 8, etc. After each round, teams with identical or near identical scores are paired. One point is awarded for a win, ½ point for a draw, and 0 points for a loss. At the end of the tournament, the program with the most points is the winner. During the computer chess tournaments, there have always been clear winners; however, it has sometimes been necessary to break ties for second and third place by scheduling play-off games or by using other tie-breaking methods.

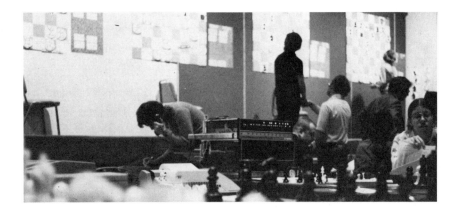

Figure 1.1 The 1975 ACM Computer Chess Championship, Minneapolis.

One aspect of a computer chess championship which contrasts sharply with human tournaments is the absence of reverent silence. Since the moves are being calculated by machines (often several hundreds or thousands of miles away from the tournament site), the human participants usually sit by their terminals and openly discuss their predictions for their computer's next move or try to explain why the previous move was made. As each move is communicated to the terminal, the operator makes the move on the chess board in front of him, punches his chess clock, and records the move. His opponent then types the move into his terminal, so that his program can begin computing its response. And so it goes—each time one of the computers completes its calculations, the move is displayed on the terminal, the operator then makes the move on the board, his opponent inputs that move through his terminal, the other computer calculates a response and then transmits it to its terminal, etc.

These activities go on simultaneously at several boards. The tournament director (an international chessmaster) augments these activities by providing a running commentary for all observers, discussing tactical maneuvers, potential traps, etc. with the aid of large display boards (see Figure 1.2). Audience participation has become a lively characteristic of all these tournaments. Members of the audience vocally second guess the tournament director; the audience joins the fray; they laugh; they talk; they boo; they applaud; they heckle. This is one of the factors which has drawn hundreds of spectators to the tournament each evening. Another reason is, of course, the curious phenomenon of computers trying to play chess.

Figure 1.2 David Levy, Tournament Director, comments on White's losing position in SORTIE vs. CHESS 4.4 of Round 1. The game ended as follows: (25) . . . B–B4; (26) K–N1 RxP; (27) RxR, RxR; (28) P–N4, R–R8ch; (29) K–N2, N–B5ch; (30) K–N3, R–QN8 mate.

These tournaments have been played under a uniform set of rules. Games are played at a speed of 40 moves per program in the first two hours and then 10 moves every 30 minutes thereafter. The tournament director has the right to adjudicate a game after five hours of elapsed time. If a team encounters technical difficulties (machine failure, communications failure or error, or program failure), the tournament director may allow them to stop their clock as long as necessary, but not to exceed 30 minutes, in order to restore their system. The tournament director may grant a team permission to stop their clock three times during the course of a game, but the *total* time for such stoppages may not exceed 30 minutes.

There may be no manual adjustment of program parameters during the course of a game. In the case of failures, the program parameters must be reset to their original settings if it is at all possible. Information regarding castling status, *en passant* status, etc., may be typed in after a failure. If the computer asks for the time remaining on its clock or its opponent's clock, this information may be provided. However, the computer must initiate the request for information.

The tournaments

In a brief chapter such as this it is not possible to cover all the tournaments nor to present all the game scores. The present summary necessarily had to focus on the highlights and therefore many exciting games are not cited. The interested reader should consult Professor Newborn's recent book [73] which provides a detailed account of the first four National tournaments as well as commentary and game scores for the early International competitions.

The first computer/computer chess match was held in 1966 and 1967 between a Soviet program developed at the Institute of Theoretical and Experimental Physics in Moscow and a U.S. program developed at Stanford University. Four games were played simultaneously with moves being communicated by telegraph. The match started in November 1966, continued into 1967, and ended with a three-points-to-one victory for the Soviet program (two wins, two draws).

It was not until 1970 that a full-fledged tournament was organized by Prof. Newborn at the 1970 ACM Annual Conference in New York, August 31 to September 1. By this time a number of programs had been developed in the United States and there was a great deal of interest in comparing their relative strengths. One of the first hurdles to be overcome was to develop a tournament format which would be interesting to watch and which would also provide a reasonable measure of comparison. I quote from Prof. Newborn's book [73, p. 51]:

> The rules that governed play were formulated several weeks before the tournament. Meeting to decide on the rules were Keith Gorlen, Dennis Cooper, Tony Marsland, and the author. The rules were relatively easy to agree upon with the exception of one. We all

agreed that each computer should be required to make all its moves within some arbitrary time allotment, but Marsland felt that the allotment given to each computer should depend on the speed of the computer; faster computers should receive less time than slower ones. The rest of us felt that it would be impossible to handicap the computers fairly; there were other factors besides speed that made one computer "better" than another. Thus, while it certainly was not the ideal solution for all involved, it was decided that all computers should receive equal amounts of time to make their moves. A rate of 40 moves in the first two hours and 10 moves every subsequent half hour was agreed upon. The rules also included time-out provisions in the case of system failures, communication failures, etc. These time-outs were frequently used in the 1970 and somewhat less in the 1971, 1972, and 1973 tournaments.

So, in 1970 this first tournament was held. It attracted six participants. Computers from Illinois, Texas, New Jersey, and two in New York City were connected to the Hilton Hotel by telephone. One minicomputer was at the tournament site. The atmosphere was captured by Prof. Newborn [73, p. 52] as follows:

> At 5:30 each evening the games were scheduled to begin, but more typically they began around 6 P.M. It was a rare event throughout the tournament when all three games were simultaneously in progress. Almost always at least one computer was having difficulties. However, in general, the better programs were more reliable, and in turn the better games usually had fewer interruptions. Each evening there were several hundred spectators in attendance, including computer specialists and chess experts. The most notable chess experts were Pal Benko, one of the top players in the United States, who seemed somewhat unsure of the future potential of computers in the chess world, and Al Horowitz, former chess editor of the New York Times, a long-time skeptic regarding their potential.

> Throughout the tournament there was a most casual and informal atmosphere in the Rhinelander Room. Good moves were met with cheers from the audience; bad moves were hissed. The programmers discussed moves they expected their computers to make, reporters interviewed the participants, and Berliner ate his sandwiches. Berliner, an old pro of the human chess tournament circuit, came well stocked with food each evening.

After the success of what was called "The First United States Computer Chess Championship," the ACM sponsored and the U.S. Chess Federation sanctioned championships in 1971 (Chicago), 1972 (Boston), 1973 (Atlanta), 1974 (San Diego), and 1975 (Minneapolis). In 1974, Mr. James Parry of the University of Waterloo organized the First Canadian Computer Chess Championship. Also in 1974, Mr. David Levy, Prof. Newborn and the author organized the First World Computer Chess Championship in Stockholm. In 1975, another Canadian tournament was

5

held during the 1975 Canadian Open Chess Championships in Edmonton, Alberta, and the first German tournament was organized in Dortmund, with eight German programs competing. Summaries of many of these tournaments, including game scores, have appeared in the ACM SIGART Newsletter, a periodic publication of the Special Interest Group on Artificial Intelligence.

The reader may judge the progress which has been made in the past decade in chess programming by examining the game scores which follow, starting with the Soviet Union vs. USA match in 1966–67 and going to the latest (1975) ACM tournament. These game scores have been annotated by Craig Chellstorp, one of America's promising young senior masters.

The Soviet Union vs. USA match, 1966–67

In late 1966 and early 1967, a chess match was arranged between a Soviet program and an American program. The third game in this four game match was surprisingly well played. Since each game was played by correspondence, each computer used considerably more time for move-calculation than the 3 minute limit which is characteristic of the later tournaments.

WHITE Program from the Institute of Theoretical and Experimental Physics, Moscow [Soviet M-20 Computer]		BLACK Kotok-McCarthy Program, Stanford [IBM 7090]	
1. P–K4	P–K4	2. N–KB3	N–QB3
3. N–B3	B–B4	4. NxP!	

Giving White a slight advantage.

4. . . .	NxN	5. P–Q4	B–Q3
6. PxN	BxP	7. P–B4	BxN+
8. PxB	N–B3	9. P–K5	N–K5
10. Q–Q3	N–B4?		

Better is (10) . . . P–KB4; (11) PxPep., NxP, with equality.

11. Q–Q5	N–K3?

After this move Black is lost. Necessary is (11) . . . P–Q3; (12) PxP, QxP! leaving White only slightly better.

12. P–B5	N–N4

Loses a piece but (12) . . . N–B1; (13) B–QB4, Q–K2; (14) B–QR3, P–Q3; (15) O–O is also hopeless for Black.

13. P–KR4	P–KB3	14. PxN	PxP(N4)
15. RxP!			

The most efficient; the rest is an execution.

15. . . .	R–B1	16. RxP	P–B3
17. Q–Q6	RxP	18. R–N8+	R–B1
19. QxR mate			

First United States computer chess championship (New York, 1970)

The first tournament contained the kinds of elements which have made these tournaments always exciting, and sometimes frustrating: great expectations from Hans Berliner's program J. Biit (Just Because It Is There), some delays due to software and hardware problems, a program with a bug that caused it to select the worst, rather than the best, moves, and occasionally, some solid chess. The tournament director was Jacques Dutka, a mathematician and former chess master. The program, CHESS 3.0, developed by Larry Atkin, Keith Gorlen, and David Slate of Northwestern University won the tournament with three points.

In the first round, Berliner's program, J. Biit, was paired against Marsland's program. This game has the dubious distinction of making the *New York Times* (Sept. 2, 1970) in a story headlined as "Chess computer loses game in king-size blunder."

WHITE The Marsland Program		**BLACK J. Biit**	
[Burroughs B5500]		**[IBM 360/91]**	
1. P–QB4	N–KB3	2. P–Q4	P–K3
3. Q–Q3?			

Too early for this queen sortie. (3) N–QB3 is more natural.

| 3. . . . | N–B3 | 4. N–KB3 | P–Q4 |
| 5. N–K5? | | | |

Moving the piece twice so early in the game costs a pawn; (5) P–K3 was still equal.

| 5. . . . | PxP | 6. QxP(B4) | B–N5+? |

Stronger was simply (6) . . . QxP.

| 7. B–Q2 | BxB+ | 8. KxB?? | |

Strange! After the natural (8) NxB, NxQP; (9) P–K3, White would have a little development as compensation for the pawn.

| 8. . . . | NxN | 9. Q–B5 | N–K5+ |
| 10. Resigns! | | | |

After (10) . . . NxQ, all of White's developed pieces will have been captured!

7

In the second round, the tournament favorite, J. Biit, was paired with a relatively unheralded program written by three students from Northwestern University. CHESS 3.0 played surprisingly well and won the game and eventually the tournament.

WHITE J. Biit		BLACK CHESS 3.0	
[IBM 360/91]		[CDC 6400]	
1. P–Q4	N–KB3	2. P–QB4	P–K3
3. N–QB3	B–N5	4. P–K3	BxN+
5. PxB	N–B3	6. P–Q5	N–K2
7. PxP	P(B2)xP	8. R–N1	N–B3
9. B–Q3	Q–K2	10. N–B3	P–K4
11. B–B5	P–K5	12. N–Q4	Q–B4

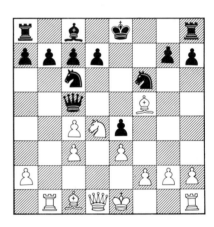

Figure 1.3 Position after (12) N–Q4, Q–B4. J. Biit (White) vs. CHESS 3.0 (Black), New York City, 1970.

13. R–N5?

After an interesting opening White begins to go astray. Better is (13) N–N5, K–Q1; (14) B–KR3, with complications.

13. . . .	QxP	14. Q–N3	QxQ
15. PxQ	NxN		
16. P(K3)xN	O–O?		

The king is safe in the center. Better is (16) . . . P–B3, and if (17) R–K5+, K–B2; (18) BxKP?, P–Q3, winning the exchange.

17. O–O?!

When a pawn down one must keep the initiative. More active was (17) B–QR3, R–K1; (18) K–Q2.

17. . . .   P–QR3!

If now (18) R–N4, then N–Q4 or (18) R–B5, K5, then P–Q3! snatches an exchange.

18. R–B5?

Overlooking the previous note but after R–R5, P–Q3 White has no compensation for the pawn.

18. . . .	P–Q3		19. BxB	PxR
20. B–K6+	K–R1		21. PxP	R(R1)–K1
22. B–QB4	N–N5		23. B–K2	N–K4
24. B–K3	P–KN3		25. R–Q1	R–B2
26. R–Q4	N–B3		27. R–Q2	K–N2

Inaccurate. Stronger was (27) . . . R–Q1.

28. B–QB4	R(B2)–B1		29. R–Q7+?	

Too soon! Instead (29) B–KN5, N–K4; (30) B–Q5! picks off a pawn.

29. . . .	R–K2		30. RxR	NxR
31. B–Q4+	K–R3		32. B–K5	R–B1
33. P–R4	P–B3		34. B–K6	R–K1
35. B–KB7	R–Q1		36. B–QB4	R–Q8+
37. K–R2	N–Q4		38. P–KN4	P–KN4
39. PxP+?				

(39) P–R5 containing the Black king would give better drawing chances. Now White has no hope.

39. . . .	KxP		40. K–R3	N–B5+
41. BxN	KxB		42. B–K2	R–Q7
43. B–B1	RxP		44. B–B4	R–B6+
45. K–R4	RxP		46. B–N8	P–K6
47. B–B4	RxB		48. PxR	P–K7
49. P–N5	P–K8=Q+		50. K–R5	Q–KR8 mate

In the third round, the two programs which had been defeated by CHESS 3.0 were paired against one another. COKO III, written by Dennis Cooper and Ed Kozdrowicki, built an early advantage that eventually slipped away. The program finally managed to eke out a draw against J. Biit while the audience howled in laughter as the final blunders (both kings moving away from the action!) were played on the display board.

WHITE COKO III			**BLACK J. Biit**	
[Univac 1108]			**[IBM 360/91]**	
1. P–Q4	P–Q4		2. N–QB3	N–QB3
3. B–B4	B–B4		4. N–N5	R–B1
5. P–QR4	P–K3		6. N–KB3	N–B3
7. P–K3	N–K5		8. B–Q3	B–QN5+
9. P–B3	B–Q3		10. BxN	BxB(K5)
11. BxB	PxB		12. O–O	P–QR3
13. N–R3	O–O		14. P–QN4	Q–B3
15. P–R5	N–N1			

Up till now the play has been quite reasonable, but here I would prefer (15) . . . N–K2 heading for the kingside.

16. R–B1   N–B3?!

Not the most active!

17. Q–K2   Q–N3   18. Q–Q1?!

Why not (18) KR–Q1?

18. . . .   B–Q6   19. R–K1   R(KB1)–Q1

A developing move but too automatic. More constructive would be (19) . . . R–B2 followed by doubling on the file.

20. Q–Q2   B–K5!

Cunning! Now White, rather than admit his mistake (21) Q–Q1!, loses a pawn.

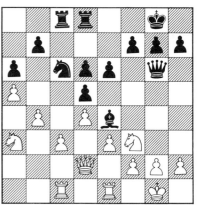

Figure 1.4   Position   after   (20) Q–Q2, B–K5!. COKO III (White) vs. J. Biit (Black), New York City, 1970.

21. N–R4	Q–B3	22. P–B3	QxN
23. P–N3	Q–N4	24. PxB	PxP
25. R–B1	P–B3	26. R–B4	P–Q4
27. R–R4			

Where is this rook going?

27. . . .	R–B2	28. R–Q1	R–K2
29. R–K1	P–K4	30. Q–Q1	PxP
31. P(K3)xP	P–KN3	32. N–B2	P–K6?

Too soon! Black should be content with (32) . . . P–KB4 followed by a gradual kingside advance.

33. Q–B3   R–K5?

Giving up two pawns instead of one.

34. RxR	PxR	35. QxP(K4)	P–B4
36. Q–K6+	K–N2	37. QxP(K3)	Q–N5
38. Q–B4	QxQ	39. PxQ	P–R4?

Not the way to get a passed pawn.

40. P–R4!

By locking up the kingside White enters the endgame with two extra pawns.

40. . . .	K–B3	41. N–K3	R–KR1
42. P–Q5	N–R2	43. N–B4	N–N4
44. R–K3?			

Much stronger was (44) R–K6+ followed by (45) N–K5, winning easily.

44. . . .	R–QB1	45. N–N6	RxP
46. R–K6+	K–B2		
47. N–Q7!			

White has lost time and a pawn but this idea is still strong enough to win.

47. . . .	N–B2	48. N–K5+	K–B1
49. R–KB6+	K–N2	50. RxP(N6)+	K–R2
51. R–N5?			

The passed pawn is all powerful and should be saved. (51) P–Q6 wins immediately.

51. . . .	NxP	52. RxP(R5)+	K–N2
53. RxP(B5)	R–B8+	54. K–R2	R–B7+
55. K–N1	R–B8+	56. K–B2	R–B7+
57. K–K1			

White allows his king to be cut off, making the win very difficult. Correct was (57) K–B3 followed by (58) K–K4.

57. . . .	R–KR7	58. R–N5+	K–R2
59. R–R5+	K–N1	60. R–N5+	K–R2
61. N–Q3	N–B3	62. R–KB5	K–N3
63. R–K5	RxP	64. R–QB5?	

After (64) R–K7, R–R2; (65) RxR, White would have excellent chances to win.

64. . . .	R–R8+	65. K–K2	R–R7+
66. K–K3	R–R7	67. K–B3	R–R6
68. K–K3	N–N5+	69. K–K4	N–B3+
70. K–K3	N–N5+	71. K–K2	K–B3
72. R–KN5			

Black has given a lot of checks but lost ground. With (72) R–B7 White would win another pawn.

72. . . .	R–R7+	73. K–B3	N–R7+
74. K–K4	R–K7+	75. K–Q5	R–Q7
76. K–K4	R–K7+	77. K–Q5	R–Q7
78. K–Q4	N–B6+?		

Forking the king and rook but losing by force.

| 79. K–K3 | RxN+ | 80. KxR | NxR |
| 81. PxN | KxP | 82. K–K3?? | |

Wrong direction! (82) K–Q4 followed by taking the queenside pawns wins easily.

82. . . .	K–B4	83. K–B3	K–K4
84. K–K3	K–Q4	85. K–Q3	K–K4
86. K–K3	K–Q4	87. K–Q3	K–K4

Drawn by repetition.

KAISSA vs. the Soviet Public (Moscow, 1972)

In January 1972, the Soviet newspaper *Komsomolskaia Pravda* sponsored a two-game match, pitting the Soviet program KAISSA against its readers. Every week, the readers would mail in their suggested moves for each game (KAISSA played White in one game and Black in the other), and the most recommended moves were made against KAISSA. The final results were: the Soviet public 1.5 points, KAISSA 0.5 points; a surprising outcome given that Boris Spassky was only able to manage the same score against *Komsomolskaia Pravda's* readers the year before. Presented below is game one of the match, which ended in a draw. The quality of KAISSA's play reflects its advantage in playing a correspondence match. Calculation time sometimes ran over 1 hour per move. This is much more helpful than the 3 minute limit which is set for tournament play.

WHITE KAISSA		**BLACK** Readers of	
[ICL 4/70]		**Komsomolskaia Pravda**	
1. P–K4	P–QB4	2. N–QB3	N–QB3
3. N–B3	P–Q3	4. B–N5	B–Q2
5. O–O	P–KN3	6. P–Q4	PxP
7. BxN	PxN	8. BxP	R–N1
9. B–Q5	B–N2		

Avoiding the clever trap. If (9) . . . PxP; (10) BxP, RxB?; (11) Q–Q4!, which wins an exchange.

| 10. P–QN3 | N–B3 | 11. B–K3 | Q–B2 |
| 12. Q–Q4 | P–QR4 | 13. B–QB4 | O–O |

14. R(R1)–K1	B–B3	15. P–K5	BxN
16. PxP	PxP	17. PxB	N–R4
18. Q–Q3	B–K4	19. B–Q4!	

White must play actively else Black will start to work on the weakened kingside.

19. . . .	K–N2	20. R–K3?	

Why not QxP?

20. . . .	P–B3	21. R(B1)–K1	N–B5
22. QxP	R(N1)–B1	23. P–QR4?	

White has finally snatched the QBP but now overlooks Black's threat. More prudent was (23) K–R1.

23. . . .	Q–Q2!		

Winning the exchange.

24. BxB	P(B3)xB	25. K–R1	Q–R6
26. R–KN1	N–Q4	27. QxP(R5)	R–QB4?

Why not simply (27) . . . NxR followed by (28) . . . QxP+?

28. Q–R7+	R–QB2	29. Q–R5	R–QB4
30. Q–R7+	R–KB2	31. QxR(B5)	PxQ
32. BxN	R–B5	33. RxP(K5)	RxP(B6)!

Black forces a draw as otherwise White's QRP would become too strong.

34. BxR	QxB+	35. R–N2	
Declared drawn.

First world computer chess championship (Stockholm, 1974)

Northwestern University's program, CHESS 4.0 (and its earlier versions), had won all four U.S. championships by the time that IFIP sponsored the first world tournament in Stockholm in August of 1974. Thirteen programs entered the tournament: four from the United States, three from Great Britain, and one each from Austria, Canada, Hungary, Norway, Switzerland, and the Soviet Union. At each board, the flags of the competing countries showed that computer chess had indeed become an international activity (see Figure 1.5). Jan Berglund, from the Stockholm Chess Club, and David Levy provided commentary in Swedish and English to the hundreds of chess players and computer specialists who crowded the tournament site each evening. KAISSA, the Soviet entry, running on an ICL 4/70 from Moscow, won the tournament.

Figure 1.5   Don Beal (left) of Queen Mary College, London (BEAL), awaits a move against OSTRICH, as Monroe Newborn checks his teletype output.

There was a large difference in the playing strength of the best and worst programs and this fact, combined with the Swiss pairing system, produced mostly lopsided contests in the first round. In the second round, CHAOS was paired against CHESS 4.0 with an opportunity to avenge its recent defeat in the fourth ACM tournament. On its sixteenth move, CHAOS made a knight sacrifice which led to its ultimate victory. David Levy commented on this move, "This is the first-ever example of a program making a positional piece sacrifice. The win is too deep for CHAOS to have seen to the end of the combination—it gives up the piece on purely positional grounds." Levy's surprise was more than justified given the usual heavy emphasis on material factors in most computer evaluation functions (see Chapter 3).

WHITE   CHAOS
[Univac 1110]

BLACK   CHESS 4.0
[CDC 6600]

1. P–Q4	P–Q4	2. P–QB4	PxP
3. N–KB3	N–KB3	4. P–K3	P–K3
5. BxP	P–B4	6. Q–K2	P–QR3
7. O–O	P–QN4	8. B–N3	B–N2
9. R–Q1	N(N1)–Q2	10. N–B3	B–Q3
11. P–K4	PxP	12. NxP(Q4)	Q–N1
13. P–N3	P–N5	14. N–R4	BxP(K5)?

Both sides have played the opening quite well but here Black should be content with (14) . . . O–O with equality.

| 15. P–B3 | B–N3 |

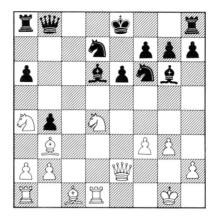

Figure 1.6 Position after (15) P–B3, B–N3. CHAOS (White) vs. CHESS 4.0 (Black), Stockholm, 1974.

16. NxP!

A Tal-like sacrifice! White receives tremendous pressure for the cost of only one piece.

| 16. . . . | PxN | 17. QxP(K6)+ | B–K2 |
| 18. R–K1 | Q–Q1 | 19. B–KB4 | K–B1 |

Forced! Otherwise (20) B–Q6 is too strong.

| 20. R(R1)–Q1 | R–R2 |
| 21. R–QB1? | |

White chucks a couple of tempos. Much stronger was (21) B–Q6! If then (21) . . . N–KN1; (22) BxB+, NxB [QxB, (23) Q–N6!]; (23) R–Q4! wins.

21. . . .	N–KN1	22. R(B1)–Q1	P–QR4
23. B–Q6	BxB	24. QxB+	N–K2
25. N–B5	B–B4	26. P–N4!	

The crusher! Even with two extra tempos Black was helpless.

| 26. . . . | Q–K1 | 27. B–R4! | |

A fine move completely tying Black up. The bishop will not run away.

27. . . .	P–N6	28. PxB	PxP
29. BxN	P–R8=Q	30. RxQ	R–R3
31. NxR	Q–Q1?!		

Black could safely resign. That White requires another 48 moves to force mate displays poor technique but the game is never in doubt.

32. K–B2	K–B2	33. Q–K6+	K–B1
34. QxN+	QxQ	35. RxQ	KxR
36. N–B5	R–QN1	37. RxP	RxP+

38. K–N3	P–N3	39. PxP	PxP
40. R–R6	R–QB7	41. R–K6+	K–B1
42. R–K5	R–B8	43. R–N5	K–B2
44. B–K6+	K–B3	45. P–R4	RxN
46. RxR	KxB	47. R–KN5	K–B3
48. K–N4	K–B2	49. R–QB5	K–K3
50. K–N5	K–Q3	51. R–R5	K–B3
52. P–B4	K–N3	53. R–R1	K–B4
54. R–Q1	K–N5	55. KxP	K–B6
56. R–Q8	K–N5	57. R–QB8	K–N4
58. P–R5	K–N3	59. R–B1	K–N4
60. P–R6	K–R5	61. R–QN1	K–R6
62. P–B5	K–R7	63. R–N8	K–R6
64. P–B6	K–R5	65. R–N7	K–R4
66. R–N8	K–R5	67. R–N1	K–R6
68. R–N7	K–R5	69. R–N8	K–R4
70. K–N7	K–R5	71. R–N7	K–R4
72. R–N2	K–R5	73. R–N8	K–R4
74. K–N8	K–R5	75. P–R7	K–R4
76. P–R8=Q	K–R5	77. Q–R4+	K–R4
78. Q–QN4+	K–R3	79. Q–QR4 mate	

In the fourth round of the Stockholm tournament, KAISSA, the Soviet program, was paired against Professor Newborn's program, OSTRICH. The American program gained the early initiative and KAISSA had to defend skillfully in order to gain an eventual win. The closeness of this match created many tense moments (see Figure 1.7).

Figure 1.7 Michail Donskoy awaits a KAISSA move to be telephoned from Moscow. (Photo courtesy of Hans Svedbark.)

WHITE   OSTRICH
[Data General Nova 2]

BLACK   KAISSA
[ICL 4/70]

1. N–KB3	P–K3	2. P–Q4	N–KB3
3. B–N5	P–Q4	4. P–K3	B–K2
5. N–B3	B–N5?!		

Indecision. (5) . . . O–O was better.

6. BxN	BxN+	7. PxB	QxB
8. B–Q3	P–B4	9. O–O	O–O
10. Q–Q2	N–B3	11. PxP	Q–K2
12. P–B4	PxP	13. BxP(B4)	QxP

Regaining the pawn with an equal game.

14. Q–Q3?

The beginning of trouble. White loses time with his next couple of moves. More natural was (14) Q–K2.

14. . . .	R–Q1	15. Q–K4	P–QN4
16. B–Q3	P–B4!		

This active move gives Black a strong initiative.

17. Q–KR4	P–K4	18. P–K4	

Forced in order to save the QBP, but after Black's reply White's bishop is dead weight.

18. . . .	P–B5
19. R(B1)–K1	B–N2?

Carelessly dropping the exchange. After (19) . . . P–KR3, Black would stand well.

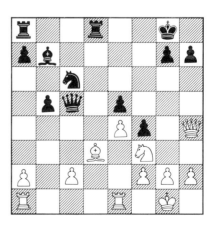

Figure 1.8   Position   after   (19) R(B1)–K1,   B–N2?.   **OSTRICH** (White) vs. KAISSA (Black), Stockholm, 1974.

20. N–N5	P–KR3	21. N–K6	Q–N3
22. NxR	RxN	23. P–QR4	P–N5
24. B–B4+	K–R1	25. R(R1)–Q1?	

Automatic, but (25) B–Q5 preparing to trade the awkward bishop was better.

| 25. . . . | N–Q5 | 26. R–QB1 | B–B3 |
| 27. P–QB3!? | | | |

A reasonable decision. After (27) B–N3, White is completely tied up.

27. . . .	PxP	28. RxP	BxP(R5)
29. Q–K7	N–B3	30. Q–KB7	Q–B4
31. R–Q3	N–Q5	32. B–Q5	B–N4
33. R–KR3!			

The correct decision. White must play aggressively.

| 33. . . . | N–K7+ | | |

Black must allow the draw as (33) . . . R–Q2; (34) Q–K8+ and (33) . . . Q–KB1; (34) QxRP are unappetizing.

| 34. K–R1 | QxP | | |
| 35. R–Q1? | | | |

Black with two pawns for the exchange stands better. Therefore White should seize his chance and play (35) RxP+! After (35) . . . PxR; (36) Q–B6+, K–R2; (37) Q–B7+, White has perpetual check.

| 35. . . . | Q–N3 | 36. R–QN1 | R–QB1 |

Black starts to wander. (36) . . . N–Q5 neutralizes White's threats.

| 37. B–K6! | | | |

Cutting the queen's protection of the KRP. Suddenly White has a winning attack!

| 37. . . . | R–Q1 | 38. Q–N6! | |

Threatening (39) R–RP+! and forcing Black's reply but . . .

| 38. . . . | Q–N2 | 39 Q–B5?? | |

Horrible! Only one more exact move (39) B–B5 and Black must resign.

39. . . .	Q–QB2	40. R–R4	N–Q5
41. Q–R3	NxB	42. QxN	B–Q6
43. R–N1	B–B5		

Curious. Snatching the pawn would leave the bishop on an ideal square.

44. Q–B5	B–K7	45. R–R1	P–QR4
46. Q–N6	P–R5	47. R–K1	B–B5
48. R–R1	P–R6		

While White flails uselessly the rook pawn marches!

49. R–QN1	Q–Q3		50. QxQ	RxQ
51. R–R3	P–R7		52. R–QB1	R–Q5
53. R(R3)–QB3	RxKP!			

The bishop is fearless!

54. R–R1	R–Q5		55. RxB?	

White panics. His game is lost but he should at least wait to get the QRP also.

55. . . .	RxR		56. P–N3	P–B6
57. P–R3	R–B7		58. R–Q1	R–Q7!?

A joke. Black toys a little before he get around to queening his king pawn.

59. R–QB1	P–K5		60. P–N4	P–K6
61. K–N1	P–K7		62. K–B2	R–Q8
63. R–B8+	K–R2		64. KxP	P–K8=Q
65. R–B2	R–Q6+		66. K–B4	P–N4+
67. K–B5	R–KB6 mate			

At the end of the regular tournament, CHESS 4.0, because of its loss to CHAOS, had not been paired with KAISSA. This was a great disappointment to both the Russians and Americans because both wished to see how these two programs would play against each other. After some discussion, an unofficial exhibition match was arranged. The game score for this encounter follows.

WHITE CHESS 4.0
[CDC 6600]

BLACK KAISSA
[ICL 4/70]

1. P–K4	P–Q4		2. PxP	N–KB3
3. P–Q4	NxP		4. N–KB3	P–KN3
5. B–K2	B–N2		6. O–O	O–O
7. R–K1	B–B4		8. N–R4	P–K4?!

A decision not to be taken lightly. Black cedes the bishop pair and allows his pawns to be broken. More prudent was (8) . . . B–K3.

9. NxB	PxN		10. PxP	N–N5
11. QxQ	RxQ		12. B–KN5	R–Q2
13. N–R3	BxP		14. P–QB3	N/5–B3
15. N–B4	P–QR4		16. B–B3!	

Quite strong! Black's position is very uncomfortable.

16. . . .	P–B3		17. B–R6	P–R5

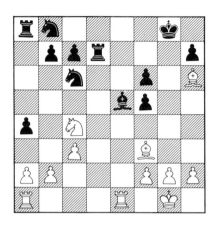

Figure 1.9 Position after (17) B–R6, P–R5. CHESS 4.0 (White) vs. KAISSA (Black), exhibition game, Stockholm, 1974.

18. R/R–Q1	RxR

No better is (18) . . . R–R3; (19) B–Q5+, K–R1; (20) B–K6.

19. RxR	K–R1	20. BxN	

White cashes in for a pawn and a winning ending.

20. . . .	NxB	21. P–KB4	P–N4
22. PxB	PxN	23. PxP	R–Q1
24. R–KB1	K–N1	25. RxP	R–Q8+
26. K–B2	N–Q1	27. B–B4	P–B3
28. K–B3?			

Up till now White has played quite well, but having reached a winning position he starts to drift. The weakness of Black's queenside pawns should give a clue as to the correct plan. Best was (28) R–QR5 taking advantage of (28) . . . R–QN8 not being playable because of (29) R–R8, winning the knight.

28. . . .	R–KB8+	29. K–K4	R–QR8
30. P–QR3	R–K8+	31. B–K3	R–K7
32. R–B2	R–K8	33. R–Q2	N–K3
34. R–Q6	N–B4+	35. K–B3	N–Q6
36. B–Q4	P–B4	37. B–K3	K–B2
38. R–Q7+	K–N3	39. R–KN7+	KxP
40. RxP	N–K4+!		

As (41) K–K4 is not playable because of (41) . . . N–N5; (42) R–R3, N–B7+; Black gets counterplay.

41. K–B4	N–Q6+	42. K–K4	NxP
43. P–N4?			

The QNP could not be saved but here (43) R–R3!, N–Q8; (44) R–B3+, K–N3; (45) K–B4 should still win. The text drops the bishop.

43. . . .	N–Q8	44. P–N5+	K–N3
45. R–R6+	K–N2	46. K–Q5	RxB
47. KxP/4	RxP+	48. K–N5	RxP?

When a piece up but short of pawns, each one should be treasured. (48) . . . N–N7 was best.

49. P–R4	R–KR6?

(49) . . . N–N7!

50. KxP/5	N–N7	51. P–R5	P–R6
52. R–KN6+	K–B2	53. R–KB6+	K–N1
54. R–KN6+	K–B2	55. R–KB6+	K–K2
56. P–R6	N–R5+	57. K–N4	P–R7
58. R–B1	N–B6	59. K–N3	P–R8=Q

There seems to be nothing better.

60. RxQ	N–K5+	61. K–B4	NxP
62. R–R6	N–B2	63. R–R7+	K–K3
64. R–R6+	K–B4	65. K–Q4	NxP

Drawn by agreement.

Fifth United States computer chess championship (San Diego, 1974)

RIBBIT from the University of Waterloo won the Fifth U.S. Championship in San Diego. It was an unusual win since RIBBIT gained a narrow victory in Round 2 when OSTRICH failed to push a passed pawn, and in Round 3 it won when TECH II from MIT ran out of time after endless computation, with a mate in two on the board. However, RIBBIT's victory against CHESS 4.0 in the final round was decisive.

In the third round, CHAOS was paired against CHESS 4.0 once more. After losing to the famous knight sacrifice at Stockholm, the Northwestern group was eager for the rematch. The game was short, and, from a Northwestern perspective, sweet.

WHITE   CHESS 4.0
[CDC 6400]

BLACK   CHAOS
[Univac 1108]

1. P–K4	P–QB4	2. N–KB3	N–QB3
3. P–Q4	PxP	4. NxP	N–KB3
5. N–QB3	P–K3	6. NxN	NPxN
7. P–K5	N–Q4	8. NxN?!	

Here (8) N–K4 is more usual.

8. . . .	BPxN	9. B–Q3	P–KN3?

This weakening move leads to difficulties. (9) . . . P–Q3 freed Black's game without making any concessions.

10. O–O	B–KN2	11. B–KB4	O–O
12. Q–KB3			

Rather awkward. (12) Q–Q2 preparing to trade the dark squared bishops was more natural.

12. . . .	Q–QN3	13. P–QB4	Q–Q5
14. PxP	B–QN2	15. Q–KN3	BxQP
16. P–QN3	QR–QB1	17. QR–Q1	Q–QN5
18. R–QB1	KR–Q1	19. B–K3	B–K5??

Overlooking White's reply. (19) . . . P–QR4 maintained equality.

20. Q–KR4!

Immediately decisive! Now rather than surrender the piece Black panics and loses everything.

20. . . .	P–Q4	21. PxP e.p.	P–KB4
22. RxR	R–KB1	23. P–Q7	Q–QN2
24. RxR+	BxR	25. P–Q8=Q	BxP
26. Q/KR4–KB6	Q–QN5	27. Q–K8	Q–K2
28. Q/KB6xQ	P–KR4	29. Q/K8xB mate	

In the fourth round, a program from the University of Waterloo in Canada and CHESS 4.0 were paired since each had won the first 3 games. RIBBIT, programmed by Jim Parry, Ron Hansen, and Russell Crook, had lost twice (once during the regular pairings and once during the playoff for second place) to CHESS 4.0 at Stockholm. San Diego was a different story, however, and RIBBIT won the match and the North American championship.

WHITE   RIBBIT
[Honeywell 6050]

BLACK   CHESS 4.0
[CDC 6400]

1. P–K4	P–QB4	2. P–QB3	P–Q4
3. PxP	QxP	4. P–Q4	PxP
5. PxP	N–QB3	6. N–KB3	B–KN5!?

(6) . . . P–K3 is safer.

7. N–QB3	Q–Q3?

In a sharp position a tempo is all important. Without knowing it beforehand (7) . . . BxN is not an easy move to find. The game might continue (8) PxB, QxP; (9) QxQ, NxQ; (10) N–N5 with complications.

8. P–Q5	N–QN5	9. B–QN5+	B–Q2
10. BxB+	KxB		

Unfortunately (10) . . . QxB is not playable due to (11) N–K5 followed by (12) Q–R4+, winning a piece.

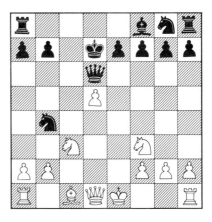

Figure 1.10 Position after (10) BxB+, KxB. RIBBIT (White) vs. CHESS 4.0 (Black), San Diego, 1974.

11. B–K3   Q–QR3?

Black's position is miserable but (11) . . . P–K3 fights on.

12. N–K5+!

Attacking and defending Q3, this wins a piece.

12. . . .	K–K1	13. P–QR3	Q–Q3
14. Q–QR4+	N–QB3	15. PxN	PxP
16. NxQBP	P–K4	17. NxRP+	Q–Q2
18. QxQ+	KxQ	19. R–Q1+	K–K3
20. O–O	N–KB3	21. P–QN4	B–K2
22. P–KR3	P–KR4		
23. KR–K1	P–KR5!		

A nice positional move. Unfortunately Black lost without much fight because of one difficult move in the opening.

24. R–Q3	P–K5	25. B–Q4	KR–K1
26. BxN	BxB	27. RxP+	K–KB4
28. RxR	RxR	29. P–KN4+	PxP e.p.
30. PxP	R–K8+	31. K–KB2	R–QB8
32. P–KN4+	K–KN3	33. N–K4	B–K4
34. P–QN5			

This pawn has a bright future but is a little slow in getting there. The technique is improved but still rather inefficient.

34. . . .	R–QB7+	35. K–KB3	R–KR7
36. N–KB2	B–KB3	37. R–Q6	K–KR2
38. R–Q5	B–QN7	39. K–KN3	RxN
40. KxR	BxP	41. P–QN6	B–QB8
42. P–QN7	B–KB5	43. N–QB6	B–QB2
44. R–Q7	B–KB5	45. RxP	B–Q3
46. P–N8=Q	BxQ	47. NxB	K–KN3
48. R–KB5	K–KR3	49. N–Q7	P–KN3

23

50. R–KB6	K–KN4		51. K–KN3	K–KR3
52. N–K5	K–KN2		53. P–KN5	K–KN1
54. NxP	K–KR2		55. P–KR4	K–KN1
56. P–KR5	K–KN2		57. P–KR6+	K–KR2
58. N–KB4	K–KR1		59. P–KN6	K–KN1
60. K–KN4	K–KR1		61. R–KB8 mate	

Sixth North American computer chess championship (Minneapolis, 1975)

With a Canadian program, RIBBIT (now called TREE FROG), as the current champion, and with two other Canadian entries in a field of twelve, the 1975 ACM tournament became the North American championship. CHESS 4.4 regained the title when it defeated TREE FROG in the final round. Three programs tied as runner-ups: TREE FROG, CHAOS, and a completely new program called ETAOIN SHRDLU. This newcomer ran on a tiny NOVA 1200 from Boulder, Colorado, and did amazingly well to end up, as a result of tie-breaking points, in third place. One new feature of this tournament was a simultaneous exhibition in which David Levy played against eleven of the programs. CHESS 4.4 participated in the exhibition on two different computers, a CDC Cyber 175 and a CDC 6400. Levy won ten of the games and drew against TREE FROG and against CHESS 4.4 playing on the Cyber 175.

In Round 3, CHESS 4.4 was paired once again against CHAOS. Both programs were run on larger machines than in prior tournaments to take advantage of the extra computing power. CHESS 4.4 ran on the Cyber 175 located in Minneapolis at Control Data Corporation headquarters. CHAOS ran on the new Amdahl 470 which had recently been installed at the University of Michigan. Both teams had improved their programs since their previous meeting at San Diego and thus both expected a difficult contest. At this point in the tournament, both were 2–0 and so either had the opportunity to win the championship. One of CHESS 4.4's earlier wins had come at the expense of a new program from Bucknell named SORTIE (see Figure 1.11).

WHITE   CHAOS
[Amdahl 470]

BLACK   CHESS 4.4
[CDC Cyber 175]

1. P–Q4	N–KB3		2. P–QB4	P–B4
3. P–Q5	P–K3		4. N–QB3	PxP
5. PxP	P–Q3		6. P–K4	P–KN3
7. B–K2	B–N2		8. N–B3	O–O
9. O–O	R–K1		10. N–Q2	N–R3
11. P–B3	N–B2		12. P–QR4	P–N3
13. N–B4	B–QR3		14. B–N5	P–R3
15. B–R4	P–KN4		16. B–B2	N–R4
17. P–R5?				

Figure 1.11 Steve Becker (left) of Bucknell University (SORTIE) congratulates David Slate of Northwestern (CHESS 4.4).

Until now both sides have shown a sophisticated knowledge of the opening but this sally is immediately fatal. Better was (17) N–K3.

17. . . .   N–B5   18. PxP   PxP

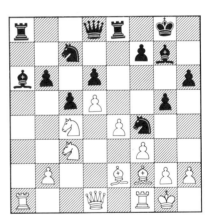

Figure 1.12 Position after (18) PxP, PxP. CHAOS (White) vs. CHESS 4.4 (Black), Minneapolis, 1975.

19. B–K3   B/KN2xN?

Temporarily winning a pawn but stronger was (19) . . . NxB+; (20) QxN, P–QN4 winning an exchange due to threat of (21) . . . P–QN5.

20. PxB	BxN	21. BxB	RxR
22. QxR	N/QB2xP	23. B/QB4xN	NxB
24. BxP/QB5	NxP	25. B–N4	N–K7+
26. K–R1	N–B5	27. R–Q1	Q–R1

28. BxP	QxQ	29. RxQ	N–K7
30. R–QN1	R–QB1	31. P–R3	R–B3
32. B–K5	K–R2	33. R–K1?	

The smoke has cleared leaving a fairly balanced position with Black's passed pawn neutralized by White's fleet bishop. Here, though, White should protect his second rank. (33) R–N2, P–KB3; (34) BxP, N–N6+; (35) K–R2, NxKP; (36) B–Q4, N–B4 left even chances.

33. . . .	R–B7	34. K–R2	P–N4
35. R–QN1	R–B4	36. B–Q6	R–B3
37. B–B8	R–B7!		

Black maintains his advantage with this move. Now White should try (38) RxP but after (38) . . . N–B5; (39) R–N6, P–KR4! Black remains better.

38. R–QR1	N–B5	39. R–KN1	K–N3
40. B–N4	P–B4	41. PxP+	KxP
42. B–Q6	R–QN7	43. K–R1?	

(43) BxN must be tried as otherwise White will be unable to free his pieces.

43. . . .	K–B3?		

Why not (43) . . . P–N5?

44. BxN	PxB	45. K–R2	P–N5
46. R–QB1	P–N6	47. R–B6+	K–N4
48. R–B5+	K–N3	49. R–B6+	K–R4
50. R–B5+	K–N3	51. R–B6+	K–N4
52. R–B5+	K–B3	53. R–QN5	K–N3
54. K–N1	R–N8+	55. K–R2	K–N2

If Black is to try and win he must march his king to the queenside. It's only protection from checks however will be in front of the QNP, therefore the pawn must not advance. (55) . . . K–B3 was the only try.

56. R–N4	P–N7	57. R–N6	K–B2
58. P–R4	K–N2	59. P–R5?	

White can draw by simply keeping the rook on the QN file. This advance loses the RP to a clever maneuver.

59. . . .	K–B2	60. R–N8	K–K3
61. R–N7	K–B4	62. R–N5+	K–B3!

A key square! White is now in zugzwang, e.g., (63) R–N4, K–N4; (64) R–N5+, K–R5! Nevertheless that was a better choice.

63. P–N3	PxP+	64. K–N2	K–K3
65. R–N3	K–B4	66. R–N6	K–N4
67. R–N5+	K–R5	68. R–N8	KxP

The position is now winning for Black as White is defenseless against a sacrifice of the Black KRP on KR6 followed by Black's rook checking and queening the pawn. Despite the inaccuracies the general play of this ending shows a clear improvement over earlier efforts.

69. R–N5+	K–N3	70. R–N6+	K–B4
71. R–N5+	K–K3	72. R–N6+	K–Q4
73. R–N5+	K–B3	74. R–N3	P–R4
75. P–B4	P–R5	76. R–N8	K–Q4

(76) . . . P–R6+!

77. R–N5+	K–K5	78. R–N6	K–B4
79. R–N5+	K–N5	80. R–KN5+!	KxP
81. R–N4+	K–K6		

A nice try but Black sidesteps the stalemate.

82. R–N4	K–Q6	83. R–N5	K–B6
84. R–QB5+	K–N5	85. R–B6	R–N8+
86. K–R3	R–KR8+	87. K–N2	K–R4
88. R–B5+	K–R3	89. R–B6+	K–N2
90. R–K6	P–N8=Q	91. R–K7+	K–B3
92. K–B3	Q–B4+	93. K–K2	P–N7
94. Resigns			

In the fourth and final round, CHESS 4.4 with a 3–0 record and TREE FROG (née RIBBIT) with an identical record met to decide the championship. The participants and the audience were interested to see if the Canadian program could retain the title for another year.

WHITE CHESS 4.4   **BLACK TREE FROG**
[CDC Cyber 175]   **[Honeywell 6080]**

1. P–K4	P–Q4	2. PxP	N–KB3
3. P–Q4	NxP	4. N–KB3	B–N5
5. B–K2	P–K3	6. O–O	N–QB3
7. P–B4	N–B3	8. N–B3	B–N5
9. P–Q5!			

Securing a slight advantage.

9. . . .   B/QNxN?

(9) . . . PxP should be played. The text leads to a bad ending.

10. PxN	QxQ	11. RxQ	B–N5
12. PxP	R–QN1	13. P–KR3	B–KB4
14. P–R3	B–B4?		

(14) . . . B–K2 was better.

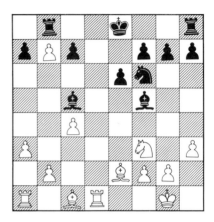

Figure 1.13 Position after (14) P–R3, B–B4?. CHESS 4.4 (White) vs. TREE FROG (Black), Minneapolis, 1975.

15. P–KN4?

(15) P–QN4 would be very strong.

15. . . .	B–B7	16. R–Q2	B–N6
17. N–Q4	BxN	18. RxB	P–K4
19. R–Q2	RxP	20. P–N5	N–K5
21. R–Q5	P–KB3	22. B–R5+	K–K2
23. B–B3	P–B3	24. R–R5	B–B7!

The only move but it would have been even better last move.

25. P–N4   R/1–QN1?

(25) . . . R–QB1 had to be tried. Now Black is lost.

| 26. B–K3 | NxP/4 | 27. BxN | PxB |
| 28. RxP/5+ | K–Q3 | 29. R/1–K1! | |

Much stronger than (29) RxNP.

29. . . .	R–KB2		
30. R–K6+	K–B2	31. RxP+	K–Q1
32. R/6–K6	R–N3	33. R–K8+	K–Q2
34. B–Q5	R–B4	35. R/1–K7+	K–Q3
36. B–K6!			

The clincher. Black is helpless.

| 36. . . . | R–QB3 | 37. BxR | BxB |
| 38. P–B5+ | Resigns | | |

A new feature of the 1975 tournament was an exhibition in which David Levy, an International Master, played 12 programs simultaneously (see Figure 1.14). Despite the many tournament games pitting machine against machine and the occasional informal game with a machine against a human opponent, there had never been an exhibition in which one man played several computers at one time. Levy has made a sizeable wager with several academicians [67] that he will be able to beat any computer program in a 10-game match up until 1978. For this reason, his simultaneous exhibition generated considerable interest at the Minneapolis tournament. Two of the twelve game scores are presented. Both involve games between CHESS 4.4, the tournament champion, and Levy. In the first game, CHESS 4.4 ran on a CDC 6400 located at Northwestern University.

WHITE   CHESS 4.4   **BLACK   David Levy**
[CDC 6400]

1. P–KB4	P–Q4	2. N–KB3	N–KB3
3. P–K3	B–N5	4. P–QN3	P–B3
5. B–N2	N/1–Q2	6. B–K2	BxN
7. BxB	Q–B2	8. O–O	P–K4
9. PxP	NxP		
10. B–K2?			

White can not afford to keep the two bishops. (10) N–B3 was better.

10. . . .	B–Q3	11. N–B3	P–KR4
12. P–KR3	N/4–N5!?		

Figure 1.14   The Tournament Director plays a simultaneous exhibition against twelve programs. Results: Levy wins ten, draws two.

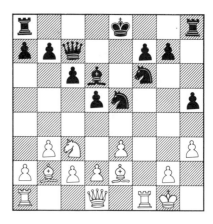

Figure 1.15 Position after (12) P–KR3. CHESS 4.4 (White) vs. David Levy (Black), simultaneous exhibition, Minneapolis, 1975.

A sharp continuation apparently leading to a draw.

13. PxN	B–R7+	14. K–R1	PxP
15. BxP	B–N8+	16. KxB	Q–R7+
17. K–B2	Q–R5+	18. K–B3?	

(18) K–N1, N–N5 is also bad but after (18) K–K2, Black seems to have nothing better than (18) . . . QxB+ with perpetual checks.

| 18. . . . | NxB |
| 19. R–R1 | Q–B7+! |

Overlooked by White, this leads to a nice finish.

20. KxN	P–KB4+	21. K–N5	Q–N6+
22. KxP	O–O+	23. K–K6	R–B3+
24. K–K7	Q–Q3 mate		

In the other game between CHESS 4.4 and Levy, the machine had the Black pieces. Early in the match, Levy effected a queen trade apparently hoping to initiate the end game as soon as possible. Levy is a firm believer that computer programs are especially inept in the end game. This game did nothing to change this conviction.

WHITE David Levy   **BLACK CHESS 4.4**
                              [CDC Cyber 175]

1. P–Q3	P–K4	2. P–KN3	N–QB3
3. B–N2	P–Q4	4. N–KB3	N–B3
5. O–O	B–K2	6. P–B3	O–O
7. P–QN4	P–K5		

The correct reaction to White's queenside advance. Black is at least equal.

8. PxP	PxP	9. QxQ	RxQ
10. N/3–Q2	B–KB4	11. N–B4	B–N5
12. R–K1	BxP/7!		

Alertly snatching a pawn.

13. N/1–Q2	BxN	14. NxB	R–Q6
15. B–N2	P–QN4	16. N–R3	R–N1
17. R/R–Q1	N–K4		

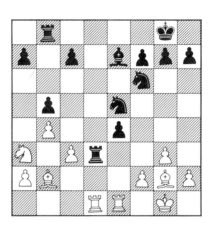

Figure 1.16 Position after (17) R/R–Q1, N–K4. David Levy (White) vs. CHESS 4.4 (Black), simultaneous exhibition, Minneapolis, 1975.

| 18. RxR | NxR | 19. R–K2 | NxB |
| 20. RxN | P–B4! | | |

Opening up the scope of the bishop, Black is playing very well.

| 21. PxP | P–QR3 | 22. N–B2 | R–QB1!? |

Another finesse but simply (23) . . . BxP; (24) N–N4, BxN was also good.

| 23. N–N4 | RxP | 24. NxP | R–B3 |
| 25. N–N8?! | | | |

White chooses to defend with two passed pawns for a piece rather than play (25) N–N4, RxP; (26) N–B2 and defend a pawn down.

| 25. . . . | R–N3 | 26. P–QR4 | RxN |
| 27. PxP | R–QB1?! | | |

(27) . . . R–N3!

28. P–N6	R–N1	29. B–R3	N–Q4
30. P–N7	NxP	31. B–B8	K–B1
32. R–B2	B–B3	33. K–N2	K–K2
34. R–Q2	P–N3	35. R–Q7+	K–B1
36. R–Q6	B–K4	37. R–QB6	P–B3?

This weakens Black's K3 and makes the win more difficult. After (37) K–K2 intending B–Q3 and N–Q4–B3–Q2–B4 Black would win without difficulty.

38. R–B4	K–B2	39. K–B1	P–B4
40. R–B5	K–B3	41. R–B6+	K–N4
42. R–B5	B–Q5	43. R–B4	B–R1
44. R–B7	P–R3	45. R–B6	B–K4
46. R–B5	B–N2	47. R–B7	B–B3
48. R–B6	B–R1		

Finally safety, but White has a lot of play now.

49. R–B5	K–N5	50. R–B6	K–R4
51. R–B5	N–R5	52. R–N5	B–B3
53. P–R3	N–B6	54. R–B5	B–Q5
55. R–B4	B–R1	56. R–B5	K–N4
57. P–N4	B–Q5	58. R–B4	B–K4
59. R–B5	K–B3	60. R–B6+	K–N2
61. R–B5	B–Q5	62. R–B7+	K–B3

Drawn by agreement.

Another case of weak play in the ending spoiling an otherwise fine effort.

Significance

One often hears criticism of the large investments in time and money which have gone into the computer chess tournaments. Why, some say, should ACM or IFIP sponsor tournaments where the quality of the chess is, at best, Class B or C? What possible benefits can come from programs playing programs? To answer these questions, one only has to experience the enthusiasm which is generated by these events. For the participants, the tournaments and panel discussions have been a unique forum for comparing notes and testing new ideas. Even though a master-level program may still be far in the future, the annual tournaments have shown that improvements can be made in a steady incremental fashion. This may be too slow for some, but nevertheless, progress is progress. The consistently large and ever faithful audience is testimony to the excitement which is generated by these annual competitions. Much credit is due to David Levy for his lively and provocative commentary. With his help, many computer specialists spend enjoyable evenings during their annual convention discussing chess programming. These events have been a useful education to chess players and the public in what computers can and cannot do.

It is interesting that the chess programmers themselves do not need any special rationalization or justification for what they do. Writing a chess program is fun and challenging. No other justification is needed. From their perspective, the fuss which has been made over computer chess during the past six years in somewhat amusing. When a journalist writes: "If computer chess were an intercollegiate sport, Northwestern would be known as a powerhouse!" the CHESS 4.5 team just smile and return to the difficult task of developing more efficient evaluation and tree-searching mechanisms.

The publication of this book is due in no small part to the world-wide interest which has been generated by the computer chess tournaments. These events have had an important and useful impact. We have all become aware of how difficult it is for a computer to deal with problem environments like the game of chess. From our present perspective it seems that computers may never be able to play chess as skillfully as human grandmasters. But this is, in fact, the central question that the rest of the book addresses. After reading the next seven chapters, maybe you will be ready to make your own judgment on this matter.

Editor's note: Recent developments and game scores for 1976, 1977, and 1978 are presented in the appendices.

Human chess skill

Neil Charness
Wilfrid Laurier University

2

Should a computer be more like a man?

At one point in *My Fair Lady*, Henry Higgins cries out in exasperation: "Why can't a woman be more like a man?" Higgins, as you may recall, was an expert linguist who had taken on the seemingly impossible task of transforming an uneducated Cockney flower girl into a very proper high society lady. The task was a close analogue to the classical Turing test.[1] The requirement was really that Higgins' protege successfully *simulate* the behaviour of a high society lady such that no observer would suspect otherwise.

No doubt many computer programmers have uttered similar cries of anguish in the process of getting their proteges, computer chess programs, to reach equally high standards of excellence in chess play. Should a computer be more like a man when it comes to playing chess? The argument for a more exact simulation of human chess players has been forcibly advanced by former World Chess Champion, M.M. Botvinnik [18]. He has suggested that since humans seem to be suited quite well to solve "inexact" tasks like choosing a move in a chess game, and computers are not, teach the computer to behave like the human.

On the other hand, a second school of thought is to consider that computers, because they operate differently than humans (at least on the "hardware" side), might perform better by adopting procedures that are maximally efficient for them (but not necessarily for humans). Thus one

---

[1] A. M. Turing [95] proposed a test in 1950 to decide if machines could think. The test involved having a human and a computer in separate rooms answer questions asked by an observer who could only communicate on a teletype. If the observer could not distinguish which was which, the computer was deemed capable of thought.

could imagine a successful chess playing program which would not play the same way a human does. Indeed, no current program does, and some of these programs play a reasonably good game of chess.

Perhaps the clinching argument in favour of the first line of thought is that if your goal is to develop a program which can beat the best human player, a guaranteed solution is to have the program simulate human playing methods almost exactly. This way you can capitalize on the computer's "inhuman" ability to avoid making mistakes in calculation.

The reason for this not so idle speculation about humans and computers lies in the failure of some predictions that have been advanced about computer chess. Not too many years ago, when the first generation of chess-playing programs appeared, some rather dire predictions were made. Before too long the best chess players in the world would be nonhuman, that is, computers.[2] The present generation of programs have not even achieved the more modest goal of playing master-level chess. If major advances do not occur between now and 1978, several professors of artificial intelligence are in danger of losing a somewhat weighty bet with David Levy, an international master chess player [67].

What has gone wrong? I think it is fair to say that the problem has little to do with "debugging" already capable chess programs (correcting programming errors). Rather, the primary reason for lack of progress has to do with our failure to appreciate the complexity of the task and our lack of understanding of how the human chess player performs the task. What characteristics do good human players possess that poorer players and programs do not? How does the human go about solving the problem of choosing a move?

The choice-of-move problem

Chess is a game that involves the alternation of moves by two armies: White and Black. The goal of the game is to checkmate the opposing king. This is accomplished when the enemy king is placed in check by one (or two) opposing pieces in such a position that escape is impossible because all flight squares are occupied by friendly pieces or controlled by opposing ones and when there is no possibility of capturing the checking piece(s) or blocking its (their) attack.

Few games are won by the strategy of trying to reach such a "mating" position directly. Instead, in high-level games, players strive for more modest goals like winning material or acquiring a positional advantage, knowing that it is possible to transform such "winning" positions to mating positions. Thus, in choosing a move from an initial position, the player attempts to transform it into one where he obtains a winning advantage, or one where he more closely approximates that goal.

[2] One such overly optimistic prediction was made by Simon [86] when he predicted in 1958 that a computer program would be world champion within 10 years.

Since chess is a finite game with a limited number of legal positions, it is possible, in theory, to generate all possible legal continuations. This can be done by generating all legal moves, the opponent's legal replies, the counter-replies, etc., until terminal positions are reached where either the White king is checkmated, the Black king is checkmated, or a drawn position has resulted. Then, by tracing his way back through the "tree" of possible moves, the player can find the best move for his side by using the so-called "minimax" procedure. He chooses the path which maximizes his outcome, given that both he and his opponent choose the move with the highest value for their respective sides at each level in the tree. (See Frey's chapter for a more detailed analysis.)

A quick piece of mathematics will convince the reader that the approach of exhaustive search through all legal positions is not a particularly efficient way to play chess. If from an initial position there are 10 legal moves for you, 10 legal replies for your opponent to each of your moves, 10 legal counter-replies to each of his replies, etc., then to look ahead only 6 half-moves (plies) you would need to evaluate $10^6 = 1$ million terminal positions. When you consider that in a typical master level game there are on average 42 moves (84 plies) in a game and an average of 38 legal moves per position,[3] the number of positions which could theoretically be explored is 38^{84}.

But as de Groot has pointed out [32], the number of master game positions that could arise is somewhat more constrained. He has estimated that the average number of good moves in a given position is 1.76. Also, the average number of moves in a master game is 42—i.e., 84 positions. Thus it seems that the number of positions to be explored in an "exhaustive" master search shrinks to 1.76^{84} or about 4.2×10^{20} positions. To illustrate how big that number is, consider that less than 10^{18} seconds have elapsed since the earth was formed some 4.6 billion years ago. Obviously, a chess player must search *selectively* among the exponentially exploding number of positions as he attempts to look ahead.

No doubt, many misconceptions about chess mastery were inspired by recognition of the difficulty of the search problem. One popular belief was that the highly skilled player calculated many more moves ahead than the amateur and hence could foresee combinations leading to winning positions which his opponent could not. Another view held that masters examined many hundred of continuations before choosing a move. The poor amateur, who could scarcely keep track of a handful of moves, would of course be no match for the formidable "thinking machine" called the chess master. Some of these myths were accepted by early investigators of human chess skill (see, for instance, Binet [15]). As we will see later, these misconceptions were demolished by de Groot and his coworkers in Holland. A simple refutation can be easily demonstrated by altering the depth of search for current chess programs. Adding a few plies does not

---

[3] See de Groot [31, p. 14, 19] for a derivation of these values.

produce tremendous changes in performance. What is gained by adding more look ahead capacity is rapidly lost in time spent evaluating the hundreds of thousands of new terminal positions. The only feasible solution to this exponential explosion is to use a highly selective search through the relevant branches. But how does one decide what is relevant and what is not?

The role of perception

"He saw everything!" is invariably the complaint of the chess player who loses a game. Other variants to this lament are: "I completely missed (seeing) his move" or "How could I overlook that move?" It is no accident that the operation "seeing" is an element in all those statements. In the final analysis, *perception* seems to be the key to skill in chess.

It is not usually the case that one player calculates so many variations that he generates the correct one where his opponent, who has searched less completely, does not. As is obvious from the previous analysis, both players are restricted to looking at a mere handful of possible positions. The difference between two players is usually that one looks at the promising moves, and the other spends his time going down blind alleys. This, in a nutshell, is what de Groot discovered in his research into the determinants of skill in chess in the early 1930's and 1940's.

At first de Groot tried to determine why some players were better than others by examining their thought processes. To do this, he showed chess players unfamiliar positions and told them to choose a move and think out loud while doing so. He recorded their verbal statements by hand and attempted to estimate their statistics of search. His subjects ranged from the world's best chess players—Grandmasters like Alekhine, Keres, Euwe—to club players who would be rated as Class A to Class C on the USCF rating scale.[4] Table 2.1, derived from de Groot, gives the results for position A (see Figure 2.1) by five Grandmasters and five experts.

The results are rather surprising and serve as a convincing refutation for the myths mentioned earlier. The only measure which clearly differentiates the Grandmasters from the experts is the one giving the estimated value of the chosen move. Four of the five Grandmasters chose the objectively correct move. None of the experts picked that move. Furthermore, as de Groot shows elsewhere [31, p. 128], all of the Grandmasters mentioned the correct move at some time in their analysis. Only 2 of the 5 experts ever mentioned the correct move in their analysis.

---

[4] Arpad Elo [36] has derived a method for rating players by comparing their performance against each other in tournaments. In the USCF (United States Chess Federation) system, the standard deviation is 200 rating points and the scale runs as follows: Class E: below 1200, Class D: 1200–1399, Class C: 1400–1599, Class B: 1600–1799, Class A: 1800–1999, Expert: 2000–2199, Master: 2200 and above. Titles such as international Grandmaster (approximately 2500) are awarded by FIDE, the world chess body.

TABLE 2.1   Choose a move task
              Position A (After de Groot [31])

Protocol structural variables	Grandmasters (N = 5) Mean (Standard error)		Experts (N = 5) Mean (Standard error)	
1. Time to decision (minutes)	9.6	(1.50)	12.8	(2.85)
2. Number of fresh starts	6.6	(1.75)	6.4	(1.57)
3. Number of different first moves	4.2	(0.58)	3.4	(0.68)
4. Maximal depth calculated (plies)	6.8	(0.91)	6.6	(1.36)
5. Total number of move considered	35.0	(10.66)	30.8	(8.14)
6. Moves/minute [(5)/(1)]	3.5	(0.59)	2.5	(0.53)
7. First moves/minute [(3)/(1)]	0.45	(0.05)	0.29	(0.04)
8. Value of chosen move (best move rated 9)	8.6	(0.40)	5.2	(0.20)

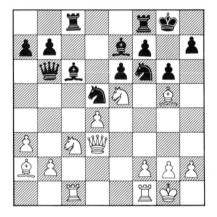

Figure 2.1   De Groot's position A with White to play. The best move is BxN/5!

It is also enlightening to observe that the average depth of search, for Grandmaster and expert alike, has shrunk from mythical levels such as 40 plies to a mere 7 plies. Also, the "hundreds" of continuations supposedly explored has dropped to an average of 35 moves in total (the range being 20–76 for Grandmasters).

Quite clearly, there was something about position A that attracted the Grandmasters' attention to the correct move, but not the attention of the experts. An argument can be advanced that the two groups *perceived* the position quite differently.

The role of perception became much better defined when de Groot modified a task used in an early Russian investigation [33]. He again permitted his subjects to look at a chess position taken from an unfamiliar game but limited the exposure to a few seconds. Then, after the players had reflected upon and organized what they had seen, they were encouraged to recall the position. Stronger players did so by calling out the positions of the pieces verbally. Weaker players were permitted to place pieces on an empty board.

The results of this experiment were striking. Grandmasters and masters recalled almost all the pieces correctly—approximately 93 percent of 22 pieces. Experts recalled 72 percent correctly, and class players recalled about 51 percent correctly.[5] William Chase and Herbert Simon [22, 23], at Carnegie–Mellon University, replicated and extended this finding by adding a novice to their group of subjects and carrying out a valuable control procedure. Their master scored 81 percent, the A player 49 percent, and the novice 33 percent with a 5 second exposure to "quiet" middle game positions taken from master games. But when randomized (scrambled) versions of chess positions were shown for 5 seconds, everybody, including the master, recalled only 3 or 4 pieces correctly—fewer pieces than were recalled by the novice with structured positions.

Chase and Simon were thus able to conclude that the superior performance of the master was not due to extraordinary visual memory capacity, but rather to a chess-specific capacity. This conclusion parallels earlier ones by Djakow, Petrovsky, and Rudik [33] and de Groot [31]. These studies in perception suggest it is not the thought process but the perceptual process that seems to differentiate chess players according to skill level.

Because recall ability seems to be the most sensitive measure related to chess playing ability, it becomes important to discover how players perform the recall task. Simon and Gilmartin [85] have produced a model of the task that is embodied in a computer simulation called MAPP.

In this model, Simon and Gilmartin make a series of assumptions about the information processing capacities of humans. They assume, on the basis of much psychological research, that people possess two memory systems: short-term memory (STM) and long-term memory (LTM).[6]

Human memory

Short-term memory apparently has a limited capacity. This memory system represents what you are currently aware of, and it is therefore sometimes referred to as working memory or immediate memory. The limited capacity aspect of STM is best illustrated by the difficulty people have remembering a new, unfamiliar telephone number which they have just looked up. Unless they rehearse the 7 digits, they are likely to forget them before they can dial the number. Furthermore if people are given 2 such numbers in quick succession they have virtually no chance of recalling both of them accurately.

This observation does not prove that the capacity of STM is 7 digits. If the two phone numbers are familiar ones (e.g., home and office), most people have no difficulty at all remembering them, but they do run into

---

[5] De Groot used a rather complicated scoring procedure whereby he awarded points for pieces placed correctly, and as well, for remembering spatial relations between pieces and material balance. He subtracted points for misplacing, adding or omitting pieces, as well as for interchanging pieces, shifting them over one file, and being uncertain. (See [31, p. 223].)

[6] There is also good evidence for the existence of a very short-term memory. This memory holds information sent from the sensory system for about ¼ of a second.

trouble if they are given 7 familiar phone numbers. From various experiments, George Miller [72] concluded that the capacity of STM is 7 *chunks*, plus or minus two. A chunk is a psychological unit—a familiar unit to the person. It is a shorthand code which can later be decoded to recover all the information it represents. It is essentially a label or symbol which designates or points to specific information in long-term memory.

Short-term memory is sometimes conceptualized as a storage bin with seven locations or slots. The organization of STM is temporal. Items can be entered serially as each is attended to. Once all seven slots have been filled, however, something must be lost if new information is to be processed. Usually the oldest item is replaced by the newest. Fortunately we have the ability to rehearse the contents of STM and the capacity to recode information and store it in a more permanent memory: LTM. Storing information in LTM takes time. Simon [83] has estimated that it takes about 5–10 seconds per chunk. Because of its small capacity and relatively long transfer time, STM is the major bottleneck in our ability to process information.

Long-term memory is the permanent storehouse of all that we know. It is virtually unlimited in capacity—barring certain neurological disorders, we can continue learning until we die and never exhaust our storage capacity. Items such as your phone number, your name, and the alphabet are stored in LTM. Information that is used frequently or which is intentionally practised or recoded resides permanently in LTM. Information in LTM is used to interpret and restructure information transmitted from the senses to STM.

A fascinating property of LTM is its organization. Information in LTM seems to be highly interconnected. This property contrasts sharply with most computer memory systems, where information is said to be location addressable. That is, one piece of information is linked to another by a location tag: e.g., "go from this cell (300) and get the contents of cell 385." Barring the existence of other pointers to cell 385, the only other way to retrieve its contents is via an exhaustive search of all memory cells —a highly inefficient way to retrieve information. The only practical way to get that information is to start from cell 300. What happens if the entry cue is changed slightly such that it no longer activates cell 300? The information in cell 385 cannot be retrieved.

Human LTM appears to be content addressable. That is, functionally similar items seem to be filed in the same location.[7] Items may be grouped together on the basis of semantic similarity (meaning), phonetic similarity (sound) or other categorizations. An example of successful retrieval based on semantic similarity occurs for most English speakers when they are

---

[7] Location is not meant to refer to an exact place in the brain. Memory capacity is apparently diffused throughout the brain, with some exceptions: e.g., language information which, for most people, is present primarily on the left side of the brain. Location thus refers to functional location of information—which may mean a series of neural pathways not occupying the same physical location.

asked for synonyms for "speedy." In short order people often report back words like "quick," "rapid," "swift," "fast." Your ability to retrieve information via phonetic cues can be demonstrated when you are asked to name words which rhyme with "bat." Words and concepts are not cross-listed under every possible category, however. For instance, most people have considerable difficulty in responding quickly to the demand "name words whose fourth letter is 'a.' "

When the memory system is confronted with a cue which is not directly associated with the desired information, it can often search the general area where the information is stored. This type of search is really a form of problem solving. Thus there are many possible paths to get from one piece of information to another, even when the items were never activated together before: e.g., name a type of dog that rhymes with "folly."[8]

Despite the highly connected structure of LTM, there are many occasions when information may not be accessible. There is a distinction between inaccessibility and absence. This distinction often underlies the difference in sensitivity between recall and recognition. "Who was Lyndon Johnson's Vice President?" Although many readers may not know the answer immediately, they may "know" that they know the answer and this knowledge may induce them to do a prolonged memory search. If the question were rephrased as a recognition task—Was Nelson Rockefeller, Richard Nixon, Hubert Humphrey, or Henry Kissinger, Lyndon Johnson's Vice President?—many more readers will select the correct answer, thereby demonstrating that the information was present in memory.

On the other hand, people often know that they do not know an answer and refuse to do much searching at all: "What is the first name of this writer's wife?" The reader, on analyzing the question might have gone to the location in memory where this information, if it existed, would be found and discovered that there was nothing present under that category.

Obviously, the more information there is stored in LTM, the more things can be recognized and labeled, provided that the information is stored in an organized fashion. Simon and Gilmartin postulated in their model that better chess players have more chess patterns (which they can thus recognize) stored in LTM than poorer players. In the short time available for looking at a chess position in the de Groot task (5 seconds), they assume that everybody is restricted to storing 7 chunks in STM.[9]

---

[8] One way this problem might be solved is by a *generate and test* method. Generate a new letter for the "f" and then test the resulting sound pattern to see if it forms a word in the dog category. See Newell and Simon [75] for an excellent discussion of methods of problem solving.

[9] Given the previous estimate of 5–10 seconds per chunk fixation time, this assumption is quite reasonable. The main problem with this parameter is that it was estimated from experiments in learning verbal materials. Charness [20] has obtained evidence suggesting that virtually all the information extracted during a 5-second exposure to a chess position is stored in LTM. This issue has not been satisfactorily resolved yet.

The key to the mystery of performance in the 5-second task is provided when you consider that the master's average chunk size may be 3–4 or more pieces, e.g., the castled king position in Figure 2.1, whereas the novice's chunk is a single piece on a square. Thus $7 \times 3 = 21$ pieces for the master, but $7 \times 1 = 7$ pieces for the novice. The idea that everyone has the same-sized STM is given further support by the condition of presenting scrambled chess positions. In that situation there are no longer any recognizable patterns larger than single pieces for the master, and he sinks to the level of the novice.

An analogy to the chess board situation for master versus amateur is the case of a child learning to read versus an adult who is already a skilled reader. When the child looks at this page he "sees" a page filled with letters which he must slowly and effortfully recombine and read as words. The adult, however, quickly and effortlessly "sees" the page as a series of words and possibly phrases (which may then have to be effortfully recombined into sentences compatible with his current knowledge about human chess skill). Both the adult and the child look at the same page but they produce very different encodings or descriptions of it, based on the size of the pattern they can use for effortless recognition.

The specific model developed by Simon and Gilmartin is considerably more complex than is outlined here—it describes how patterns are originally learned and later recognized, which pieces will be attended to, how the patterns are reproduced—but the reader can easily perceive its explanatory power.

The simulation does a very good job of imitating strong and weak players by simply altering the number of patterns which are stored in LTM. Simon and Gilmartin estimated the size of the vocabulary of patterns that a master would theoretically need to perform the recall task as well as he does. They arrived at an estimate of about 50,000 patterns—which is roughly the same size as the vocabulary of recognizable words for an adult speaker of English.

Does this research mean that all one needs to do to become a Grand-master is to sit down and memorize 50,000 chess patterns? I can hazard a guess that if you attempted to do this you would undoubtedly perform as well as the Grandmaster on the recall task, but your chess play would hardly improve. How then is it possible to link up this vast knowledge of patterns with chess skill?

Chase and Simon have suggested that the correlation between perceptual skill and chess skill can be accounted for by assuming that many chess patterns are directly associated with appropriate plausible moves. That is, when the master looks at a chess position his recognition of familiar con-figurations of pieces triggers certain "productions" into action. A produc-tion is a behavioral unit which has two components: a condition side and an action side. It can be modeled by a statement of the form: if condition X exists, do action Y. A chess production might be: if pattern X, consider move (plan) *Y*; or, more concretely: if there is an open file, consider moving a rook to it. This can be illustrated by way of a more complex example. Most skilled chess players will recognize the smothered mate position illustrated in Figure 2.2. White, if on move, can mate in 4 moves (or less) via (1) N–B7 ch., K–N1; (2) N–R6 dbl. ch., K–R1 (if K–B1, Q–B7 mate); (3) Q–N8 ch., RxQ; (4) N–B7 mate. Changing nonessential elements of the position (moving the black QRP to QR3) does not change the mate. Other changes, however, make a big difference: e.g., moving the black KRP to R3 or interchanging the black queen and rook.

Humans are probably sensitive to the critical features of such a position. They do not store a copy of each possible smothered mate position or each back row mate position, etc. They probably abstract more general descriptions. In the case of this type of smothered mate the features are probably propositions like: queen on open QR2–KN8 diagonal; knight capable of reaching KB7 in one move; opponent's king on KR1 hemmed in at KN2 and KR2. Probably the latter feature together with one of the former is sufficient to trigger the plan: try to reach a smothered mate position. One can come up with many other examples of such typical tactical plans which are part of every skilled player's repertoire.

Now there is a potential explanation for why, in position A (Figure 2.1), the Grandmasters all considered the correct move, but only a few experts did. There were probably certain features in the position which quite automatically, *when recognized*, elicited the appropriate move. Only those players who recognized the features and possessed the appropriate productions would generate the correct move for subsequent evaluation.

Parenthetically, it also becomes reasonable to speculate about questions like: why does a "highly intelligent" individual when playing chess, miss obvious moves? Moves are only "obvious" when the patterns they spring from are recognized.[10] One can also ask why masters do so well in

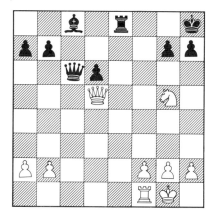

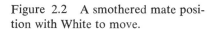
Figure 2.2 A smothered mate position with White to move.

[10] See Botvinnik's text [18] concerning Norbert Wiener, p. 61, for another explanation.

simultaneous exhibitions,[11] where they have only a few seconds to choose a move. If masters automatically generate appropriate plausible moves, these moves will usually be good enough to beat all but the best players at the exhibition. A similar explanation will probably also suffice to explain a master's superiority at speed chess—where the entire game is played in less than 10 minutes. Indeed, if the perceptual process is so important for skilled play, it becomes possible to understand the idiosyncracies of a Bobby Fischer, who insists that the lighting in the tournament hall, the size of the board and the size of all the pieces, all be optimized.

The first few seconds

Following the analysis of de Groot, and Chase and Simon, much of what is critical to choosing a move in chess appears to occur in the first few seconds of exposure to a new (or changed) position. In those first few seconds the skilled player has constructed his internal representation of the position. This phase is usually accompanied by a series of eye movements which fixate on parts of the board or diagram. As Tikhomirov and Posnyanskaya [92] and others have shown, these fixations are made on the functionally important or salient pieces. That is, in the first few seconds when an expert is told to choose a move, he first explores the relations which bind the pieces into functional units, i.e., chunks. Only later does the pattern of eye movements trace out the paths of pieces when they are moved in the "mind's eye." What are the relations which bind pieces into a chunk? Chase and Simon examined the pattern of pauses in a simple perceptual task. The task required that chess players reconstruct a position seen on one board onto a neighbouring board. Players had to glance back and forth between the two boards (presumably to transfer pieces chunk by chunk), and their head movements and reconstruction were recorded on videotape. It was found that chess players paused significantly longer when placing a new piece if the piece had fewer relational links with the previously placed one than if it had many such links. These relations were of two types: chess functional like attack and defence and visual-spatial like proximity, color, and type of piece. If two successively placed pieces had a large number of these relations in common, the latency between their placement was quite short. The function relating interpiece latency and number of shared relations is shown in Figure 2.3.

Thus these researchers were able to use the criterion of a latency greater than 2 seconds to indicate a chunk boundary. Apparently, even during the first eye movements, the skilled chess player is sensitive to important functional relations among pieces.

This phase of perceptual organization was first postulated by de Groot

---

[11] In a simultaneous exhibition the master plays many opponents at once, usually 20 or more, moving steadily from board to board, playing a move at each board.

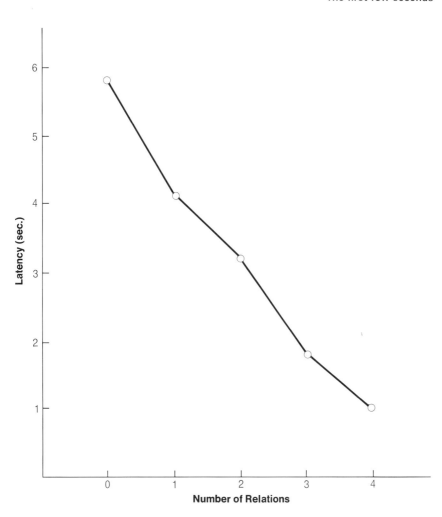

Figure 2.3   Research data on interpiece placement latency in a task where the subject is asked to set up a chess position while viewing the position. (Adapted from Chase and Simon [23], with permission.)

when he noticed that players in his choose-a-move task were initially silent. De Groot notes that it is during this time that the player obtains the "sense" of the position. He recognizes patterns, discovers the state of material balance,[12] and starts generating plausible moves or plans. Following this phase, the thought processes look quite similar for master and less-skilled player, although the paths they explore are quite different.

[12] Material balance refers to how many pieces are present in each army. A position is considered balanced when the same number of pieces of each type are present, or if there is equivalent material present.

Search through the tree of moves

Much of what we know about the analysis procedure which players use in evaluating a move comes from the work of de Groot and that of Newell and Simon [75] and Wagner and Scurrah [98]. Briefly, they found that players explored their candidate moves one branch at a time by a method called progressive deepening. (These authors all used the same procedure: having their subjects think out loud and recording their statements.) Players choose an initial move for consideration and then generate the consequences to some depth, usually no more than 6 or 7 plies. They may then reexplore the same base move by returning to the initial position and then considering new countermoves further down the line. Opinions differ on the rules for generation of a search episode (or line of moves), but they all seem to hinge on the evaluation which is extracted from the terminal position.

One aspect of progressive deepening which seems quite nonintuitive is that the same move may be taken up again later in search. This resumption of an abandoned line is not necessarily the result of a player's having forgotten his analysis. Rather, it indicates that the player may have changed his conceptualization of what is required in the position. Thus a move which is rejected because it failed to lead to the win of material may again be taken up in the context of trying to gain a positional advantage. Much of the human's search through the tree of possible moves is goal directed and the goals may well change as new information is integrated into the knowledge base about the initial position.

Virtually every line of moves mentioned by a player in these experiments was terminated by an evaluative statement. That is, the players noted an advantage or disadvantage for the line of moves. Statements were made like: "not sufficient," "that seems to win a piece," "(the move) will probably win" (see de Groot [31, p. 409]). Of course, that is the goal of dynamic analysis—to reach an evaluation of a move by exploring and evaluating some of its outcomes. One hopes that the "some" in the previous sentence encompasses all of the relevant continuations.

Terminal positions in search are evaluated statically. Some feature or property of the position is usually cited in the evaluative comment, usually just one feature. In this respect, virtually all chess playing programs differ radically from the human. Machines usually rely on a polynomial weighting function to evaluate a position. That involves counting up the pros and cons of a large number of features such as material balance, mobility of pieces, safety of the king, and control of the center. It may be the case that the human conceals the calculations which he goes through to reach an evaluation, and merely mentions the feature with the greatest weight. At present, though, there is no evidence to suggest that the human does go through such an elaborate procedure. One possible reason why only one feature is mentioned is that the line of moves under examination has probably been generated in response to a particular board goal. The evaluation procedure is then reduced to determining if that goal has been met.

As was mentioned earlier, the moves that a player examines are not a random subset of all legal moves. To cut down on searching irrelevant moves, people (and some programs) search heuristically. That is, they use information about chess to help them generate and evaluate a restricted number of moves. Winning a knight for a pawn, all other things being equal, is known to be good. Similarly, any move which will win the "exchange" is evaluated positively. Other heuristics which help chess players focus their search are rules of thumb like: in the opening, move your king to safety by castling; control the central squares of the board; develop your pieces to places where they have high mobility. These principles are typically espoused in chess books.

Such heuristics are valuable because they provide general rules which can be filled by specific types of moves. On the other hand, they are too general to act as hard and fast rules which, when followed, enable a player to play well. That is, they do not act as *algorithms*[13] for playing chess.

Another type of heuristic process which is often found in human play is to make use of information generated in searching a specific move. A particular move found somewhere along a line of investigation may itself become a candidate as a base move. Or certain propositions about relations between pieces may be used to generate new plans or moves. For instance, a player may notice that in following one continuation that one of his opponent's pieces becomes tied down to the defence of another piece. This may elicit the idea of attacking the tied down piece in order to win the other piece—a theme called attacking an "overloaded" piece.

Visualizing positions

All this analysis is carried out in the player's head. How do players keep track of the new positions generated in analysis? Keeping track involves memory and some imagery and is susceptible to spatial errors. Occasionally a blunder can be traced directly to the "imagining" operation. A player will fail to "notice" that moving a piece to a certain square blocks another piece from giving check at a later critical moment. (For an amusing account of just such an hallucination see *Chess Treasury of the Air* [94, p. 273].)

The role of visual imagery in chess has long been of interest to psychologists. It was initially investigated to explain the ability of chess masters to play "blindfold" chess. In this situation the master plays a game entirely in his head—he hears the moves of his opponent (in chess

---

[13] An algorithm is a specific set of rules (i.e., a recipe) which, if followed exactly, will guarantee a successful result. The algorithm for long division is a good example of such a procedure. A particular long-division problem you face may never have been solved before, but you have no trouble doing it.

notation) and then replies with his own moves without ever seeing the board.

At first it was thought that the blindfold player had an image of the board much like that of a photograph or picture—namely that the shape of the pieces, the color of the squares, were all present in vivid detail. Binet in 1893 refuted this view after interviewing many masters. He concluded that the representation used by blindfold players was quite abstract. For instance, a player would know that there was a knight in a certain relation to other pieces in a particular position, but he would not have an image of a particular carved knight. He might know the knight was white, but he wouldn't *see* a certain shade of white.

The reader can easily convince himself that one does not form a detailed image of an entire position. Imagine an empty chessboard. "Place" a bishop on QR3. Name the farthest square the bishop can reach on the long diagonal. Now put a real bishop on a real board and do the same. The time taken to answer KB8 should be markedly different in the two cases. (Parenthetically, how many of you chose a white bishop? Or did the bishop in the imaging case have a color? Such *generative memory* is quite abstract.) Similar conclusions about the nature of the representation of the board were reached by de Groot, and by Reuben Fine in his article on blindfold chess [43].

Apparently the ability to imagine pieces on squares in a chess position is also correlated with chess skill. I conducted an experiment [20] where players were given chess positions verbally, piece by piece, via chess notation. After hearing a position dictated in this fashion at a fairly brisk pace, the players attempted to reproduce the position. Two groups of players were tested: Class A (mean rating = 1870) and Class C (mean rating = 1458). The order in which pieces were read made a large difference in recall, but beyond that, the A players recalled 14 percent more pieces per position, on average. That all players fared poorly when the pieces were "scanned" randomly indicates that they did not perform the task by "imagining" pieces on squares. Rather, they attempted to remember the pieces by remembering the relations which bound them together into chunks. The most favourable scan was one which consecutively named pieces with many relational links.

Evaluation

As was mentioned earlier, the reason for extensive dynamic analysis (search) by players was to evaluate the consequences of a candidate move. Static evaluation of the position after a move is almost never sufficient to judge it accurately. In essence the whole problem of choosing a move in chess comes down to choosing a move that can be correctly evaluated as being superior to others. Or, in a nutshell, the player must decide: does one move leave him with a better position than all others? The decision is extremely simple in the case of giving check and recognizing that it is mate. In most positions, however, the evaluation process is complex.

The point of searching deeply (many moves into a continuation) is to find a position which can be evaluated confidently. The stop rule for search is apparently just that—reaching a position which is recognized as static (or quiescent) and which can be evaluated as good or bad. The more skilled player—the one with more patterns in memory—should, in theory, be able to recognize a terminal position (dead position) sooner than a less skilled player. We *should* be surprised by de Groot's finding that Grandmasters and experts search as deeply into a position. If the above analysis is correct we might expect the Grandmaster to search *less* deeply before reaching a position which can be statically evaluated. Perhaps the apocryphal anecdote in this regard is the one attributed to Reti. When asked to tell how many moves ahead he typically looked when calculating a combination, he is reported as having said "as a rule not a single one" (see [94, p. 39]).

Again the realization occurs that the number of patterns stored in memory may be instrumental in understanding evaluation. It is probable that the chess patterns which are stored in memory are associated not only with information about plausible moves, but also with evaluative information. For instance, most skilled chess players rapidly evaluate the diagram in Figure 2.4 as a win for White. They undoubtedly recognize that in this type of position, with white a pawn ahead, white wins. But if you add either a pair of knights (one for each side), a pair of bishops, a pair of rooks, or a pair of queens to the position with the sole restriction being that no exchanges are forced, most skilled chess players will rate the position as drawn. In this instance, they recognize that in this type of position, with one side ahead a pawn but all pawns on the same side of the board, there is no forced win. Thus, for the skilled player, there is no problem in deciding to transpose to the former or the latter position when contemplating a series of piece exchanges in an earlier part of the game.

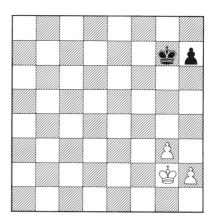

Figure 2.4   A position which is a clear win for White. If rooks, knights, bishops, or queens are present, however, and no exchanges are forced, the position would be a draw.

The player merely needs to generate these two terminal positions and recognize that one is a win, the other a draw. There is no need to calculate (tree search) any farther.

The more accurately a player can classify positions as positive, negative, or neutral, the more likely he is going to defeat an opponent who has less accurate evaluations—particularly if they both search the same continuations. (How many chess playing readers have been faced with the agonizing decision either to "close" a position or exchange pieces and open it up and have been unable to choose because they could not evaluate the resulting positions accurately? After the game, your opponent graciously points out that you should "obviously" have chosen the other alternative.)

It is possible, following this line of reasoning, to speculate on how masters make "intuitive" moves or sacrifices. Perhaps what is meant by an intuitive move is that the player has *recognized* that the resulting position is of a type where an attack almost always succeeds. He doesn't need to calculate out all the details. He knows that when he does search later for a combination he will find it.

Motivation

One elusive aspect of chess skill that psychologists have not come to grips with particularly well is the "will to win." Some players are characterized by their fierce desire to win at all costs. Others are content to seek draws and take few risks. How important is desire? What makes one player an attacker and another a maneuverer? If one player constantly looks for an opportunity to sacrifice material, he is of course more likely to head for positions in which this happens. Another who is more comfortable fighting in closed positions is more likely to play for those sort of positions.

One would have to predict, however, that any Grandmaster should play the same move in the vast majority of situations. This is of course implied by the fact that there is rarely more than one good move in a position, as de Groot has shown. Also, what we mean by chess mastery is that the player has to a large extent mastered the problem of choosing the best move.

There is some interesting data from Tikhomirov and Vinogradov [93] which suggests that if a player is not permitted to get involved in the game emotionally his problem solving ability decreases. Using galvanic skin response (GSR) as a measure of emotionality, these investigators discovered that as players neared a solution to a chess problem or discovered a critical line they showed an emotional response—a swing in galvanic skin response. Tikhomirov and Vinogradov then tried an interesting experiment. They asked the players to attempt to eliminate any emotion or arousal (control the GSR device) during problem solving. If subjects were successful in following these instructions, they solved problems of moderate difficulty but were quite unsuccessful with the more difficult ones. The inference, though speculative,[14] to be derived from this work is that unless a player is fully involved in a game, emotionally as well as cognitively, he may not perform at his best.

Thus there is some evidence to favour an oft-expressed opinion. Namely, that a player who has just arrived at a tournament from a previous one is unable to do his best because he is "all played out" and "emotionally exhausted." (A more sanguine explanation is that his opponents have looked at his recent games and prepared opening novelties against them.)

The road to mastery for man and machine

The process of choosing a move seems to involve perception as a primary component, and in particular, the recognition of thousands of stored patterns. It may seem surprising, but chess is not so much a game of deep thinkers as one of skilled perceivers. Perception apparently holds the key to understanding why the master barely glances at a position before seizing on the correct move, where the novice spends hours staring at a position and never generates the winning move.

Perception operates in two main areas: generating plausible moves and statically evaluating terminal positions. Not only will a plausible move be perceived more quickly by the master, but his long experience with many patterns on the board (50,000 or more) translates into the advantage of being able to evaluate the resulting position more readily.

The process of searching through the tree of possibilities, i.e., dynamic search, is surprisingly similar for both master and class player. They both search to a similar depth; they both examine about as many moves. The reason they end up with such different moves is that one goes down blind alleys whereas the other examines the critical variations.

How does the master build up this repertoire of patterns and chess-specific knowledge? Simon and Chase [84] suggest that it is a matter of practice. You cannot become a concert pianist by practicing one hour a day. Similarly you do not become a master chess player by thinking about chess one hour a day. Simon and Chase observed that it apparently takes a player nearly a decade of intense preoccupation with playing chess to become a Grandmaster—even child prodigies like Capablanca, Reshevsky, Fischer, and others were not exceptions.

Practice does not mean staring at and memorizing 50,000 patterns. It means learning to recognize types of positions and the plans or playing methods which go with them. The reason why the information necessary to become a master does not appear readily in chess books is that it is

[14] There is still much disagreement among psychologists over the interpretation of a change in GSR. In this case a change may be indicative more of concentration than emotion. It may reflect the degree of cognitive strain involved in searching many plies deep. See for instance Leedy and Dubeck [65].

primarily nonverbal; many patterns are difficult to describe in common language terms. Apparently, advice should take the form of: when you see this (pattern description), consider trying this plan. (Some current chess books are attempting to use this approach.) Also, the heuristics which appear in chess books are just not precise enough to cover the many concrete situations which occur over the board. Only the slow process of storing and classifying thousands of patterns seems to work.

As de Groot put it, for the master player "there is nothing new under the sun" ([31, p. 305]). Each position summons up typical playing methods or plans. Perception leads to playing method, which leads to search for the effects of specific moves.

This analysis may offer a rather discouraging picture to chess player and programmer alike. Unless somehow we can systematize and classify thousands of patterns and their appropriate playing methods, there is going to be no shortcut to mastery of chess. Kotov [60] has outlined what he feels are the fundamentals for becoming a Grandmaster. They can be summarized in five points:

1. Know opening theory
2. Know the principles behind typical middle games positions (methods and moves)
3. Be able to assess a position accurately
4. Be able to hit the right plan demanded by a given position
5. Calculate variations accurately and quickly

Almost all of these principles can be subsumed under three general principles: recognize patterns, know their value, and know their corresponding playing methods.

Will the computer reach and finally surpass the best of its human tutors? That day may be some time away unless some of the built-in advantages of humans are incorporated into chess programs. Humans have two major advantages over computers. They have both a vast knowledge base about chess and a set of procedures for efficient manipulation of that base. Master players possess an enormous amount of highly organized chess knowledge. They can recognize thousands of patterns and can evaluate them and generate plans for them. The latter point is an important one: human players are goal directed when playing chess. They know hundreds of heuristics that help structure their search. Computers also use heuristics but often the heuristics are not sensitive enough to the context of the board position.

The second advantage that humans have over most computer programs is the ability to modify their knowledge base. One aspect of this modification process is learning. Humans are learners *par excellence*. They continually add new information to their knowledge base. Chess players learn both specifics: e.g., "I'll never play that move in the Ruy Lopez opening again" and general principles: e.g., "To win this ending I must retain pawns on both sides of the board."[15]

Another type of modification that humans perform quite nicely (as do some complex programs: e.g., Winograd's language comprehension program [100]) is inference—inductive and deductive reasoning. This process is a form of problem solving which seems quite effortless for adults. Suppose you hear the following: "Eliot is a better chess player than Neil. Neil is a better chess player than Peter." Someone now asks you: "Is Eliot a better chess player than Peter?" Most adults rapidly answer "yes." Yet nowhere in either of those two sentences was there any stated relation between Eliot and Peter. By using your knowledge of relationships (that *better than* is a transitive relation for chess skill) you correctly inferred (deduced) that there was a link between Eliot and Peter. Inference is invaluable for chess play. It is this very process which underlies the "method of analogies" discussed in Frey's chapter.

Unfortunately, neither of these two capabilities is present to any sophisticated extent in present computer-chess programs. Thus the key to master level chess by computers would seem to be to provide them with a dynamic knowledge base—a large set of patterns, evaluations, and playing methods (board goals) which can be accessed, sometimes quite indirectly, and modified. Researchers have begun to make considerable headway toward understanding human chess play. If the principles of play uncovered by this research effort are implemented successfully in computer programs, the phenomenon of master level play by the computer may soon appear. Programmers ought to ask themselves: Why can't a computer be more like a man?

---

[15] That computer chess programs are not capable of such sophisticated self-modification need not dictate against the attainment of master level play. Programs function as models of performance. They can be considered to represent the knowledge state of a chess player at one instant in time. Programmers can step in to modify a program, thus acting as the learning component for the program. Admittedly this feedback loop is slower than the human's, but it is not in principle a limiting factor in reaching master level performance—eventually. Examine the other side of the coin: just because human chess players are capable of learning does not guarantee that they all become Masters.

An introduction to computer chess

3

Peter W. Frey
Northwestern University

Chess has been an intriguing problem for individuals interested in machine intelligence for many years. Claude Shannon, the American mathematician, first proposed a plan for computer chess in 1949 [81]. The literature on mechanical chess-playing prior to this time reveals that the early automatons were merely facades which concealed a skilled human player [50]. Shannon believed that chess was an ideal problem for experimentation with machine intelligence since the game is clearly defined in terms of allowed operations (the legal moves) and in the ultimate goal (mate). At the same time, chess is neither so simple as to be trivial nor so complex as to be impossible. Shannon felt that the development of a credible chess program would demonstrate that "mechanized thinking" was feasible.

Shannon's prescription for machine-chess was not modeled on human chess play. As Charness describes in Chapter 2, humans master chess by capitalizing on their vast memory capacity and by organizing information in terms of meaningful piece configurations, plausible moves, and likely consequences. Several million years of evolution have provided the human with a tremendously complex visual pattern-recognition system and a large memory capacity. These permit man to assimilate newly acquired information in such a way that it may be subsequently recalled by using any one of many different retrieval cues. Human problem solving is critically dependent upon recognizing similarities among patterns and recalling information relevant to the specific situation at hand. The modern high-speed computer lacks both of these skills. Pattern-recognition skill in computers is still at a primitive level. Computer memories are large and fast but are organized simplistically in such a way that retrieval strategies based on structural or conceptual similarities are difficult to implement.

54

The computers that were available to Shannon in 1949 were much less powerful than our present machines. Shannon also had an additional handicap in that much less was known about human memory or human information processing at that time. For these reasons it is surprising that Shannon's proposal for machine chess is remarkably similar to the methods widely used today. Two of the strongest programs, KAISSA (the Institute for Control Science, Moscow) and CHESS 4.5 (Northwestern University, Evanston, Illinois), use sophisticated implementations of the basic strategy suggested by Shannon.

Machine representation of the chess board

A modern computer consists of a central processing unit, a memory unit, and multiple devices for the input (e.g., a card reader) and the output (e.g., a high-speed printer) of information. The central processor can perform simple operations such as addition, subtraction, and conditional branching on numbers that are transmitted to it from memory. After the designated calculations have been performed, the "results" are transmitted back to memory. Input and output operations, because of their slow speed, generally involve auxiliary devices that interface directly with the machine's memory. Most computer memories are quite large, ranging in size from several thousand computer "words" to hundreds of thousands of computer "words." A "word" is a binary string (e.g., 01101001011 . . .) in which each bit[1] can take on only two values, generally represented as 0 and 1. A typical computer word consists of 8 or 12 bits in minicomputers and 48 or 64 bits in the high-speed giants. A 64 bit word is especially convenient for chess programming for a reason that most chess players can easily guess.

Shannon suggested that the chess board be represented by having 64 computer words each represent one of the squares of the chess board. Each word in memory can be thought of as a simple mailbox that will hold one piece (i.e., word) of information. Just like a mailbox, each word in memory has a specific address such that the central processor can gather information (e.g., several numbers) from specific memory addresses and —after performing several calculations with these numbers—store the result in one of these same addresses or into a new address according to its instructions.

Shannon suggested that each piece be designated by a number (+1 for a White pawn, +2 for a White knight, +3 for a White bishop, etc.; −1 for a Black pawn, −2 for a Black knight, etc.). Each of these numbers would be stored in the memory address that represented the square on which the piece resided. An empty square would be represented by having a zero stored at the address representing that square. More recent programs have followed this procedure, except a 10×12 board is used rather

[1] "Bit" is an abbreviation for "binary digit", either 0 or 1.

than an 8×8 board with a unique number, such as 99, stored at the address of all squares which are "off-the-board." In this way, the edges of the board can be easily detected. Using this system, the central processor can examine the contents of each memory address and determine if a piece exists on that square and if so, what its type and color is. If the central processor "examined" the address which represents KB4 (f4) and noted a -3 stored at that address, it would "know" that a Black bishop resided on KB4.

Legal moves from any given position can be determined quite easily by simply noting the mathematical relationship among the squares. Assume an assignment of memory addresses to the squares of the board as depicted in Figure 3.1. QR1 is assigned address 22, QN1 becomes address 23, QR2 becomes 32, QR3 becomes 42, QR8 becomes 92, and KR8 becomes 99. All addresses between 1 and 120 that are not depicted in Figure 3.1 would be assigned a value such as 99 because each represents a "square" that is off the board. Now if a knight is located on any square, the 8 potential squares to which it might move can be calculated by adding the following offsets to its present address: $+8$, $+19$, $+21$, $+12$, -8, -19, -21, and -12. For example if a White knight resided on KB3 (square 47) its potential move squares are $47+8$ or 55, $47+19$ or 66, $47+21$ or 68, $47+12$ or 59, etc. Potential king moves can be calculated in a similar manner by using the offsets of -1, $+9$, $+10$, $+11$, $+1$, -9, -10, and -11. After calculating the address of each potential move square, the machine must check the present contents of the new address to determine if the move is legal. If the address contains the number 99, the proposed move is illegal since the new square would be off the board. If the address contains a positive number, the move would be illegal since a positive number indicates that a white piece is already occupying the square. If the new address contains a negative number, the White piece can legally move to the new square[2] and capture the Black piece that occupies the

Figure 3.1 "Mailbox" representation of the chess board.

92	93	94	95	96	97	98	99
82	83	84	85	86	87	88	89
72	73	74	75	76	77	78	79
62	63	64	65	66	67	68	69
52	53	54	55	56	57	58	59
42	43	44	45	46	47	48	49
32	33	34	35	36	37	38	39
22	23	24	25	26	27	28	29

[2] If the White piece were a king, the machine would also have to determine if the square were attacked by an enemy piece.

square. Finally if the new address contained the number zero, it would represent an empty square to which the White piece could legally move.

Calculation of legal moves for a sliding piece such as a bishop, rook, or queen is slightly more complicated. Assume a White bishop is located on square XY (e.g., 35, where $X=3$ and $Y=5$). Examine address $X+1$, $Y+1$ (i.e., 46); if this address contains a positive number the bishop cannot move to this square; if this address contains a negative number, the White bishop can move to the square (capturing a Black piece) but can move no further along this diagonal; if the address contains a zero, the bishop can move to this square, and address $X+2$, $Y+2$ (i.e., 57) should be examined next. In this manner, each of the four potential directions for a bishop move can be checked until an edge (99) or another piece is encountered on each. After $X+1$, $Y+1$ (46), $X+2$, $Y+2$ (57), $X+3$, $Y+3$ (68), etc. are examined, the machine then needs to look at $X+1$, $Y-1$ (44), $X+2$, $Y-2$ (53), etc. and then $X-1$, $Y+1$ (26), $X-2$, $Y+2$ (17), etc. and finally $X-1$, $Y-1$ (24), $X-2$, $Y-2$ (13), etc. In this way, the machine can determine legal moves in all four potential directions for the bishop.

The legal moves for a rook can be determined in a similar fashion. Assume a rook on square ZW (e.g., 67, where $Z=6$ and $W=7$). Examine address Z, $W-1$ (66), Z, $W-2$ (65), Z, $W-3$ (64), etc.; then examine address Z, $W+1$ (68), Z, $W+2$ (69), etc.; next look at address $Z+10$, W (77), $Z+20$, W (87), etc.; finally examine address $Z-10$, W (57), $Z-20$, W (47), etc. In this way, the legal moves for a rook can be determined. For a queen, the legal moves for bishop and rook need to be considered in conjunction. Thus Shannon provided a relatively neat prescription for making pseudolegal moves in chess by machine. I use the term pseudolegal because I have failed to discuss the intricacies involved in determining the legality of moving a pinned piece or considering castling or an *en passant* capture. These additions make our mechanical move generator more complex but do not threaten the feasibility of Shannon's approach.

There is a more modern way to represent the chess board that was first suggested in the late sixties by a Russian computer-chess group [2] and discovered, apparently independently, by the Northwestern computer-chess group (see Chapter 4) and by Berliner [12] at Carnegie–Mellon. Assume, for example, that one is programming a large computer that has a 64-bit computer word. Now instead of assigning one computer word for each square, we will assign 1 bit of each 64 bit computer word to a square. Next we will represent the chess board in terms of 12 words. One word will represent all White pawns by setting a bit to 1 if a White pawn resides on that square and to zero otherwise. A second computer word will represent all Black pawns in the same manner (i.e., 1= piece present, 0= piece absent). A third word will represent all White knights, a fourth for all White bishops, and so forth for all the pieces such that six words are used for the White pieces and six words are used for the Black pieces. In addition to pieces, we can use this procedure (called "bit maps" or "bit boards") to represent other information about the chessboard. Thus, we can have one word that represents all White pieces, one word for all Black pieces, one word for all squares attacked by White pieces, one word for all squares from which a bishop or queen could pin a particular piece against the king, etc. The power of this bit map procedure for expressing chess relationships is limited only by the programmer's skill in selecting important patterns.

The advantage of this approach becomes more apparent when one considers the instruction set for a modern computer. In addition to the common operations of addition and subtraction, the computer can perform Boolean instructions such as "logical-and" and "logical-or." For example, if we have two 8 bit words, say 01011100 and 11010011 and perform an "and" operation with the two words, the result would be 01010000. The new word would have a bit set (i.e., a 1) only at those positions where a 1 appeared in both of the original words. The "or" operation sets a bit in the new word at each position where a 1 appears in *either* of the two original words. For our example case, an "or" operation would produce 11011111. These operations can be applied to chess programming with highly desirable results.

Consider generating all legal moves for a White knight on KB3. First, the central processor "fetches" a bit map from memory that has a bit set for each position representing the squares to which a knight on KB3 could move. In this schema, central memory would contain 64 bit maps representing potential moves for a knight from each of the 64 squares on the board. Secondly, the central processor would fetch a bit map representing the positions of all White pieces presently on the board. The central processor would then negate (change 1's to 0's and 0's to 1's) the White piece map and then "and" this new map with the knight move map. The resulting bit map would represent all pseudolegal moves for the knight. Notice that move generation in this case involved two "fetch" instructions and two "Boolean" instructions. The Shannon "mailbox" procedure requires many more computer operations to determine the same result.

Consider a simple problem in chess. During the middle game, White decides to examine his attacking possibilities. He poses the question, "can I fork Black's queen and king with one of my knights on this next move?" Answering this question requires an assessment of several subgoals such as

1. Does there exist a square that is a knight's jump away from both the Black king and Black queen?
2. Is there a White knight positioned such that it can jump to the forking square in one move?
3. Is the forking square undefended by Black?

For a human, the answers to these three questions can be determined at a glance. For a machine, the answer is more difficult to determine.

If we start at the goal and work backward using Shannon's mailbox method, we first need to add the eight Knight offsets (+8, +19, +21, etc.) to the Black king square and then store these eight locations. Next we add the eight knight offsets to the Black queen square and compare the resultant of each addition to the eight stored values. If we find a match, then we must test the square's contents to determine if it is on the board (i.e., not 99) and if no White piece presently occupies the square (i.e., not a positive number between 1 and 6). If we find a match and the address does not contain a positive number, we have determined that a forking square exists.

Next we must determine if one of our White knights is located a knight's jump away from this square. This can be done by adding the eight knight offsets to the address of the forking square and then checking to see if any of these contain a +2 (a White knight). Finally, we need to determine if the forking square is attacked by a Black piece. This would be a tedious operation if we needed to check the legal moves of each Black piece to see if it can attack the forking square. Generally the attack squares for each piece are usually calculated and stored at the beginning of each move calculation. These data can then be used repetitively during the subsequent analyses of potential moves. In any event, the machine must execute at least 50 computer instructions in order to answer the question in an affirmative manner.

On the other hand, let us examine a bit map approach to this same question. First, we would "fetch" bit maps from memory for the potential knight moves from the Black king's square, from the Black queen's square, and from the White knight's present square. Next, the machine would fetch a bit map from memory representing the location of all white pieces. This map would be negated (a Boolean "not" operation, all 1's becomes 0's, all 0's become 1's) and the resultant map would be compared using an "and" operation with the resultant map produced by "and"ing the other three bit maps. If this final map were nonzero, a forking square exists. Finally, a bit map representing all squares attacked by Black would be "and"ed with the previous result. If this last operation produced a map containing all zeroes, one would know that the forking square was not being attacked by Black. Note that the bit map approach answers the same question, but uses only 5 "fetch" instructions, 1 "not" instruction, and 4 "and" instructions. A very significant increase in machine efficiency.

At present, many computer programs use bit maps which are oriented toward move generation and basic relationships among the pieces. There is no reason, however, why these bit maps cannot represent complex relationships such as "all squares accessible to a particular bishop in three moves given the constraints of the present board configuration." The advice-taking program developed by Zobrist and Carlson [101], which has been "tutored" by Charles Kalme, makes extensive use of bit maps as part of its pattern recognition scheme.

Static evaluation functions

Shannon [81] proposed that a move be selected by considering potential moves by White, replies by Black, counter-replies by White, etc. until relatively static terminal positions were reached. This examination of move sequences is commonly referred to as the look-ahead procedure and will be discussed at length shortly. Shannon proposed that each terminal position be evaluated in a mechanical way. He suggested a crude evaluation function which examined the material balance (9,5,3,3,1 for queen, rook, bishop, knight, and pawn, respectively), the relative mobility for each side (number of available legal moves), and pawn structure (penalties for doubled, backward, and isolated pawns). In his appendix he suggested additional factors for consideration such as control of the center, pawn structure adjacent to the king, passed pawns, centralized knights, knights or bishops in a hole, rooks on open files, semiopen files, or on the seventh rank, doubled rooks, attacks on squares adjacent to the enemy king, pins, and other factors. The idea was to weigh each of these factors according to its importance and then add all items together to determine the value of the terminal position. Once these values have been determined, the machine can select a move which would "lead toward" the most desirable terminal position.

Other factors for a general evaluation function have been suggested by Shannon's successors. Greenblatt and his associates at MIT [48] have included a "piece-ratio change" term that encourages piece exchanges when the machine is ahead in material and discourages piece exchanges when it is behind. The MIT group also included a king-safety term that encourages the king to remain on the back rank when queens are on the board. Church (see Chapter 6) has suggested that the king safety term should include the number of moves required before the king can castle. Turing [96] suggested a king-safety factor that "imagines" a queen on the king's square and subtracts points for the number of legal moves which the queen would have from that square. It is important to realize that king safety becomes less important as the number of pieces on the board diminishes and that in the end game the king-safety term becomes a hindrance. In the end game, for example, the Northwestern program (see Chapter 4) adds evaluation points if the opponent's king is close to the edge of the board.

In writing an evaluation function for a chess program, it is essential that efficient computer instructions be employed because this aspect of the program is used repetitively (i.e., ten thousand to 100 thousand times during each move selection). For this reason it is probably best not to include every conceivable evaluation term in the function since each new term means a small increment in the time which is required to evaluate each terminal position. A good evaluation function is one that assesses the critical aspects of the position in question and does this as efficiently as possible. For each new term which is added to the evaluation function one must ask if the chess information gained is worth the cost in computation time that this additional assessment will require. The time requirement is important, of course, because computers play chess using the same tournament rules as humans, such as requiring 40 moves in the first two hours of play.

The structure of the evaluation function is dependent on the type of look-ahead procedure which is employed. In a program such as Berliner's [12], the emphasis is on evaluating a small number of terminal positions (e.g., 500) in a very thorough manner and therefore a highly complex evaluation function is necessary. In programs in which a very large number of terminal positions are examined, the evaluation function must be very fast and thus simplistic. For example, the "Technology" chess program by Gillogly at Carnegie–Mellon [46] examines only the material advantage (or disadvantage) for each terminal position and looks at as many as 500,000 terminal positions before selecting a move in tournament play. At present it is not clear which strategy will eventually lead to the best machine chess although our present best model, the human, clearly uses the former approach rather than the latter.

Our experience in computer chess over the past few years seems to indicate that future chess programs will probably benefit from evaluation functions that alter as the general chess environment changes. Such "conditional" evaluation functions will consider the type of opening, the stage of the game, the pawn structure, and the king defenses and then construct an evaluation function appropriate to the particular position. Computer programming techniques that use a hierarchical structure involving "discrimination nets" and "decision tables" are useful for this purpose. This modification would make the machine's evaluation procedure more similar to human analysis.

The look-ahead procedure

The most obvious way to examine future moves which might occur in a chess game is to generate all legal moves for the side on-the-move, all legal replies for his opponent, all legal counters, etc. until the possible sequences of moves and counter-moves seem to be sufficiently deep to make a terminal evaluation appropriate. As Shannon [81] pointed out in his classic paper, this "type-A strategy" has a serious drawback. The number of legal moves at each position (on the average, about 38) and the depth which seems necessary for reasonable play (6–10 plies), generate an enormous number of terminal positions. For example, a 2-ply (i.e., one move for each side) analysis of all legal moves, assuming 38 moves at each position, would generate 1444 terminal positions. A 4-ply analysis would generate 2,085,136 terminal positions. A 6-ply analysis would generate 3,010,936,-389 terminal positions! This difficulty with the exhaustive look-ahead procedure is referred to as the "exponential explosion" since the number of terminal positions increases exponentially with depth.

The look-ahead procedure is often discussed in terms of a "game tree" since a diagramatic depiction of the possible sequences of moves leads to a structure that branches out much like a tree. The original position is like the trunk of a tree which leads to several moves (the major limbs) which in turn lead to counter-moves (the large branches) which lead to counter-counter-moves (the small branches), etc. The point at which one branch subdivides into many smaller branches is called a "node" of the tree and represents an intermediate board position in the game tree.

Shannon suggested that the exponential-explosion problem be solved by examining only a small subset of the potential legal moves at each node. He labeled this approach as a "type-B strategy." If one makes a 6-ply analysis examining only 5 continuations at each node instead of 38, the number of terminal positions would be 5^6 rather than 38^6 or "only" 15,625 positions. Since there are never more than 5 reasonable moves in any given position [31], this suggestion appears to have great merit. One merely needs to select 5 "plausible" moves at each node and examine these continuations while ignoring all others. To implement this approach, the machine must be able to determine which of the potential moves at each node are most reasonable. The machine subroutine which is designed for this purpose is called the "plausible-move generator."

Human chess players have a great facility for selecting reasonable moves and reasonable replies at each node. The ability of skilled players to play a respectable game of "speed" chess (e.g., 5 seconds per move) demands this. This human ability seems to be perceptual (see Chapter 2) since it is unlikely that the consequences of each move can be examined thoroughly in 5 seconds. When de Groot [31] studied the protocols of skilled players, he reported that the experts failed to select the best move because it was not even considered in their verbal analysis of the position. Apparently, their "plausible-move generators" were not as discerning as the ones used by the grandmasters. The success of Shannon's "type B" strategy depends upon our ability to develop a plausible move generator for the computer. History has shown that this is a very difficult problem. Most computer chess programs contain fatal blind spots in this regard and this severely limits the quality of their play.

Let us assume for the moment, however, that it is possible to develop a reasonable static evaluation function and a reasonable plausible-move generator for our machine. Given these two basic functions, how can we use them to decide which move to select when confronted with a specific game position? How do we construct a game tree and then use it to select our move? There are actually several procedures for doing this.

The method initially suggested by Shannon involves the "minimax" procedure proposed by von Neuman and Morgenstern [97] in their classic book. A move is selected by "looking ahead" in the game tree from the base position to some predetermined depth. At each node the machine assumes that the player who has the move will select that alternative that is "best" for him. "Best" would be defined in this case by the static evaluation function. If White has the move from the base position and if the static evaluation function is represented such that large numbers reflect an advantage for White (and small numbers favor Black), then the machine will maximize (choose the pathway leading to the largest evaluation) at the odd nodes (i.e., White's turn to move) and will minimize (choose the pathway leading to the smallest evaluation) at the even nodes (i.e., Black's turn to move). This process of alternately choosing the maximum value and minimum value leads to the descriptive name of "minimaxing."

The machine's procedure for analyzing a game tree can best be explained by using an example. Let us assume a starting board position with all pieces and pawns in their original position. White, as always, has the first move. Assume that the machine analyzes to a depth of 4 half-moves (4 plies) and uses its plausible move generator to develop the game tree depicted in Figure 3.2. The squares represent a position in which it is White's turn to move and the circles represent a position in which Black has the move. The pathways between successive positions each represent a potential move which seems plausible to the machine. The nodes of the game tree can be generated in many different orders, but generally a "depth-first" procedure is used. That is, the first branch is explored to its maximum depth before the machine starts on a second branch. An alternate procedure would be a "breadth-first" search in which all the nodes at one level are explored prior to examining nodes at a deeper level. The nodes in Figure 3.2 are numbered in the order in which they would be generated if a "depth-first" search had been employed. The machine would first examine (1) P–K4, P–K4; (2) N–KB3, N–QB3, evaluate the terminal board configuration and then store this value. Next, the machine would examine (1) P–K4, P–K4; (2) N–KB3, P–Q3 apply the static evaluation function, and store the result. Next, the computer would explore (1)

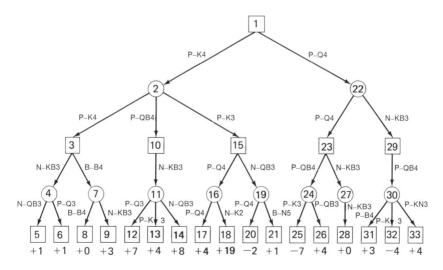

Figure 3.2   Sample game tree for the opening position in chess.

P–K4, P–K4; (2) B–B4, B–B4, evaluate, and store the result. This procedure would continue until the entire game tree in Figure 3.2 had been generated and an evaluation calculated for each of the 17 terminal positions.

After each position is evaluated, the value is returned to the level above (the immediate parent) and it becomes the "best value so far" for that node. Each additional descendent of this same parent node is examined in the same fashion, and when a value is obtained for each terminal position, the value is compared to the best value found so far. If the value associated with the most recent evaluation is better for the side to move than the best value so far, the new move is stored in memory and its value becomes the new "best value so far." After all of the descendents of each node have been examined, the best value so far and the move associated with that value are "backed-up" to the level above. This process is continued until a value and a move for the current position are determined.

For expository purposes, let us assume a simple evaluation function for the opening which is computed as follows. Let LW and LB equal the number of legal moves for White and Black respectively, let CW and CB equal the minimum number of moves required for White and Black to castle respectively, and let SW and SB equal the number of central squares (K4, K5, Q4, Q5) attacked by White and Black respectively. Our evaluation function is then defined as: $(LW-LB)+[3 \times (CB-CW)]+[3 \times (SW-SB)]$. The larger the number, the better the position from White's point of view. The numbers which appear underneath each terminal position in Figure 3.2 represent the result of applying this evaluation function to each of these positions. The intermediate calculations are presented in Table 3.1. Note the laborious calculations necessary for even a very simple evaluation function such as this one.

To select a move, the computer would apply the minimax procedure to this game tree. The two terminal positions "sprouting" from node 4 would be examined and the minimum evaluation (it is Black's turn to move) would be "backed-up" to node 4 ($+1$). The two terminals "sprouting" from node 7 would be examined next and the minimum evaluation would be "backed-up" to node 7 ($+0$). In a similar manner, "backed-up" values for nodes 11, 16, 19, 24, 27, and 30 of $+4$, $+4$, -2, -7, $+0$, and -4 respectively would be selected. Next, the machine would maximize at node 3 (it is White's move), "backing-up" that value from its descendents, nodes 4 and 7, which is largest ($+1$). Maximizing at nodes 10, 15, 23, and 29 would produce "backed-up" values of $+4$, $+4$, $+0$, and -4 respectively. Moving toward the base node again, "backed-up" values for nodes 2 and 22 would be selected by minimizing since it would be Black's turn to move. Thus node 2 would have a value of $+1$ and node 22 would have a value of -4. Finally, the machine would select a move at the base node by maximizing between nodes 2 and 22 and this would lead to the selection of node 2 (i.e., P–K4). Although this minimax procedure can lead to some confusion when it is applied by humans, it is easily

TABLE 3.1   Preliminary calculations used by a primitive evaluation function

Terminal position	Legal moves		Moves to castle		Center squares attacked	
	White	Black	White	Black	White	Black
5	27	29	2	3	3	3
6	27	32	2	3	3	2
8	33	33	2	2	2	2
9	33	27	2	2	2	3
12	27	29	2	4	3	2
13	27	29	2	3	3	2
14	27	25	2	4	3	3
17	38	34	3	3	3	3
18	38	22	3	3	3	2
20	33	35	3	3	3	3
21	31	33	3	2	3	1
25	30	34	4	3	3	3
26	30	29	4	4	3	2
28	29	29	3	3	4	4
31	30	24	4	3	3	3
32	30	28	4	2	3	3
33	30	23	4	2	3	2

followed by a machine. The choice rule at each node is precise and therefore the machine only needs to remember whether to minimize or maximize at odd-ply levels and vice-versa at even ply levels. The operation of selecting the largest or smallest value for the potential descendents at each node is trivial for the machine. Thus the minimax strategy provides a workable procedure for the machine to use in selecting a move.

Backward pruning

Although Shannon apparently never implemented his plan for playing chess by computer, Newell, Shaw, and Simon [74] did and soon discovered that much of the laborious tree-searching involved in the minimax procedure can be avoided. The reason can be easily demonstrated by examining Figure 3.2. Assume that the computer generates nodes sequentially in the depth-first order depicted in Figure 3.2 and evaluates each terminal node as soon as it has been generated. After all of the descendents of node 4 have been generated and the resulting terminal positions have been statically evaluated, the machine can "back-up" the appropriate evaluation to node 4. In the present case, this would be a value of $+1$. Now at node 3, it is White's turn to move so that the larger of the values backed-up at nodes 4 and 7 will be selected. For this reason, the machine can determine in advance that node 3 will eventually have a value which is $+1$ or larger. The value would never be less than $+1$ since White could always select the pathway leading to node 4. Given this information, the computer can deduce that it is a waste of time to generate and evaluate node 9. The reason for this is that the evaluation value for node 8 is less than $+1$ and black will choose the descendent of node 7 with the smallest value. Therefore node 7 will have a final backed-up value which is 0 or less independent of the value eventually computed for node 9. Since 0 is less than $+1$, White will choose the pathway to node 4 and not the pathway to node 7. Therefore it is senseless to examine any further descendents of node 7 once a value has been found which is equal to or less than $+1$. This reasoning can be applied throughout the tree. When the branching factor (i.e., the average number of descendents for each node) is high, this procedure will lead to a substantial reduction in the number of nodes in the game tree which need to be generated and evaluated. In the example presented in Figure 3.2, this "pruning" procedure would eliminate nodes 9, 19, 20, 21, 29, 30, 31, 32, and 33 from the minimax search. When the game tree involves more descendents from each node (say 25 instead of only about 2 in our example) and the tree extends to 5 or 6 plies in depth, this "backward-pruning" method can lead to a tremendous saving in search time.

The technical name for this procedure is the α–β algorithm because the value for the move which is currently best for White during the tree search is labeled α while the value for Black's best move so far is called β. This α–β algorithm has made the minimax procedure feasible in many problem-solving tasks where it would otherwise be totally unrealistic because of time constraints. The beauty of this modification is that it always produces the same result as the full minimax procedure [59]. One factor that is very important to the efficiency of an α–β minimax tree search is the order in which the moves are generated and tested. If White's best moves and Black's best replies are considered first, a great many weaker alternatives need not be examined. For example, if White considers QxP and Black can reply BxQ, it is wasteful for Black to generate and evaluate 34 other moves which do not involve the capture of White's queen. If the queen capture is examined first, White "knows" that QxP is a "losing" move and there-fore should not be attempted. Moves such as BxQ are called "refutation moves" since they refute the opponent's previous move(s). By examining refutation moves first, the machine can reduce the number of nodes in the tree by a substantial amount. The efficiency produced by proper ordering of the moves is enormous since each pathway eliminated early in the tree also eliminates all the potential descendents that would "sprout" from that pathway.

Present computer-chess programs place great emphasis on ordering the moves at each node such that strong moves will be examined first. To do this, the program uses "heuristics" (i.e., general rules-of-thumb) that provide useful information concerning what kinds of moves in a particular situation will lead to rapid pruning. One important heuristic is that of examining all capturing moves first. Captures are common pruning moves since they refute any previous move by the opponent which has left a piece *en prise*. Captures also reduce the size of the game tree by eliminating pieces from the board. This usually has the effect of decreasing the number of legal moves that can be generated from each node. A decrease of a few moves in a tree growing exponentially has a surprisingly large effect.

Another commonly used heuristic is to have the program store previous refutation moves in some other part of the game tree and to try these moves again in each new position of the tree. In some situations Black, for example, may have a move that is strong against a variety of moves for White. In this type of situation, poor moves by White can be most efficiently "pruned" from the game tree by always examining first this one move for black each time it is Black's turn to move in the tree search. Because this procedure involves remembering previous refutation or "killer" moves, it is often referred to as the "killer heuristic."

It is interesting to note that this look-ahead minimax procedure is essentially a blind search. It is only after the sequence of moves has been generated and the terminal position evaluated that the machine can determine if this prior activity was worthwhile. This process bears some resemblance to Darwinian evolution. Reproduction in biological organisms produces new variations in a somewhat haphazard fashion. These variations are acted upon by natural selection (i.e., nature's evaluation function). Selection among the new variations occurs by a retrospective process. Only those variations that survive the rigors of the natural environment persist long enough to reproduce. The minimax procedure works in a similar retrospective manner, selecting those variations that "survive" the scrutiny of the evaluation function. The success of this "blind" search process in biological evolution indicates the feasibility of the procedure. However, biological evolution has taken millions of years while the selection of chess moves must occur in 3 minutes or less. The weakness of this process, therefore, lies in its inefficiency rather than in its ultimate feasibility.

In a recent article in *Artificial Intelligence*, a Russian group [3] has suggested a technique for making the tree search more efficient. Their idea is based upon the observation that the machine's calculations in the game tree are highly repetitive. For example, there might be a position on the board in which (1) NxP, PxN; (2) BxP, BxB; (3) RxB, RxR; (4) QxR, QxQ or some similar exchange is possible. In order for White to determine that these exchanges are not worth initiating, the machine must examine all captures on this square in all possible orders. Unfortunately, at each new node in the tree where it is White's turn to move, this same potential set of captures may exist and thus need to be refuted each time by generating all possible capture sequences. Most programs would refute NxP several thousand times in this way at various locations in the game tree. Obviously this is highly wasteful since most of the positions in the game tree are highly similar and the outcome of this exchange will be the same in almost all of these cases.

The Russians have suggested a procedure which they call "the method of analogies." The strategy is to examine refutation moves in detail and determine all factors which are necessary for this refutation to remain true. This is really a case of theorem-proving since it attempts to establish a set of postulates that must be true for the refutation to remain effective. The actual proofs are quite complicated and involve such information as the number and types of pieces bearing upon a particular square, the absence of any pieces which might block the attack pathway of a sliding piece, and the pin status (relative and absolute) of pieces involved in the exchange. If such a plan is implemented, the move NxP could be rejected after checking a few board features rather than having to generate and test all sequences of captures each time. This strategy could produce a very significant improvement in middle-game play since it would produce rapid pruning in the game tree and would thereby eliminate many pathways from further search.

There are tree-searching methods that are different from the $\alpha-\beta$ mini-max procedure. General discussion of these are provided by Nilsson [77] and by Slagle [88]. In Chapter 7 of this book, Harris describes one of the more powerful alternatives which is similar to progressive-deepening as described by de Groot [31].

Quiescence

In using the look-ahead game tree approach, it is often difficult to determine when a node should be considered terminal and ready for evaluation. A major source of error is the premature evaluation of a node giving an erroneous impression of the advantage or disadvantage of that position. The problem for the machine is to avoid applying the "static" evaluation function to a position that is not static or "quiescent." If an evaluation is made on an active node, such as one representing a position in the middle of a piece exchange, the calculated value may be grossly in error. It would be a blunder of major proportions to evaluate a position after RxQ if the next move for the opponent was BxQ. The notion of quiescence applies to material evaluations and also in a more subtle way to positional evaluations. For example, a knight or bishop may have to move to a relatively unfavorable square in order to eventually reach its "post" in a hole or in some other desirable position. If an evaluation is made while the knight or bishop is "en route," the machine may conclude that the necessary sequence of moves is not worth examining any further. Unfortunately, it has been very difficult to program a machine to "understand" whether a position is active or static.

Many programs try to compensate for this lack of understanding by always examining capture sequences to their end until no additional captures exist. Unfortunately even this approach is oblivious to pins or other positional moves that guarantee a gain in material for the opponent. Checks on the king can also lead to serious problems. In many positions a series of checking moves can proceed for 10, 12, or 14 plies without really accomplishing anything. Unfortunately, the machine is weak at discriminating between "aggressive" checks and "useless" checks. In order to prevent an exponential explosion of the game tree, most programs place a limit upon the number of checks which can be pursued without an immediate gain of material or mate. In most cases, this limit is about 2 extra plies. Thus, if a tree search were structured for a 5-ply search in general, checks might be pursued to 7 plies and captures out to 12 or 15 plies, whatever was necessary to exhaust the different sequences of captures. These procedures clearly improve the quality of play. It would be preferable, however, for the machine to be able to assess the quiescence of a position directly and terminate its search on this criterion rather than at some fixed depth which has no rationale other than the time limit for choosing a move. Harris amplifies this point in Chapter 7.

It might seem reasonable to solve this problem by searching the game tree to great depth and thereby looking far enough ahead to compensate for a less-than-perfect evaluation function or for a poor notion of quiescence. It has been easier to increase the search depth by acquiring faster machines and developing more efficient tree-search procedures than it has been to improve the machine's evaluation function or its notion of quiescence. Depth of search, in and of itself, produces a considerable increase in the machine's degree of "understanding." Many chess concepts are clearly depth dependent. With a fixed 2-ply search supplemented by a check and capture search, the machine will completely miss a simple forking manœuvre. With a 4-ply search, however, the computer appears to develop an "understanding" of the fork and will select moves to avoid this simple trap.

Greater depth can be achieved in the middle game if a very primitive evaluation function (such as an analysis of material only) is used. Additional depth might also be obtained by developing a special central processing unit with an instruction set including chess operations. Even with the blinding speed available with modern hardware, this approach would still have an optimistic limit of around 8 ply for a full-width search during the middle game. This does not augur well for brute force solutions to machine chess since most good human players find it necessary to calculate to 12 or 14 plies at least once during the middle game. Time will tell whether hardware innovations will permit future machines to substitute brute strength for finesse. The mathematics of the situation, however, are highly unfavorable to the brute strength approach.

Plausible-move generators

For those who have concluded that a brute-force, full-width search (i.e., Shannon type-A strategy) will never be able to look ahead far enough to play acceptable chess, there is a second method, that of selecting only a few of the progeny at each node for further examination (i.e., Shannon type-B strategy). This can be dangerous since a move excluded from the game tree can never be made across the board. If the machine were successful, however, in developing a good plausible move generator such that only 3 moves, on the average, sprouted from each node, the depth of search could be increased dramatically. A 12-ply search with 3 sprouts per node produces 531,441 terminal positions. With 30 sprouts per node, the number of terminal nodes becomes 810,000 after only 4 ply. This type of calculation has convinced many people, including Shannon, that emphasis should be placed on developing an accurate plausible-move generator.

The Greenblatt program [48] attempts to select the most promising moves at each node. The search width for tournament play is usually set at 15, 15, 9, 9, and 7 moves for the first, second, third, fourth, and fifth ply, respectively. Moves are selected that cause pieces to attack squares in the center and near the enemy king. Moves that block opponent's pieces or unblock friendly pieces are also considered. Priority is given to attacks on weak pawns, pinned pieces, pieces defending other pieces, etc. All checks are investigated within the first 5 ply. All captures are examined within the first 2 ply. Priority is given to considering a few moves of several different pieces rather than many moves of only one or two pieces. In all, Greenblatt uses about 50 heuristics for computing the plausibility of the different descendents at each node.

Berliner [12] also places great emphasis upon reducing the branching factor at each node. He feels that a successful move generator will average only 1.5 descendents from each node in the tree. Because of this belief, he is willing to accept very long computation times for determining plausible moves and thereby restrict his game tree to 500 nodes or less. This approach more nearly approximates human chess play than do the brute-force procedures. The success of Berliner's approach will depend very heavily upon his skill in transmitting a tremendous amount of chess knowledge to the machine.

The difficulty of building an "intelligent" plausible-move generator can best be illustrated by citing several examples. Consider the board position depicted in Figure 3.3, taken from a game between Kirdetzoff (White)

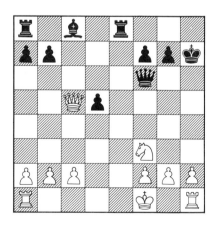

Figure 3.3   Position after 16 moves between Kirdetzoff (White) and Kahn (Black), Copenhagen, 1918.

and Kahn (Black) played in Copenhagen in 1918. Black, with the move, has several plausible lines of play. Developing the bishop seems reasonable since it would also double his rooks. The queen pawn is *en prise*, so moves that defend it are plausible. White's QN pawn can be captured with resultant pressure on White's queen rook. All of these moves are reasonable. The winning move for Black, however, was QxN! Play continued (17) PxQ, B–R6+; (18) K–N1, R–K3; (19) Q–B7, QR–K1; (20) R–KB1, R–K8; (21) White resigns. The move Q–B7 for White was necessary to prevent R–N3 mate. This is a nice example of Morphy's sacrifice, clearly demonstrating that a positional advantage can be worth much more than a material advantage. For a machine, however, losing a queen for a knight is an "unthinkable" exchange and would probably not survive a superficial plausibility analysis. If QxN is not even entered into the game tree, it can never be selected as the across-the-board move.

A second example of this same idea is taken from a recent game between Adorjan (White) and Tompa (Black) in the 1974 Hungarian championship. After Black's 27th move (N–R4), the position depicted in Figure 3.4 was reached. In this active position, White has a number of seemingly aggressive moves. Play continued (25) QxN!, PxQ; (26) R–N3+, B–N2; (27) N–B5, Q–B1; (28) NxB, PxP; (29) N–K6+, K–R1; (30) BxP+, P–B3; (31) RxP!, Black resigns. Again we observe a queen sacrifice that gains a positional advantage at a major cost in material.

In both of these examples, a sacrifice in material was followed by a series of moves ultimately leading to victory. However, these subsequent moves were not an uninterrupted sequence of checks or captures and therefore the value of the queen sacrifice could not be easily analyzed with a deep but narrow tree search. Most programs place heavy emphasis on material factors simply because this strategy is necessary to maintain reasonable play. If the machine were to give positional factors equal weight, it would routinely throw away its material in unsound sacrifices. In the great majority of cases, a loss of a piece is tantamount to losing the game.

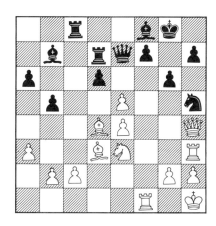

Figure 3.4 Position after Black's 27th move, Adorjan (White) vs. Tompa (Black), Hungarian Championship, 1974.

The use of a reasonable plausibility function seems to automatically exclude the brilliant sacrificial moves which add flair and excitement to chess.

In addition to material sacrifices, there are other excellent moves often missed by a plausible move generator. Figure 3.5 depicts a tactical position with White to move. Black has a pawn advantage and White's queen is presently *en prise*. White can win a pawn by (1) QxQ+, RxQ; (2) BxP or can simply hold his position by moving the queen to defend the bishop such as Q–N5 or Q–N8+. Each of these moves would be highly plausible for a machine since they win or "save" material. The correct move, however, is one which leaves both the queen and bishop *en prise*, namely B–Q6. If Black responds with QxQ, then R–B8 is mate. If Black responds with RxB, then Q–N8+ leads to mate. If Black captures the bishop with his knight, then QxQ+ wins. Only a dynamic analysis indicates that B–Q6 is correct and thus a plausible move generator that selects moves on a static basis would most certainly exclude B–Q6.

A final example is depicted in Figure 3.6. In this position, Black has a material advantage and it is White to move. There are a large number of potentially plausible moves but the correct move is one that seems, at least superficially, to be unsound. The proper move is Q–R6, virtually

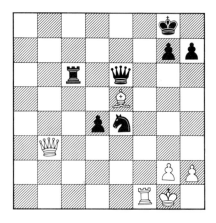

Figure 3.5 The best move for White seems plausible only after considerable analysis.

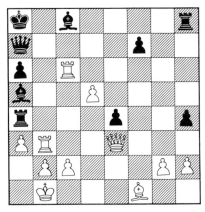

Figure 3.6 White can launch a winning attack with a move that, on the surface, appears to be unsound.

destroying Black's game. Few, if any, computer programs would consider this move plausible on the basis of a static analysis of the position. Only dynamic analysis would show that the rook is "riveted" to the back rank and therefore cannot capture the queen.

One of the characteristics of chess as a research environment for analyzing heuristic search is that the most promising continuation is often not discernible from a superficial analysis of the position. This is clearly evident in the examples just cited. Techniques based on a hill-climbing strategy, such as forward pruning, face serious problems in this type of search environment. Berliner has recognized this inadequacy of traditional forward-pruning search procedures and has developed a coping strategy he calls the "causality facility" [12]. This technique permits his program to discover an important problem deep in the search tree and to pass this information down to lower levels of the tree. The new insight is then used to restructure the search at shallow levels. This approach more nearly approximates a human search process and provides a viable alternative to the full-width search strategy.

Selective searching, deep in the game tree, can lead to additional problems whether it results from forward pruning or is part of a quiescence analysis following a limited-depth full-width search. If the tree-search is not tightly structured and firmly controlled, the machine can get lost at some deep level of the tree and spend hours trying to select the proper variation in a chess environment in which each pathway leads to an exploding number of potential continuations. This problem plagued the TECH II program from MIT at the 1974 ACM tournament in San Diego and has been discussed in some detail by the authors of COKO [61].

Full-width searching

The difficult problems associated with forward pruning have encouraged several programmers to employ a full-width search strategy. Both the Northwestern group and the Russian group [2] develop game trees in which all legal continuations are examined from each node out to a fixed depth. This full-width search is supplemented at the terminal nodes by a narrow search of potential exchange sequences and a few checking moves. The obvious weakness of this strategy is that deep searches are not possible. Berliner [12] has discussed the blunders that inevitably accompany shallow searching. Two of the most common problems are the absence of long-range planning and a special phenomenon Berliner has labeled the "horizon effect."

These problems can be demonstrated by reference to Figure 3.7, which is a slight variation of Figure 1.10 of Berliner's thesis [12]. In this position, with White to move, there is a clear and obvious win that even a chess novice can recognize after a moment's thought and a bit of counting. The White rook pawn is closer (in moves) to its promotion square than the Black king and its advance cannot be impeded in any way.

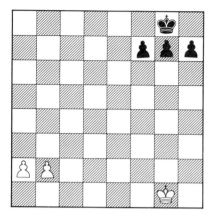

Figure 3.7   White to move and win.

This observation, however, involves long-range planning (being aware that pawn promotion is desirable and that this goal is highly relevant to the present situation) as well as some dynamic computations to determine if the desired goal can be attained. Unfortunately for the machine, a shallow search recognizes only those outcomes that exist within the search horizon so that the promotion of the pawn is not discovered until the event becomes part of the game tree.

On the basis of a static analysis of this position, the machine notes that Black has three pawns and White has only two and thus assumes that Black has the advantage. If the machine were White and were offered a draw, it would readily accept even though this would be utter folly. Static evaluation can be very misleading.

To get a clear idea of the problem, let us analyze Figure 3.7 by having the Northwestern program (CHESS 4.4) conduct a full-width search on this position using the α–β minimax strategy. With a 3-ply search, the machine (Control Data Corporation 6400) examines 148 nodes in the game tree in 0.3 seconds and selects a principal variation of (1) P–N4, P–B4; (2) P–R4. Based on this 3-ply search, the machine evaluates the position as favorable to black with a rating of -107 (a pawn is worth 100 and the minus sign indicates that Black has the advantage). Obviously, the machine "misunderstands" the position since the correct move is P–R4 and White has a clear win.

By deepening the search, we can attempt to enlighten the machine. With a 5-ply search, the computer examines 990 nodes in 2.1 seconds and selects a principal variation of (1) P–N4, P–B4; (2) P–R4, P–N4; (3) K–B2. The machine is still blind to the promotion opportunity and now evaluates the position at -115. The selected first move, P–N4, could easily lose the game to a competent opponent.

With a 7-ply search, the computer examines 4523 nodes in 8.6 seconds and selects a principal variation of (1) P–N4, P–B4; (2) P–R4, P–N4; (3) K–B2, P–R4; (4) K–N3. The evaluation function now is set at -116. The machine is still totally blind to its clear opportunity. With a 9-ply search, the machine finally discovers the clear advantage of pushing its rook pawn. This occurs because a 9-ply search involves 5 moves for White and the pawn can reach the eighth rank in 5 moves. In conducting this search, however, the machine makes use of the "horizon effect" to delay the pawn promotion. In the 9-ply search, the computer examines 48,273 nodes in 96.5 seconds and selects a principal variation of (1) P–R4, P–R4; (2) P–R5, P–R5; (3) P–R6, P–R6; (4) P–R7, P–R7+; (5) KxP. Its evaluation function improves by about 100 points since it believes that it can win a pawn. In fact, the machine selects P–R4 because it anticipates that this move will lead to a pawn capture! It does not understand that Black's sacrifice of a pawn does not prevent the ultimate promotion of White's rook pawn. Since the pawn sacrifice "pushes" the pawn promotion over the machine's horizon (i.e., beyond 9-plies) the computer assumes that the promotion has been permanently prevented. This ridiculous strategy of self-delusion plagues the machine in many different environments.

The position in Figure 3.7 demonstrates several major weaknesses of a full-width shallow search. The machine's evaluation indicating that Black has the advantage shows why a static evaluation emphasizing material is a poor substitute for a dynamic analysis of the position. Secondly, the pawn sacrifice by Black indicates the foolish behavior which is engendered by the horizon effect. Thirdly, the absence of long-range planning becomes painfully evident when the machine copes with this position by examining 48,273 positions in 96 seconds (at a million operations per second) instead of simply counting squares. At the end of all this labor, the computer picks the right move for the wrong reason. The machine would need an 11-ply search in order to select the right move for the right reason. Clearly, a conventional full-width search is not the right approach for positions such as the one in Figure 3.7.

The problem with long-range planning becomes painfully evident when a machine competes against a human. In the simultaneous exhibition between David Levy and twelve different machines (Minneapolis, October, 1975), CHESS 4.4 as White walked into a devastating mating attack developed by Levy over a sequence of many moves (see Figure 1.15). Levy, taking advantage of the weakened king side after Bird's Opening, carefully positioned his queen [(7) . . . Q–B2], his king bishop [(10) . . . B–Q3], and both knights [(2) . . . N–KB3 and (9) . . . NxP/K4] to bear down on the hapless White King.

Because it has no long-range planning, the machine had considerable difficulty "understanding" the purpose of Levy's opening strategy nor did it anticipate the piece sacrifices. From the machines perspective, these sacrifices involve the loss of material by Black without any immediate compensation. Without even a vague idea of Levy's long-range plan, the machine was quite happy to accept the material and thereby increment its evaluation function. After castling king-side, the machine had to take steps to thwart Black's attack. It made a fatal mistake with (10) B–K2, retreating the bishop to avoid losing the minor exchange. It could not afford this lost tempo because a developing move such as (10) N–QB3 was essential. The machine, however, lacking a long-range planning facility, had no idea that defensive maneuvers were necessary.

The "horizon effect" that appeared with the 9-ply search in the previous end-game example can also cause much more malevolent effects. Berliner has provided a clear example of one such disastrous situation in Figure 1.3 of his thesis [12]. Figure 3.8 presents this position with White to move. White's white-squared bishop is trapped and cannot be saved. Therefore White's strategy should be to get as much as possible for the bishop. The problem for the machine, however, is that the bishop capture can be delayed by sacrificing material worth less than the bishop. If these material sacrifices can push the eventual capture of the bishop over the search horizon, the machine will " believe" that it has saved the bishop.

Let us examine the way in which the Northwestern program deals with this position. With a 2-ply search, it examines 211 nodes in 0.6 seconds and selects a principal variation of (1) B–QN3, P–QB5. It's evaluation is 247 since it has a bishop advantage. It does not realize that the bishop is trapped because its 2-ply search examined only those capture sequences which might be initiated by White at the end of the principal variation. With a 3-ply search, it discovers that B–QN3 does not work and then "invents" a foolish plan to save the bishop. It examines 1137 nodes in 3.4 seconds and decides that (1) P–K5, PxP; (2) N–Q5 is its best strategy even though its evaluation function decreases to 176. The machine observes that if (2) . . . PxB, then (3) NxB+ or if (2) . . . NxN, then (3) RxN, PxB; (4) RxB. In each case, the machine's analysis past the third ply is based only on a direct sequence of captures. The problem here is that the machine's tactics merely delay the loss of the bishop by sacrificing an additional pawn and giving up a positional advantage. The machine fails to understand this position until it conducts a 6-ply search, examining 168,774 nodes in 442 seconds. At this depth, it selects a more promising principle variation of (1) B/2xP, PxB/5; (2) P–K5, N–R4; (3) PxP,

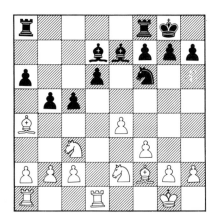

Figure 3.8 White to move [from Berliner (12)].

B–KN4. With this variation, White exchanges the bishop for two pawns and maintains a positional advantage.

Another instance of the horizon effect occurred at the 1975 ACM computer chess tournament in Minneapolis. CHESS 4.4 (White) and TREE FROG (Black) competed in the fourth round for the championship (see Figure 1.13). With its twelfth move, White placed a pawn on the seventh rank. Because CHESS 4.4 places a high value on a pawn in this position, it was unwilling to give up the pawn without a battle. Unfortunately for CHESS 4.4, it could not find a viable plan to save the pawn, so it used the horizon effect to engage in a bit of self-deception. Its next few moves served to delay the eventual capture of the pawn. The move, (13) P–KR3, provided a delay by forcing Black's queen bishop to retreat as did the move, (14) P–QR3, forcing Black's king bishop to move. The next move, (15) P–KN4, maintained this delay strategy by continuing these harassing tactics. Each of these moves served to delay Black's capture of the White pawn on the seventh rank and thus "successfully" pushed this capture beyond the search horizon. The price that CHESS 4.4 paid for this folly was that the positional advantage it had gained through its first twelve moves was virtually dissipated and its pawn structure on the king side was seriously weakened. Not until Black captured the aspiring pawn on (19) . . . RxP did CHESS 4.4 resume its usual solid game. The partisan observers from Northwestern gave a collective sign of relief when the pawn finally succumbed to the Black rook.

The horizon effect can lead to the meaningless sacrifice of material and the loss of positional advantage when the machine would otherwise have an excellent game. If a rook or queen becomes trapped and cannot be saved, the horizon effect will encourage the machine to offer up an endless procession of pawns and minor pieces to delay the eventual capture. In this instance, a tree search of 9 or 10 plies (not presently possible in the middle-game) might not find the correct continuation. This problem can only be solved by having the program terminate its search at each node only when the position is truly quiescent. Thus it is clearly necessary to improve the machine's ability to discriminate between active and non-active nodes.

The opening

The look-ahead procedure is relatively weak for selecting good moves in the opening. The opening emphasizes the development of pieces to squares where they can effectively do battle some 20 or 30 plies later. Since these future battles are beyond the machine's look-ahead horizon, it must develop its pieces purely on heuristic grounds (e.g., control the center, knights before bishops, prepare castling, etc.). Because these rules of thumb often lead to imprecise play, many programmers have decided to use a common human strategy, i.e., memorize many of the standard openings and play them by rote. The computer can easily be programmed to play "book" openings. There is no reason, other than the work involved, why a machine could not have an opening library which covered as many as 100,000 positions. Most tournament programs now have between 3000 and 10,000 positions in their libraries.

Since moves can be accessed from this library very quickly, machines play the opening at blinding speed and it is often difficult for human observers to move the pieces about the board fast enough to keep up with the play. A library of openings not only insures the machine a decent level of performance in the early going but also conserves valuable clock time for the middle game where some lengthy calculations may be necessary. In science, however, we have a law (called Murphy's law) which states that if something can go wrong, it will and in a way which will cause the most damage. Sadly enough, this principle applies with a vengeance to computer play with a memorized opening library.

Sooner or later, regardless of the size of the library, the machine will exhaust its store of predigested moves and will have to think (i.e., calculate) on its own. The problem arising is that the board position it encounters when leaving its opening library is not of its own making. The grandmaster's "plan" or "idea" in selecting the opening moves is not available to the machine so that it must rely upon its own static evaluation function to determine whether its pieces are in their "proper" positions. Of course, the machine decides that they are not because its evaluation function is much less sophisticated than that of a grandmaster. The end result is that the machine devotes its first several moves to rearranging its pieces into a new configuration more compatible with its evaluation function. In doing this, it usually loses several tempos and often gets itself into an inferior position. It is interesting that the machine's failing in this regard is not that dissimilar to the difficulty that some novice players have when they laboriously memorize book after book of openings without learning the theme or idea behind each opening.

It is probably unrealistic to expect that computer chess will be played without a library of openings. If improvements do occur in opening play, therefore, they will probably result from organizing the library to store more than just a sequence of moves. For each position the library should catalog both a move and thematic information concerning the type of strategy which is appropriate to this position. This could be done by giving the library the capability of modifying the static evaluation function when the machine leaves the library. The modified function might encourage the movement of certain pieces to particular squares or to control certain squares. Even minor revisions along these lines would produce a major improvement in machine play during the late opening and during the early middle game. Since the machine must survive the opening and the middle game in order to reach the end game without a lost position, it is probably appropriate to devote considerable effort to this problem.

An interim solution which has been adopted by most tournament chess-programming teams is to carefully select "book" openings compatible with their machine's style of play. If the machine's evaluation function emphasizes material rather than positional factors, the program will appear strongest in tactical positions. Thus the programmers can select library moves that quickly lead to active positions. If the evaluation function carefully considers pawn structure, the opening library can be structured to produce positions which permit pawn doubling or pawn isolation. Considerable skill is required to artfully select those openings which make the most of the machine's playing style.

The end game

Levy [67] and other observers have felt that the end game is the most difficult problem for machine chess. The end game requires highly specialized knowledge that is used relatively infrequently. The winning plan may involve an exact sequence of 20 or more moves. A full-width search to this depth is totally impossible. For this reason, it may be necessary to abandon the $\alpha-\beta$ minimax procedure in the end game and adopt an alternate strategy.

One promising plan is to structure the heuristic band-width search (see Chapter 7) to examine only those portions of the game tree relevant to some specific goal, such as pawn promotion. This strategy requires the machine be able to recognize the beginning of the end game and then determine which goals are feasible. The pattern recognition these decisions require is not an easy problem for a machine but it is one that must be solved if this approach is to be successful.

A second strategy is to analyze specific types of end games in some detail and then to develop specific programs to deal with each of these in an algorithmic fashion. Thus the machine will have a detailed set of instructions for every position it might encounter in a king and rook versus king ending or a king and pawn versus king ending. This approach is discussed in detail in Chapter 5. If this strategy can be generalized to more complex end games, it may provide a partial solution to this problem.

Improvement through competition

One of the advantages of research on machine intelligence in a chess environment is that new ideas, once implemented, can be easily evaluated in tournament play. Academicians have many ideas that persist in the literature simply because their truth or falsity can not be easily tested. This is unfortunate because it slows the pace of progress. Chess programming has the advantage that new ideas can be implemented and tested within a period of a few weeks. Several innovations in Northwestern's program were tested in a few early morning sessions simply by playing the new version of the program against the old version and noting the outcomes.

The annual computer chess tournaments held by the Association for Computing Machinery provide a national testing ground for chess programmers. This annual competition is useful for uncovering the important weaknesses which most programs inevitably have. It is true that these tournaments are expensive but their value could be maintained by restricting each machine to 20 or 30 seconds per move instead of 3 minutes. A "blitz" tournament would still provide each programming team with an opportunity to test their innovations but at a much reduced cost in machine time and in long-distance telephone expenses. At the same time, the audience enthusiasm that Mittman discusses in Chapter 1 would probably be augmented because the games would proceed at an exciting pace.

Greenblatt [48] has avoided the ACM tournaments and has entered his program exclusively in human tournaments. In addition to developing a USCF rating for his program, this competition has provided a broader test of the program's skill then would be the case for machine tournaments. Humans show much greater diversity in playing style than do present computer programs and this characteristic may be an important aspect of the testing environment. Tournament play against humans also provides some special opportunities not present in machine tournaments. With human opponents, the opening library can be used more effectively than with machine opponents. With two machines, book-after-book of openings can be read into each with neither gaining an advantage. With play against a human, however, the enlargement of the machine's library should have beneficial results. Secondly, the human's propensity for an occasional blunder (such as inadvertently leaving a piece *en prise*) should work to the machine's advantage. Such events never occur in computer tournaments. Thirdly, most human players are unaware of the common weaknesses of Shannon-type chess programs and thus would not be able to capitalize so easily on these shortcomings. It is interesting that the Northwestern program has competed very favorably in the few human tournaments it has entered. Slate and Atkin have been surprised at the relatively poor play exhibited by the machine's opponents. It is often difficult for humans to adjust to the machine's unnatural style of play and many face it with unjustified trepidation; their play suffers accordingly.

For example, CHESS 4.5 recently entered the Paul Masson American Class Tournament in California (July, 1976). Playing on a large scale Control Data Cyber 170 system, the program was matched against 5 human opponents in the B section who had an average rating of 1735. The machine won all five matches. This result was quite surprising because the program at a conceptual level is clearly in the C class or below (see Hearst's chapter for a more thorough discussion of this). Apparently the machine's abilities to avoid miscalculation and to never miss an opportunity seem to provide a certain amount of compensation for its conceptual inadequacies.

Future prospects

Chess, as a problem environment, is representative of a large class of problems that machines have been unable to master. The "cycle time" for the human brain is relatively slow (4 or 5 operations per second as compared to several million per second for modern computers). Despite this, humans clearly outclass machines as problem solvers. Through evolution, man has developed specialized skills to compensate for the slow speed of biological information processing. Two major developments are prominent in this regard. One is the large degree of parallel processing that occurs very early in the visual and auditory systems. This permits complex pattern recognition, an essential ingredient in human problem solving. A second important development is a sophisticated storage and retrieval mechanism for accessing information. Machine representations of knowledge lack the richness and semantic meaningfulness of human memory. The computer needs to emulate the human brain in being able to recognize key features of a position, to know which actions are appropriate to these features, and to implement tactics that are thematic with an appropriate long-term strategy. Developments in these areas are essential for "intelligent" machine chess.

David Levy [67] has a bet with several academicians that no computer chess program will be able to beat him by 1978. His prospects for winning this bet are quite good considering that no present program has yet attained even an expert level of play. Given the tremendously difficult conceptual problems involved, Levy may even have an outside chance of winning such a bet if the deadline were extended for another decade.

CHESS 4.5—
The Northwestern University
chess program

David J. Slate and Lawrence R. Atkin
Northwestern University

4

CHESS 4.5 is the latest version of the Northwestern University chess program. CHESS 4.5 and its predecessors have won the U.S. Computer Chess Championships in 1970, 1971, 1972, 1973, and 1975, placing second in the 1974 U.S. Tourney and also in the first World tournament held the same year. This chapter will describe the structure of the program, focusing on the practical considerations that motivated the implementation of its various features. An understanding of not only what CHESS 4.5 is, but also why it turned out that way, is necessary if one is to appreciate its role in the present and future development of chess programming.

In the spring of 1968, engineering students Larry Atkin and Keith Gorlen launched Northwestern University's computer chess program in their spare time. Later in the year, then physics graduate student David Slate began his own effort. By mid 1969, the two groups had joined forces and produced their first successful program, CHESS 2.0. Between 1969 and 1972, CHESS 2.0 was gradually refined into CHESS 3.6. In that period, Atkin, Gorlen, and Slate all became professionals in the computing field. Gorlen left Northwestern in 1970 but continued for some time to contribute ideas to the program, whose development continued under Atkin and Slate. The story of that first era of chess programming at Northwestern is told in detail in Larry Atkin's masters thesis [5]. This chapter will concentrate on the "modern" era of our program, comprising CHESS 4.0 and the minor improvements that have led to CHESS 4.5.

Background

In the spring of 1973 we (Larry Atkin and David Slate) faced the bleak prospect of yet another imminent computer chess tournament. By this time we had gotten over the initial thrill of winning the U.S. Championships. In fact, the annual ritual had turned into an annual chore—we could think of better things to do with our time than going through the motions of preparing for another tournament. In April we could no longer push the problem of ACM 1973 out of our minds. There seemed to be four alternatives:

1. Do not enter at all
2. Enter last year's program (CHESS 3.6)
3. Make modifications to CHESS 3.6
4. Write a whole new program

The possibility of not entering at all we finally discarded partly out of cowardice. We knew that our absence would be noticed, and we were afraid to answer the embarrassing questions that would inevitably greet our sudden and premature retirement from competition. Besides, we enjoyed getting together with other chess programmers, and perhaps we secretly enjoyed the competition at least as much as we disliked it.

We quickly ruled out entering CHESS 3.6. If there is anything more useless than yesterday's newspaper, it is last year's chess program. Our interest in the tournament lay in the chance to test something new and different, not to find out whether the other programs had improved enough to smash our old program. We knew, despite our unbeaten record and a well-developed myth about the "solidity" of our program, that our luck must soon give out. The bubble would burst, and the gross weaknesses of CHESS 3.6 would suddenly pour out in a series of ridiculous, humiliating blunders. For CHESS 3.6 was the last in a series of evolutionary changes to our original chess program, written in 1968–1969, and it faithfully carried most of the original design deficiencies. CHESS 3.6 was, like the dinosaur, a species about to become extinct. Basically a Shannon type-B program, it had a depth-first, α–β, more-or-less fixed depth tree search. A primitive position evaluation function scored the endpoints and also doubled as a plausible move generator earlier in the tree by selecting the "best n" moves for further exploration. Rudimentary as they were, CHESS 3.6's evaluation and tree search were just adequate to make "reasonable-looking" moves most of the time and not hang pieces to one- or two-move threats. Apparently this was enough to play low class C chess and, for a while, to beat other programs.

We could have tried to improve CHESS 3.6 by yet another notch. But that would have required expending much effort for rather little return. The design deficiencies of CHESS 3.6 went much deeper than the mere fact that it was an old-fashioned program that depended on the searching of large trees filled with unlikely positions. It was poorly documented and not very modular. The instructions that formed the evaluation function were nearly unreadable. Figuring out how our old program worked was like deciphering hieroglyphics, and adding anything to it was like writing in ancient Sanskrit. One glance at the listing told us that the program had outlived its usefulness. It had taught us how not to write a chess program. It had sharpened our skills, brought us into contact with other chess-programmers, and broadened our perspective to the point where we could see CHESS 3.6 as the hopelessly archaic creature that it was. No, it had become too painful even to look at CHESS 3.6 anymore, let alone work on it.

Thus, by a process of elimination, we were forced to write a whole new program, despite the limited amount of time (four months) available for doing so. Fortunately, one's second chess program grows much more quickly and smoothly than the first.

The development of CHESS 4.0

We had realized by April, 1973 that our view of a strong program—one that would play master-level chess—would be very different from CHESS 3.6. It would conduct very smart specialized, narrow, deep searches of the game tree. It would evaluate positions in a subtle, thorough fashion. The criteria for searching and evaluating would come from a large data base of chess knowledge to which chess players could contribute in an easy-to-use language that spoke of squares, pieces, and moves, rather than binary bits. In time, one would be able to instruct the program in methods of modifying its "knowledge pool" based on its own playing experience. Knowing all this, of course, didn't help much as far as the 1973 ACM tournament was concerned. We had to settle for something much less ambitious in the dwindling weeks that remained. So we chose instead to write a program which in terms of chess-playing methods was not very different from CHESS 3.6, but which in its architecture was more in the spirit of our vision of a strong program.

Some features of CHESS 4.0 were designed before we started writing code. Others developed as we went along, and the finishing touches went in just hours before the first game of the tournament. The criteria for adding something to the program were that it be simple to write, simple to understand, and easy to test. There was little time for experimentation or testing or the fine tuning of parameters. The description which follows details the essential features of this program and compares its design to that of its predecessor.

Program structure

In terms of its organization, CHESS 3.6 was a mess. Not only was it difficult to modify the evaluation function—it was difficult even to find it in the listing of the program. So in 4.0 we decided to combine the tree searching and evaluation decisions and put them into one routine, called "EVALU8." The rest of the program performs utility functions in an efficient and straight-forward manner. These include input/output of the moves and the processing of various commands that the user can type in to adjust parameters, debug the program, set up certain positions, etc. Other utility routines are concerned more directly with playing chess. They can generate moves, manage the tree search, and perform other tasks when called upon to do so by EVALU8. Much of the programming effort has gone into the design and construction of the support routines rather than the chess-playing heuristics themselves. To illustrate the technical problems involved, some of these routines will be examined in detail later.

EVALU8 is responsible for a node in the tree. It returns a score and/or a best move for each node. It may call for tree searching to be done outward from that node to aid in its decision making, but control returns to it when each of these searches is complete. Since these searches invoke EVALU8 again at greater depths of the tree, EVALU8 is recursive and reentrant. When EVALU8 calls for such a search, all the data relevant to the current node are saved, and the board and other data are updated to reflect the move that is being searched. When searching of the move is complete, the data for the parent node is restored and control is returned to EVALU8 to continue processing that node. The purpose of such a structure is to eliminate, at least in principle, the artificial separation that exists in many programs (including CHESS 3.6) between node evaluation and tree searching.

CHESS 3.6 was a mixture of FORTRAN and assembly language (for CDC 6000/CYBER machines). Although we would have liked to use a high-level language, we felt that neither FORTRAN nor other languages available at the time offered the right combination of efficiency and power of expression. In writing CHESS 4.0, we used assembly language so we could have complete control over the instructions that were generated. For EVALU8, which contains all of the "chess decisions," we used high-level assembly language macros, which give the "illusion" of a higher-level language.

Data base

For each position in the look-ahead tree, CHESS 3.6 maintained certain data related to that position that were useful for evaluation and move generation. The largest part of this was a table specifying which pieces attacked which squares. This table suffered from two major problems: it had to be regenerated from scratch for each position in the tree, and it had no clean, simple format that might have more general utility. In 4.5, we chose a simple data format which could be used for many purposes, including the construction of attack tables which could be incrementally updated as the tree search stepped from node to node. Incremental updating means altering only those aspects of positional information that actually change due to a move on the board. The attack tables after (1) P–K4, for example, differ only slightly from those before, and much time is saved (although more code is required) if the changes are computed rather than the entire tables. The basic data element in CHESS 4.5 is the bit board.

The bit board is a string of 64 binary bits specifying some subset of the 64 squares on the chess board. Each bit that is set to one represents a square that is a member of the set.

Examples of such sets are "all the squares attacked by the White queen," "all the Black rooks that are on the seventh rank," etc. Some bit boards are permanent (incrementally updated from node to node), and some are temporary (generated and discarded as needed by EVALU8). Bit boards, which were described by Adelson-Velskii *et al.* [2], are simple, yet can express a variety of notions concisely. Machine instructions exist on the CDC 6400 and most other computers to efficiently perform often desired operations on bit boards, like set functions "and," "or," etc., and such things as counting the elements of a set and finding the next member of a set. The incrementally updated attack tables, from which most move generation is done, are called ATKFR and ATKTO. ATKFR is a set of 64 bit boards which give, for each square, all the squares attacked by the piece, if any, that resides on that square. ATKTO is the transpose of ATKFR, giving, for each square, the locations of all the pieces that attack that square.

Some data in forms other than bit boards are also maintained incrementally during the tree search. Assorted variables, like the current level in the tree, the current values of α and β, and the move being searched are needed for book-keeping purposes.

Hash tables

In addition to the raw data kept in the data base, there are some functions that are computed for a large number of positions in the tree. Some of these functions are time consuming, so we would like to avoid these calculations whenever possible. One scheme for saving time is to save the value of every function computed in a table and look up its value (rather than recomputing it) whenever possible. In order to be advantageous, the table look-up scheme must be faster than the function it is replacing. CHESS 4.5 uses three hash tables to store previously computed results.

Material balance is the most important term in the evaluation of a position. It is a fairly complicated function of only the number of each type of piece on the board. The exact function is described in more detail later. For now, we will just describe how the values are kept in the hash table.

One word in the data base (the material balance signature word) contains the number of each type of piece for each side:

w score	wq	wr	wb	wn	wp	b score	bq	br	bb	bn	bp
10	4	4	4	4	4	10	4	4	4	4	4

The left half of the word contains the counts of the White pieces, and the right half holds the Black pieces. The White score (w score) is the value of the material balance function for this count of White and Black pieces; the Black score (b score) is the negation of the White score. The numbers indicate the number of bits in each field. Each time that a move affecting the material balance (i.e., a capture or pawn promotion) occurs, the appropriate counts are updated. The program must now find the value of the material balance function. It first computes a very simple function of the material balance signature word and uses that value as an index into the material balance hash table. If that entry in the table matches (i.e., has the same number of each type of piece), the score is immediately available and is saved in the material balance signature word. If, however, the hash table entry is different, the value of the function must be computed, and the value and signature are placed into the table.

The hash function used to probe the table must have a number of characteristics. First, it must be fast. In particular, it must be faster than the function it is replacing. Second, it must distribute the positions that are likely to occur in a single search. Thus, the removal of a single piece from the material balance signature should always change the value of the hash function. Finally, if possible, the function should be symmetric with respect to Black and White. That is, a material balance signature should hash to the same location if the Black and White piece counts are reversed. For positions where both sides are about even, this doubles the utility of the table.

The hash function actually used is the sum of the White side of the signature (taken as a 20-bit number) and the Black side of the signature exclusive "or"ed with the absolute value of their difference, folded over (with an exclusive "or") to get a 7-bit number. The reader may verify that this function does indeed have the three desired characteristics.

The pawn structure hash table operates in a similar manner. The pawn structure on a file is dependent only on the locations of pawns on that file and the two adjacent files. The pawn structure signature has 18 bits (6 ranks by 3 files) for each side, indicating the presence or absence of a pawn on each of those squares.

The trans/ref table was added in the summer of 1975 and is the main difference between CHESS 4.5 and 4.2. It is a hash table of chess positions kept in auxiliary core memory (ECS) and is used for two purposes: to store previously computed evaluations and to store best moves. A similar hash table was mentioned by Greenblatt [48]. Our table has a user-adjustable capacity of from 256 to 65536 positions. In tournament play we have used from 8192 to 32768 entries depending on the availability of storage. The utility of the table is based on the graph of move sequences that is grown not being strictly a tree, because different branches may lead to the same position or node of the graph. Consider the position of Figure 4.1. The two sequences of moves: (1) N–KB3, N–QB3; (2) B–B4 and

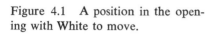

Figure 4.1 A position in the opening with White to move.

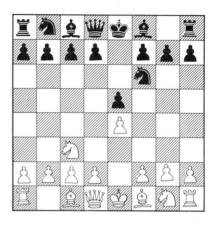

(1) B–B4, N–QB3; (2) N–KB3 both lead to the same position because White has transposed his first and second moves. If a score has been saved from the first occurrence of that position, it can be used for the second, and we may avoid the whole subtree that would otherwise have been grown from that node. Another example is that of a piece that moves from one square to another in two steps, stopping at any one of several intermediate squares. For example, in Figure 4.1, the two sequences: (1) N–KB3, N–QB3; (2) N–KN5 and (1) N–KR3, N–QB3; (2) N–KN5 are equivalent. There are situations in which the same position may recur several times. In Figure 4.1, the white bishop may stop at any of K2, Q3, B4, or R6 on its way to QN5, resulting in the same position after 3 ply providing Black's intervening move is the same each time. Of course it may not make sense for the bishop to take two moves to get to QN5, but this makes little difference to a full-width search. Because of α–β cutoffs, not all such equivalent move sequences occur even in a full-width search, but the killer heuristic, described later, helps maximize the occurrence of equivalent branches. Although the above examples are all 3-ply long, there are many varieties of transpositions and multiple pathways creating equivalent branches of length greater than 3 ply.

Strictly speaking, positions reached via different branches are rarely truly identical, because the 50-move and three-time repetition draw rules make the identity of a position dependent on the history of moves leading to that position. This effect is small, and therefore we decided to ignore it. Differences in positions due to *en passant* pawns or castling status are correctly handled by the program.

The table contains the computed evaluation of the position as well as the predicted best move from the position. Since, in general, not all positions in the tree can fit in the table, a priority scheme decides which are worthy. The main criterion is the ply depth at which the position occurred, with preference given to shallower positions.

Move generation

Earlier versions of our chess program had a very simple mechanism for generating moves. The board was scanned, square by square, until a piece that belonged to the side on the move was encountered. The moves for this piece were then generated, and these new positions were scored.

With the introduction of the data base indicating which squares are attacked by each piece, move generation became more efficient. With the exception of pawns, a piece can move to any square that it attacks, unless that square is occupied by a friendly piece. Thus, to generate all of the moves of the knight from KB4, all that the program must do is to intersect (i.e., logical "and") the bit board representing all attacks from KB4 (i.e., ATKFR[KB4]) with the complement (i.e., logical "not") of the bit board representing the location of all friendly pieces. The squares that are left represent the valid destination squares for the knight, and it is a simple matter to translate this bit board into a list of moves.

A similar procedure can be used to determine which pieces (if any) can move to a particular square. All moves that move a nonpawn piece to a specific square can be generated by examining the bit board representing all squares that contain pieces that attack that square, intersected with the set of squares occupied by the side to move.

Generating pawn moves is not so simple, but here, too, there is an advantage to using a bit board representation. It is possible to generate the moves of all the pawns simultaneously. The bit board representing the location of all pawns belonging to the side to move is shifted one rank, producing the set of all squares that are directly in front of a pawn. That, in turn, is intersected with all the empty squares on the board. The bits which remain represent the destination squares of all pawn moves where the pawn advances one square. This bit board can then be intersected with all squares on the third rank, shifted forward one more rank, and again intersected with the empty squares, producing all moves where a pawn moves forward two squares. Similarly, pawn captures are generated by shifting the pawns forward one rank, to the side one file, and intersecting with the location of all enemy pieces. Even *en passant* captures can be generated by including the "*en passant* square" (that square that a pawn passed over on the last move, if any) as the location of an enemy piece.

The move generator in CHESS 4.5 has two routines. One is GENTSL, which generates all moves to a set of squares, and the other is GENSFL, which generates all moves from a set of squares. These routines have been constructed in a way which prevents the generation of the same move twice at a given node in the tree. This is accomplished at practically no expense by a very simple trick. Upon initial entry to a node, two bit boards are produced: the set of valid originating squares, GENFR, is initialized to be the set of all squares from which pieces can move (i.e., the location of all pieces belonging to the side on the move), and the set of valid destination squares, GENTO, is initialized as all other squares. Each time GENTSL is called, it intersects its parameter with GENTO (so that it does not generate any moves to squares that it has already generated moves to) and removes those squares from GENTO. Similarly, GENFSL intersects its parameter with GENFR and removes those squares from GENFR.

Now comes the real trick. Rather than using the "complement of the bit board representing the location of all friendly pieces" to determine if a square attacked by a piece is a valid move, GENFSL uses GENTO, thereby generating only those moves that GENTSL has not generated. Correspondingly, GENTSL uses GENFR instead of "the set of squares occupied by the side to move." In effect, neither routine will generate a move unless both:

1. The from-square was not a parameter to an earlier call to GENFSL, and
2. The to-square was not a parameter to an earlier call to GENTSL.

The move generator produces pseudolegal moves, moves that would be legal if leaving or moving a king into check were legal. A number of obvious schemes for generating only legal moves have been suggested, but they have weaknesses that require an excess of special-case code and are therefore difficult to implement and debug. Consider the problem of generating only strictly legal moves from the class of positions similar to Figure 4.2. The pseudolegal moves for White include five king moves and two pawn moves. Of these, the only illegal move is PxP *en passant*. It is illegal because it removes the *two* pieces protecting the White king from being in check by the Black rook. In fact, most of the moves generated by the program are legal. Rather than spending time trying to determine if a generated move (which may never be searched anyway) is legal, CHESS 4.5 defers this test until a more convenient time. If the move is actually searched, the data base will be updated, and it is then simple to determine that the king is sitting on a square that is attacked by an enemy piece.

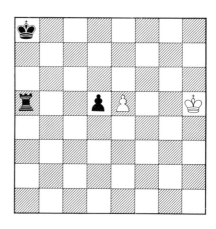

Figure 4.2 Position after Black plays P/Q2–Q4.

Tree-searching strategy

As stated earlier, CHESS 3.6 had a plausible move generator based on its evaluation function. Moves were ordered on the basis of preliminary scores produced by that function, and best n, plus some captures, checks, and other "threatening" moves, were searched from each position in the tree to a fixed depth limit. Other moves, except for certain special cases, were discarded as being unworthy of search. At first, we were going to implement a similar scheme in CHESS 4.0. However, with only a month or two remaining before the tournament, we changed our minds. Although our plausible-move generator sounded plausible enough, and differed not very much from methods employed in several other chess programs, we had built up profound dissatisfactions with it over the years. A suggestion by Peter Frey triggered some thoughts on the matter, and as a result we dumped selective searching in favor of full-width searching, ostensibly a more primitive algorithm. In CHESS 4.5, all legal moves are searched to the same depth. Beyond that depth, only a limited "quiescence" search of captures and some checks is conducted. One may think of the quiescence search as a tool employed by EVALU8 to refine the tactical accuracy of the scores it produces for the positions at the horizon of the full-width search. At each node in the capture search, the side to move is given the choice of accepting the evaluation score or of trying to better it by trying capture moves.

The principal motivation for switching to full-width searching was a desire for simplicity. Simplicity was important to ease the testing and debugging that had to be crammed into a short period of time. The easiest way to avoid all the complexities of generating plausible moves is to do away with the plausible-move generator. The trouble with plausible-move generators is that they have to be very clever to avoid discarding, at ply 1, good moves whose merit even a meager 5-ply search would discover. This is true for both tactical and strategic moves. Thus a move that appears "quiet" (to a naive plausible-move generator) at ply 1 may pose a threat at ply 3 and win outright at ply 5. With CHESS 3.6 and other Shannon type-B programs, whether the right move is played often depends on whether, by sheer accident, that move is inadvertently included in the "best n," n being about 8 or so moves, at the base of the tree. This problem is discussed in some detail in Chapter 3.

Some programs try to alleviate this problem by setting the "width" (number of moves looked at) higher near the base of the tree than at deeper ply levels. This works up to a point, but there are still too many moves whose consequences look good at 5-ply but are ranked no better than mediocre (20th or 30th or even worse) at the first ply where they are capriciously discarded by a well meaning, but stupid, plausible-move generator. The main cause of this phenomenon is that most plausible-move generators and evaluation functions are so near-sighted that they are apt to become suddenly aware of a feature of the position at, say, 5-ply that totally eluded them at 4-ply. This characteristic, which will become clear in the description of our evaluation function, gives rise to the "horizon effect" described in detail by Berliner [12] (see also Chapter 3).

The proper way to conduct a selective search lies in such techniques as long-range planning, piece pathway analysis, recognition of patterns, analysis of causality of events in the tree search (see Berliner), and other devices that are not perfected in a period of a few months. So, instead, we took the coward's way out and made all of the moves "plausible." We made the pleasant discovery that the elimination of the move-ranking process, which required applying the evaluation function to each move, saved a great deal of time. It saved so much, in fact, that together with the 300 percent speedup of CHESS 4.5 over CHESS 3.6 due to greater efficiency, CHESS 4.5 is able to look at all the moves in the same time that CHESS 3.6 took to search a fraction of them. The lesson learned was not that selective searching doesn't work, but that unless it is done cleverly it is no better and may be worse than full-width brute-force searching.

The implementation of full-width searching had immediate beneficial results. At last we had a program whose behavior we could explain simply. When it searched to 5 ply it found everything within that range, including both tactical combinations and positional maneuvers, some of which were obscure and ingenious. Although the endpoints of the tree were still subject to the gross defects of the primitive heuristics of the evaluation function, we had freed the search leading up to them from those defects, and thus unencumbered, the search was able to make up for some of them.

In Figure 4.3 White may win by maneuvering the knight to KB5. A smart plausible-move generator or evaluation function would identify the Black pawns at Q6 and KR6 as targets and construct the pathway that the knight should take to attack them. But, in this position, the evaluator of CHESS 4.5 is just lucid enough to know that eating the Black pawns is good for White. It also has a vague desire to make passed pawns and to centralize pieces like knights. None of these factors justify evaluating the move N–KB2 as good for White. But an 8-ply (plus capture sequences)

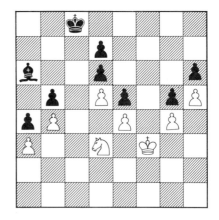

Figure 4.3 An endgame position with White to move.

search of all the moves makes the surprising (to the program) discovery that a Black pawn is won by force in 5 moves: N–B2, N–Q1, N–K3, N–B5, NxRP.

Besides simplicity, a full-width search rewards its creators with "peace of mind." The following daydream (or nightmare) illustrates the psychological hazards associated with the standard "best n" tree-search approach.

Imagine yourself at a computer chess tournament. In a complicated position your program has the opportunity to shine by finding the right continuation or to embarrass you by making a blunder. You are reduced to a mere agent of the machine—communicating moves between it and its opponent and reporting the time on request. While anxiously waiting for the machine's decision, you speculate about what move it will make. It is difficult to infer the program's thinking processes. By combining an estimate of the machine's ability with an analysis of the structural features of the position, you decide that:

1. The program will very likely make the right move.
2. The program will very likely make the wrong move.
3. The machine's move will depend on seemingly irrelevant factors that are difficult to estimate.

In Cases 1 and 2 the suspense is relieved—one has peace of mind. Case 3, however, is hard on the nerves. Often one likes to be surprised by one's program, but not in positions where there is something straightforward to be done. A full-width search sharply reduces the number of incidents of Case 3 by eliminating the "seemingly irrelevant factor" of whether a tactically crucial move at a low ply level happens to lie just within the best-n group or just outside of it.

By now the reader is surely wondering what is the nature of an evaluation function which requires deep tree searching to enable it to recognize phenomena that appear obvious to most human players. So we will now describe the evaluator and return later to the tree search to actually show how we have made some small headway in overcoming the enormous branching factor that hangs like an albatross about the neck of brute-force searching.

The evaluation function

The CHESS 4.5 evaluation function was derived from that of CHESS 3.6, with the addition of perhaps 30 percent more chess knowledge, but is similar in spirit. The code was completely rewritten in assembly language macros that combined greater clarity with greater efficiency. The whole function was produced in a few weeks shortly before ACM 73 and has remained almost unchanged in the two and a half years since.

Basically, the function adds several easily computable factors together. The dominating term is material. The remaining terms are rules of thumb designed to give the program a vague positional sense. Rather than expressing some theoretically rigorous chess principles, these factors merely improve somewhat over "aimless" moves. The design motive for the evaluator appears to be a self-fulfilling prophecy: we knew that it was going to be primitive and would thus depend heavily on tree searching. To do such deep tree searching would require that the evaluator do its work quickly, and so it wouldn't have the time to do anything clever, and thus would have to be primitive.

Material balance

Material constitutes by far the biggest term in the function. The total of the nonmaterial terms does not usually exceed the value of about a pawn and a half. The theory of a materially dominated evaluation function is that whether and how quickly one is winning correlates well with having a favorable material balance, where material balance is dependent only on what pieces are on the board and not where those pieces are. CHESS 4.5 gives the pieces "standard" values: pawn = 100, knight = 325, bishop = 350, rook = 500, and queen = 900. It modifies this sum by a "trade-down" bonus that encourages the winning side to trade pieces but not pawns. The total function, expressed from the winning side's point of view, is: Total material advantage = minimum (3100, MS), where: MS = minimum (2400, MD) + MD*PA* (8000–MT)/[6400*(PA+1)]. MD is the material difference computed by adding the standard values of each piece and subtracting the total of the side with the least material from the side with the most (the winning side). PA is the number of pawns possessed by the winning side. MT is the total material on the board, i.e., the sum of the material of both sides.

As an example of how the function works, consider a material configuration in which each side has all its original pieces, except that Black has lost a bishop. Then MD = 350 and MT = 2*4050–350 = 7750. Also PA = 8 since White has all his pawns. Then compute: minimum (3100, MS), where MS = minimum (2400, 350) + 350*8 (8000–7750)/ [6400*(8+1)] = 362. Minimum (3100, 362) = 362, which is, therefore, the total advantage. Suppose a pair of knights are now traded off. The MT changes to 8100–350–2*325 = 7100, but MD and PA remain the same, and the advantage comes out to 394. Therefore, the trade-down bonus for exchanging knights is 394 − 362 = 32 or about one-third of a pawn. Actually, the material advantage is truncated to the next lower multiple of a quarter of a pawn by the program, so this difference would be less accurately represented. This function is, of course, so simplistic that it fails badly in many situations. In particular, it gives the wrong answers for such trivially drawn endgames as king and bishop against king and king and knight against king. To take care of a few of these situations, a table of exceptions is maintained which is searched before the usual computation is performed. Also, the trade-down bonus has the probably unfortunate property of decreasing the importance of positional terms relative to material terms as the material advantage, and hence the bonus, increases.

Hung pieces

It is important not to overlook pieces that are subject to immediate capture by the side to move. In CHESS 4.5, these pieces are not considered by the evaluation function but are instead relegated to the quiescence/capture search, described in detail later. Pieces that are subject to capture by the side not on move are presumed likely to escape. Although the responsibility for an accurate prognosis of the future of these pieces is shifted to the capture search, that search, as we shall see later, fails to accept this responsibility. A term in the positional score helps to correct this oversight.

Positional evaluation

The nonmaterial terms depend on which of two phases the game is in: one set is used for most positions, while a simpler set serves in "mop-up" situations—endgames in which there are few pieces and one side has an overwhelming material advantage. The regular positional evaluation is the sum of the attacked piece term, which depends on which side is on move, and several piece position terms, which do not. These piece position terms are computed for both sides. Terms for White pieces are added to the total score, and those for Black are subtracted from it.

Attacked-piece term

A piece subject to profitable capture by the side not on the move is penalized a small amount, not because its capture is considered likely, but because the tempo presumably used up moving to safety detracts from the quality of the position. A threatened piece is defined here simply as a nonpawn piece attacked by a smaller piece, or one attacked by an equal or larger piece and not defended. The definition of attack and defense here does not distinguish situations in which the attacker or defender is pinned or otherwise overloaded. If there is only one threatened piece, the penalty is 16. If there are more than one, the situation is more complicated. Prior to 1975 and CHESS 4.5, an extra penalty of 22 was assessed in addition to the 16. We had noticed, however, that CHESS 4.0 and 4.2 would sometimes judge favorably positions, reached in the tree, in which the computer was on move but suffered from multiple hung pieces. Of course the question of whether a piece must really be lost should be decided either by a very clever static analysis or by the quiescence search, which, unfortunately, was at ease only in searching captures by the side on move, and not defenses or retreats. Often, the best defense to such a double threat, especially in the strange positions reached in the tree, is itself a capture which will be found by the capture search. So one could "play it safe" by penalizing a much larger amount than just 38. However, that would play havoc with the program's dependence on the fact that nonmaterial evaluation terms are always small, a fact that the program makes considerable use of. So instead, for CHESS 4.5, we made a last minute change to penalize the doubly threatened side by setting its total positional score to the worst value that side has yet experienced in the tree. This is usually worse than the pre-4.5 penalty. The change seems to have a beneficial effect in some positions.

Pawns

Earlier versions of our program have always involved an evaluation of pawn structure and CHESS 4.5 follows in that tradition. The basic idea is that doubled, backward, and isolated pawns are bad, and passed pawns and some advanced pawns are good. Doubled pawns are 2 or more pawns of the same color on the same file. Isolated pawns are those for which there are no friendly pawns on either of the adjacent files (or single file for rook pawns). Passed pawns are those whose journey to the 8th rank is no longer impeded by blocks or attacks by enemy pawns. The penalties for doubled and isolated pawns are fixed at 8 and 20 respectively, independent of the stage of the game and independent of surrounding nonpawn pieces. Two types of backward pawns are recognized: a "very backward" pawn is currently undefended by other pawns, could not be defended by advancing other pawns, and, if advanced one rank itself, would be immediately confronted by attacks by enemy pawns on both adjacent files without any compensating defenses by friendly pawns. A "lightly backward" pawn is similar to a very backward pawn except that if advanced one rank the number of enemy pawn attacks it would encounter would exceed the number of pawn defenses by 1, rather than 2. Penalties for very and lightly backward pawns are 8 and 4. Passed pawn bonuses are computed by multiplying the square (2nd power) of the rank number (2 to 7) by a factor whose basic value is 2.3 but which is modified by the status of the square in front of the pawn. If this square is blocked by an enemy piece, the factor is reduced by 0.7. If attacked by an enemy piece, it is reduced by 0.4, and if defended by a friendly piece, it is increased by 0.3. Thus if a passed pawn is on the fifth rank and the square on the sixth rank ahead of it is defended by a friendly piece but blocked by an enemy piece, the bonus would be $(2.3 - 0.7 + 0.3)*5*5 = 48$, or about half the material value of the pawn itself. If a pawn is part of a 3-file majority (the 3 files including and adjacent to the file the pawn is on have more friendly than enemy pawns on them), then a bonus is awarded equal to 1.6 times how far the pawn has advanced (rank number minus 2). All pawns in general receive additional bonuses for advancing depending on what file they are on: multiply the rank number minus 2 by one of the factors (0, 0, 3.9, 5.4, 7.0, 2.3, 0, 0) corresponding to the pawn's file reckoned left to right from queen rook to king rook. Note that only the four center files currently have nonzero values.

Each of the different pawn bonuses or penalties is awarded independently. For example, a pawn can be both passed, doubled, and isolated. However, only one pawn is counted for each file, so that, for example, the doubled pawn penalty is exacted only once for White pawns on K4 and K5. A few other evaluation terms involve pawns in combination with other pieces and are described elsewhere.

Rooks

Rooks are given bonuses for square control, king tropism, doubling, open and semiopen files, and seventh-rank occupation. Square control means in this case the number of squares attacked by the rook including squares occupied by enemy or friendly pieces. Each square is worth 1.6.

King tropism is a measure of nearness to the enemy king. The factor −1.6 is multiplied by the minimum of the vertical and horizontal distances between the rook and the king. The vertical (or horizontal) distance is the absolute difference between the rank (or file) numbers of the rook and the king. This term, therefore, is a penalty for distance rather than a bonus for closeness.

A doubled rook is a rook on the same rank or file as another friendly rook, without intervening pieces, and is awarded 8. Since both rooks are counted separately, a pair of doubled rooks is credited 16 altogether.

A rook is awarded 8 for standing on an open file, which is one which contains no pawns, and 3 for standing on a semiopen file, which is a file on which there are no friendly pawns but at least one enemy pawn that is not defended by other enemy pawns and which cannot move forward a single square without being attacked by one or more pawns.

The bonus for a rook on the seventh rank is 22.

Knights

Knights are evaluated for king and center tropism and development. Center tropism is a peculiar measure of the closeness of a knight to the center of the board and is computed as 6 minus twice the sum of the rank and file distances from the center of the board to the square the knight is on. This value is then multiplied by 1.6. Example: consider a knight on QB3. Numbering files and ranks from 1 to 8, the knights coordinates are 3,3. The center of the board is 4.5, 4.5, so the center closeness is $[6−2*(4.5−3+4.5−3)] = 0$. A knight on KR5, however, has closeness $[6−2*(8−4.5+5−4.5)] = −2$, and so would be credited $(−2)*(1.6) = −3.2$ (hence penalized 3.2, since the credit is negative).

King tropism, for knights, is computed differently from that of rooks. We compute 5 minus the sum of the rank and file distances between the knight and enemy king and multiply the result by 1.2. Example: a knight on KN5 and an enemy king on KR8 are 1 file and 3 ranks apart, so the tropism bonus is $[5−(3+1)]*1.2 = 1.2$. By contrast, if the knight were still on KB3, the bonus would be $[5−(5+2)]*1.2 = −2.4$. Thus the knight would gain 3.6 points of king tropism by moving from KB3 to KN5. Like bishops, development of knights means not being on the back rank, the penalty being 9.4.

Bishops

Bishops are evaluated for square control and development. Bishop square control is computed differently from that of either rooks or queens. The value 7 is subtracted from the number of squares that the bishop directly attacks (or defends), not counting squares occupied by friendly pawns. The result is multiplied by 2.4. Development is defined, as for knights, simply as whether or not the bishop is on the back rank. A penalty of 11 is exacted if it is.

Queens

Queens are evaluated for square control and king tropism. The queen square-control term is counted differently from that of rooks. Only squares not attacked by enemy pieces or pawns are counted. Each square is worth 0.8. Like rooks, queens are penalized in proportion to the minimum of the horizontal and vertical distances to the enemy king. The number of files or ranks is multiplied by -0.8, or half as much as for rooks.

Kings

Kings are evaluated for safety from attack and for center and pawn tropisms (if endgame). King safety is a primitive measure that is designed only to impart a vague tendency to protect the king, such as a reluctance to wander into the center of the board during the opening. Like other positional terms, it is not sufficiently large to offset the value of a sacrificed piece. Basically, the king-safety term is the product of two factors: one, a measure of how important it is for the king to be guarded at this stage of the game, and the other a measure of how well guarded the king is. The importance measure is $(NP + QB - 2)$, where NP is the number of nonpawn enemy pieces, and QB is 2 if the enemy has a queen, else 0. If the importance comes out zero or below, then king safety is ignored. The effect of the importance factor is to encourage the side whose king is exposed to trade pieces, especially queens, and to encourage his opponent to avoid such trades. In the opening position, the importance is 8. Trading queens reduces it to 5. The guardedness measure itself is the sum of several terms. These are computed as penalties for vulnerability rather than bonuses for safety.

The program assumes that a king is safer on one of the corner squares KR1, KR2, KN1, KN2, QR1, QR2, QN1, QN2 than elsewhere. A king is punished 3.1 for not sitting on one of these "sanctuary" squares. Actually, the program is lazy and considers all 16 corner squares alike, so that a king that has somehow wandered to his opponent's sanctuary also avoids the penalty. Such a situation rarely comes up, however. Note that in the opening board position, the contribution of the sanctuary factor to the total positional score is $8*3.1 = 24.8$, which means, roughly, that a king receives about a ¼ pawn bonus for castling short.

A king on one of the first-rank sanctuary squares (QR1, QN1, KR1, KN1) is penalized 0.8 for being "cramped," which means not having at least one square next to it, on the second rank, which is not attacked by any enemy pieces and not occupied by a friendly pawn. This term, which is one of the very few additions to the evaluation function since 1973, was designed to help overcome a tendency toward vulnerability to back-rank mates that we observed in tournament play (see Harris's comments on this theme in Chapter 7). Although CHESS 4.0 did not actually get mated, its failure to push one of its king-side pawns made it vulnerable to mate threats that cramped its game. The success of this evaluation term has not been determined.

The king-safety term also determines whether the king is "sheltered" and whether opponent pieces are attacking the squares adjacent to the king. To help prevent the king from sitting on a barren region of the board devoid of the protection of friendly pawns and pieces, the king is penalized if there are not at least two friendly pieces or pawns on squares adjacent (within one king move) to it. It there is only one such piece, the penalty is 1.6, and if none (a bare king), 3.1. If no friendly pawn stands on the same file as the king, a fee of 4.1 is charged. If no friendly pawn stands on at least one of the files adjacent to the king, the king is docked 3.6. For example, if the king-bishop, knight, and rook pawns are all missing, a king on KN1 is penalized for lack of both direct and side pawn cover: $4.1+3.6 = 7.7$. Before any piece trades, when importance $= 8$, the positional score contribution would be $7.7*8 = 61.6$. Fines are levied if at least 2 squares adjacent to the king are attacked by enemy pieces. The penalty is $1.2*(NAT-1)$, where NAT is the number of such squares attacked. This concludes the description of the king-safety term.

When a sufficient amount of material has been traded, the king acquires a desire to come out of hiding and roam toward the center of the board and toward whatever pawns lie on the board. The threshold is reached when enemy material falls below 1500 in value (e.g., a rook, bishop, knight, and 3 pawns). When the material is that low or less, the king is suddenly penalized for distance from the center. The penalty is 2.3 times twice the sum of the rank and file distances from the king to the center of the board. See the section on knights for a similar measure.

The king in the endgame is also penalized for wandering away from any remaining pawns. The penalty is $7.8*(ATPD-6)$, where ATPD is the average of the "taxicab" distances of the king to each pawn, friendly or enemy. The taxicab distance is the sum of the rank and file distances, as if the king could move only horizontally or vertically to approach the pawn. This term was inspired by observing ours and other chess programs reach an ending with kings and locked pawns and then draw by repetition because the kings moved aimlessly back and forth.

Mop-up evaluation

The mop-up evaluator is assigned positions in which one side has a material advantage of at least 400 points (4 pawns) and the other side has no more than 700 points worth of material. In addition, the winning side must have at least one queen or rook, or must have no pawns and at least minimum mating material in minor pieces (B+N, B+B, N+N+N, or more). All positions in the tree not satisfying these criteria are assigned to the regular position evaluator. The no-pawns criterion was based on the notion that it is easier to promote pawns than to checkmate with minor pieces alone.

The mop-up evaluation consists of two phases, the stalemate guard and the checkmate drive. The stalemate guard is a quick check for stalemate done only in the case of a lone king. If the king has no moves but is not in check, the draw score is set and EVALU8 exits. The checkmate drive is the sum of several terms:

1. The king getting mated has a great desire to avoid the edges and corners of the board. The mating side is credited 4.7*CD, where CD is twice the sum of the rank and file distances from the king to the center of the board. (See the sections on knights and kings in the regular positional evaluation for a similar measure.) Example: for a king on KB3: 4.7*2* (4.5−3+4.5−3) = 28. If the king is driven to KN2, then we have 4.7*2* (4.5−2+4.5−2) = 47, for an increase of 19.

2. A few plies of search are enough to show effects on the center tropism term by moves of the sliding pieces (rooks, bishops, queens) that restrict the enemy king. However, the king and his knight(s) must get close to the target king before having an effect, and so a term is added to encourage this approach: for each king and knight on the winning side add 14 minus the sum of the rank and file distances from the king or knight to the enemy king. Multiply the total by 1.6.

3. A minor factor is also added which seems to help position the winning king properly in the final stages of difficult checkmates, such as K+B+B vs. K. If the winning king is on the third or sixth rank or the queen-bishop or king-bishop file, it is awarded 2.

Special evaluations

Checkmate and stalemate are recognized during tree searching when no legal moves are found. Except for the mop-up evaluations, stalemate is not recognized by the evaluation function itself at the endpoints of the tree. Repetition of position is detected by comparing the position to be evaluated with a table of the fifty most recent positions in both the tree search leading up to the current node and the recent history of the actual game. The "fifty-move" rule is incorporated in spirit by pulling scores towards the draw value as the number of moves since the last pawn push or piece capture approaches 50. The draw score itself is not set to 0 but is modified by a "contempt" factor that depends on estimated ratings of the program and its opponent, which are set prior to the game. Another parameter pretends to know how negative the evaluation can get and still have the "better" player play for a win. These factors are usually set (for the computer tournaments) so that CHESS 4.5 will still play for a win, avoiding repetitions, etc., even though it is a pawn down. This is done so that the program will not become panic-stricken and seek a draw after having played a gambit from its opening book.

Tree searching in CHESS 4.5

Here we look at CHESS 4.5's tree search in detail. In summary, it looks simple (and simple-minded) enough: the search consists of a series of iterations terminated when a preset time threshold is exceeded. Each iteration is a complete α–β depth-first search of all the legal move sequences (except those eliminated by α–β cutoffs) out to the nominal depth of the iteration, with extensions beyond that depth only for sequences of capture moves (of almost unlimited depth) and also for checking moves one or two ply beyond the nominal depth. The depth of the first iteration is 2 and each subsequent iteration is a ply deeper than the preceding one. To gain efficiency, an iteration uses move-ordering and score information saved from previous iterations.

The key phrase in the above summary is "all the legal move sequences." Textbook accounts of computer-chess algorithms usually touch on the futility and foolishness of such brute-force searches, drawing analogies to the number of grains of sand in the Sahara Desert or perhaps the number of atoms in the universe. In fact, it does require some maneuvering to compute a positional score at each endpoint and still achieve depths of 4–6 ply in the middle game and up to 9 or more in the endgame. It is important to order the moves so as to get many α–β cutoffs. In a full-width search the difference between poorly-ordered and well-ordered searching is large, and so CHESS 4.5 devotes pages of code to move ordering. It is ironic that the lazy programmer, hoping to escape the brain-racking task of selective searching (forward pruning) by searching all the moves, is forced to devote his energies to move selection anyway so as to get the near-optimal ordering necessary to make the full-width scheme feasible. The difference is that mistakes in move selection are not as fatal to full-width searches, since they only affect efficiency, whereas they can doom a forward-pruning program by completely eliminating a crucial move from consideration. However, in CHESS 4.5 we succeed in cheating nature a little by using almost no chess knowledge in our move ordering. This way we have kept true to our principles, one of which is that "chess knowledge" is something that belongs in our "next" chess program. Actually, as you shall see in what follows, there is nothing magical in our ordering heuristics. In fact, at least as much of our programming effort has been devoted to another principle of full-width searching, which is to spend as little time as possible at any given node in the tree. It is at this dubious endeavor that our program excels. On a CDC 6400 CHESS 4.5 processes from 270 to 600 nodes (calls to EVALU8) per second.

The BASE module

The BASE module processes the base of the tree (the position on the actual board), whose ply level we define as zero. First, BASE looks this position up in the openings library. If found, the stored move is made immediately. Usually, it is not found. Then all the legal moves from this position are generated and tried, with instructions that the resulting ply-1 positions be processed by the PREL module, which assigns preliminary scores by using the evaluation function. The capture search is not done, but a very brief analysis of hung pieces is performed and the result is folded into the score. BASE also tells the search to omit the $\alpha-\beta$ minimax calculations that are usually performed. The moves are then ordered on the basis of these preliminary scores.

The iterations come next, starting with a 2-ply search. BASE tries out each move in order of preliminary scores from best to worst, with instructions that the resulting ply-1 positions be processed by the FULL module and that the $\alpha-\beta$ minimax procedure be employed. This means that the score expectation variables α and β will be maintained at each level of the tree. Before each iteration starts, α and β are not set to $-(\infty)$ and $+(\infty)$ as one might expect, but to a window only a few pawns wide, centered roughly on the final score from the previous iteration (or previous move in the case of the first iteration). This setting of "high hopes" increases the number of $\alpha-\beta$ cutoffs. If the final score does not lie within this window, however, all of the moves must be re-searched with lower expectations. Each time that a BASE move comes back with a better score than any of those preceding, that move is placed at the head of the list so that it will be searched earlier in subsequent iterations. Under certain conditions BASE will terminate an iteration prematurely and use the best move found so far. This may happen, for example, if the time consumed by the current iteration is judged excessive by the time-control monitor. The time is checked before each new move is tried out by BASE.

Another way an iteration can terminate early is in the case of an "obvious" move. Since the program continues to try new iterations until a preset time threshold is exceeded, there is usually little correlation between the difficulty of a position and the time spent pondering it. In 1974, the "obvious-move" feature was added to spare us further embarrassment at having to wait a minute and a half for CHESS 4.0 to respond pawn-takes-queen (assuming only one way to capture), which any of the spectators could have played after a moments thought. Now, when CHESS 4.5 finds a move which was judged clearly superior by preliminary scores (i.e., at least 156 points better than any of the others) and has maintained its first place thru every iteration up to the last one, then the last iteration is terminated after examining only this move to ensure that it hasn't worsened by more than 156 points. Now pawn-takes-queen takes only perhaps 35 seconds and CHESS 4.5 prints out "that was easy" to the amusement of all.

The FULL module

The FULL module handles nodes at depths 1 thru $n-1$, where n is the iteration depth. Since end-point evaluation is done at depth n or beyond, FULL is concerned mostly with more searching. The order of operations is very important in maximizing efficiency. FULL tries first to avoid any searching at all. Then it tries to search moves in an order likely to produce a quick α–β cutoff. Here is the detailed flow of the FULL module, divided into phases:

A. Repetition check. The position is matched against previous positions in this branch and also against up to 50 previous positions in the actual game. A match indicates a position repetition, which is scored as a draw, even if it has only occurred once. FULL then exits immediately. To speed up the comparison, the number of moves since the last irreversible one (piece capture or pawn move) is stored, so that no comparisons need be done beyond that point.

B. Transpositions/refutations table look up. Here we are interested in the evaluations stored in the trans/ref table that was described earlier. The table is probed, and if a match with a table entry is found, the stored evaluation is retrieved. Depending on the α–β values in effect at the time the position was stored, the value may be a true score, an upper bound, or a lower bound. The α–β values at the time of retrieval are also important in determining the applicability of the stored value to the present position. There emerge three cases:

1. The value is completely valid, in which case the current node is assigned this value, and FULL returns without further tree searching or evaluation.
2. The value is partially useable, in which case processing continues, but with a narrowed α–β window that will increase efficiency of searches done in the subtree grown from this node.
3. The value is useless, in which case processing of this node must continue as if no match had been found.

Values in the table are good only for the current search iteration. The utility of the table increases with the depth of the iteration and the simplicity of the position. The effect of increasing depth is significant because of combinatorial effects on the number of transpositions and multiple pathways. Thus a faster machine makes better use of the table than a slower one, provided that enough space is available to store the table. On a CDC 6400 in complicated middle game positions, the table reduces search times by from zero to about 50 percent. In simple endgames the benefit is much greater, showing gains of a factor of 5 or more, with a resulting gain in search depth of up to two or three additional plies.

C. Check evasion. If the side to move is in check, and the depth is n–1, the program branches to a special routine to efficiently generate moves to get out of check, and the remaining phases are skipped. See phase C of the MINI module for the details of the algorithm. FULL phase C is skipped during the first (2-ply) iteration.

D. Main variation. The main predicted sequence of moves from the previous iteration was saved, and, if we are still following that sequence, we search the predicted move. Since the BASE module also searches the main variation first, this sequence is the first one searched in each iteration.

Unlike some other programs which generate all of the moves from a given position before searching any of them, CHESS 4.5 tries to generate only a few at a time and thereby save time if one of the early moves turns out to be a refutation. In phase D, all the moves of one piece are generated and saved for use by other phases, and the particular move found in the main variation is selected from the generated list and searched. For bookkeeping reasons, the move from the main variation cannot be passed directly to the tree search but must be generated by one of a standard set of move generation routines. The tree search is instructed to send the resulting position to the FULL module if it occurs at depth $n-1$ or below and to MINI if at depth n. This is true of subsequent phases as well.

E. Transpositions/refutations table. The look up of the current node in the trans/ref table described previously may have retrieved a move that had been found—probably in a previous iteration—to be the best (or a refutation) in this position. This move is now searched. Most, but not all of the main variation moves also show up in the trans/ref table. Each move in the move list is flagged when searched, so that a move is not searched redundantly by different phases.

The principle of phases D and E is that a move found to be good for a particular position in a previous iteration is also likely to be good for this same position in the current iteration in which scores are computed one ply deeper. This principle has not proven to be as valid as we had originally thought, especially at the deeper ply levels close to depth n of the iteration. In fact, recent tests suggest that phase E might be more effective if it followed the captures (phase F) and the killer moves (phase G) rather than preceding them, since its skill in selecting moves, while significant, appears to be less than that of these other phases. Phases D and E are skipped during the first iteration because there are no previous iterations from which moves could have been saved.

F. Captures. All of the capture moves are generated by this phase. There is a routine named GENFSL that generates all moves from a given set of squares and also a routine GENTSL that generates all moves to a set of squares. Captures (except for *en passant* pawns) are generated simply by calling GENTSL with the set of squares containing enemy pieces. Then they are tried out, in order of decreasing estimated gain, down to an estimated gain of zero. The estimated gain defines a loose ordering of the captures and is simply the value of the captured piece if that piece is undefended, or its value minus the value of the capturing piece if defended.

Examining the captures first has a large effect on search efficiency. First, the full-width search involves lots of crazy moves and thus contains many weird positions in which pieces are left hanging. A capture is a refutation move more often than would be the case in positions reached in a normal chess game. Second, at a node at which any one of several moves would serve as a refutation, it is better to choose a capture than a noncapture, because the subtree grown from it is smaller. Not only does the capture simplify the board, reducing the number of legal moves, but it reduces the number of potential exchanges on the board, thus cutting down the capture/ quiescience search done at the endpoints. A capture also reduces the opponent's reasonable options for one ply, thus improving α–β cutoffs.

The importance of searching capture moves early became more apparent in 1974, when a predecessor of phase E was implemented. Since phase E passes refutation moves from one iteration to the next, the refutations chosen in the first iteration greatly influence the rest of the search. In CHESS 4.0, the killer heuristic (phase G) took precedence over captures. In 1974 we put the captures before the killers and observed a two-to-one speed-up in many positions. Rarely did the change produce a slower search.

G. Killer moves. The killer heuristic has been used by other chess programs and is basically an inexpensive attempt, based on superstition, to find a quick refutation move. Consider the position in Figure 4.4. White is threatening N–B7, forking the Black queen and rook and winning the exchange. Most of the Black moves do not avoid the fork. Once the program discovers (by accident, as usual) that (1) P–K4 is answered sharply by (1) . . . N–B7, it would do well to remember N–B7 and try it early against the other Black moves from the diagram. This principle goes by the name of the "killer heuristic," and N–B7 is the killer move. Phase G concentrates on the idea that the immediate offspring of a given parent node are often similar enough to be susceptible to the same killer move. So, in CHESS 4.5, from and to squares of the last refuting or best move at each ply level are saved in the "killer" table so as to be retrieved by phase G the next time the same ply level is reached, which is when a new move is tried from the same parent position, unless all those moves have been exhausted. Of course the killer move may not be legal at some of these nodes, in which cases it is ignored. Generation and listing of the move is accomplished as in phase D, once it is determined that a piece of the proper side stands on the from-square. If the killer move is best or causes a refutation, then of course it will be saved to be used again for the next offspring. However, if a different move proves best, then it will replace the killer table entry for that ply level and will be used the next time. A

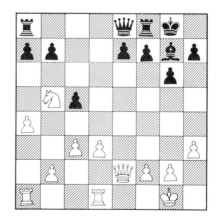

Figure 4.4   Black to move must defend against the knight fork.

move that captures the piece the opponent just moved is an exception. It is not put into the table since it most likely refutes only that one move.

In 1975, for CHESS 4.5, an enhancement was made to the killer heuristic that is related to the transpositions/refutations table. For phase B to be most effective, the killer heuristic should be used as often as possible, since the use of the same move over and over increases the number of transpositions. Suppose that, most, but not all, of the moves from a given parent node can be refuted by a single move. Then this move will be used over and over until one of the offspring positions is reached for which it does not work. For that node a different move will be found to be best and will be stored in the killer table. Then perhaps follows a series of offspring nodes for which the original killer move would once again serve as a refutation. However, knowledge of it has been lost since its place in the table has been taken. It might be rediscovered and thus reappear in the table, but it is likely that some other move would take its place, and would serve as a competent refuter, except for its negative effect on the frequency of transpositions. So for CHESS 4.5 the table was expanded to hold two entries per ply level—first and second most "popular" killers, together with popularity counts for each one. Both killers are tried in phase G, the most popular one first. When a FULL node is exited, the best or refuting move (if any) is compared to those in the table. If already in the table, its popularity is upped by one unit. If not, it replaces the lower entry and acquires a popularity of one. Thus a long-standing killer move, with many quick refutations to its credit, will not be hastily lost.

H. Killer of 2-plies lower. This phase tries out the most popular killer move of 2 plies shallower in the tree. This move is of no use, of course, if it already forms part of the current branch, since it can't be played twice in succession. This phase sometimes produces a refutation when the previous attempts did not.

I. The rest of the moves. The previous phases attempted to find a quick refutation move, or, if not that, then at least a good move that would set a respectable α–β expectation value. If there was no refutation found, then phase I must set about the business of searching the remainder of the legal moves. Of course any of these may still cause a refutation and terminate the search. First the rest of the moves are generated and added to the end of the moves list, which already contains some moves generated but not searched by previous phases. To impose some admittedly very weak chess sense on the order of these moves, they are generated in three steps:

1. Moves of hung (attacked and undefended) pieces
2. Moves of other attacked pieces
3. All other moves

Then the complete list is searched from beginning to end in two passes. Pass 1 covers only moves of pieces to squares not attacked by enemy pieces, and pass 2 includes all remaining moves.

In 1974, a time-saving feature was put into this phase, for nodes at ply level $n-1$, to take advantage of the evaluation function being dominated by the material balance. Consider a move m at ply $n-1$ (i.e., a move that results in a position at ply n and therefore is eligible for terminal evaluation), and suppose that m is neither a capture nor a check. Then the material score after the move m is the same as that before m. The positional score after m is not known before m is searched but is presumed, as we shall see in the description of the MINI module, to lie within the relatively narrow bounds of the minimum and maximum positional scores so far encountered in the whole search. Therefore, the total score after m can be predicted to lie in a certain range. The capture search conducted beyond move m can alter the score, but only to the advantage of the opponent of the side playing m. So already at ply $n-1$ a maximum value can be placed on the move m. If this value is less than the minimum expectation specified by current values of $\alpha-\beta$, then the move m is discarded without ever being searched. This algorithm has its greatest utility in branches in which an early move gives up much material for no good reason, so that most of the moves at ply $n-1$ are discarded as unable to win it back. In some positions the saving approaches 50 percent. The requirement that m not be a check stems from the effect of a check being unpredictable at level $n-1$. A few other criteria for the ineffectuality of move m are investigated before m is discarded—these involve the 50-move and repetition-draw rules.

J. Cleaning up. When all the phases are complete, FULL confirms that at least one legal move was found. If none were, then a draw is scored if the side to move is not in check, and a checkmate is scored otherwise. This checkmate score is larger the smaller the ply number so as to prefer fast checkmates over slow ones. If there was no checkmate or stalemate, then the best move (if any) is saved for the trans/ref and killer tables. If the ply level is one, the lack of a best move may be due to the rejection of all the moves by the artificially narrow $\alpha-\beta$ window that was imposed at the start of the search. In that case, the window is enlarged to relax the opponent's expectations, and phase I is reexecuted to try all the moves again. If this re-searching is not necessary, then FULL is done, the position is abandoned, and control is returned to the parent node one ply level back.

The MINI module

The MINI module completes the tree search. MINI processes all nodes at or beyond depth n, the terminal depth of the current iteration.

A. Repetition check. The check for repetition of position is done the same way as in the FULL module.

B. Transpositions table look up. The table is inspected as in the FULL module. Even at the "terminal" depth of the iteration, an evaluation from the table can still save considerable work—notably, the computation of the positional score and the capture and check-quiescence searches.

C. Check evasion. If the king is in check a branch is made to a special routine that generates moves that specifically try to get out of check. All of these moves are searched, so the effective terminal depth in this case is $n+1$. Phase C of the FULL module also may branch here if the king is in check at level $n-1$. The use of this special routine saves time because the move generation usually done in the FULL module does not screen out moves that leave the king in check. These moves are rejected only after tree-search control has updated the board and data base, a time-consuming process (1.5 millisecond or so on a CDC 6400), and then finds the resulting position illegal. In positions in which the king is already in check, most of the moves are illegal. This phase avoids generating most of these moves by considering only the following plausible alternatives:

1. Try to capture the checking piece
2. Try to move the king to an unattacked square
3. Try interpositions
4. Try an *en passant* pawn capture

Checkmate is scored if all these remedies fail.

D. End-point evaluation. This phase provides a score using either the regular or mop-up function described earlier. The regular evaluation is done in two steps. First, the material score is computed. This is done very quickly, because values are saved in a hash table and used over and over. All positions which contain the same number of pieces of each type have the same score. The number of pieces of each type form the "material signature," which is incrementally updated during the search, and is the key to the material balance hash table.

Now comes a time-saving trick. Our positional score is crude and is therefore weighted lightly. It would be nice if we could avoid calculating it at all. This can be done if the positional score is presumed to lie within certain bounds and these bounds bear a certain relation to the current values of α and β. Rather than compute analytically the extremes of values taken on by the evaluation function, we assume, somewhat erroneously, that the positional score will lie within certain limits.

Consider the preliminary scores given out by the PREL module for the purpose of sorting the moves at the base node. When the first iteration begins, positional scores are presumed to lie within a window whose limits are 75 points above and below the average value of the positional components of all these preliminary scores. This range is approximately one and a half pawns wide. Then each time a positional score is found outside these limits, the range is stretched just enough to include it. Usually the range of scores encountered during the search somewhat exceeds 150 points, so the limits become the minimum and maximum positional scores encountered so far in the search.

To make use of this information, we note that the α–β algorithm treats all scores less than or equal to α alike, and all scores greater than or equal to β alike. If a score is less (greater) than α (β), it doesn't matter by how much. Now the total score is the sum of the material and positional terms. If the material term is so low that the addition of even the assumed maximum positional score could not pull it up to α, then the positional score need not be computed at all. This is similarly true if the material term is so high that even the minimum positional score could not pull it down below β.

If the base position is relatively quiet, perhaps 50 percent of the end-point positions in the tree actually require positional scores. If the base position is tactically alive, and there are many forcing moves, this fraction may drop to as low as 10 percent. It seems to take about three times as long to process a node with full positional scoring as to process one without. For some reason that is lost in antiquity, we do not use this same trick in mop-up positions. It is not as important there, however, since the mop-up evaluation function is much faster.

The material and positional scores are added together and tapering, based on the 50-move rule, is folded in. The resulting score is not the final judgment on the position, however, but is considered only one of several alternatives, available to the side on the move, which are all mini-maxed together. The side to move has the choice of accepting the computed score (standing pat) or of trying captures (and perhaps checking moves) which might improve it. Of course it is possible that the just-computed score is enough to cause an $\alpha-\beta$ refutation and so eliminate the need for further searching from this node.

E. Capture search. The capture search tries out capture moves in order of decreasing estimated gain, as in phase F of the FULL module, except that even moves with negative estimated gain may be tried. There is a criteria for rejecting some capture moves *a priori*. The material score (assuming a successful capture) is computed. If this score, plus the most favorable possible positional score, is not enough to reach the current $\alpha-\beta$ expectation, then there is no sense trying it, since in the position resulting from the capture the other side will have the option of "standing pat." Positions resulting from the capture search are fed back into the MINI module, except that the transpositions table lookup is bypassed. Because the look up is bypassed, the storing of new information in the table for this position also does not take place. As a result, scores and best moves for positions within the capture search are not saved for use by the MINI module in subsequent occurrences of these positions. Also, the check-evasion code of phase C is bypassed for nodes more than 2-plies beyond the nominal depth n of the current iteration. In 1975 pawn promotions were added to the capture search on the grounds that they also immediately change the material balance.

So the main business of the capture search is to explore sequences of capture moves, with each side having the option at alternate levels of accepting the existing material balance or of trying more captures. The depth of these branches is limited only by the maximum capacity (30) of certain arrays. In practice, branches of 10 to 15 ply are not uncommon, although their utility is doubtful. Theoretically, the search could explode and hangup indefinitely looking at unlikely piece exchanges, but it usually fades out because of its self-limiting nature: each capture removes a piece from the board and so reduces the potential for further captures. Typically, the capture search constitutes about 20 to 70 percent of the total search. On rare occasions the search does blow up and this fraction reaches as high as 95 percent. It is quite likely that when the capture search exceeds 50 percent or so of the total, it is no longer cost effective in comparison to using just the primitive static exchange analysis such as is done in the PREL module. This hypothesis has not been tested, however.

The capture search is a special case of a tactical "quiescence" search—a search whose purpose is to reach "quiet" positions in which the static evaluator will in theory make more reliable decisions. However, the presence of capturable pieces on the board is not the only feature that makes a position tactically nonquiescent, nor is a search of capture moves alone a sufficient remedy. That our quiescence search is top-heavy with captures is due mostly to its simple, self-limiting nature and our laziness. A balanced quiescence search containing the most promising capture, threat, and threat-evasion moves, together with sophisticated time-control to prevent explosions, could yield much more accurate tactical analysis. Harris discusses this in some detail in Chapter 7.

F. Check-quiescence search. For nodes satisfying certain strict criteria, a more general quiescence search replaces the simple capture search of phase E. The *raison d'etre* of the check-quiescence search is fear of embarrasment—the embarrasment of falling into a three-move mate after having spent a minute-and-a-half doing a 4-ply search.

This phase averts the majority of such mates by essentially adding 2 additional plies onto branches in which the last 2 moves by one side were checks. Of course, these additional 2 plies would not prevent a 4-move mate (after a 4-ply iteration) or a 3-move mate in which not all of the three moves were checks. But we considered these possibilities either less likely or less embarrassing. The exact criteria for check-quiescence searching are that:

1. The node be at depth n or n+1
2. The last 2 moves (in the current branch) of the side to move be checks
3. The side to move not be winning by more than 400 points (a little less than a rook) as measured by the current α–β expectation value

If these criteria are met, all capture, pawn-promotion, and checking moves are searched, with the resulting nodes fed back to the MINI module. First, capture moves are searched in order of decreasing estimated gain. There is no special routine for generating only checking moves, so all the moves are generated and the checks selected from them. Check-quiescence finds mating combinations for both sides and also some checking sequences that lead to a win of material. It does not add more than a few percent of search time as averaged over a whole game. However, at the drop of a hat (or the slightest relaxation of the strict criteria for its application), check quiescence blows the search sky-high. This accounts for the severe limitations on it and illustrates the necessity for tight controls on a quiescence search.

This concludes the description of the MINI module and in fact the entire tree-search algorithm. We are now in a position to examine an example in detail. For simplicity, we will analyze the position depicted in Figure 4.5, in which each side has only a few legal moves. White has a king, Black a king and a pawn. It is clear that White's task is to stop the Black pawn from queening. The initial expansion of the base position indicates that White has six legal moves:

Move	PREL score
K–K4	–116
K–B4	–114
K–N4	–106
K–K5	–121
K–K6	–129
K–B6	–127

These are K–N4, K–B4, K–K4, K–K5, K–B6, K–K6 when ordered by score. K–N4 heads the list because the evaluation function encourages the king to be near the pawn. Its preliminary score, however, does not differ very much from that of any of the other moves, since the evaluation function does not understand that the pawn will be captured two half-moves later.

Below are shown the actual trees of the first 2 iterations. In parentheses are the module that generated the move (B = BASE, F = FULL, M = MINI), and also, for MINI and FULL, the letter of the phase within that module.

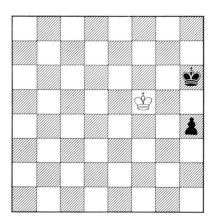

Figure 4.5 White with the move can capture the Black pawn.

2-ply iteration

Ply 1		Ply 2		Ply 3	
K–N4	(*B*)	K–N3	(*F*.I)	KxP	(*M*.E)
		K–N2	(*F*.I)	KxP	(*M*.E)
		K–R2	(*F*.I)	KxP	(*M*.E)
		P–R6	(*F*.I)	KxP	(*M*.E)
K–B4	(*B*)	K–N3	(*F*.G)		
K–K4	(*B*)	K–N3	(*F*.G)		
K–K5	(*B*)	K–N3	(*F*.G)		
K–B6	(*B*)	K–R4	(*F*.I)		
K–K6	(*B*)	K–N3	(*F*.G)		

(1) K–N4 is the first move searched at the base node because of its PREL score. FULL tries out all 4 responses: (1) ... K–N3, K–N2, K–R2, and P–R6, and the MINI capture search finds they are all met by (2) KxP. The next 3 moves tried by BASE, (1) K–B4, K–K4, and K–K5, are all refuted by the killer move (1) ... K–N3, since α–β now reflects White's expectation of winning the pawn, something which MINI did not see as possible after these moves. The BASE move (1) K–B6 is refuted by (1) ... K–R4, the killer K–N3 having been tried and found illegal. But (1) ... K–N3 comes out of hiding to refute the last BASE move, (1) K–K6. Thus (1) K–N4 is best and so retains its position at the head of the moves list.

3-ply iteration

K–N4	(*B*)	K–N3	(*F*.D)	KxP	(*F*.D)
		K–N2	(*F*.I)	KxP	(*F*.F)
		K–R2	(*F*.I)	KxP	(*F*.F)
		P–R6	(*F*.I)	KxP	(*F*.F)
K–B4	(*B*)	K–N3	(*F*.E)	K–K3	(*F*.I)
K–K4	(*B*)	K–N3	(*F*.E)	K–Q3	(*F*.I)
K–K5	(*B*)	K–N3	(*F*.E)	K–Q4	(*F*.I)
K–B6	(*B*)	K–R4	(*F*.E)	K–K5	(*F*.I)
K–K6	(*B*)	K–N3	(*F*.E)	K–Q5	(*F*.I)

Once again, (1) K–N4 is tried first. The FULL responses, (1) ... K–N3, K–N2, K–R2, and P–R6, are still answered by (2) KxP, which, however, is found by FULL instead of MINI, since it lies within the 3-ply horizon. In response to (1) ... K–N3, (2) KxP is a main variation move. All other moves besides KxP are discarded by the time-saving feature of phase I, since they cannot (within the horizon) meet the established expectation of winning a pawn. In response to (1) ... K–N2, K–R2, and P–R6, (2) KxP comes from the FULL capture phase and is a simple α–β refutation. The next three BASE moves, (1) K–B4, K–K4, and K–K5, are refuted, as in the 2-ply iteration, by (1) ... K–N3, which is recalled from the trans/ref table. Notice that in response to (1) ... K–N3, only one move is tried in each of the three cases. Once it is confirmed to be legal (to avoid getting into the checkmate or stalemate code), the others are discarded by the phase I time-saving feature. Finally, the last 2 moves at BASE, (1) K–B6 and K–K6, are refuted similarly to the previous ones. So the 3-ply iteration discovers the same simple truth that the 2-ply iteration did, that (1) K–N4 is best because it quickly wins the Black pawn. The predicted moves are (1) K–N4, K–N3; (2) KxP.

Although the base position is trivial, CHESS 4.5's search exhibits many of the features seen in much larger trees in more complicated positions. Note that because of α–β cutoffs and the time-saving feature, the tree does not appear to be "full width." The whole 3-ply search here was completed in about 100 milliseconds. In a tournament game the search would have gone out to perhaps 12 ply to get the same result, since the program lacks the sense to see that since White can force a position in which all material is gone, the game is necessarily drawn.

Program performance

Experience shows that the features of the present evaluation function coupled with a brute-force search of 3 to 10 plies (about 5 in the middle game) are sufficient to motivate CHESS 4.5 to do something "constructive" in most positions. Of course, what is constructive to the program may be a blunder to a Master, but at least the program rarely lapses into shuffling pieces back and forth aimlessly. In a typical game against a weaker opponent, the program keeps busy by maneuvering, with varying degrees of success, to optimize its notions of pawn structure, piece mobility, and general motion of pieces towards the enemy king, while it waits for a tactical blunder by its opponent. Once the program obtains a substantial material advantage, it can usually promote pawns and win more material until its mop-up algorithm drives the enemy king to a mate. Sometimes it wins in the middle game with a direct assault on the king without having to promote pawns.

Conclusions and perspective

What have we learned from the experience of creating CHESS 4.5 and its predecessors? Although CHESS 4.5 is more-or-less a Shannon type-A program, it is only one arbitrary example of a large number of possible programs that would fit into that same category. So one should be careful not to draw too many conclusions about the prospects of Shannon-type programs in general. The features of its evaluation function and tree search were determined often by the whim of the moment. Certainly they were not the result of a comprehensive, steady, and coherent research plan designed to exhaust the potential of brute-force tree searching. Sometimes we have been mistakenly pictured as hard-working, government-financed, full-time exponents of the "big tree." In reality, the program has been a part-time effort, with long stretches of inactivity punctuated by occasional panicky spurts of attention.

Now, having related CHESS 4.5's unsystematic mode of development, we can reflect on what it is we have really constructed. CHESS 4.5 can be approximated by the following theoretical model: Imagine that we have an evaluation function f that—when applied to any chess position—yields a numerical value, dependent on that position alone, which in some sense measures how well White is doing. A positive value means White has the superior winning chances, and the larger the value, the greater is the likelihood and imminence of victory. Now imagine a chess program which generates the moves from the base node and applies f to each of the ply-1 positions reached by those moves. Then, clearly f can be used to order the moves and in particular to select a "best" one from among them, so that we have a full-width 1-ply search. Here f is understood to consist of not only a static score but also the results of any quiescence search applied. Now imagine a program which applies that same function f to all of the ply-2 nodes of a full-width α–β 2-ply search. Heuristics may be used to order the second ply moves so as to produce more cutoffs, but these affect only the speed and not the result of the search and are not of interest here. This 2-ply program also picks a best move from the base node. If one chose to disable α–β, the program would produce a score for each of the base moves, just as the 1-ply search did. In fact we could pretend that the 2-ply search was really a 1-ply search, but with a different evaluation function applied at the ply-1 nodes. Now imagine an n-ply search with the same function f applied at the ply-n nodes. Once again we can pretend that the backed-up values at ply 1 were determined by some imaginary evaluation function applied directly at ply 1. This imaginary function embodies the real nature of the program, since it picks the move the machine would actually make. In mathematical terms, it is as if we had a depth operator that, when applied to an evaluation function f, yielded an imaginary "smarter" function f_n that, applied merely at ply 1, would simulate the results of a full-width n-ply search that applied f to its endpoints. What is the relation of f_n to f itself? The answer to this question should give us an understanding of the full-width search technique. Obviously $f_1 = f$ and f_2 has similarities to f but also some important differences. For example, if f understands (because of a capture search or static analysis or whatever) that it is bad to make a move that leaves one of one's own pieces attacked and inadequately defended, then f_2 understands that it is good to make a move that forks two enemy pieces, since at 2 ply at least one of the forked pieces is still capturable. And f_3 understands additionally that it is good to make a move that prevents a forking maneuver by the opponent. The point is that if f contains a particular chess concept such as material gain, then the depth operator in a peculiar way transforms, enriches, and extends the concept, by expressing the result of projecting this concept out to the endpoints of an n-ply search. This notion holds for positional ideas as well. If f likes knights in the center of the board, then f_5 finds 3-move pathways to get them there. So the full-width search program deals not just in the ideas imparted to it by its author but also in subtle extensions of them coaxed from the program by a costly expenditure of computing time. The basic axiom of full-width searching is that given a reasonable f, f_{n+1} is better than f_n, so that given enough time, we might as well do another iteration. But what is a reasonable f? Is it enough that the values of f correlate positively with the game-theoretic values (win, lose, draw)? Tests that pit CHESS 4.5 against itself at time odds tend to confirm the basic axiom fairly strongly. However, the f of CHESS 4.5 is quite rudimentary, and the search depths achieved are necessarily low. There are many interesting aspects, beyond the scope of this discussion, to the question of what happens to f_n as one increases n while keeping f fixed. One example is the questionable validity of the assumption made by our search model that the opponent will use the same algorithm as the computer in choosing its moves. Thus as n increases, the program "sees" more, but it also assumes erroneously that its opponent will necessarily see the same things. (See Michie [103] for a discussion of this and related topics.) If we do assume that f_n in general improves with n, then do different f's (or different aspects of the same f) improve at different rates? We conjecture that the better f already is, the more it will benefit from a deeper search. If this is true, then we should work on improving the quality of evaluation functions, rather than on small increments in search efficiency. This brings us to the next topic of discussion: what might one do to improve CHESS 4.5?

There is controversy over how to write better chess programs. Some think that gradual changes to a program like CHESS 4.5 are the way to go. Others think that CHESS 4.5 is heading in the wrong direction and an entirely different approach is needed. It is our belief that both of these positions are valid, and that, in fact, one could arrive at a radically different and more powerful program even by "gradual" changes to a brute-force tree-searcher like CHESS 4.5. The weakest parts of CHESS 4.5 are its evaluation function and quiescence search—its f, the brains of the program. Our present f is blind to the simplest phenomena. The evaluator gladly accepts a position in which the computer is a knight ahead although its king is out in the center of the board surrounded by hostile enemy queens and rooks. In a king-and-pawns endgame, that a passed pawn is outside the square of the king and so queens by force is discovered only by a grueling 9-ply search. The list goes on and on. But why is the program so devoid of chess knowledge? It is not because we are deliberately trading it for speed of execution. For example, in a position in which the king is surrounded by enemy pieces, the program is still wasting time worrying about doubled pawns. In these situations more knowledge would probably save time in the evaluation. Similarly, some sensible heuristics in the quiescence search would restrict it to a balanced selection of tactical tries rather than letting it get lost in a forest of capture moves. It is not quite true to say that we don't know how to feed additional knowledge to the program. Certainly we could teach it something about the square of the king. Our problem is that the programming tools we are presently using are not adequate to the task. Too much work is needed to encode the sizeable body of knowledge needed to significantly improve the quality of play. The macro language developed for EVALU8 is hopelessly inadequate. If we had put in a few hundred man hours writing statements in this language, we could have substantially improved the evaluator between CHESS 4.0 and CHESS 4.5. Instinctively we have recoiled from such an effort. Intuition tells us that "there ought to be an easier way" and that our time would be better spent finding it than in hacking away at make-shift solutions, especially if we are aiming our sights at the shimmering mirage of master-level play.

This lack of programming tools has plagued the whole field of computer chess. With the proper tool one might accomplish in a day a job that had been put off for years. Although serious efforts are underway to overcome this deficiency, the number of people working on this is surprisingly small, and their research is still in its infancy. When this research begins to produce results, the domination of the computer-chess tournaments by old-fashioned programs like CHESS 4.5 will come to an end.

These programming tools could be developed at several levels. Each successive step should be more sophisticated and should take computer chess closer to the realm of artificial intelligence. The first step for our group might be just a modest structured programming language with records, sets, lists, other user-defined data types, macros, and user-defined operators. Within this language one would embed definitions of data elements and operators which are suitable for chess programming. Modularity, simplicity, and elegance would be stressed. For the last few years we have given some thought to the problem of what language to use as a base and what kinds of chess-specific data types and operations to embed in it. Completing this task will probably take more time than actually implementing a chess program within the finished design. This design will not look very impressive to a computer scientist, but it should make chess programming a lot easier for us. Still, this design will go only a limited distance in solving what we see as two major problems in chess programming: the difficulty of specifying chess specific knowledge to the program and of representing this knowledge internally. It will be awkward to express chess notions in the form of statements of a conventional programming language, even if the data-types and operators have been custom designed. The next logical step therefore would be to develop a language for expressing statements about chess which would not require an understanding of computer programming. The program would preprocess these statements and convert them into an internal form (perhaps linked lists or some other form of associative data base) for use during actual execution. The TYRO program of Zobrist and Carlson [101] is an experiment in this direction. The language would be tailored for ease of use by the person writing it, perhaps resembling a subset of English. Eventually one would like to be able to introduce strategic concepts of the kind strong players use. A hypothetical example might be: "In positions of the classical variation of the King's Indian Defense, Black should try to establish control of QB4 before developing his queen's knight."

What is the role of the quiescence search in a full-width brute force program? Presumably, as more chess knowledge is introduced into the program, the quiescence procedure will share in this bounty and become cleverer in the way it selects moves to be searched. Although the quiescence search as a whole may, like the evaluation function, depend only on the terminal position at which it is conducted, the processing of nodes within the quiescence subtree need not have this restriction. In fact, information would ideally be passed along the branches of the subtree as in Berliner's tactical analyzer [12]. A smart quiescence procedure should have all the characteristics of a selective (Shannon type-B) search. But if we pretend to be able to do selective searching, what is the sense of grafting such a search onto a full-width procedure? Why shouldn't selective searching be used throughout? One might ask: "What is a smart search like you doing in a dumb program like this?" The answer is that as the quiescence becomes more sophisticated, it can be entrusted with greater responsibility. In the limit, the quiescence procedure would take over and become the whole search as the number of full-width plies is reduced to one. And so the transition from an old-style program to a modern one would be effected. But does this method of transition make sense, with an intermediate stage in which full-width searching and smart quiescence searching co-exist? A plausible justification is that it provides a method of handling time control in a "production" situation such as a tournament chess game. The problem of time control is very important in a chess program. When the program spends time searching a subtree or evaluating a position it implies a decision as to the cost-effectiveness of that search or evaluation. Only a few percent of the chess positions encountered in tournament play permit a complete solution by a program in a reasonable amount of time. It will be difficult to build time-control decisions into every nook and cranny of the program's thinking processes and yet this capability is essential for a selective search. For the present it may be possible to isolate the time-control process in a simple way by using iterated searching and by restricting the quiescence and evaluation procedures so that they cannot blow up. In a position in which the program's knowledge is small, so that its complete search takes only—say—5 seconds, the safest way (if we believe in the basic axiom mentioned above) to utilize additional time is to add another 1-ply layer of full-width searching to the base of the tree. As we have pointed out earlier, leaving out moves early in the tree is dangerous. The deeper the tree extends, the more intelligent must be the criteria for pruning at shallow nodes.

The speculative model of chess-program evolution sketched above is only one of several possible routes to stronger programs. We believe that the common element of any such efforts is that they involve the addition of more intelligence to chess programs. This intelligence may take many different forms. The Russian group of Adelson-Velskiy, Arlazarov, and Donskoy [3] have expressed strong belief in brute-force full-width searching. But they believe they can greatly improve the depth of search by the intelligent use of knowledge of the rules of chess to prune away branches of the tree. The program would do this by rigorously proving that these branches lead to positions not necessarily identical to others already seen, but similar enough so as to have the same evaluations. On the other hand, some groups believe, perhaps rightly, that an advanced chess program will need to do very little tree searching. In any case, the whole effort to build more intelligent chess programs is just beginning, and I believe we can look forward to some very interesting results over the next several years, even including programs that are able to monitor their own performance and use the information gathered to alter their algorithms and thus learn on their own.

PEASANT:
An endgame program
for kings and pawns

Monroe Newborn
McGill University

5

Tournament chess programs have had considerable difficulty in playing the endgame. The game scores presented by Professor Mittman in Chapter 1 and by Newborn [73] provide ample evidence of this weakness. Levy [67] has frequently pointed out this shortcoming. It is not clear whether the poor play which is generally observed is due to a basic weakness of the Shannon–Turing minimax approach [81, 82, 95, 96] as Harris suggests (see Chapter 7) or whether it is because the evaluation functions that have been used were not intended for the endgame. To examine this question, a program was written which uses a conventional α–β minimax search procedure but employs an evaluation function and tree-pruning heuristics which are specifically tailored for the endgame.

Our program plays chess when there are only kings and pawns on the board. Work on the program, called PEASANT, began in 1973 when the author held a visiting appointment at the Technion in Haifa, Israel. Israel Gold, a member of the Technion's chess team and an undergraduate student in the Department of Computer Science, assisted with the programming. Additional program refinements have been implemented more recently at McGill University with the help of Leon Piasetski, an International Master. The program is written in FORTRAN IV for the IBM 360/370 Series computers. It consists of about 2000 instructions and requires about 25,000 words of storage. During execution, the entire program resides in core memory. It is capable of searching around 18,000 terminal positions per minute when executing on the IBM 370/158. About 800 hours of programming work have been invested in the program.

PEASANT is based on the Shannon–Turing approach. It is designed to perform a tree search to some arbitrary fixed depth. A minimax decision strategy is implemented by using the α–β algorithm [45, 59, 77]. In addi-

119

tion, the program employs forward-pruning to eliminate many king moves at depths short of the fixed depth. The net effect is that positions involving 3 or 4 pawns can be searched to a look-ahead depth of around 10 ply. ONEPAWN, a special algorithm, developed by Piasetski and myself, statistically evaluates positions in the tree having only one pawn on the board. Another special algorithm developed primarily by Piasetski (named TWOPAWN) statistically evaluates *most* positions in which one side has two pawns. It reverts to a regular tree search when it arrives at a position it cannot evaluate.

This chapter is organized in several sections. The first section describes a special set of chess-playing rules which the program uses. The program itself is then described in some detail. The third section analyzes the performance of the program by examining a number of endgame positions from Fine [44] and the final section presents some observations.

The rules of play

PEASANT is written to play with the two kings and with as many as eight pawns per side on the board. The rules of chess are modified slightly in order to simplify the program's structure. When a pawn reaches the eighth rank, it automatically becomes a queen. In addition, the queen is not allowed to move and thus is not able to check the opponent's king. Promotion to a minor piece is not permitted. White is defined as the winner if (1) Black's king is in check and has no legal moves to prevent its capture on the next move (the usual definition of a checkmate) or if (2) White has more queens than Black and it is White's turn to move. A position is defined as a draw if (1) it is repeated for the third time or if (2) both sides have an equal number of queens on the board and there are no queening moves for the side to move. The 50-move rule is not programmed and neither side has the capability of offering or accepting a draw.

These rules cause only a small percentage of the games to be played differently than they would be played with the usual rules. The changes however make programming considerably easier.

A description of the program

The program is described by considering its data structures, the criteria for declaring a node terminal, the scoring function, the algorithm for generating, ordering, and forward-pruning moves, and the special subprogram that evaluates all positions which have only one pawn.

Data structures

The board is stored in a 64-word, 8 × 8 array. At any given time in the tree search only one board is retained in memory; subroutines incrementally update and restore this board as the search progresses. White pieces are represented by positive numbers and Black pieces by negative numbers with a pawn indicated by a 1, a queen by a 5, and a king by a 6. The number 0 is stored in the array for each of the squares which are empty.

In addition, two separate lists are kept (one for Black and one for White) which record the pieces which are currently present and the XY coordinates of each piece. These lists require 30 computer words for each side since each is limited to a maximum of 10 pieces and 3 items of information need to be stored for each piece. The king and its coordinates appear at the top of each list. Pawns are then placed on these lists in the order of their advancement. This is done to increase the probability of an α–β cutoff in the search since moves are generated for pieces on these lists from top to bottom and statistically it seems best to try to move the most advanced pawn first. The piece lists are also incrementally updated and restored as the search progresses. When a White (Black) piece is captured, it is "crossed off" the list by changing its value to a -1 $(+1)$. A zero (0) denotes the end of each piece list.

A large 1000-word list is employed to remember the moves which are currently being considered at each ply in the tree. The first 50 positions in the list are reserved for the moves at the first ply, the next 50 positions are reserved for the moves at the second ply, etc. The program can therefore search to a maximum depth of 20 plies. Each move is represented by a sign digit followed by nine decimal digits, all of which are stored in a single four byte word. The sign digit is a plus or minus to indicate that the move was made by White or Black. The second digit indicates the type of piece which moved (1 = pawn, 6 = queen). The third digit is reserved for information about captures. If a capture occurred, this digit is set to the position of the captured piece on the opponent's piece list. The fourth digit records the position of the piece which is being moved on its own piece list. The fifth and sixth digits indicate the XY coordinates of the initial location of the piece and the seventh and eight digits indicate the XY coordinates of the destination square. The ninth digit indicates the type of move which occurred (0 = transfer of a piece from one square to another, 1 = conventional capture, 2 = en passant capture, 3 = pawn promotion). All other words on the list (i.e., unused data locations) are set to zero.

A 20-word list is maintained to remember which move at each ply is currently under study. Thus move pointers are available for a twenty ply search. The values for α and β are stored in a separate 22-word list. These values are determined for terminal positions by invoking the evaluation function. For nonterminal positions, values are determined by backing-up terminal values using the minimax rule. The search also employs a 20×20 triangular array which keeps track of the principal continuation and two special 18×80 arrays which store certain 3 move continuations and the scores associated with them.

Processing at each node

Processing at each node begins with a series of tests to determine whether to consider the node a terminal node and if so what score to assign to it. If a node is not found to be a terminal node, it is considered a nonterminal node. At each nonterminal node, all moves are initially generated and placed on a list. The list is then examined and the best moves are placed at the top. Moves which are judged to be "obviously" bad are eliminated.

With the exception of one class of nodes, *all nodes found to be terminal nodes at depths less than the maximum search depth correspond to positions that the program is able to declare won or drawn.* The exception is the class of nodes that are identical to nodes found earlier in the search and that are arrived at again through a permutation of moves. The scoring function gives credit for winning as quickly as possible by giving less credit for wins at deeper plies. In particular a win by White at ply i receives $200 (i-j)$ points less than a win at ply j for $j<i$. A win is considered as a position in which one side has more queens than the other and the side with fewer queens has just made a move. A win also occurs if the side to move is in check and has no legal moves. A won position at ply d (for White) receives a score of $6000-200*d$.

Each node which is generated is examined to determine whether it should be classified as being terminal or nonterminal. A node is considered terminal

1. If it is at the maximum preset depth
2. If one side has exactly one or two pawns and the other side has none.
3. If there is one or more queens on the board and the last move was not a promotion
4. If a pawn is closer to its promotion square than the enemy king and can outrace any enemy pawn with a move to spare
5. If the depth of the node is equal to that of a previously examined node where a win can already be guaranteed
6. If this same board position has occurred previously at this same depth in the tree
7. If the side to move has no legal moves
8. If the position is identical to a parent position which occurred 4-plies earlier in the tree
9. If the side that is ahead makes a move which permits the opponent to force a draw by repetition

Each node which meets one or more of these criteria is declared terminal and is scored. In Cases 8 and 9, the position is scored as a draw. In Case 7, the position is a loss for the side to move if its king is in check, otherwise it is a draw. In Case 6 the position is given the score which was computed for the previous position. In Case 5, the position is given a "bad" score for the side on-the-move. In Case 4 where a pawn is free to run, the score is computed as $6000-200*d-400*p-100*(1-c)$ for White where d is the depth (in plies), p is the number of moves to the promotion square, and $c = 1$ if White is on-the-move and -1 otherwise. In Case 3 where a pawn has been promoted, the position is scored as a win if the opponent cannot capture the queen on the next move or cannot promote one of his own pawns on the next move. In case 2, ONEPAWN or TWOPAWN is called to evaluate the position. ONEPAWN evaluates positions with only one pawn on the board as described below. TWOPAWN evaluates positions in which one side has two pawns and the other side has none. In some cases, TWOPAWN is not able to return a score and recommends a deeper search.

In Case 1 where the node is declared terminal because the maximum search depth has been reached, the position is scored for White as $10*$ (MATW–MATB) $+ 5*$(WP–BP) $-$ (ADVW–ADVB) $+ K_1 + K_2 + R$. MATW and MATB are the number of White and Black pieces on the board, WP and BP are the number of passed pawns for each side, and ADVW (ADVB) is the number of moves that the most advanced White (Black) pawn must make before promotion. K_1 is a factor giving credit for having the king near the pawn(s); 5 points are deducted for every square that separates the king from the "center of gravity" of the pawn(s). K_2 awards 3 points if the king has "opposition." R gives credit for having a passed pawn out of reach of the enemy king, a situation that is not enough, in general, to guarantee a win but one that is a very strong advantage. Ten points are awarded for every square that such a pawn is advanced.

If none of the above nine conditions is satisfied, the node is classified as nonterminal. In this case, all legal moves are generated and then examined for ordering. Captures and promotions are placed at the top of the list. Moves selected by the "killer heuristic" (see Chapter 3) are placed next on the list. Moves by the king to a square on the edge of the board are eliminated if the move list would otherwise contain 8 legal king moves. Moves by the king which take it more than 2 columns or 3 rows away from the nearest piece are also eliminated. These last two rules comprise the forward-pruning component of the tree search.

The king vs. king and pawn subprogram (ONEPAWN)

When a node is classified as terminal because there is exactly one pawn on the board (i.e., Case 2), a special subprogram named ONEPAWN is called and the position is scored by this routine. All positions are correctly evaluated by carrying out a short series of tests. The program first determines the pawn's square and the opponent's king's square and then checks to see if the potentially winning side's king is on a square which yields a won position. For example, if a White pawn is at QB4 and a Black king is at KB2, White wins if it has the move and if its king is on any of the squares marked by an "X" in Figure 5.1. Otherwise the game is drawn. A short series of tests determines whether the White king is on a marked square. This same "mask" is used if the pawn and Black king are on squares QB3 and KB3 or QN4 and K2 respectively. A different mask, shown in

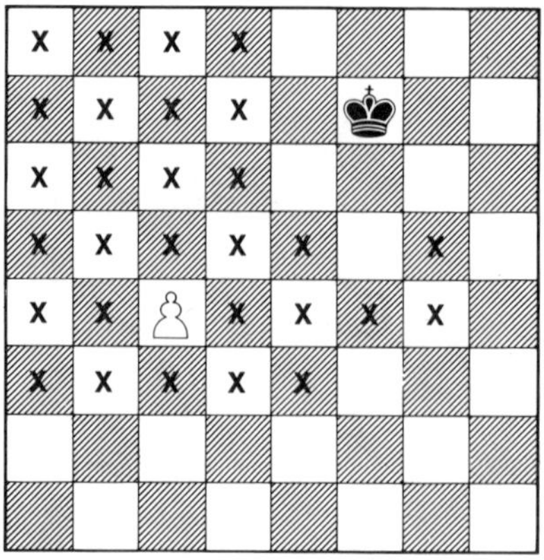

Figure 5.1 The White pawn will queen if White has the move and the White king is located on any of the squares marked with an "X."

Figure 5.2 is used if the White pawn is on QR4 and the Black king is on Q2. ONEPAWN has about 300 masks covering all possible piece configurations.

If the position is won for White it is assigned a score of $6000 - 200*d - 400*p$, where d and p are defined as before. If the position is drawn, credit is given for pawn advancement and for having one's king near the pawn as described previously.

The program's performance

In order to illustrate the program's strengths and weaknesses in king and pawn endgames, we asked it to solve a series of problems from Fine's *Basic Chess Endings* [44]. A limit of two minutes of CPU time was allowed for each problem involving search depths of from 4 to as many as 13 plies. The program responded with the principal continuation for successively increasing search depths, the score of the continuation, the number of terminal nodes scored, and the CPU time consumed. Of the 16 positions tried, PEASANT selected the correct move for 11 of them. In several

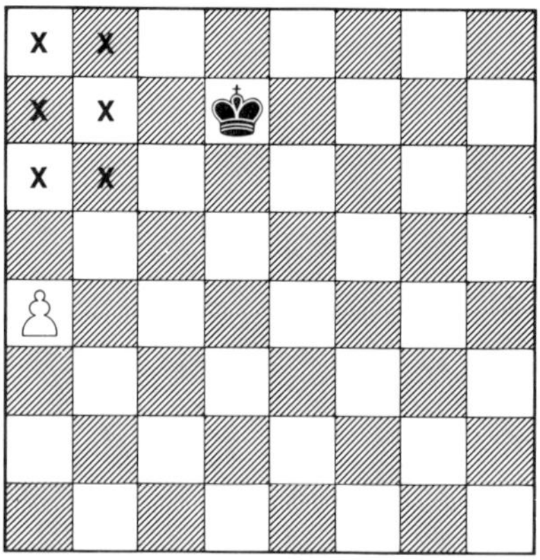

Figure 5.2 The White pawn will queen if White has the move and the White king is located on any of the squares marked with an "X."

problems the correct move was selected for reasons somewhat secondary to the main theme. In others, PEASANT had no understanding of the real considerations involved in solving the problem.

The problems can be grouped into several categories based on the program's ability to solve them:

(1) Simple races to promote passed pawns where concepts such as critical squares [103] or opposition or zugzwang do not enter. Four problems from Fine [44] fall in this category: Problems 51, 61, 80, and 82. These positions are presented in Figure 5.3. The program did reasonably well on these. In Problem 51, the program directly selected P–Q5 and saw the win with the passed pawn out of reach of the enemy king. This solution required only a 5-ply search. In Problem 61, a search of 8 plies found the win with P–N6. In both Problems 80 and 82 the program failed to find the

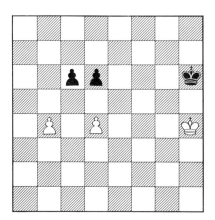

Problem 51: White to move

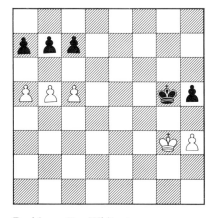

Problem 61: White to move

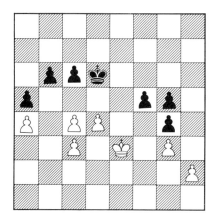

Problem 80: Black to move

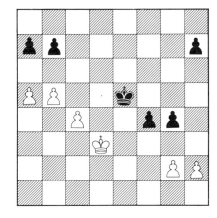

Problem 82: White to move

Figure 5.3   Endgame positions from Fine [44].

win although it made the correct moves, P–N4 and P–B5 respectively, at several depth settings. In each case, a search of approximately 18 plies would be necessary to envision the win. In both problems it was sidetracked by its opponents delaying moves with the net result that the win was pushed over the search horizon. In Problem 82, for example, at 9 plies PEASANT sees: (1) P–B5, P–B6! (a delaying move); (2) PxP, PxP; (3) K–K3, K–Q4; (4) KxP, KxP; (5) K–K4. If Black were unable to make the delaying move, the program would see that (1) P–B5, K–Q4; (2) P–B6, PxP; (3) P–N6, PxP; (4) P–R6 gives it a passed pawn out of reach of the enemy king.

(2) Problems that involve the concept of critical squares or opposition or zugzwang. This is best shown by Problem 70 although Problems 25, 53, 58, 67, and 76 all involve these principles. These problems (see Figure 5.4) require a very deep search—far too deep for PEASANT to carry out in its present form. A minimum of a 20-ply search is necessary to solve any of these problems as the program now exists.

For Problem 70, the program selects K–N2 at all depths (4 to 12 plies) instead of the correct move K–N1. For Problem 25, the program selects P–R3 with a shallow search (4 and 5 plies) and selects K–R5 with a deeper search (9, 10, and 11 plies). The correct move, K–N5, is selected with searches of 7 and 8 plies but for the wrong reason. On Problem 53, the program selects P–Q4 with a shallow search (4 and 5 plies) and K–Q4 with searches of 6, 7, and 9 plies. The correct move, K–K4, is selected with an 8-ply search but again for the wrong reason. On Problem 58, the program vascillates between P–B5 and the correct move, P–Q5, but does not see the win. For Problem 67, the program selects the correct move, P–N4, for the wrong reason with a shallow search and then switches its preference to K–B4 with an 8-ply search. Finally, on Problem 76, the program has no idea of what is needed, and selects P–R4 at depths of 4, 7, 8, and 9 plies. K–R2 is selected by a 6-ply search and the correct move, P–B4, is chosen by the 5-ply search.

(3) Problems for which the correct move is forced for reasons not necessarily related to the ultimate winning strategy but forced by immediate considerations. This includes Problems 26, 42, 90, and 100A. These positions are presented in Figure 5.5. In both Problems 26 and 42 the program must play the correct move (K–Q5 and K–K4, respectively) or immediately feel the negative consequences of another move. In Problem 90, searches less than 6 plies don't reveal that the advanced pawn on K6 can be defended. In searches of depths 6 and 7, the program sees this and changes its move from P–K7 to the correct move, P–K4. It does not see the win however. The continuation presented by Fine is 37 plies and involves Black queening a pawn that is immediately captured by White's king (which is free to roam the board while Black's king must remain near K1 to prevent the advanced White pawn from queening). White then queens two pawns, the first of which also falls immediately and the second of which queens with a check giving White an extra move to prevent Black's last hope on N7

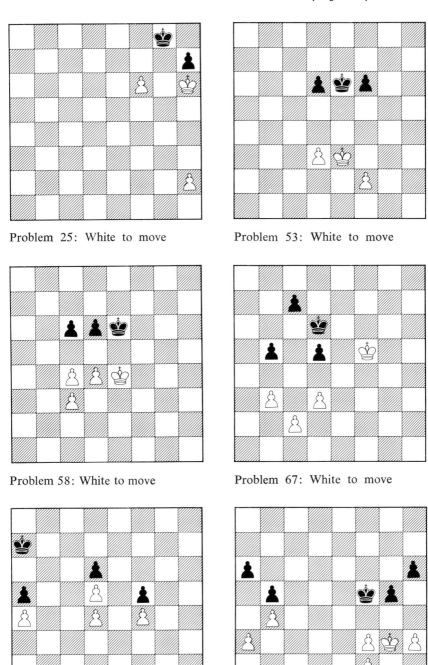

Problem 25: White to move

Problem 53: White to move

Problem 58: White to move

Problem 67: White to move

Problem 70: White to move

Problem 76: White to move

Figure 5.4   Endgame positions from Fine [44].

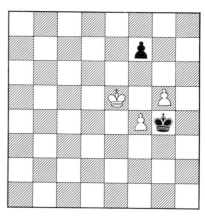

Problem 26: White to move

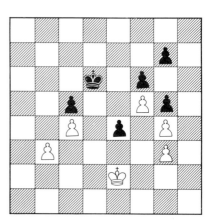

Problem 42: White to move

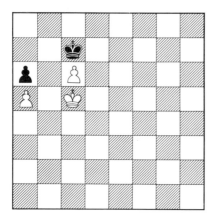

Problem 90: White to move

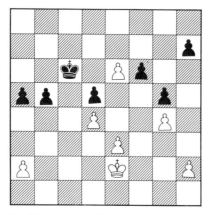

Problem 100A: White to move

Figure 5.5 Endgame positions from Fine [44].

from queening! Fine's continuation (1) P–K4, PxP; (2) P–Q5+, K–Q3; (3) K–K3, P–N5; (4) KxP, P–R5; (5) K–Q4, K–K2; (6) K–B4, P–N6; (7) PxP, P–R6; (8) K–B3, P–B4; (9) PxP, P–N5; (10) P–N4, P–R4; (11) P–N5, P–R7; (12) K–N2, P–R8=Q+; (13) KxQ, P–R5; (14) P–N6, P–N6; (15) P–Q6+, KxP; (16) P–N7, K–B2; (17) P–K7, P–N7; (18) P–N8=Q+, KxQ; (19) P–K8=Q+ could be viewed as involving a series of delaying moves by Black. In Problem 100A, the program selects the correct move, K–B2, at all depths but not because it sees the win. The move is selected simply because all other moves lead to immediate disaster.

Problem 29 (see Figure 5.6) is simple enough for the program to find the correct continuation in an 11-ply search. It involves only three pawns and Black has only one move in each position. The tree grows very slowly

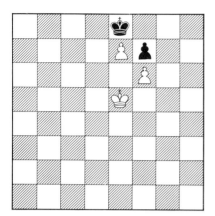
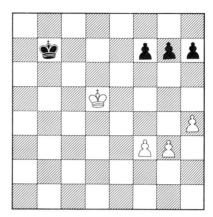

Problem 29: White to move   Problem 66: White to move

Figure 5.6   Endgame positions from Fine [44].

and at a depth of 11 plies, the tree contains only 1966 terminal nodes. The search takes only 6.3 seconds.

In Problem 66 (see Figure 5.6) the White king must prevent Black's king from coming to the defense of its own pawns. At a depth of 8 plies, the maximum depth attempted by the program, the function of the White king is not realized by the program although at a depth of 9 plies, White should see that (1) K–Q6, P–R3; (2) K–K7, P–B4; (3) K–K6, P–N3; (4) K–B6, P–N4; (5) KxP gains a pawn. The 8-ply search consumed 59.6 seconds and a 9-ply search would probably have required about 3 minutes.

A detailed analysis of these end-game positions indicates how difficult the task is for a Shannon–Turing program. PEASANT would have to search to a depth of about 25 plies in order to solve Problems 25, 53, and 58. This would require about 1000 hours of CPU time. Position 70 would require a 30-ply search (25,000 hours). Positions 90 and 100A would require about 40 plies (over 300,000 years). Obviously, the Shannon–Turing approach will need quite a few refinements if it is to cope successfully with these difficult positions.

Final observations

The level of play shown by PEASANT is superior to that of tournament programs in king-and-pawn endgame situations. The weaknesses of the tournament programs reflect the fact that they were not designed with the endgame in mind. The present level of play by PEASANT is fairly respectable and yet there remains considerable room for improvement. The program's scoring function is not very sophisticated nor are its decisions which classify a node as terminal or nonterminal. Furthermore, the pro-

129

gram needs a more knowledgeable algorithm for forward pruning which would allow searches along very select lines. In this respect, an approach similar to Newell, Shaw, and Simon's seems best [74]. Moves for the king deep in the tree must only be generated for very specific reasons— for example, moves that tend to move the king nearer weak pawns, tend to move the king nearer pawns that need protection or, tend to reduce the opponent's king's access to good squares. Pawn moves need not be generated deep in the tree if there is no possibility that the pawn can eventually queen.

The scoring function can be improved by adding subprograms similar to TWOPAWN for cases involving 1 pawn vs. 1 pawn, 2 pawns vs. 1 pawn, and 2 pawns vs. 2 pawns. We are presently working on this. In these subprograms, an attempt is being made to classify as many positions as possible as won or lost and then examining the remaining positions with a shallow tree search in order to arrive at one of the solved positions. The scoring function must also understand the concept of critical squares although this seems to be a very difficult problem. The scoring function must recognize when one of the kings is forced to move within a small area in order to stay within reach of a passed pawn. In addition, it must recognize and give credit for certain special pawn positions, such as those that involve one passed pawn supporting another.

A great deal of work and careful thought will be required to implement each of these proposed refinements. Until these projects are completed it will not be possible to judge the true limit of the Shannon–Turing approach. In the meantime, we will be satisfied with slow and steady progress. If we can improve the program in an incremental fashion, we should gradually be able to clearly identify the more serious weaknesses of this approach.

It is important to recognize that the endgame in chess is an incredibly difficult challenge. To appreciate this complexity and to gain a better understanding of our present level of accomplishment, the reader should test a friend on these 16 positions. Our program selected the correct move for 11 of the 16 problems in an average time of 10 to 15 seconds each. It would be nice if our program could solve all of these problems, but this may be an unrealistic expectation given the complexity of the task and the short timespan of our efforts.

Plans, goals, and search strategies for the selection of a move in chess

Russell M. Church and Kenneth W. Church
Brown University

In the spring of 1970 at the Adriatic resort town of Herzeg-Novi, the strongest speed tournament of all time was held. Of the twelve participants, all but one was a grandmaster. Bobby Fischer won the double round robin with the amazing score of 19 points (out of a possible 22). The time limit for each game was 5 minutes, and it was reported that Fischer spent only half his allotted time on the average [4].

The quality of play of grandmasters at speed chess is surprisingly high caliber. It would be easy to confuse such games with games played by strong players at regular tournament speeds. It is unlikely that any game played by a computer program would be confused with a game played by a strong player.

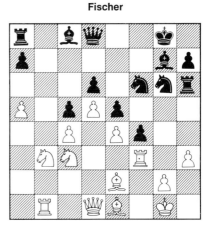

Figure 6.1 Korchnoi vs. Fischer.

Fischer

Korchnoi
24 Be1 ...

Consider two positions from that speed tournament. In the first position Black played (24) . . . Nh8. After it was played, the point was obvious. Fischer wanted to post a knight on g5 where it would be poised to be sacrificed at the appropriate time for White's pawn on h3. The route is h8–f7–g5–h3. The difficult part of that move was deciding on the goal; its execution was straightforward. We do not know how many seconds Fischer thought before making the move, but it is likely that the move was made after only a few seconds of reflection. In that time it would not have been possible to trace the implications of all possible moves and replies to a depth of 8 ply (i.e., 4 moves and 4 replies) or greater. Other methods of analysis make this an intuitively appealing move, however, and the intuition was correct in this case.

In the second game, White sacrificed the exchange with (24) Re7. Although he undoubtedly saw other less dramatic ways to win in this overwhelming position, the move he chose led to a checkmate eight moves later. Again, we do not know how many seconds Fischer spent before playing the move, but certainly it would not have been possible to trace the implications of all possible moves and replies to a depth of 16 ply. Again, other methods of analysis make this an appealing move since the Black king is stuck in the center of the board, surrounded by the power of white pieces, and devoid of power of its own pieces. By general principles, a checkmate probably is present in this situation, and again the intuition was correct.

The basic purpose of this chapter is to describe how it is possible for excellent chessplayers to play strong chess even at blitz speeds. This is a simpler problem than the attempt to understand how excellent players choose a move under normal tournament conditions [31]. Psychologists have had little to say about the methods people apply to the solution of serious, intellectual problems. If a person is allowed to think deeply about a matter, and does so for several minutes, the complex thought processes

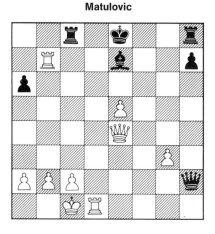

Figure 6.2 Fischer vs. Matulovic.

are virtually inaccessible. Physiological records are of essentially no value. Although some aspects of the brain waves may be characteristic of thinking, there is no analysis of the brain waves that reveals the content of the thoughts. The location of eye fixations can be recorded accurately, but the excellent play of many chessplayers under blindfolded conditions demonstrates that a great deal of thinking about a position can occur in the absence of sensory input from the location of the pieces. Physiological measures of emotional activation can be recorded with equipment similar to that used in lie detection, but such methods are not likely to do more than identify certain periods in the game when the player believes the position has reached a critical stage. The direct introspective methods [31, 75] offer somewhat more information regarding complex thought processes, but they are far from satisfactory. A person can be asked to describe what he is thinking about while he is analyzing a position, but there is the danger that the process of talking out loud can influence the process of thinking, i.e., that the measurement of the phenomenon distorts the phenomenon that is measured. The retrospective method of asking a person to describe how a move was chosen after the analysis is complete undoubtedly suffers from large recall losses over the period of several minutes. Both introspective methods assume that the thought processes are conscious, although it is realistic to assume that many of them occur automatically and rapidly and are inaccessible to introspection. Some ideas have emerged from the introspective evidence (e.g., the concept of progressive deepening), but the difficulties with current attempts to understand thought processes during several minutes of analysis are considerable, and the progress since de Groot's original work has been slight.

Psychologists have had much greater success in dealing with events that occur rapidly in time, e.g., decisions that occur within fractions of a second or, at most, a few seconds. The general approach is to infer the nature of thought process from the way in which the decision time varies with small increases in the difficulty of the task. The best example of the approach is the line of research beginning with Sternberg's [90] study of speed of recognition that an item was (or was not) included in a small set of symbols that a person had been asked to memorize. The results were that the speed of recognition of items included in the set (and those not in the set) was a linear function of the size of the memory set, which was varied from one to six items, and that the slope of the function was about 45 milliseconds per item. The conclusion was that the person rapidly (at 45 milliseconds per item) searched the list of items in the memory set in a serial (rather than a parallel) manner, and made a decision only after all items had been examined. In the Sternberg memory task most subjects would say that the correct answer was immediately obvious and they were not consciously aware of any search strategy. This is a case in which an analysis of reaction time led to the identification of a search strategy of which the person had no conscious awareness.

A chessplayer in a blitz game may also have little awareness of the

133

search strategies he is using to choose a move—the decision appears almost immediately. Our aim is to attempt to understand what search strategies are, in fact, being used in such situations.

The chapter begins with a description of three search methods: forward search, pattern analysis, and problem reduction. Our major message is that forward search has been overemphasized, and that pattern analysis and problem reduction have been underemphasized, in most current discussions of how people choose a move in chess. We, next, briefly describe some data from an experimental study that supports the idea that, even at the level of the individual move, chessplayers are guided by goals, and that they immediately respond to patterns. Finally, we describe a program to play chess that follows these principles.

Search strategies

Many of the search strategies that are used to find a move in chess are examples of general problem solving techniques that are used to deal with diverse mathematical problems [78, 99]. Most problem solvers, e.g., chessplayers, are familiar with these techniques, even though they do not have readily accessible names for them. A formal classification of problem solving techniques is a reasonable first step toward understanding the conditions under which a person uses any particular approach to discovering a move in chess. It also alerts us to the large number of different approaches that are possible for solving a particular problem. In this section, we will consider only three of the problem-solving methods: forward search, pattern analysis, and problem reduction.

Forward search

One method for choosing a move in chess is to generate legal moves and replies to some depth, and then evaluate the resulting position. This is the search method that Shannon described in his influential article which demonstrated that a digital computer could be programmed to play the game of chess [81].

Shannon correctly observed that the method he was proposing to program a computer to play chess could be called "trial and error." The method he proposed is now widely known, and it was closely related to a plausible interpretation of human thought processes. He wrote,

> The thinking process is considered by some psychologists to be essentially characterized by the following steps: various possible solutions of a problem are tried out mentally or symbolically without actually being carried out physically; the best solution is selected by a mental evaluation of the results of these trials; and the solution found in this way is then acted upon.

The general approach is to consider all possible combinations of moves to a depth determined by the practical limitations of space and time. Then

134

a move is selected which maximizes the evaluation function on the assumption that the opponent will also attempt to maximize this evaluation function from his point of view at each choice point. (See Chapter 3 by Frey in this volume for a more complete description.) The forward-search approach has one major strength. If there is a decisive series of moves within its horizon, a complete forward search is certain to find it. This makes it particularly accurate in shallow tactical situations.

The depth of search permitted by this approach is surprisingly limited. There are about 30 legal moves in a typical chess position. This means there are about 900 possible positions after White and Black have each moved once, about 1 million possible positions after two moves, and 1 billion after three moves. We can think of these alternatives as a branching tree that is quickly getting out of control. To keep the number of positions to be evaluated within manageable limits various heuristics have been introduced to prune the tree in both width and depth. With restrictions of this sort, however, there is the danger that the program will stop analyzing a line of play prematurely. Tree-searching programs should not terminate a search when the side which is evaluated to be ahead has a piece *en prise* or is vulnerable to a forced checkmate. To prevent this, various heuristics have been introduced to continue a search until a position becomes quiescent. These modifications of search do not alter the fundamental approach described by Shannon. In each case, a standard evaluation function is applied to a large number of positions generated by a trial and error procedure.

In their book *Human Problem Solving*, Newell and Simon [75] devoted a chapter to the description of programs which have been written to play chess. All of them use Shannon's approach. In their summary Newell and Simon wrote:

> They are all very much of a type: forward search through a subtree
> of the tree of legal moves, selection heuristics, static evaluations,
> minimaxing.

In summarizing the history and basic ideas of computer chess, Newborn [73] wrote, "All the chess programs that have ever been written and that are of any significance today are based on Shannon's ideas." It is certainly true that all programs that have been entered in the ACM Tournaments, and any other programs that would have a chance to challenge the stronger programs in those tournaments (e.g., Greenblatt's MacHack) have used the forward-search methods proposed by Shannon.

How well do the strongest computer programs play the game of chess? Shannon believed that a computer programmed in the manner he suggested "would play a fairly strong game at speeds comparable to human speeds." He noted that the computer has several advantages over a human player:

1. It can make individual calculations with much greater speed.
2. Its calculations will be free from errors.

A human player may occasionally overlook the power of one of the pieces as a result of laziness, carelessness, overconfidence, boredom, or anxiety. As a result, a person may not have complete confidence in his initial calculations, so he may take extra time to repeat a calculation that has already been made. Despite these arguments, in practice, the best computer programs do not play a strong game of chess, even when spending an average of two or three minutes per move. In speed chess the quality of play deteriorates considerably.

Many teams of skilled programmers and chessplayers—working at Northwestern, MIT, Carnegie–Mellon, and elsewhere—have tried to modify the Shannon approach to improve the quality of play. This improvement has consisted of increasing the efficiency of searching the branching tree structure, earlier elimination of unpromising lines of play, greater depth of analysis of the more promising lines of play, and improvements in the evaluation functions. Although considerable work has been conducted along these lines since 1967, the improvement in the quality of play has not been substantial. In 1967 Greenblatt's program at MIT was playing at the Class C level; similar comments could be made about the strongest programs available in 1975. Even this may overstate the quality of play since there are important qualitative differences between computer chess and the chess played by Class C players. It would probably be easier to teach a novice to beat a computer program than to beat a Class C human player. (See Chapter 8 by Hearst for some specific recommendations.)

Pattern analysis

The most reliable method for choosing a move is based upon complete pattern recognition. Particularly in the openings, a chess player has associated many positions with specific moves. When the player recognizes the position as one which has been previously encountered, the associated move can be executed without any analysis. Such moves can be made quickly and accurately.

In the middlegame, it is not likely that the player will have encountered the complete position previously, but aspects of the position may include familiar patterns. For example, certain tactical elements (e.g., pin, discovery, x-ray, skewer, overworked piece, trap, and fork), certain structural features of the pawn formation, and other features of the position may be immediately recognized as patterns. These patterns will not be associated with specific moves, but with goals that the player might attempt to realize, and various plans to achieve these goals.

The recognition of winning and drawing endgame patterns may be an essential factor in the choice of moves at any stage of the game. A player who attempts to work out a complicated rook and pawn endgame that his opponent recognized would be at a substantial disadvantage. As in the case of middlegame features, endgame patterns will normally be associated with goals and plans rather than specific moves. The treatment of the legal move as the elementary unit of chess thinking is concrete but undoubtedly misguided.

Problem reduction

An alternative approach to choosing a move can be called "problem reduction." If the problem is not a simple one (i.e., solved by one move or by pattern recognition), then it can usually be reduced to several simpler ones. The aim is to reduce each of these problems to primitives.

Problem reduction is used frequently in choosing a move in chess. Its application to cases in which there is no interaction between areas of the board is obvious; the remainder of this section is based upon cases in which the person first selects a goal, and that goal serves to guide the selection of a move. In many positions the key problem is to find a meaningful idea to pursue. Given the idea, the move is not hard to find. For example, a person may identify an opponent's backward pawn and search for a piece that might be effectively posted in front of it; or a person may identify a knight forking square (a square that, if occupied by a knight, would put two pieces *en prise*) and search for a knight to occupy the square or threaten to occupy the square. In Figure 6.1 Black identified a target and found a safe route for the knight to attack the target. In other cases, power may be transferred to certain areas, holes, or posts. In other cases, the goal may be to increase king protection, or to improve pawn structure, or to utilize an open line.

This method takes advantage of a problem with the answer being easier to solve than the same problem without an answer. The same person who unerringly identifies an unusual queen sacrifice when told there exists a mate in three might often fail to find the correct move in over-the-board play when no specific goal is given. Even general hints about a goal, e.g., "the opponent's last move was a blunder," or "you now have a winning position" can serve as important guides to the selection of the best move.

Problem reduction can be used to build two trees: one forward from the current position and the other backward from the desired position. Since the number of branches is greatest at larger depths, there will be fewer nodes when problem reduction is used. If the subproblems are further subdivided, then there will be an increased savings. The process repeats recursively until the problem is reduced to primitives or a subproblem is reached with a poorly defined goal.

How is a player able to choose a reasonable move in a few seconds? There is not time to evaluate a million different positions, or even many dozens. Instead, a person would look for some weakness in his opponent's position to exploit or for some weakness in his own position to correct. This kind of intuitive play can be very rapid since it requires evaluation of relatively few positions, and it may be superior to the systematic trial and error approach of current programs that play chess according to the Shannon proposal.

The major advantage of problem reduction is that the quality of positional play is much improved, and most moves can be reasonably chosen on positional considerations alone. With only a few nodes to investigate, there is ample time to find subtle positional points.

The major difficulty of problem reduction is in tactical situations. Although many complications can be avoided by conservative positional play, serious tactical problems still may arise a few times in a game. Most tactics fall into one or more categories, such as pin, discovery, skewer, trap, fork, overwork, deflection, and pawn promotion. It is easy enough to identify most of these tactical possibilities, and many of them may be correctly solved by thorough static analysis.

Search strategies in the movement of the pieces

Even at the level of mentally moving a piece, a person uses methods other than systematic forward search. To identify the nature of the pattern transformations explored by a human subject while looking at a chess position, Church [26] employed extremely simple and artificial positions. Each position contained only one White piece and the Black king. The subject simply reported whether or not the king was in check as quickly as possible consistent with reasonable accuracy.

One approach that the subject might have taken toward this task can be called "forward search." For forward search a person generates perceptual transformations and then evaluates them. For example, the person could mentally move the rook in each of its four directions and then decide whether or not the king had been encountered.

An alternative approach can be called "problem reduction." In problem reduction the person first identifies a goal, and that goal serves to guide the perceptual transformations. In the present experiment, the person's goal is to assess the power of the piece upon the king. If a person employs problem reduction in this position, he would generate moves only in the direction of the goal. Our current opinion is that this goal-oriented approach is characteristic of all serious problem solving.

The task was as follows: A person was seated in front of an oscilloscope. When he was ready for a trial, he pressed the space bar with his thumb. This led to an immediate display of a chessboard with two pieces randomly located on the board—a White rook (capital R) and a Black king (small k). If the king was in check the subject pressed the left switch; otherwise, he pressed the right switch. His task was to respond as quickly and accurately as possible. The display continued for one second after the decision so that the person could see whether or not he made the correct response, and then the oscilloscope went blank. When ready, the person initiated the next trial. A session consisted of 1000 trials, which took approximately 40 minutes.

The same procedure was used with the bishop, and with the queen. The results for one subject are shown in Figure 6.3. The error rate was low

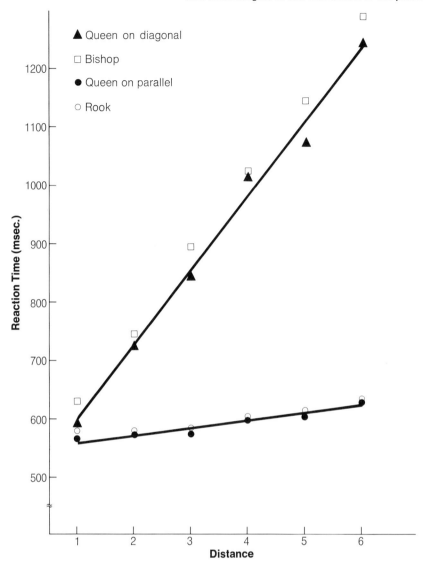

Figure 6.3   Mean reaction time as a function of distance between White piece and Black king.

(about 3.5 percent), and times for these trials were not included in the figure. When the rook and king were in checking relationship, the greater the distance between the pieces, the slower the reaction time. The time to recognize the power relationship between a rook and king was a linear function of the distance between the pieces. The processing speed was about 10 milliseconds per square. The time to recognize the power relationship between a bishop and king was also a linear function of the dis-

139

placement between the pieces. The processing speed was about 132 milliseconds per square. Figure 6.3 also shows the same data for the queen and king in cases in which there is a checking relationship between them. The speed of correct perception of the checking relationship along a rank or file was approximately the same for queen and rook; along a diagonal it was approximately the same for queen and bishop. This is an important result which demonstrates that a person must decide which of the legal directions to move a piece *before* beginning to move it mentally.

The subject was definitely not employing a trial-and-error, forward-search, strategy. If the person mentally moved the queen in all its eight legal directions and the bishop in all of its four legal directions, the time required to recognize a check on a diagonal should be greater for the queen than the bishop. A similar argument leads to the conclusion that the time required to recognize a check on a rank or file should be greater for a queen than a rook. Since the speed of the queen was like the rook on the ranks and files and like the bishop on the diagonals, the person must have recognized the relationship between the pieces prior to making the mental movement.

In a related experiment, the pieces displayed were a White knight (capital N) and the Black king (small k), and the subject's task was to press the left switch if the king was in check or if it could be put in check by a single move; otherwise, the person was instructed to press the right switch. Chessplayers (A–C ratings) were much faster in this task than nonplayers but, more interestingly, the relative difficulty of the different positive patterns differed for players and nonplayers. The nonplayers were faster on the immediate check case than the check-in-one-move cases, but the various check-in-one move cases were processed in approximately the same time. The players, on the other hand, made the correct decisions more rapidly when the knight was close to the king (within two ranks or files) and more slowly when the knight was further away. Apparently, the nonplayers made their decision only after mentally moving the knight; in the cases in which the knight and king were close together, the players immediately responded on the basis of the pattern. This is consistent with Botvinnik's [18] treatment of the movement of the pieces.

These results suggest that pattern recognition and goal-oriented problem reduction, rather than trial-and-error forward search, are used by chessplayers even on a simple problem of assessing the power relationship between two pieces.

A program to play speed chess

Our primary reason for programming a computer to play chess is to understand how strong chess players are able to choose good moves under severe time constraints. In our description of alternative search methods we have presented various arguments in support of the idea that chessplayers are guided by goals and that they respond to patterns. Some experimental evidence was also presented which was consistent with that view. We now describe our attempts to simulate the accurate first impressions of a strong player on examining a chess position for only a few seconds. The process of writing a computer program to play chess according to the principles assumed to be true for strong chessplayers has disciplined our thinking. When our program does not execute a strong move in a particular situation, it is clear that we have not yet captured the essence of the behavior of strong chessplayers in such a position.

A second reason for programming a computer to play strong chess is simply to respond to the challenges of accomplishing this end, regardless of the differences between the methods employed by the computer program and people. It may be that the two motivations for chess programming are not incompatible. Botvinnik [18] has written that a program to play strong chess "must be modelled on human thought processes." We have adopted this as a working assumption, and this implies that the two purposes for writing chess programs (to simulate human thought and to play strong chess) are complementary.

The program we have written to play chess used the principles we assume strong players use in speed chess. The program is designed as a fast, intuitive system for chess. It is written in the LINC and PDP–8 assembly languages (mostly the latter), and it is executed on a PDP-12 minicomputer. The computer has an oscilloscope, a teletype, and 8 K of core memory. The only mass storage device is magnetic tape, and this is rarely used during a game. At the present time, the program chooses a move in about 4 or 5 seconds.

When the computer has chosen a move, the move is printed on the teletype, and the new position is displayed on the oscilloscope. The person replies by typing a move in algebraic notation. This returns control to the computer to plan the next move.

Goal orientation

Alexander Kotov [60], a Soviet Grandmaster, has emphasized the importance of selecting a plan in his book, *Think Like a Grandmaster*. He wrote:

> . . . it is better to follow out a plan consistently even if it isn't the best one than to play without a plan at all. The worst thing is to wander about aimlessly. (p. 148)
>
> You notice a desirable objective, plan how to achieve that objective, carry out the plan and then repeat the process all over again and so on throughout the game. (p. 140)

After an analysis of a large number of computer chess games, Newborn [73] characterized the essential weakness as "an obvious lack of long-range planning." We have been particularly impressed by the aimlessness of many moves played by the forward search approach. Current chess programs often lead to a sequence of moves that are not related to each other. This can be seen at all stages of the game, but it is probably most obvious in the endgame. Planning is also a problem for the novice chessplayer. After he has successfully achieved what control he can in the center, developed his pieces, and castled his king, he may be at a loss for a continuation. Without a plan, he makes uncoordinated moves or merely waits for opportunities to arise. By the time contact is initiated by the opponent, the game may be lost.

Our program is always following a plan. Our method is simply as follows:

1. Describe the position (static analysis)
2. Select a goal based on the position, and select a plan based upon the goal and the position
3. Discover the move that is most consistent with the plan selected

Several plans may be available to attempt to realize a particular goal. If there are no moves which have a positive evaluation with respect to the goal, a new goal is chosen and the procedure is repeated. If no additional goals are identified, and this occasionally happens to human players as well as computer programs, the first unrefuted legal move is made. When the program runs out of ideas in this manner, we are alerted to study the particular position to identify what goal the program should have had in the particular position.

This method is designed for the discovery of plausible moves, and our logic is not always perfect. For example, we sometimes make assumptions which we do not bother to test. In practice some verification of the adequacy of the move should be made by forward analysis. We have decided to proceed without any verification. The absence of this self correcting feature allows the programmer to recognize inadequacies easily.

Data structure

Most basic facts about a chess position can be conveniently represented in a table—an 8×8 matrix corresponding to the squares of a chessboard. Space is reserved in core memory for 32 different board representations of a given position. When necessary, additional board representations of a given position may be stored on magnetic tape.

The 64 squares of a board representation may be filled with symbols in one of three formats (identification, power, or value). The *identification format* identifies the color and type of piece associated with a square (e.g., a White bishop); the *power format* represents the number of each type of piece associated with a square (e.g., 2 pawns and 1 bishop); the *value format* consists of a signed integer associated with a square. Each of these formats is used for diverse purposes. For example, the value format is used for recording the material value of the piece occupying a square, the number of moves required by a knight to move to a square, etc.

Tables can be used to represent features of the actual position, hypothetical transformations of the position, and ideal patterns. Descriptions of many of the types of board representations we are now using are given in the next three sections. The answer to many questions about a chess position can be readily obtained by examination of the appropriate board representations. In some cases, these may represent a complex arithmetic or logical combination of several board representatives.

Most decisions regarding the move can be made from logical or arithmetic manipulations of various 8×8 matrices representing alternative ways of viewing the position. Each chessboard matrix is given a table number, and various manipulations of the information in the table can be done with standard subroutines, e.g.,

1. Operations on a single table
   Clear the table
   Find the maximum or the minimum entry of the table
   Sum the entries in a table, or sum a selected group of entries
   Count the number of positive, negative, or zero entries
2. Operations on pairs of tables
   Copy all entries of Table A which are less (equal, greater) than a constant into Table B
   Mask all entries in Table A with a particular bit configuration, and deposit the result in Table B
   Add a constant to each entry in Table A and deposit the sum in Table B
3. Operations on triplets of tables
   Matrix addition and subtraction. Add each entry in Table A to the corresponding entry in Table B (or subtract B from A) and deposit the result in Table C
   Conditional copying. Copy entries of Table A into Table C, if certain conditions exist in the corresponding cell of Table B

The extent to which our program relies upon board representations, table manipulations, and plans can be seen by the allocation of space to various purposes:

Board representations	0.28
Table manipulation	0.08
Plans	0.28
Move generation	0.11
Teletype	0.14
Oscilloscope	0.05
Lists	0.03
Other	0.03

Our program does maintain several short lists (which will be described later). These lists, and the routines required to service them, take very little space. Although the same chess information can be coded either in terms of lists or tables, chessplayers are more likely to think in terms of board representations than in terms of lists. The major advantage of tables over lists is that they can be meaningfully combined with simple logical or arithmetic operations.

Goals of the opening

At the present time three opening goals have been formulated: book, pattern-seeking, and center control.

Book. Lists of specific opening lines have been selected from a standard reference source [39]. A particular line is played until the opponent deviates. Then the remainder of the book is searched for any rote continuation that has been stored. If none is encountered, the program returns to the center control plan. Altogether about 4000 positions are stored for use when the computer is White, a somewhat smaller number when the computer is Black. There is currently no basis for transposition back into a book line once the computer has left it.

Pattern seeking. The goal is to achieve a particular pattern (e.g., that characteristic of the King's Indian Reversed). The plan is simply to make moves to achieve this pattern unless another move produces a more favorable material outcome.

Center control. In this section we will describe the way in which moves are selected by a plan designed to achieve the goal of control of the center. The desired final pattern of center control is not well defined, so a minimum of forward analysis (1 ply) is used to determine whether or not progress is being made (hill climbing).

The approach can be seen best by example. We will describe the basis for the selection of a move in the position shown in Figure 6.4, which was reached after the following sequence of moves:

Computer vs. Person

| 1. e4 | e5 | 2. Nf3 | Nc6 | 3. Bc4 | Bc5 | 4. 0–0 | Nf6 |
| 5. Nc3 | 0–0 | 6. d3 | d6 | 7. Be3 | Be3 | 8. fe3 | Bg4 |

Person

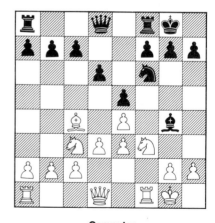

Figure 6.4 Computer vs. Person.

Computer
8 ... Bg4

The last seven moves of the computer were generated by a plan designed to achieve control of the center (i.e., book moves and pattern seeking were not used). The program took about 4 or 5 seconds per move, and no verification was employed. The center-control plan, as described later in this section, is obviously very elementary, but it often leads to a natural move when adopted in the appropriate situations.

A static analysis of the position is conducted as follows: a position table, in identification format, is maintained throughout the game to indicate the occupant of each square. Fourteen additional board representations are always calculated. (Separate representations of the following seven tables are kept for the White and Black pieces).

1. Mobility tables. The mobility of the pieces to each square is represented in power format. A piece is said to have mobility to a square if it is legal to move the piece to that square. For example, the White mobility table on square d5 would have a bishop and a knight since these are the two White pieces that can move to this square in one move.

2. Power tables. The power of the pieces to each square is represented in power format. A piece has power on a square if it is legal to move the piece to that square *if the square were occupied by an opponent's piece.* Any piece can have power on a square to which it cannot legally move—it can have power on a square occupied by another piece of the same color. The pawns have mobility to squares over which they have no power. In Figure 6.4, the White power table on square d5 would have a bishop, a knight, and a pawn since these are the three White pieces that could capture a Black piece on that square.

3. Safety tables. Each square is filled with the value of the maximum piece that would be safe on that square. Figure 6.5 presents the safety table for the position depicted in Figure 6.4. The calculation of the safety of a particular square for a White piece is based upon a combination rule for corresponding squares of the White and Black power tables. For example, in Figure 6.4, White has the power of a pawn, a knight, and a bishop on square d5; Black has the power of a knight on d5. This square

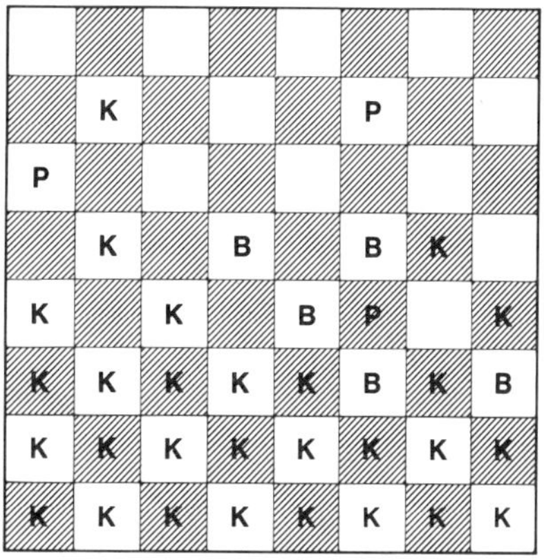

Figure 6.5 White safety table for position in Figure 6.4. The letters refer to the white piece of greatest value that would be safe on a square. (P = pawn, B = bishop, and K = King)

on the White safety table would be safe for a knight; this square on the Black safety table would not be safe for any piece. The initial calculation is based upon the examination of each square independently of all other squares. A recalculation of the safety of a square is necessary if some of the pieces with power on the square are pinned or overworked. (See the discussion of the position in Figure 6.6.)

4. Discovery block table. Identification of the piece that serves as a block for discovery power. For this table, and the remaining three tables, some definitions would be useful. A piece is considered to have *indirect* power on a square if it has direct power on the square after any single piece is removed from the board. If the piece removed is of the same color as the piece with power, then the indirect power is called *discovery* power. If the piece removed is of the opponent's color, then the indirect power is called *pin* power. In both cases the removed piece is called a *block*, and the additional squares on which the pieces have power after the blocks are removed are called targets. In Figure 6.4 seven of White's pieces serve as blocks for discovery power. For example, the queen is a block since both rooks have additional direct power if the queen is removed.

5. Discovery target table. The additional squares on which the pieces have power after the discovery blocks are removed (in power format). For example, if the pawn block at d3 were removed, White would have the power of a bishop on e2 and f1, and the power of a queen on d4, d5, and d6.

6. Pin block table. Identification of the piece that serves as a block for pin power. In the position shown in Figure 6.4, White has pinned only one piece (the pawn at f7), and Black has pinned only one piece (the knight at f3). The White and Black pin block tables would each have only a single entry to identify these pieces.

7. Pin target table. The additional squares on which the pieces have power after the pin blocks are removed (in power format). In the position shown in Figure 6.4, White has additional power of a bishop on g8 when the block is removed, and Black has additional power of a bishop on e2 and d1 when the block is removed. These squares are identified in the White and Black pin target tables.

In addition to the tables which are calculated in all positions, there are many tables that are calculated only in selected positions. Two such tables are described now; others are described in the middlegame and endgame examples.

1. Mobility from the squares. The mobility of the pieces from each square is represented in value format. This is particularly useful in securing development, restricting mobility of opponent's pieces, and dealing with potentially trapped pieces.

2. Vulnerability. For any particular square the minimum potential attacker of that square can be represented in identification format. For example, if White plans to castle kingside the vulnerability of the square to which the king will be moved (g1) is a matter of some importance. It

146

is especially critical if the opponent has a piece that can reach one of these squares in one move (check the Black mobility table), and if White has no defenders on the square (check White power table). Of course, this is a very superficial treatment of king safety, but a more thorough analysis can be conducted by consideration of more data of the sort found in the board representations.

Our program also maintains three short lists for each side as follows:

1. Mobility. Each legal move is represented by the origin and destination squares of the move.
2. Power. Each item in the power list is composed of the square from which the power originates and the destination square of the power.
3. Indirect power. Each item is composed of the square of the piece that is blocked, and the square of the block, and the square on which there would be additional power if the block were removed. This list includes both discovery power (when the blocking piece is the same color as the blocked piece) and pin power (when the blocking piece is the opposite color from the blocked piece).

There is also a list of moves, in the same format as the mobility list, to preserve a record of the game.

The center control plan that was used consisted of the following 10 considerations:

1. Material. This has value of the material consequence of the move.
2. Pawn trades. This has the value of 1 if a White pawn captures something and 0 otherwise.
3. King safety. The minimum number of White moves necessary for the king to castle.
4. Indirect safety. This has the value of 0 if the piece that White moves can be made *en prise* by a single Black move, and 1 otherwise.
5. Development. The number of pieces off the first rank.
6. Tempo gain. This has the value of 1 if a Black piece is *en prise*, and 0 otherwise.
7. Mobility. The number of legal moves by the White pieces.
8. Center power. The sum of the power of the White pieces in a rectangle near the center (files c–f and ranks 4–7).
9. Discovery avoidance. This has the value of 1 if Black has discovery target power on a square occupied by a White piece and 0 otherwise.
10. Pin avoidance. This has the value of 1 if Black has pin target power on a square occupied by a White piece, and 0 otherwise.

In the position shown in Figure 6.4 there are 36 legal moves to consider. The first move that is tried (Bb5) is initially assumed to be best, and it is evaluated according to each of the subroutines. The result of each test is a numerical value (possibly only pass–fail).

At the present time we are using the values 10, 35, 35, 50, 99, and

300 for the pawn, knight, bishop, rook, queen, and king, respectively. To find whether or not a piece is *en prise*, we use matrix subtraction (A − B = C). Table A is the White safety table in value format, and Table B is the position table in value format. In other words, the value of the piece on each square is subtracted from the maximum-valued piece of the computer that is safe on the square. If the computer now has a piece on a square on which it is not safe, Table C has a negative entry. (Forks and other double attacks are shown by multiple negative entries.) The sum of the largest negative entry (i.e., the most-valuable piece that is *en prise*) and the value of any captured piece is the material consequence of the move. The accuracy of the result, of course, depends upon the tactical completeness of the calculation of the safety table. After Bb5 all entries in the White safety table (Figure 6.5) are greater or equal to the corresponding entries in the position table (Figure 6.4), and no piece has been captured. Therefore, the material consequences of this move are null.

The first proposed move (Bb5) does not involve a capture by a White pawn, so it is given a value of 0 on the second priority. It does not involve castling, so it is given a value of 0 on the third priority. The move is indirectly unsafe since a single Black move (a6) can put the bishop *en prise*. The calculation is done without actually generating each of the person's replies to the proposed move. Instead it is performed by the following combination of tables:

1. For each square find the possible attackers on the square to which the bishop proposes to move. For example, a pawn on a6 would be such an attacker.
2. For each square find the pieces the person can move to the square. This has already been calculated as Black's mobility table and it shows, for instance, that a pawn can be moved to a6.
3. From (1) and (2) above a conditional copying routine records on each square the minimum actual attacker of the square to which the bishop proposes to move. In this case, the pawn on a6 is an actual attacker.
4. Find the maximum-valued piece of the person that is safe on each square (assuming a piece with mobility to the square has moved to the square). In this example, a Black bishop would be safe on a6. Record the actual attackers which are safe. The pawn on a6 is recorded.
5. Record each piece that is less valuable than the computer's piece. The pawn on a6 is recorded.

The result is that the move is given a value of 0 on the fourth priority of indirect safety.

The first candidate move (Bb5) does not remove any additional pieces from the back rank so the fifth priority (development) is recorded as four pieces off the back rank. The move does not put a Black piece *en prise* so the value of the sixth priority, tempo, is 0. This determination is made by the same matrix subtraction approach used for material assessment of the first priority.

The number of legal moves by White after the first proposed move (Bb5) is determined by a count of the number of bits set in the White mobility table. This number, 33, three fewer than in the base position, is the value on the seventh priority of mobility. After the first proposed move (Bb5) the knights have power on four center squares and the bishop has power on two (c6 and d7). In the base position the bishop had power on three center squares (d5, e6, and f7).

The first proposed move does not change Black's indirect power on White's pieces, so the move scores 0 on the final two priorities, avoidance of discoveries and pins. Although this first move is tentatively considered best, it does not improve the base position according to any of the 10 conditions.

The next move (Ba6) is evaluated on the first priority, material. Since the square a6 is safe only for a pawn (Figure 6.5) and is now occupied by a bishop, the bishop would be *en prise*. Since no piece was captured, the second candidate move is worse than the first in terms of material consequences. When a new candidate move is worse at any priority than the move currently considered best, it is rejected. No evaluations are made at lower priorities. When a new candidate move is better at any priority it is considered the best move so far, and it is evaluated at all lower priorities. When a new candidate move is equal to the best at any priority, it remains a candidate and it is evaluated at the next priority. Thus, if two moves are equal in all respects, the first one is chosen.

In the position in Figure 6.4 the move that is finally evaluated as best is Qd2. We can readily see that there are no better moves based on the first five priorities. It does not lose material, and no move gains material. It does not involve a pawn trade or castling, but no other move does either. It is indirectly safe, i.e., Black cannot safely attack the queen in one move [(9) . . . Ne4 is rejected since e4 is not safe for a black knight]. The move Qd2 does develop a piece, and only three other moves do so (Qe2, Rf2, and Kf2). (The unnatural nature of Kf2 as a developing move has led us to refine our definition of development.) None of these four alternative moves gains a tempo, but the two queen moves (Qd2 and Qe2) gain more mobility than the alternatives. The basis for the choice of Qd2 over Qe2 is that the former breaks the pin, i.e., Black's bishop no longer has remote power on White's queen.

Goals of the middlegame

At the present time the selection of middlegame goals is limited to the following:

1. Kingside attack with pieces
2. Kingside attack with pawns and pieces
3. Queenside attack with pieces
4. Queenside attack with pawns and pieces
5. Target. A concentration of forces on a weak point

The position in Figure 6.6 can be used to illustrate the selection of a move in a middlegame position. We will assume that a static analysis of the position has led to the goal of increasing power on the queenside (defined as the 16 squares in the upper lefthand side of the board), and that the plan simply consists of three subroutines: material, tempo, and queenside power. This is not a particularly good plan, and it is not one our program typically uses, but it does exemplify several themes we have been describing, and it is easier to deal with than one which contains many more subroutines.

Each of the 42 legal moves are tried and evaluated with respect to the priorities of the queenside attack plan. In the example, only 10 moves survive the first-priority consideration, material. There are six moves of the attacked piece (Ra5, Rb5, Rg5, Rc4, Rc2, and Rcc1) and four moves which defend the attacked piece (Qc4, Qb5, Qe3, and Rdc1).

The move Rd5 is not included among the safe moves since the pawn at e4 is pinned. The target (the Q at e2) is found not to be safe if the pawn block at e4 is removed. Since the target does not have a tempo-gaining move, the power of the pawn at e4 is removed from squares d5 and f5, and the safety of these squares is recalculated. In this case, the square d5 is found to be unsafe for any piece, so the move Rd5 leaves a piece *en prise*.

The move Nb3 is not included in the list of safe moves because the White queen would then become overworked. The program identifies those squares that need all of their defenders (c5, e4, and d1). It finds that two of these squares share a single defender (e4 and d1), and that there is no communication between these two squares for such a defender, i.e., the queen cannot capture a piece on e4 after capturing a piece on d1, or vice versa. Therefore, the move Nb3 leaves a pawn *en prise*.

Olafsson

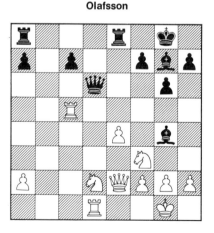

Figure 6.6   Tal vs. Olafsson.

Tal

18 ... Qd6

The next priority, tempo, has already been described in the center-control plan. It has the value of 1 if a Black piece is *en prise* and 0 otherwise. From the ten possible moves, only three survive this test: Rg5, Qc4, and Rdc1. Both Qc4 and Rdc1 gain tempo by adding not direct power but discovery power on the Black pawn on c7. The move Rg5 is unnatural, and it exemplifies the need to refine the concept of tempo. The easiest way for us to identify errors in our logic or weak definitions of terms is to play games with the program and recognize its unnatural moves. In this case, it might be desirable to add additional tests such as, (1) after the forced reply, is the resulting position preferable to the position before the tempo-gaining move, and (2) does the opponent have a tempo-gaining move upon the piece just moved?

The final priority of this plan is queenside power. If this does not uniquely define a move, the first best move will be chosen. The amount of queenside power is defined as the sum of power over the 16 squares in the upper left-hand side of the board. The power on a square is inversely related to the material value of the pieces that could capture an enemy piece occupying the square. Since a pawn can chase away a queen, a pawn is considered far more powerful (although, obviously, far less valuable) than a queen. In this case, after Rdc1, the additional power of a rook on three of the queenside squares (c5, c6, and c7) is greater than the additional power of the queen on the four squares (c5, c6, c7, and d5) after Qc4. This definition of queenside power uniquely narrows the list of possible moves to Rdc1. As it happened, Tal played this move and lost. According to the annotator, Larsen, this was an error. Nevertheless, if computer programs can make the type of errors that Grandmasters make, this is clearly a remarkable improvement.

Goals of the endgame

At the present time the program recognizes only three basic goals in the endgame, and it uses only a few rudimentary plans to accomplish these goals. The goals are:

1. Basic mate, e.g., rook and king vs. king
2. Pawn promotion
3. Target

To make the discussion more concrete, we will use the position in Figure 6.7 to describe the approach to selecting a move in an endgame.

Suppose a person is shown the position in Figure 6.7 for the first time and asked to select the best move for White. How would the person deal with a position of this sort? His major problem is to decide upon a goal and a plan to accomplish this goal. The decision must be based on a thorough static description of the position. Normally, during the course of a game, a player builds up a large amount of information regarding the current position. When a new move is made, most of this information

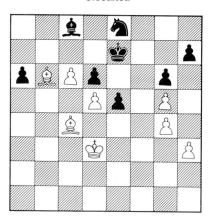

Ciocaltea

Hort
43 ... Ne8

Figure 6.7 Hort vs. Ciocaltea.

still remains relevant, but some information must be updated. Primarily to simplify the coding, we have recalculated the static description of the position rather than updating it. The updating approach is psychologically more realistic, and it is faster, but the two approaches will lead to the same move decision.

The purpose of the description of the position is to obtain some qualitative understanding of the position on which to base a goal selection. It is not enough to know that White stands better. The basis for an advantage must be known in order to know how to proceed. The following type of description would be satisfactory for rapid chess:

An examination of the position table leads us to classify the position as an endgame, so one of the endgame goals will be used. A static analysis of the pawn structure is applied to a copy of the position table which excludes all pieces. Because of the large number of pawns, the goal of a basic mate is not used. The two possible remaining goals are to promote a pawn or attack a pawn target.

The position of the pawns is evaluated with respect to such features as whether or not they are doubled, isolated, protected, or backward, and the number of squares behind the pawns. For example, Black's pawns at a6 and e5 and White's pawn at c6 are passed. The next step is to select a specific goal. The existence of a passed pawn leads to the tentative selection of the pawn promotion goal.

Another table is calculated which defines the remote power of the pawns. This consists of a board representation filled with values representing the number of moves required by a pawn to have direct power on each square. The calculation is terminated when the pawn reaches a square which is occupied or which is not safe for a pawn. Black's remote-pawn power table contains no entries that indicate that Black's pawns have no mobility to safe squares. White's pawns have some mobility to safe squares.

(The table would have a 1 on square c7 and h4, a 2 on square h5, and a 3 on square h6.)

A plan to implement the pawn promotion goal is used only if the opponent does not have control of the square in front of the passed pawn. The square c7 is currently safe for a pawn (as seen in the White safety table). However, an analysis including the remote power of the pieces gives a different conclusion.

A board can be filled with values representing the minimum number of moves on an otherwise unoccupied board required by a king (or knight) beginning on a given origin square to reach any destination square. For example, after White has moved c7, the remote-king table from the origin square of c7 would have a 1 on d7 and a 2 on e7; the remote-knight table would have a 1 on e8 and a 2 on f6.

A somewhat slower but more general routine, fills a board with values representing the minimum number of moves on an occupied board required by a piece (excluding pawns) to move from a given origin square to any destination square. This calculation is not continued in a given direction when the piece reaches an occupied square or one on which it would be *en prise*. The distance between the origin and the destination (goal) square is the number in the destination square. This table is always examined with backward analysis. To find a path between the origin and the goal square, forward analysis would begin at the origin and generate (by moving to square containing a number one greater than the number of the current square) many paths in various directions. Backward analysis begins at the goal square and generates (by moving to squares containing a number one less than the number of the current square) all paths from the goal to the origin without starting down any blind alleys.

Since the square c7 is remotely unsafe for a pawn, the goal of pawn promotion is discarded, and the final goal of attacking a pawn target is selected. Examination of the Black remote-pawn power table shows Black has three pawns that cannot be protected by other pawns (the pawns on h7, d6, and a6). The squares h7 and d6 are currently protected by as much as White could ever attack them with. The square a6, on the other hand, is only defended by one bishop. White could eventually attack it with a bishop and king. The remote power of the king table from a6 is shown in Figure 6.8. Since Black cannot defend with anything else, White can eventually win control of a6 and capture this pawn. The route from the current location of the king (d3) to the location of the target pawn (a6) is found to be c3–b4–a5. In the actual game, Black resigned after White played Kc3 because the logic is so simple. However, the solution by forward search is at the nontrivial depth of 9 ply before a material advantage is realized.

Before the program will play many endgames in a reasonable manner it will be necessary to improve the basis for the selection of a goal, to improve the manner of implementation of the goals, and (particularly) to increase the number of different goals. For example, it is critical to decide

Figure 6.8 Table of remote power of king from square a6 for position in Figure 6.7.

whether the play is for a win or a draw, and plans aimed at achieving a draw must be added. No defensive goals have been implemented at any stage of the game. They can be added more easily after a large number of aggressive plans are available since a successful defense usually requires an accurate assessment of the nature of the opponent's threats. The major purpose of this section was to show how a goal oriented approach can be used to select a specific move in an endgame. For a program to use problem-reduction methods successfully, it is necessary for it to have easy access to information of the sort described in this section.

Evaluation

At the present time our program is incomplete. It often chooses an inappropriate goal, it runs out of plans, and it makes several characteristic blunders. These deficiencies are in the process of being corrected, and improvements are relatively easy to make for several reasons:

The approach is simple enough that we can nearly always correctly anticipate the move that will be chosen by the program. When an unexpected (usually weak) move is chosen, it is easy to understand the exact nature of the problem by one of the following debugging aids:

1. Full information regarding the static analysis is immediately available on the oscilloscope, or it can be printed on the teletype. That is to say, the content of any table can be made available in a readable format.
2. The computer's move can be taken back (type *R*, for restore) and the operator can examine the dynamic basis for the choice of a move from the console by stepping through a particular subroutine or stopping at selected parts of the program.

Since the computer's selection of a move takes only 4 or 5 seconds, many different positions can be examined in a short session. In addition, the operator can create and modify positions from the teletype in various ways:

1. Move a piece from one square to another
2. Remove a piece from a square
3. Create a piece on a square
4. Clear the board
5. Initialize the position

This means that a programmer can quickly and easily obtain a thorough understanding of the nature of play of the program in various types of situations.

Plans are easily added or modified by individuals unfamiliar with computer programming or the details of our program. Most of the plans are built from standard components, e.g., material, mobility, pawn structure, tempo, king safety. The modification of a plan proceeds as follows:

The TRY routine is a master rountine which makes it possible to try each of the legal moves, and to test each of them according to several subroutines. The form of the call is:

$$\text{TRY}; k; S_1; \cdot S_2; \ldots; S_n; \ldots S_k$$

where k is the number of subroutines and S_n is the nth subroutine. In the case of the center-control plan (described earlier), the call is:

TRY; 10; MAT; PTRADE; KSAF; ISAFE; DEV; TEMPO; MOB; CENPOW; DAV; PAV

where each of the arguments refer to the name of some subroutine. For example, MAT refers to the material value of the move. This can be considered to be an evaluation function (a vector quantity rather than a single value) applied at ply 1. Of course, this particular evaluation function is used only if a description of the position leads to the decision that control of the center is the essential goal in the situation. Redefinitions of the concepts (e.g., TEMPO) and addition of new concepts requires some experience with assembly language programming and some knowledge of the structure of our program, but anyone can easily implement alternative plans by reordering the components, or by adding or deleting components.

If the primary interest of a person were to write a program to win games in competition with people and other programs, should the program seek to simulate the thought processes of strong chessplayers? By the objective criterion of consistent performance in ACM tournaments, the Northwestern program is probably the strongest one currently available. That its performance was demonstrably improved after the elimination of the "plausible-move analyzer" supports the notion that existing chess programs can be improved by reducing their similarity to the decision methods of human chessplayers. No psychologically meaningful program has the playing strength approximating the Northwestern program. Our program certainly does not at the present time, and Berliner's tactics analyzing program which selectively deals with plausible lines of analysis in much the same way that a master analyzes a situation does not play at the level of programs entered in the ACM tournaments [10]. Nonetheless, there is considerable room for improvement in the quality of play by computer programs. This gives some credibility to our final paragraph which is a statement of faith that programs which simulate the thought processes of chessplayers will eventually play stronger chess than the current generation of full-width tree-searching programs.

It is our belief that the speed and quality of decisions by people and computer programs are improved when goal-oriented rather than trial-and-error procedures are used. Our expectation is that the program we are developing will follow the methods used by Class A players when they are playing rapidly, and that it should reach their level of play under those conditions. We are convinced that if one wants to design a computer program to play chess successfully, one must simulate the thought processes of strong players. Strong chessplayers cannot learn to make better decisions by examining existing programs that play chess; but better programs to play chess can be written if they are based on human thought processes.

The heuristic search: An alternative to the alpha–beta minimax procedure

Larry R. Harris
Dartmouth College

7

Many current computer chess programs use a full-width tree search (e.g., CHESS 4.5 from Northwestern (see Chapter 4), KAISSA from the Institute of Control Science, Moscow [2], and TECH II from MIT). Other programs, such as Berliner's [12], attempt to perform a highly selective search using extremely sophisticated heuristics. Recent improvements in chess play have come primarily from the programs using the "brute force" procedure. In particular the Northwestern program improved markedly when its plausible move selector was replaced by a full-width search. The development of specialized computer hardware, such as the chess-specific central processor which is being developed at MIT, will further benefit this "brute-strength" approach.

Let us assume for the moment that full-width searching could achieve master level play in the midgame, a rather generous assumption given the role of quiescence in tactical play. This will allow us to focus our attention on the impact of using this technique during other stages of the game. In the endgame the ability to search 12-ply ahead, the anticipated capability of the chess-specific hardware, will have little impact on searching lines that require 30 to 40 ply to develop. It seems clear that at least for the endgame, a more sophisticated board evaluator is needed. Thus, despite the recent gains made with the full-width search technique, it is inevitable that chess programmers must eventually provide a means for representing and using chess knowledge.

This chapter addresses the problem of selecting a search mechanism that can more effectively use sophisticated chess heuristics. There is a better searching algorithm for using sophisticated heuristics than the α–β minimax full-width search. This is obvious since human masters do not use the α–β procedure and they clearly play better chess. An alternative search philosophy for machine play might be modeled more closely on the way the chess masters search. The notion of information-gain per evaluation will be our yardstick for comparing our new technique to the α–β procedure.

Consider a search philosophy that constantly orders the potential lines of play on the basis of their interest or merit. The interesting lines would be investigated first and the information gained would be used to update our notion of what should be evaluated next. In this way our evaluation time would be invested more heavily on the playable or interesting lines rather than the absurd ones. Furthermore there would be no maximum ply limitation. If an interesting line required an analysis of 10 or 15 ply, this would be done as a natural consequence of our strategy. We would terminate the process only when our evaluation of all the lines indicated that an accurate assessment was possible.

How would such an algorithm compare to the way in which humans search the move tree? What we have described is very much akin to what de Groot [31] called "progressive deepening" when describing the analysis of a chess board by Grandmasters. The analysis proceeds only on the interesting lines, which are evaluated repetitively, each time probing more deeply than the previous analysis. The finer points of implementation, however, are different. It is certain that Grandmasters do not maintain an ordering of *all* lines of play as we have suggested. Furthermore when the analysis switches from one line of play to another, this jump is usually quite small for humans, i.e., the two lines are usually relatively close in some analytical sense. This may not be the case for the computer algorithm, since the definition of the most interesting line of play may change quite drastically as the search proceeds. This algorithm is an example of the formal heuristic search strategy of Hart *et al.* [53] and described more fully in Nilsson [77].

The heuristic-search algorithm provides important theoretical properties called admissibility and optimality, meaning that under certain conditions the move found by the search is the best possible in some sense and that the algorithm found it expending only the minimum effort possible. Such properties, which depend on the accuracy of the evaluation function, are very desirable. For this reason it is preferable to apply the algorithm directly, rather than altering it to more closely approximate human play.

The extension of the standard heuristic search to the game of chess is discussed in detail in Harris [51, 52]. Basically the algorithm is as follows.

1. Initialize the search tree to the current board
2. Select a line of play for expansion by moving down the tree, choosing the most "interesting" move at each level
3. Expand this line of play, extending the tree 1 level
4. Calculate the "interest" of each of the moves just generated

5. Back up (in a minimax fashion) the "interest" values for each move along the chosen line of play
6. go to (2)

The search "interest" of a move is computed by combining the results of the static board evaluator, the quiescence measure, and the depth of the move in the search tree. The algorithm terminates when the overall quiescence of the search tree becomes sufficiently small. Put another way, the search stops when it appears that the backed up static board evaluations are sufficiently accurate that no further search is necessary.

The method by which this "interest" is defined and how it orders the search process is what gives the heuristic search the necessary flexibility to cope with the very intricate environment of the game of chess. We will discuss in detail how this flexibility can be used to deal with the problems of tactics and quiescence in a natural way. The basic differences between heuristic search and the α–β minimax procedure relate to the naturalness or elegance of a solution within the heuristic search environment. The ability to search to arbitrary depth, the ability to return to a given line of play and investigate it more deeply, and the notion of overall tree quiescence and the relative quiescence of different lines of play are all elementary elements of the heuristic search paradigm. All are extremely difficult to attain using the α–β minimax procedure. Another point is that the heuristic search makes much better use of the chess program's most expensive commodity—the static evaluation function. The implication being that efficient use of the evaluation function will become more critical as more knowledgeable, and thus more expensive, chess heuristics are put into chess programs. It is to be hoped that a discussion of these points and examples of how the heuristic search deals with these problems will make clear the distinction between these two algorithms and indicate the future prospects of each.

The evaluation function is used more heavily by the heuristic search procedure because it directs the search in addition to defining the end values. Its role in directing the search will be our present focus. In searching the tree selectively, we must be careful to search all important continuations. The search must be broad enough to encompass the best move yet selective enough to avoid wasting time on the absurd lines of play. That this can be done is evidenced by human play in which an incredibly small proportion of the full move tree is searched.

We wish to view sections of the move tree as imparting information relevant to choosing the best move. The cost for this information is the time required to invoke the evaluation function. Also, from our analysis of human play we are willing to assume that adequate information about choosing the best move is contained in a *very small portion* of the move tree! Thus if we could find and evaluate just this portion of the move tree we could attain optimal play with minimal drain on our resources, and thereby receive maximal information-gain per evaluation. Two points need to be developed. First, that areas of the move tree differ in the amount of information pertinent to finding the best move. Second, that the heuristic search can in fact be directed towards investigating only these areas of the tree.

That certain areas of the move tree contain more information pertinent to best move determination than other areas of the tree should be obvious. On a simplistic level, the absurd lines of play that appear in the move tree contain almost no information relevant to finding the best move. Evaluation of these areas of the tree is wasted effort. This point seems hardly debatable. It is less obvious that the branch of the tree that actually contains the best move may also convey low information! This is really just a manifestation of quiescence. That is to say, positions that are quiet can be accurately rated whether they are good or bad. Active positions, on the other hand, cannot be accurately rated by any static evaluation function. Therefore expansion of quiet positions, and the subsequent evaluation of their successors, will impart little additional information since the original ratings are accurate. More information is gained by expanding active positions because their static evaluations are highly inaccurate. Berliner [12], in his discussion of the horizon effect, gives several examples of the serious errors that result from trying to make a static evaluation of an active position.

The information gained during the expansion of a node depends *on how active or quiet the position is* rather than on how good or bad the actual position is. For this reason the best line of play to search is not necessarily the one which is best to make across the board. This is a very important distinction to make. In recognizing this distinction between good moves to search and good moves to make, we make a significant departure from the α–β paradigm and from the standard heuristic search in which move ordering is determined essentially by the evaluation function itself.

To implement this strategy it is necessary to place emphasis on searching the active areas of the tree. To this end a second evaluation function is developed which is responsible for the measurement of quiescence. By this we mean a thorough analysis of quiescence, not the typical definition of only checks and overt captures used in many chess programs. Our strategy is to *not even attempt* to statically assess the final impact of an active feature such as a check, since this is no doubt impossible. Rather our approach is simply to detect the presence of active features, telling the search that it must continue investigating the active section of the tree in order to receive an accurate rating. The search is ordered primarily on the basis of the quiescence measure and secondarily on the basis of the static board evaluation. Thus we will be evaluating the most active positions first, thereby gaining maximal information for each evaluation. When the activity of positions is no longer a distinguishing factor we will be biasing the search towards the moves we are most likely to play. Note that positions that are rated as highly active need not be statically evaluated at all, since any such evaluation would be inaccurate anyway. Thus the search postpones the application of the static evaluator until the active lines become quiet.

Actual move selection is based solely on the static evaluation function. The quiescence measure is used only in deciding where to search, and when to stop searching. A typical search scenario might be as follows. The current board position would be expanded until the relatively active areas of the tree become discernable. At this point these active lines would be expanded since the search order is based primarily on the activity of the position. The active lines are expanded until they become quiet, at which point the static evaluator is applied and the line is no longer searched. In this way, the overall activity of the search tree is monotonically reduced until all ratings are accurate. At this point the best move is chosen solely on the basis of the static evaluations.

Since the search process depends so heavily on this quiescence measure let us discuss it in more detail. Exactly what does this quiescence measure consist of? We must include detectors of the common tactical ploys—forks, pins, and checks, since these can lead to sudden changes in material balance. These detectors are more than binary in output; they try to assess the relative importance of each feature. For example a queen pinning a pawn to another pawn is less critical than a bishop pinning the king to the queen. Our detector should reflect this distinction. No attempt is made to assess the outcome of the pin, since this static evaluation cannot be done accurately. The relative importance of each of the tactical features is scaled so that the critical ones can be searched first.

By using individual detectors to measure these tactical features we can sum their outputs and thus arrive at an overall measure of quiescence. Experience has shown that tactical detectors by themselves can not accurately measure quiescence. The detection of pawns about to queen, levers, back rank threats and sacrifices is also necessary. Let us consider each of these in more detail.

The threat of promoting a pawn often aids attacks on other parts of the board. If the search terminates before examining the impact of the promotion threat on these other attacks, serious errors in play can result. Most chess programs bias pawn promotion by increasing the value of a passed pawn as it advances. In many situations, however, the pawn never really stands a chance to queen, but pushing it aids threats elsewhere. In these cases the pawn advance is good because of the tactical threats it may create, not because it increases the value of the pawn. To rate this move as material improvement in the static board evaluator is misleading since the pawn's likelihood of surviving may actually be reduced and if the tactics elsewhere prove unsuccessful, the move could be disastrous. What is called for is a thorough investigation of the tree below the pawn move, without any commitment to actually making the move. Treating advanced pawns as a nonquiescent situation does exactly this. The position depicted in Figure 7.1 illustrates this type of situation. The move P–K7 actually

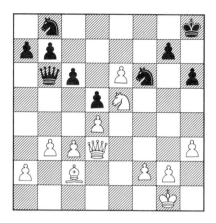

Figure 7.1 White's advanced pawn at K6 should trigger additional tree searching.

weakens the pawn since it is harder to defend as it progresses down the board. Also the chances of the pawn queening and remaining on the board are nil. Thus, rating the move P–K7 as good because it improves the value of the pawn is highly inaccurate and could lead to errors in play. The move P–K7 creates tactical threats and thus our quiescence measure should signal the search that this line of play should be more thoroughly investigated—not because it is known to be good but because it might be good. A program that would make a commitment to this move due to a static evaluation may have trouble carrying out the win. The correct, but not obvious, sequence is: (1) P–K7, K–N1 (only choice); (2) Q–R7!!ch, N*Q; (3) P–K8(Q)ch, N–B1; (4) N–N6, leading to mate.

A lever, the act of a weak pawn attacking a strong pawn formation in the hope of dissipating it, is another example of a board feature that must be detected in order to assess quiescence. In a sense a lever is a low-level exchange, pawns being traded instead of pieces. But since a lever always alters the pawn structure of both players it can seriously effect the static board evaluator. For this reason potential levers must be given high search interest to find the resulting pawn formations after the exchanges. Pawn structure changes slowly in chess, so it is worthwhile to investigate areas of the tree in which the pawn structure is likely to change radically. Fortunately these pawn structure changes are often forecasted by levers. Thus the lever detector is an important part of an overall quiescence measure.

Figure 7.2 shows a typical position in which a lever is required. White has a strong central pawn formation that Black should attack. The required move, P–QN4, is one that many computer programs would not find. In this case the long-term effects of this move on the pawn formation are quite significant. Thus, the move deserves far more "search interest" than other pawn moves. The quiescence measure is responsible for seeing that such lines are searched until they stabilize and the resulting formations are accurately rated.

Another sign of turbulence in a chess position is the back-rank threat.

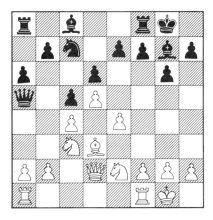

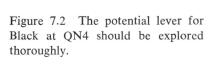

Figure 7.2 The potential lever for Black at QN4 should be explored thoroughly.

Like pawn promotion, the back-rank threat may aid tactical threats on other parts of the board. For this reason, positions with existing back-rank threats are extremely unstable and the search should not terminate at positions where the threatening player is about to move.

An example of this in computer chess play occurred in the fourth ACM computer chess tournament in a game between CHESS 4.0 and the Dartmouth program. Figure 7.3 shows the position just after Black (CHESS 4.0) played Q–R5. Black's attack, . . . Q–K8+, is futile since White can respond with K–N1 and prevent any further mobilization of Black's forces because of White's back-rank mate threat, Q–Q8+. In the present example, a 9-ply search is required to determine that Black's attack is harmless and therefore White can safely proceed with RxP.

Another element of the quiescence measure we will discuss is the sacrifice. Undoubtedly this is the most difficult detector to describe and implement, but conceptually the solution within the heuristic search paradigm is extremely elegant. Sacrifices, like other nonquiescent aspects of chess are impossible to assess statically. We must find some way to

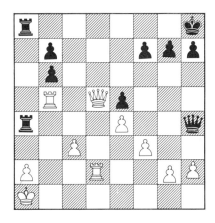

Figure 7.3 White's back-rank mate threat indicates a turbulent position.

insure that the search thoroughly investigates these areas of the tree. We do this of course, by defining all boards with "sacrifice potential" as being nonquiescent. "Sacrifice potential," however, is not easily defined. Chessmasters have a hard time expressing exactly why they consider throwing a piece away in some positions and not in others. Ideas such as king safety, mobilization of supporting pieces, and the probable outcome without trying a sacrifice often contribute to the notion of "sacrifice potential."

It is impossible to statically evaluate the impact of a sacrifice. We would like, however, to be able to trigger the idea that a sacrifice is currently worth considering. Once we have made this determination on the basis of good "sacrifice potential," the line of play would be expanded until the final outcome could be accurately assessed. When the line finally becomes quiet the static board evaluator will indicate whether the sacrifice was worthwhile.

A classic example of the inability to statically evaluate sacrifices is given in Figures 7.4 and 7.5. These positions differ only in the placement of a single pawn, yet the sacrifice Q–R5+ leads to a win in Figure 7.4 but not in 7.5. The correct moves are (1) Q–R5+, NxQ; (2) PxP+, K–N3; (3) B–B2+, K–N4; (4) R–B5+, K–N3; (5) R–B6+, K–N4; (6) R–N6+, K–R5; (7) R–K4+, N–B5; (8) RxN+, K–R4; (9) P–N3, any; (10) R–R4mate. In Position 7.5, Black's KRP is at R4 instead of R3. The queen sacrifice fails with this small change because the king can eventually hide and avoid further checks. The line is: (1) QxP+, NxQ; (2) PxP+, K–N3; (3) any, K–R3, ending the checks. Since the winning sequence involved a 19-ply search, it is unlikely that a static evaluator could distinguish Position 7.4 from 7.5. Thus a thorough search of the relevant continuations is required to determine what the outcome will be for each line of play. By defining interesting sacrifices as active features, the search

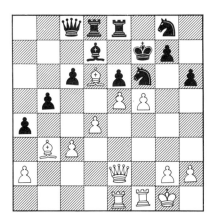

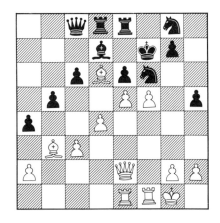

Figure 7.4 White's sacrifice, Q–R5+, leads to mate.

Figure 7.5 White's sacrifice, Q–R5+, loses.

process can investigate these lines without forcing a premature evaluation of their merit.

One hopes that these examples illustrate some of the components of a good quiescence measure. Let us now examine how it allows the heuristic search to optimize use of the static evaluator. First, it detects the areas of the tree with high search interest—namely the nonquiescent positions. Second, it directs the search towards these areas of the tree since the search is ordered primarily on the basis of the quiescence measure. Third, the heuristic search remains uncommitted in terms of making a move during the search process. It is not necessary to brand a move "good to make" just in order to search it more fully. Fourth, the application of the static evaluator is reserved for quiet positions which can be accurately rated.

With a full-width search strategy, each of these problems can be handled individually but dealing with all of them at once would be difficult. This is true because the basic premise of the α–β algorithm is that it can cut off the unrealistic lines of play without evaluating all of them at full depth. The cutoffs required are quite extensive, about 99.9 percent of the lines in a 5-ply tree will contain at least one very poor move, generously assuming that 25 percent of the roughly 30 legal moves from each position are good. The α–β procedure is remarkably effective at achieving these cutoffs *if the move ordering is correct*. Thus, before we even begin to discuss the role of a quiescence measure within the α–β paradigm we see that the ordering of moves is already tightly constrained to achieve the critical cutoffs.

If we superimpose upon this the need to search active areas of the tree until they are quiescent, we must choose between either altering the move ordering to expand the active lines first or simply dealing with the active lines in the order in which they are presented to the search. The first choice is clearly counterproductive in terms of α–β cutoffs. The second choice means that the algorithm must face many highly active nodes at the end positions without having the time to search until quiescence. The consequences of such a situation have been aptly demonstrated by Berliner [12]. Most chess programmers react to this by restricting their quiescence measure to checks and overt-captures so that the quiescence search can be made very quickly. However, we have seen examples in which far more sophisticated quiescence measures are required. Integrating a sufficiently general quiescence measure into the α–β algorithm while still maintaining the needed overall efficiency has been a major stumbling block to progress. Contrast this to the ordered search we have suggested that is designed to deal with quiescence from the very outset, using as general a quiescence measure as possible.

In conclusion, we have argued that the heuristic search formalism can make more efficient use of the evaluation function than the α–β minimax paradigm. The basis of the argument was that the heuristic search could apply the heuristic to areas of the move tree that would impart the most information-gain per evaluation. Therefore the heuristic search approach allows the program to become adequately informed about the move tree in less time than other search techniques. This reserves as much time as possible to be devoted to the execution of a very sophisticated evaluation function.

Man and machine: Chess achievements and chess thinking

8

Eliot Hearst

Indiana University

"Within 10 years a digital computer will be the world's chess champion, unless the rules bar it from competition."

Herbert Simon, 1957

"Today's chess programs are trivial opponents for master players"

Earl Hunt, 1975

Introduction

A skillful human chessplayer usually achieves the title of chessmaster by the time he is 20 years old, after five or six years of relatively serious devotion to the game. Chronologically at least, computer chess is about as old as the typical new chessmaster; computers first played complete games in 1957 and they have been participants in tournaments with human beings and fellow computers since 1966. Despite much discussion, research, revision, and competition in subsequent years—and despite contrary claims by some computer scientists—the chess programs of 1976 are not much stronger than those of 1966. A human chess enthusiast would have long since abandoned his quest for a master's or expert's rating if he had progressed at the snail's pace displayed by his computer counterparts. Rather than being "barred from competition" in serious tourneys, today's computer chessplayer would be welcomed as "just another duffer" by most of the competitors.

Both Simon and Hunt, the writers of the passages [56, 86] quoted above, are experts in the fields of artificial intelligence and computer science rather than in the game of chess. Nevertheless, Hunt's comment is an accurate one. Why was Simon's prediction premature, to say the least? And why are other researchers and computer scientists, including some contributors to this volume, almost as optimistic about the prospects of a chessmaster computer as Simon was 20 years ago—even though today's enthusiasts would admit that the appearance of a topnotch machine player will have to be postponed for a while? In large part, this optimism seems founded on the questionable belief that *technical* deficiencies (for example, in the speed, memory size, and time availability of computers) have been

167

the main obstacles hindering the development of a machine master and that these deficiencies can be corrected in the near future.

On the contrary, I think the reasons for past disappointments lie much deeper than mere technical problems and reflect a failure to understand what high-level chess performance entails, as well as a failure to appreciate the large gaps that exist in our knowledge of how human learning, memory, and problem solving operate in general. Any promising attempt to create a computer program that plays superior chess will, in my opinion, have to be based on advice from master chessplayers and on significant advances in our understanding of relevant psychological principles and processes. Unfortunately, psychologists have reached very few definite conclusions about the nature of human thinking.

In this chapter I will try to evaluate, primarily from the point of view of a psychologist and chessmaster, the achievements of computer chess and to examine some of the reasons why technologists, experimentalists and theorists in various scientific disciplines pursue work on the topic. A principal portion of the chapter focuses on an attempt to isolate and assess systematic differences between the methods by which a computer and a human being select their moves and improve their play. In other words, do the principles that control human learning, memory, and thinking correspond to those that guide the play of a chess computer? Most of my comments on this question will necessarily be rather speculative; but perhaps the remarks will stimulate research and thinking even if they prove wrong or inaccurate. At the end of the chapter there will be a consideration of whether computer-chess projects are worthy of our time, money, attention, and general support.

Why program a computer to play chess?

There are a variety of reasons that have prompted computer scientists to develop chess programs. For some workers, the technological challenge seems to provide the main stimulus; these individuals are interested mainly in determining how strong a chessplayer they can create, without any particular regard for whether the program selects its moves in ways like those a human being would use. Northwestern's project (see Slate and Atkin's description in Chapter 4 of this volume) seems to fall into this category. The current version of their program (CHESS 4.5), which in my opinion is rivalled only by the USSR's KAISSA in general playing strength, is a result of revisions of prior programs. These changes were made on the basis of specific performance weaknesses rather than on the basis of some general theoretical or conceptual model of human thinking or problem solving. Slate and Atkin's approach is a down-to-earth one and Slate himself is an expert player. The programming challenges are fun and it is easy to understand why many programmers would welcome the opportunity to participate in a computer-chess project.

Loftier goals have been expressed by researchers whose names are most closely associated with the origin and development of the fields of artificial intelligence and computer chess. These men view work on computer chess as one aspect of a general approach aimed at understanding human thinking, concept formation, and problem solving. They propose theories and hypotheses about how human beings produce satisfactory but not perfect solutions to complex, inexact problems such as many arising in master chess; and, by simultaneously performing experiments with human subjects and attempting to program computers to solve problems in ways that seem analogous to the methods a human employs, they try to assess and revise their theories. For example, Newell, Shaw, and Simon [74] stated that "we wish not only to have the program make good moves, but to do so for the right reasons" and that their work represents a "deliberate attempt to simulate human thought processes." Why do they consider chess an appropriate task for these purposes? Because "if one could devise a successful chess machine, one would seem to have penetrated to the core of human intellectual endeavor." Good chessplayers sign appreciatively when they come across this quotation! The "theoretical" approach of Simon and Newell involves the belief that lessons learned from attempts to program chess will inevitably contribute to such fields as psychology, mathematics, and economics—and, for that matter, to any aspect of life in which humans must make complex decisions and solve problems. Operation of the brain and nervous system are viewed as machine-like in nature, and therefore human thinking eventually ought to be imitated by computer analogs.

Both of these general approaches to computer chess, technological-empirical and theoretical, can be further justified by their potential *practical* applications. Computers have replaced human beings in many situations that require fairly complex "decisions," for example, landing an airplane successfully, assigning work schedules to employees, or organizing the layout and printing of textbooks. Work on computer chess could conceivably result in the development of new techniques to handle even more complex problems, for which no perfect solution usually exists (controlling inflation, diagnosing certain kinds of illness). These devices would not necessarily have to work "for the right reason" (just as an artificial hand is not controlled in the same way as a real one); their overriding criterion of success would lie in the benefits to society.

Another practical outcome of work on computer chess involves its potential contributions to education. If one could design a reasonably powerful chess program that relied on knowledge about how humans actually solve problems, its structure might prove applicable in a variety of areas besides chess. Conceivably, the computer could break down a problem into significant subgoals and steps, and expose human students successively to these intermediate problems as they progress toward a final solution by mastering previous steps. Such contributions to education might prove an important spinoff from work on computerized chess—an outcome that might allow human teachers to spend extra time advising students on how to attack even more abstract problems in their particular area of interest.

There is one feature of computer chess that is less often explicitly mentioned as a goal or motivation for those working in the field—perhaps because it seems less defensible or noble than the other goals, at least to programmers working in an academic setting. This aspect concerns the aura of competition that pervades the field. Competition among the designers of different chess programs is keen, perhaps as keen as among human beings competing in serious tourneys, and this factor may in some cases account for why technological refinements, discoveries, and gimmicks are often not well publicized by their originators. Admittedly, competition is not absent from the motivation of researchers in any field of science; but failure to disseminate specific new ideas and findings, once their merit has been established, is relatively rare in scientific work (a scientist's reputation is primarily based on public communications about his new findings and ideas.) Why should one worker in computer chess have to spend months or years rediscovering what another group had implemented some time ago? The lines of communication are not wide open among computer-chess programmers, and this has probably hampered general progress on the topic. The publication of a book like the present volume, composed of contributions from several different groups of workers, may reflect a growing awareness that more cooperation, rather than more competition, will benefit everyone concerned.

Past achievements of computer-chess programs

Most outsiders, and a surprising number of workers within the field of computer science, hold unrealistic beliefs concerning the strength of computer chess programs. Since the layman's stereotype of a chessmaster portrays him as a person with a prodigious memory and lightning calculational abilities, it seems quite natural to presume that a computer, with its vast capacity for memory storage and rapid calculation, should be able to compete on a par with human experts. Chessmasters are often asked by new acquaintances whether they can hold their own against a computer. When confronted in this manner, the master does not know whether to be insulted or entertained; perhaps his most common (and most diplomatic) response is one of tolerant amusement.

The belief that computers are capable of high-class chess has been fostered by newspaper publicity and by exaggerated claims from computer scientists themselves. In his recent book on computer chess, Newborn [73] states that chess experts will be "surprised by the quality of the better games" and that within 15 years "it seems quite possible to develop a chess program that will compete on an even footing with a master without any new breakthroughs in the field." Kozdrowicki and Cooper [62] state that "chess-playing computers are learning quickly" and that "we have been making uniform progress since 1968."

Let's look at the facts. Greenblatt's program, MacHack Six [48], was the first to compete in tourneys against human opponents. It participated in four events in Massachusetts early in 1967 and achieved a United States Chess Federation (USCF) rating of 1400–1450 in its last two tournaments. These results placed it in USCF category Class C (at that time all players below 1600 were listed in Class C; above them were Class B players at 1600–1799, Class A players at 1800–1999, Experts at 2000–2199, Masters at 2200–2399, and Senior Masters above 2400). The same numerical system applies today, although two classes below Class C are now listed separately [Class D (1200–1399) and Class E (below 1200)].

At the end of 1974 I asked David Slate for his overall estimate of the Northwestern program's current strength. This was the program which had won every U.S. Computer Championship between 1970 and 1973 and had fought to a draw in an exhibition game against the USSR's world-champion computer (KAISSA) in 1974, after finishing second to KAISSA in the Stockholm tournament. It had also achieved a USCF rating of 1734 in one 6-round tourney with human opponents in Fall, 1974. Nevertheless, Slate's frank answer was: "High Class C, around 1550." In other words, within a 7- to 9-year period during which the most concentrated work was being performed on chess programs, there was only an increase of at most 100–200 points in the rating of the best programs.

Slate's estimate of "High Class C" as an approximate upper limit on the strength of current chess programs is supported by my own evaluation of published games from recent national and world computer championships. David Levy, an international master and computer-chess expert, rates the middlegame play of computers at approximately 1300–1500 and deplores the "lack of conceptual progress over more than two decades" of work on such projects [67]. U.S. Senior Master and computer scientist Hans Berliner [11] states that "hardly measurable" progress has been made since the first tournament programs appeared. More recently (*Chess Life and Review*, Oct. 1975) Berliner commented that the best computer programs "play at about the Class C level . . . This has been the state of affairs for about nine years now." And Zobrist and Carlson [101], who collaborated with U.S. Senior Master Charles Kalme on developing the pattern-recognition chess program described in *Scientific American* in 1973, evaluated its play as "sound novice level (1200–1500)."

In 1975 there were more than 100,000 North American players who held USCF ratings as a result of playing in official tournaments. Although it is true that the best computer programs will usually defeat the amateur chess-player who "knows the moves" and plays occasionally with friends but never in tourneys, these programs are weaker than at least 25,000 North American chessplayers—as estimated by USCF officials—and hundreds of thousands of players in the USSR. Consequently, predictions about imminent victories by computers over international masters (usually rated from 2300–2500 on the USCF scale) or international Grandmasters (usually rated above 2500) are very premature, especially in view of the lack of gradual and consistent improvement shown over the past 8 years by computer programs and in view of the absence of any significant conceptual breakthroughs. This lack of improvement seems especially blatant when technological advances in computer hardware are taken into account; consider Newborn's statement that "due to hardware advances, today's computers are several hundred times faster than they were when chess programs were first written" [73].

The USCF's current rating system, Arpad Elo's refinement of ideas originally developed by Kenneth Harkness, has been used by the USCF for 15 years and was recently adopted by the World Chess Federation (FIDE). Elo [36] supplies probabilities of a win for each player depending upon the difference in their ratings. For example, the higher-rated player will win approximately 64 percent of his games against a player ranked 100 points below him, 76 percent of his games against a player 200 points below him, and 96 percent of his games against a player 500 points below him. The chances of Northwestern program winning an extended match against an average Class B player (that is, about a 100-point difference) are not very great, and the program would be unlikely to win even a single game in a 10-game match with an Expert (a 500-point difference), who is still a step below the lowest master category. Furthermore, the best computer player falls approximately 800 points short of David Levy's rating—with less than three years to go on the famous bet Levy made in 1968. He declared that he would still be able to beat any computer ten years later. The computer must gain more than 800 points in less than three years to achieve its backers' goal and save their $2000, but it has gained only about 100 points in the past 8 or 9 years.

About the only way a current computer program could ever win a single game against a master player would be for the master, perhaps in a drunken stupor while playing 50 games simultaneously, to commit some once-in-a-year blunder, such as to place his queen where it can be taken for nothing or to overlook a forced checkmate in two moves. There is, therefore, ample justification for Hunt's conclusion, cited at the beginning of this chapter, that contemporary computer programs provide "trivial opposition" for master chessplayers.

The chessplayers among the readers of this book may enjoy the accompanying game between Russian Grandmaster David Bronstein and a computer that had previously been able to defeat him when Bronstein played without his queen (that is, at a handicap of "queen odds"). So far as I know, this is the only published game between grandmaster and computer. Bronstein did not give queen odds, but he announced a forced checkmate in 10 moves after only 14 moves of the game had passed.

In contrast to actual tournament results, another way that chess-computer enthusiasts support their optimistic claims is on the basis of examples of the best games or moves which computers have produced— often accompanied by comments from some grandmaster about the high quality of the computer's play. Readers should view such testimonials with considerable skepticism. First of all, many grandmasters are not aware

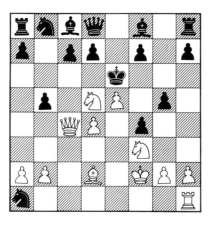

Figure 8.1 The pretty finale to a game played in 1963 between USSR Grandmaster David Bronstein and the EVM "M-20" chess computer. In this position Bronstein announced checkmate in 10 moves (that is, 19 half-moves or ply ahead), beginning with his (White's) 14th move: (14) NxNPch, QxN; (15) NxQBPch, K–K2; (16) N–Q5ch, K–K3; (17) NxPch, K–K2; (18) N–Q5ch, K–K1; (19) QxBch, Q–Q1; (20) N–B7ch, K–K2; (21) B–N4ch, P–Q3; (22) BxPch, QxB; (23) Q–K8 Mate. Other alternatives by Black lead to even quicker checkmates. The opening moves preceding this debacle were as follows: (1) P–K4, P–K4; (2) P–KB4, PxP; (3) N–KB3, N–KB3; (4) P–K5, N–N5; (5) P–Q4, P–KN4; (6) N–QB3, N–K6; (7) Q–K2, NxB; (8) N–K4, N–K6; (9) N–B6ch, K–K2; (10) B–Q2, NxBPch; (11) K–B2, NxR; (12) N–Q5ch, K–K3; (13) Q–B4, P–N4.

that standard openings (taken directly from games played by masters) are routinely placed in the computer's memory, and that its reasonable play for the first few moves may be a result of mere "thoughtless imitation" of a particular column or game in the latest edition of *Modern Chess Openings* or *Chess Informant*. Second, the *best* game out of, say, 20 games played by a Class B or Class C human player might be fairly well-played, too, even if the other 19 were very poor; a larger, unselected sample of games is needed for the master to render a reliable judgment. Third, computer chessplayers will play better in certain types of positions than in others. If the game is not very complicated and obvious strategic themes are absent, the computer's play might seem sound even to a skeptic, since the computer does not commit outright blunders—something which is typical of Class C and Class D human players.

Take, for example, the game described in detail in Zobrist and Carlson's article [101] about their computer-chess program. The contest, against Charles Kalme, is supplied below for the reader's benefit. U.S. Grandmaster William Lombardy annotated the game for *Scientific American* and concluded that it was a "remarkable game for the computer, particularly against a topflight master. My guess is that David Levy will have his hands full in 1978." However, Kalme himself commented that, of all the games he had played over the course of several years against the computer, this was by far the best. Even so

> . . . the machine was never really in the game and had no viable plan beyond the defense it was forced into. It is easy to make the best moves, in the sense of losing most slowly, if these entail meeting immediate tactical threats. . . . The method of attack by Black was particularly suitable for making the machine look good. . . . [if I want to] I can crush the machine tactically by choosing wilder lines of play.

Games of this kind remind me of ones that frequently occur in simultaneous exhibitions, in which a master usually takes on 30 or 40 opponents at one time. On such occasions masters sometimes "go easy" on certain contestants, for example, the town's mayor, the organizer of the exhibition, or the prettiest opponent. Without deliberately avoiding any forced wins, the master simply sidesteps complications, frequently offers exchanges of

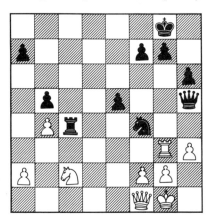

Figure 8.2 A decisive position from a game between the Zobrist–Carlson (University of Southern California) chess-computer program and U.S. Senior Master Charles Kalme, who was Black. Kalme has just played (34) . . . Q–R4 and the computer's position is now hopeless—so bad that most masters in White's position against a good player would resign the game. The complete game went as follows: (1) P–K4, P–K4; (2) N–KB3, N–QB3; (3) B–B4, B–B4; (4) O–O, P–Q3; (5) P–KR3, N–B3; (6) N–B3, O–O; (7) P–Q3, P–KR3; (8) N–Q5, NxN; (9) BxN, N–K2; (10) B–N3, N–N3; (11) P–B3, B–K3; (12) P–Q4, BxB; (13) QxB, B–N3; (14) PxP PxP; (15) R–K1, Q–B3; (16) B–K3, BxB; (17) RxB, P–N3; (18) R–Q1, QR–Q1; (19) R(3)–Q3, RxR; (20) RxR, N–B5; (21) R–K3, R–Q1; (22) Q–B4, Q–N3; (23) N–K1, R–Q8; (24) Q–B1, R–Q7; (25) Q–B4, P–QB3; (26) P–QN4, P–N4; (27) Q–N3, Q–N4; (28) P–B4, Q–R5; (29) R–KB3, R–K7; (30) Q–Q1, RxKP; (31) PxP, PxP; (32) N–B2, Q–N4; (33) Q–KB1, R–B5; (34) R–KN3, Q–R4; (35) N–K1, N–K7ch; (36) K–R2, NxR; (37) KxN, R–B8; (38) P–B3, Q–N4ch; and the game was abandoned as hopeless for White.

pawns and pieces, and builds up his position slowly. The result is inevitable—he wins anyway, unless he decides to offer a chivalrous draw. Only another very strong player could detect the opportunities the master has passed up when he plays in this fashion.

Finally, many of the good moves played by a computer program in examples of its best games may not have been made for the "right reasons," according to master judgments. There is a chance that a very good move may occur for an irrelevant or incorrect reason. The master who comments on a computer game should not take it for granted that a move was made for the same reasons he would have made the move. Only a detailed examination of the computer printout by a strong chessplayer could reveal such discrepancies. Of course, an extensive analysis of this kind is rarely performed because of the thousands of positions and moves the human must search through to make a final decision about the reasons for the computer's choice of a single move.

Although some computer scientists have declared that collaboration with chessmasters on computer-chess projects is more a hindrance than a help—because the chessmaster does not appreciate the technological problems of computer programming—the close involvement of strong human chessplayers in any serious project of this kind seems indispensable to me. Only masters can evaluate the progress of a particular program with any real accuracy, since programs rarely compete against *humans* in USCF rated tourneys. The pitting of one computer against another is not very revealing, because such games fail to provide a human standard relative to which the excellence of play may be measured. In a television interview Bobby Fischer commented: "Computers won't go anywhere unless they actually involve some good chessplayers." Newborn [73] maintains that this statement is unfair, pointing to the participation of Hans Berliner, Mikhail Botvinnik, and Charles Kalme in such projects. Several other names should be added to this list: Max Euwe, former world champion and a mathematics professor; Adriaan de Groot, a Dutch psychologist, chessmaster and mathematician; and David Levy himself.

Newborn neglected to mention, however, that virtually every one of the masters who has actually been involved in work on specific programs is pessimistic about the prospect of high-level chessplay by a computer in the near future, or at any time at all. I have already cited Berliner and Levy's strong reservations and Kalme's negative comments. de Groot [31] declared: "Persistent rumors to the contrary, . . . machine players are poor players. At best they are rather narrow specialists of mediocre ability. . . . The ideal, a program that plays master chess, still appears to be quite remote." Euwe, who was a member of the Euratom Committee formed in 1961 to investigate the problem of programming chess and who has since retained his interest in computer chess [37], now talks only about the prospect of a machine playing "passable chess."

The single optimist among this group is former world chess champion Botvinnik, an electrical engineer by profession; in 1968 he commented

[18] that a precise program is potentially available for the solution of inexact problems such as those arising in chess and that "this can be done and will be done, not in 50 years, but much sooner." However, Botvinnik [17] has recently made it very clear that he considers KAISSA's play weak by expert standards and "diametrically opposed" to the principles of the specific program on which he has been working since 1970. Although he still expresses optimism about creating a machine of master strength—an opinion that is reassuring to many workers in the field—there is no evidence so far that he is any closer to that goal than anyone else, despite the fact that he has been concerned with the problem for more than 10 years.

In summary, the past achievements of computer chessplayers are relatively small. Computer programs are not significantly stronger than they were 6–10 years ago—they still play at Class C level—despite the substantial increases in speed of computer operation over that period. Computers do play games that are free of serious errors (what the chess expert calls "one-movers"), and they probably can solve forced mates or simple combinations quite efficiently when they are explicitly programmed to do so and are presented with positions containing exact solutions [12]. There seems little or no evidence to support the claim that attainment of a master's rating by a machine requires only "faster computers" and "larger opening and endgame memories."

If any success is to occur, a new or different approach appears to be needed. An experienced chess teacher can probably take an intelligent and enthusiastic 7–10 year old child and transform him into a Class A or Class B player within a year or two. There must be something about the human brain and the way it operates that is overlooked by chess-computer programmers; perhaps the method of teaching a human and the way in which he learns are markedly different from what happens in computerized chess. Either we are telling the child something a computer programmer is not telling or cannot tell the computer, or the child is qualitatively different from the computer in his perceptual and thinking capacities. Questions of this kind are the object of attention in the next section of the chapter.

Chess thinking: Man versus machine

Some misconceptions about master chess

Many outsiders regard the chessmaster as some kind of superman; he is presumed to be a person who possesses an extraordinary memory, can calculate many moves ahead with lightning rapidity, and probably has an astronomical IQ. Since computers have an enormous memory capacity and can make specific calculations in fractions of a second, the idea of a computer chessmaster seems quite reasonable. However, if pressed for clarification about the third characteristic, high intelligence, the layman (and anyone else, for that matter) would have some difficulty answering.

As we shall see, chessmasters would probably score no higher on an IQ test than other human beings with similar family backgrounds and education; but they do have the ability, at least in chess, to acquire new ideas rapidly, to solve novel problems, to recognize and quickly evaluate similarities and differences between various complex situations, and to isolate the core of a difficult problem without much hesitation—abilities usually implied by the layman when using the word "intelligence." It is these latter qualities that probably come closer to characterizing the master's skills, and the talents of good problem solvers in any area, than do exceptional memory capacity and calculational ability.

Memory

The notion that master play is critically dependent on having an exceptional memory—in the sense of an encyclopedic move-by-move knowledge of opening variations and endgame techniques, and in the sense of amazing recall for the exact details of prior games played by himself and other masters—is erroneous. Unfortunately, this belief has been fostered by numerous chess writers, usually not grandmasters, who imply that young players should exhaustively study reams of opening analysis and retain as much specific detail as possible. Although a master must certainly know a reasonable amount of opening and endgame "theory," the form or organization of this knowledge and the way in which it is acquired (by rote or through understanding of general principles) seem to be the factors that are important in his ability to apply the knowledge effectively in actual game situations. The Russian Master Znosko-Borovsky said that chess is a game of understanding, not of memory. Danish Grandmaster Bent Larsen cautions against "learning variations, not chess [38]."

Men played master chess long before the end of the nineteenth century, when extensive and specific opening analysis first became a fixture in chess literature. Emanuel Lasker, who was world champion for 27 years (1894–1921) as well as holder of a Ph.D. in mathematics, remarked that "I have stored little in my memory, but I can apply that little." His successor as world champion, José Capablanca, often boasted that he had hardly ever opened a chess book, even early in his career, and he recommended that "chess books should be used as we use glasses—to assist the sight; some players make use of them as if they thought they conferred sight." Recent world champion Tigran Petrosian [38] summarized his views in 1974 as follows: "To study opening variations without reference to the strategic concepts that develop from them in the middlegame is, in effect, to separate the head from the body. . . . Thoughtless imitation [of moves made by masters] can actually hinder the realization of [a player's] talent." And Hungarian Grandmaster Lajos Portisch advises [38] that *your only task in the opening is to reach a playable middlegame. . . .* To all players I can recommend the following [in the opening]: *simplicity* and *economy.* [Many great masters] do not strain unduly for advantages in the opening." A book like Reuben Fine's *Ideas Behind the Chess Openings* is particularly valuable, in my opinion; Fine stresses plans and general goals, not specific variations [41].

To be fair, I should mention that knowledge of "opening theory" (very specific move-by-move analysis of openings played in recent tournaments) is probably necessary today in *grandmaster* chess, primarily for practical reasons. As Larsen says, if you know only the ideas behind the openings and your opponent knows the ideas *and* a lot of specific variations, he is likely to beat you. Because of the time limit placed on championship games (usually 40 moves in 2½ hours, an average of less than 4 minutes per move), a grandmaster cannot afford to give an approximately equal opponent a great time advantage—which might well occur if one player were unfamiliar with the latest opening subtleties.

Nevertheless, very few games between grandmasters are "over" even when one side does obtain a definite advantage in the opening. An alert player ordinarily has several "second chances" to rescue a game later on, since even grandmasters rarely conduct a full game impeccably. Fischer and Karpov have often won or drawn objectively lost positions against grandmasters of the highest strength, which also indicates that there is much more to top-level chess than mnemonic skill and encyclopedic knowledge.

Studies by psychologists [31, 54] have shown that chessmasters perform no better than other human beings on memory tasks unrelated to chess, in which they must study some material for a while and then are tested afterwards for retention of the material. Their general-memory capacities are not extraordinary at all, although of course their ability to recall meaningful chess material is excellent and varies directly with their playing strength. While studying the psychological capacities of great chessplayers in the nineteenth century, the outstanding psychologist Alfred Binet [15, 16] was surprised to discover that they do not have "photographic minds" —exact visualization of chess positions while recalling old games or playing chess blindfolded; their imagery was abstract, in the sense that specific details were often omitted. When asked to describe games played months or years ago, expert players were most likely to forget isolated moves that were not well integrated with the rest of the game. They remembered ideas, patterns, plans and the type of tactical finale, rather than individual moves. Their memory of old openings and games was organized so that they retained some general scheme, from which they could reconstruct details— just as a mathematics professor, unexpectedly called upon for proof of a theorem, does not normally "rattle it off" from memory but reconstructs it on the basis of the general methods and principles covering such situations.

Thus we see that a chessmaster does not store thousands or millions of specific moves and move-sequences in his memory—contrary to what many outsiders or weaker players may think. His memory is organized economically, in terms of general principles, patterns, and rules. Consequently, he can usually produce a good move even when surprised by an opening novelty. Probably there is nothing special about the chessmaster in this regard; the memory processes of all normal human beings—be they post-men, doctors, chefs, or orchestra conductors—are likely to operate in a similar way. Otherwise, we would have to waste time searching through a mass of irrelevant or unimportant material in solving new problems or recalling solutions to old ones.

Calculation

Another misconception about master chess concerns the master's pre-sumed ability to calculate very rapidly and deeply. Even though most non-chessplayers tend to greatly underestimate the number of possible different games that can be played—there are actually so many that a computer can only examine a small fraction of these in a human's lifetime—they do recognize that chess is a very complicated game. Edgar Allen Poe dismissed chess as a process of calculation [1], that is, seeing many moves ahead and examining numerous side variations. However, masters can play high-level chess at the rate of 1 or 2 seconds per move, which seems to demonstrate that they are not calculating far ahead (see Chapter 6 in this volume for a description of a computer program that is designed to play rapid chess without "analyzing ahead"). U.S. Grandmaster Robert Byrne [29], after remarking that memory is not a major ingredient of the great chess mind, added that calculation is not so important, either. Likewise, William Lom-bardy [29] insists that the accurate setting of goals ("combined with appropriate smoke screens") and the accumulation of small advantages—not exact calculations—are the keys to master chess: "Calculation most often comes after the goal is achieved, the moment when a winning position converts into a mathematically forced win." Most chessmasters, whether because of time pressure, sheer laziness, the risk of making a calculational error, or mere economy of thinking, actually avoid elaborate calculations during competitive play. It is rarely worth the time to delve deeply into a particular variation unless certain ill-defined features suggest to the master that an unexpected trap or combination might be hidden there.

Mikhail Tal of the USSR provides an exception to the general rule that grandmasters tend to sidestep very complicated variations in which detailed calculation is necessary. When Tal first became a contender for world championship honors in the late 1950's, his risky style of play was viewed with disdain by most grandmasters; for example, former World Champion Vassily Smyslov commented that "Tal wins by tricks. I consider it my duty as a grandmaster to beat him properly." Tal welcomed the chance to enter incredibly complicated positions, where he might sacrifice a pawn or piece for unclear compensation. He demolished all opposition (including two brilliant victories over Smyslov) on his way to the world championship in 1960, although in many games the post mortem analysis revealed that he would have lost if his opponent had calculated perfectly. Tal took advantage of his fellow masters' uneasiness and possible lack of practice at calculating precisely under the pressure of time. Of course, Tal did not win merely because he was a better "calculator". He was a fine all-round player who also had an exceptional ability to *create* positions that contained numerous tactical resources.

A year later, Tal lost the return match with Botvinnik, who is primarily a deep strategist. In their second match Botvinnik exercised extreme care and managed to avoid the complex tactical positions in which Tal excelled. Since 1961, no new world championship candidate has appeared who plays "Tal style."

We have seen that masters rely less on ability to calculate long variations than on application of general plans, techniques, and stratagems. Chessmaster and theoretician Richard Reti [64] labeled as "profane" those who think that "the superiority of the chessmaster rests in his ability to calculate far ahead." He argued that

> every player, from the weakest to the strongest, possesses—consciously or unconsciously—principles by which he is guided in the choice of moves. Perhaps, a weak player holds to primitive principles . . . such a player is already content, for example, if he succeeds in saying check to his opponent.

de Groot's comparisons of masters, experts, and weaker players, who were asked to analyze aloud while selecting a move in positions they had not seen before, revealed no major differences between the groups in the breadth and depth of their calculations (see Charness' summary of the work, especially Table 2.1, in Chapter 2 of this volume). However, I do think that masters could calculate significantly further ahead than weaker players *if it were necessary for them to do so*—for example, if the most logical first move committed the player to a subsequent sequence of action that had to be calculated 15 to 25 moves deep in order to be sure it had no fatal flaw (such as might arise in an endgame where both sides are pushing pawns toward the eighth rank or in a position where both kings are under direct attack.) In my opinion, masters avoid deep calculations not because of any severe limits placed on them by some short-term-memory process [21]—they can calculate deeply if they have to—but because their time is generally better spent in other types of analysis. How unlike computer chess, where programmers boast about the hundreds of thousands of terminal positions examined on a given move! A chessmaster is more likely to brag about how few specific variations he investigated rather than how many.

Putting decisions into words

Another widespread but erroneous belief about chessmaster play is the notion that masters can verbalize very specific criteria for their choice of a given move; presumably such criteria could then be relayed to a programmer who would instruct a computer accordingly. However, unless some specific tactical points are involved, grandmasters often explain their moves with such vague comments as "It looked good" or "That had to be the correct move." They are frequently reluctant to elaborate their reasons in detail. Very few rules are independent of the position of the pieces and the master apparently takes many global and specific factors into account simultaneously. When a master loses a game, he sometimes does not know where he made the decisive error. Current World Champion Anatoly Karpov asked Petrosian after a defeat in 1973, "Please, where did I make my mistake?" It might have taken both of them hours, days, or months before the crucial error was finally isolated.

A quotation from William James' chapter on "Reasoning" [57] is worth repeating in this connection:

> [An expert] instinctively knows that, in a novel case, this and not that will be the promising course of action. The well-known story of the old judge advising the new one never to give reasons for his decisions, "the decisions will probably be right, the reasons will surely be wrong," illustrates this. The doctor will feel that the patient is doomed, the dentist will have a premonition that the tooth will break, though neither can articulate a reason for his foreboding. The reason lies imbedded, but not yet laid bare, in all the countless previous cases dimly suggested by the actual one, all calling up the same conclusion, which the adept thus finds himself swept on to, he knows not how or why.

In psychological research [49] involving human subjects who must learn to make complex decisions based on a variety of cues, none of which is invariably correct, the subjects who produce superior judgments are frequently unable to provide a clear explanation of exactly how they do it. In real-life situations, interviewers have discovered that the more experienced stockbrokers are less able to describe their judgments than are the less experienced. The implications for computerizing *master* chess seem obvious: to raise the machine's play to a very high level, masters must articulate fairly specific rules for the programmer to use in revising his choice-of-move criteria (evaluation function), but masters find this an extremely difficult task to perform in many positions. The only alternative route for the machine to achieve master-level chess would appear to be via introduction of learning or feedback mechanisms into the computer itself, so that it may learn from "countless previous cases" as a human being presumably does. I will return to these alternatives and discuss their practicality shortly.

I do not want to leave the reader with the impression that I feel there are mysterious or mystical forces at work when a master produces these intuitive, poorly-articulated justifications for his decisions; no "soul" or "creative force" is operating that we are incapable of ever understanding. However, at present, our knowledge of basic principles of human learning, thinking, and general problem solving is so inadequate that we cannot expect easy or imminent resolution of such complex issues—unfortunately for the progress of computer chess. After more than 30 years of studying the psychology of perception, memory, and thinking, de Groot (who is one of the most analytical workers in the field) said [30]:

> My attitude toward the phenomena of perception and toward those of memory functioning, has become one of deep respect. These phenomena are highly complex, often ambiguous and very difficult to pin down in terms of a code, a model, or a program. . . . [Machine] simulation of memory functioning and, even more so, of perception has remained quite primitive compared to what humans or, for that matter, animals can do.

This type of modest and careful statement, by a person who is well versed in chess, psychology, mathematics, and computer simulation (perhaps the best qualified person to speak on the topic of this book!), stands in vivid contrast to the exaggerated and simplistic comments of many workers in the field of artificial intelligence. The latter group tends to greatly overestimate our knowledge of basic psychological processes and to underestimate the complexity of brain function. The much larger number of *interconnections* between different parts and centers of the brain than of a computer network suggests that "integrative activities" of the brain and nervous system play a critical role in human and animal pattern recognition, memory storage and retrieval, and problem solving. One wonders whether a computer will ever be able to perform such tasks on a similarly-high level unless it can somehow be equipped with interconnections and integrated, "wholistic" mechanisms of a comparable nature.

Genius and chess

Nonchessplayers commonly regard the chessmaster as a "brain" or "quiz kid" who is sure to be a success in any kind of intellectual endeavor. Of course, chessmasters like to encourage such flattering appraisals, but there is little or no evidence from psychological studies or personal observations to substantiate the belief. An admittedly crude Russian study performed with the cooperation of participants in the 1925 Moscow International Tournament failed to yield any support for the idea that chessplayers are generally more intelligent than nonchessplayers. de Groot believes that masters would score well above the average on "spatial imagination" tests of nonverbal intelligence, but he does not believe that exceptionally high verbal intelligence is an indispensable requirement. (On the other hand, a blockhead like Mirko Czentovic, a major character in Stefan Zweig's classic chess novella *The Royal Game* [102], probably could not become world champion, as he was in the story.) In my opinion, based on acquaintance and conversations with many American and foreign masters, chess champions would not score any higher on tests of verbal or quantitative aptitude than lesser players or nonplayers of comparable background. Chessmasters as well as chess computers deserve less reverence than the public accords them.

Psychological studies of human thinking and chess mastery

Chess has several features that make it appealing as a research tool for psychologists interested in human learning, memory, and thinking. It provides a rich, almost inexhaustible supply of material (positions, combinations, plans), which can be varied along various dimensions or attributes. Its visual information-processing aspects make chess potentially valuable as a task to compare with verbal (linguistic) information-processing tasks. Moreover, subjects participating in research on chess can be classified objectively into several distinctly different categories, either on the basis of USCF ratings (if they are active tournament players) or on the basis of the number of correct solutions they give to a few graded chess problems presented during a brief preliminary phase of the research. Fairly objective standards can be established for the best move in certain kinds of chess positions, and possibly even for the "creativeness" or "brilliance" of different proposed moves or ideas. Chess is a complex intellectual task, played by individuals who differ markedly in ability, and it seems to provide feasible situations for testing hypotheses about human learning, memory, and thinking. Actually, the extent of its potential as a research tool has probably not yet been realized by experimental psychologists.

Charness' Chapter 2 in this volume describes details of the systematic work on chess and chessplayers performed by de Groot in Holland and Simon and his colleagues in the USA. Some comments on the generality and applicability of conclusions from these studies appear appropriate before I turn to a comparison of how computers and human beings seem to differ in their ways of selecting a move in chess. In addition to Charness' chapter, the interested reader will find pertinent material on the psychology of chess elsewhere [16, 30, 31, 42, 43, 54, 64, 84].

Most studies performed by de Groot, Simon, and their collaborators examine the memory and thought processes of chessplayers when presented with middlegame or endgame positions from previously played games that are unfamiliar to the subjects. Reconstruction and recognition procedures are generally employed if "memory" is the focus of the research, and thinking-aloud protocols if "thinking" is the focus. The stronger the chessplayer, the better he is at reconstructing a position after brief exposure to it—provided the position is one that is likely to have occurred in an actual game (usually the positions are selected from published games between good players.) Masters do no better than beginners in recalling positions that involve pieces scattered randomly on the chessboard. In examining *thought* (move-selection) protocols when subjects are exposed to positions from unfamiliar games, Newell and Simon [75] found that humans implicitly employ "minimaxing" and "quiescence" evaluation (see Frey's Chapter 3 in this volume for a discussion of these terms) while they think aloud in this kind of situation.

Although the results and conclusions of such research certainly must be relevant for our eventual understanding of differences in chess reasoning between masters and weaker players, the unfamiliar-position task may not be ideal for generating valuable information about human chess thinking under normal conditions—which would presumably have the most applicability for computer chess. Players thinking aloud in unfamiliar positions evaluate material, examine threats, and look for possibilities of action. These findings have been used as a basis for positive comparisons with computer-chess programs, because the latter also follow such steps when they begin analysis after their opponent's move. In actual game situations, however, strong players do not ordinarily need to evaluate material or examine threats after each move. They have already judged or anticipated such factors because the position has developed from immediately prior ones with similar material balance and threats.

The late Estonian Grandmaster Paul Keres complained to de Groot about the "unnaturalness" of having to select a move in a position from a game that had already progressed 20 to 40 moves before he first saw it. Normally, a strong player makes his decisions and assesses his chances primarily on the basis of what he has analyzed on previous moves, and on the basis of his evaluation of the overall strength of his position as it fluctuates from move to move. No position changes completely with a single move. As Chessmaster Tarrasch once said: "A good chess game can be told as a series of interrelated facts."

de Groot was well aware of potential problems with his method and he usually selected positions for his subjects that did not contain extremely obvious goals or immediate forced wins, so that *once a player was oriented in the position*, his thinking ought to follow a course like that in an actual game (where no immediate forced win usually exists). Positions used to test computer programs, however, generally do contain forced checkmates or major gains of material (see Simon's MATER [8] and Berliner's CAPS programs [12]), which unfortunately are relatively trivial problems relative to high-level chess thinking.

The unnaturalness of de Groot's standard thinking-aloud procedure might be partially overcome if subjects were asked to think aloud while playing an actual game (the players would, of course, have to be placed in separate rooms, so that the plans of one player would not be revealed to the other). If chessmasters could function well in such a setting—and not lapse into long periods of silent analysis—their thinking-aloud protocols might be of great benefit to a psychologist (cf. [98]) and might also entertain chess audiences (tuned-in to both players' comments). Under such conditions, would de Groot's original estimates of the master's depth and breadth of analysis, compared to a weaker player's, be confirmed? My guess is that results from this new procedure would indicate much more difference between masters and amateurs than did de Groot's unfamiliar-position task. Besides, he reported that his "second-class" subjects took the situation much more seriously than did the grandmasters—another reason for suspecting that his findings might not hold in a competitive (public) situation. World Champion Alexander Alekhine, one of de Groot's subjects, implied that in a serious game he would go to much more trouble.

The finding that masters were able to reconstruct de Groot's test positions much more accurately and quickly than weaker players or nonplayers is in itself of relatively limited interest, in my opinion. Studies of human memory conducted as long ago as the 1880s also revealed that recall of meaningful material (for example, words or poems from one's native language) is much greater than recall of nonmeaningful material (for example, nonsense syllables or foreign-language terms). Positions taken from published games between good players are, after all, very meaningful for a master and less so for nonmasters of different playing strengths. Masters have a distinct advantage because they are more familiar with the typical patterns, formations, or "chunks" that occur in games between good players. Similarly, Morse code experts can decode a message faster and remember it better than amateurs because they presumably process the material in terms of larger units (words, phrases, sentences, etc.) than their inexperienced counterparts, who must plod along letter-by-letter.

The patterns that appear in games between topflight players are fairly stereotyped. Chase and Simon [22] described a "pennies-guessing task," in which subjects are shown "quiet" positions with pennies substituted for all the pieces remaining on the board. Masters and Class A players were quite successful in guessing which pieces stood where (readers might like to try variations of this experiment on some of their friends). de Groot [30] has determined the most frequent position of each piece after Black's 20th move in a sample of 192 games from master tournaments. As expected, a great deal of stereotypy was present in the positions that were reached. Chessplayers may be interested in the "average" position (Figure 8.3) after reaching Black's 20th move in this sample of games. The result might be somewhat different today, more than 10 years later, since the popularity of various openings has probably changed a little since then. All in all, the research indicates, probably to the surprise of very few chessplayers and psychologists, that patterns and organized configurations seem to control the play of the strong chessplayer, rather than disconnected moves of the various pieces.

Does memory of the details of a chess position depend on whether the position is one which the subject must merely memorize or is one in which he is asked to discover a winning move? So far as I know, not very much research, if any, has been performed along these lines. My guess would be that good players, asked to solve a problem without being told they would later have to recall the details of the position, would make more and perhaps different errors when recalling the position than if they received equivalent time but were merely asked to memorize the position. Their recollection in the former case would probably be very schematic, focusing on salient features and unusual aspects, and overlooking unimportant details such as the exact material situation and pawn formations on the

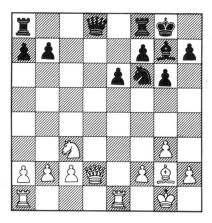

Figure 8.3 The "average" position reached after Black's 20th move in a sample of 192 master games. It was created by, first, selecting the most probable material situation at that point in the games (usually two pawns, one bishop and one knight had been exchanged and removed from the board by the 20th move) and, second, placing the remaining pieces on their most likely squares at that time. The position is taken from de Groot [30], who calls this the "stereotyped chess position *par excellence*." (Reprinted by permission of John Wiley and Sons; copyright 1966.)

opposite side of the board from where the action is. Such research seems worthwhile to perform and might yield results that vary significantly depending on the amount of time since original exposure to the positions.

In de Groot's standard (simple memory) task, he found that the reconstruction errors of strong players often involved placement of a piece on a good square *for that type of position*. Similarly, Chase and Simon [22] observed that reconstruction errors often involve displacement of a piece a square or two away from where it actually stood, but from which the piece still preserved its crucial function in the position; that is, its correct *relative* position was remembered. The recurrent conclusion from all this work is that strong players think about positions and remember them in terms of sets of integrated functional units, rather than as conglomerations of scattered squares and wooden pieces.

Computer and man as learners and thinkers in chess

Most workers in the field of computer chess agree that one should strive for a program that selects its moves in ways as similar as possible to the manner in which a human being makes such decisions. For example, Newell, Shaw, and Simon [74] argued that "any information-processing system—a human, a computer, or any other—that plays chess successfully will use heuristics generically similar to those used by humans." Botvinnik [18] stated that we must make the machine "in our image"; "the program must be modeled on human thought processes." Of course, it is conceivable that a machine could be programmed to play good chess even though it operates in a way radically different from its human counterpart, but there is no evidence today indicating that such an approach is feasible or preferable.

As noted earlier, merely because a machine chessplayer frequently makes good moves or seems to be adopting sensible plans, according to judgments of experts and masters, does not guarantee that the processes or reasons by which it came to those "decisions" are the same or very similar to those used by a human being. A correct move might be selected for a wrong or irrelevant reason. A computer that performs at a USCF Class C level may not choose its moves via methods which a human Class C player uses, and it may make quite different kinds of mistakes.

Let us now examine some of the major differences between the ways in which computer and man seem to select and analyze chess moves. Computer scientists interested in chess projects are certainly aware of most, if not all, of these discrepancies and would be happy to take them into account in future work—if only they knew how. However, until they are able to do so, one can question whether a computer of expert or master strength is really a practical possibility.

Computer programs of today do have certain advantages over the human chessplayer. If no technical problems occur during a game, the best-constructed programs will never commit simple blunders, such as leaving a queen or bishop to be taken for nothing or overlooking a checkmate in one or two moves. The computer will never fall victim to fatigue or inattention, and it will store and retrieve thousands of specific opening variations better than a human. Even though technical breakdowns occur occasionally during computer-chess performances, the computer offers benefits of speed and reliability that are lacking in most human chessplayers, especially the lower-ranked ones. It would probably be easier for a master player to give queen-odds successfully to a Class C or Class D *human* chessplayer than to a Class C or Class D computer program, because the master can generally count on several bad blunders from the human but not from the computer.

Most other differences between human and computer chessplayers strongly favor the human. Some of these distinguishing features involve not so much differences in general processes of learning or thinking as differences in the weighting of various specific criteria for move selection (that is, evaluation functions). The more systematic, general differences will be considered first and then the specific ones.

Massive tree search versus focused or restricted search. Computer programs generate all possible first moves, prune some of these to retain the most plausible alternatives (a step which often eliminates sacrifices and other uncommon moves that a strong human player might consider), and then continue the analysis for 4 or 5 half-moves along many different branches. Some programs, notably CHESS 4.5 and KAISSA, search all the legal moves to a fixed depth. The search typically ends, and a move is selected, after tens or hundreds of thousands of terminal positions have been evaluated, certain specific algorithms have been applied, and "quiescent" positions are presumably achieved in the main variations arising from the selected move.

In contrast, a human chessplayer, whether master or not, ordinarily considers very few first moves (masters often examine only one; see de Groot [30]), analyzes a few sample variations, and then decides on his move. As Hunt [56] states: "Humans restrict their search space to *feasible* solutions." Likewise, in one of the very first articles on the psychology of chess, published almost 70 years ago [28], Cleveland remarked on the selectivity of chess thinking, and the grasp of essentials and "position sense" that characterize strong players. The unfortunate computer must examine thousands of irrelevant moves or variations, many of which are refuted by the same basic idea. Furthermore, good or bad ideas discovered in one branch of a computer tree may not be transferred to other branches, because their general importance is not "recognized" by the computer. Simon and Chase [84] discuss a similar weakness of the PERCEIVER program, which notices attacks and defenses but has no processes for organizing and remembering this information.

Thus the human being—novice or master, young or old—never applies a brute-force approach to any but the simplest chess positions, whereas such massive tree-searching is typical of the computer. High on the human's list of heuristics is "overlook x, y, z, etc."; he conforms to William James' dictum that "the art of being wise is the art of knowing what to overlook." Hans Berliner [10] believes that naiveté concerning the value of generating an immense number of move possibilities is common among nonchessplayers and computer scientists. He suggests that his "well-meaning friends" in computer science need to find a better method than massive tree searching if they want to develop stronger computer chessplayers.

Starting-from-scratch versus long-range planning. While a computer is selecting a move, it makes little if any use of information discovered during analyses of prior moves; it almost literally must start from scratch. Therefore, not only is the analytical process extremely wasteful—because the same possibilities have to be rediscovered and evaluated again and again, as if new knowledge always went in one ear and out the other—but long-range planning is very difficult to arrange. The program is frequently "distracted" by relatively unimportant factors that arise from move to move and temporarily affect its plausible-move generator or terminal evaluation-function values.

On the contrary, human chessplayers, particularly the stronger ones, select their moves primarily on the basis of a plan or typical technique for handling that kind of position, as determined mainly by relatively permanent aspects of the position. Pawn formations, for example, are very important in guiding a master's choice of moves; if the pawns on the queenside are arranged in a certain way after his opponent has declined the Queen's Gambit, a master will probably pursue the "minority attack" on the queenside and hardly consider any moves which do not contribute to this well-known strategy. The master's general goals in such a position may not shift for many moves unless the opponent's replies force a radical revision of strategy, or suggest to the master that another plan would now be even more effective, perhaps in combination with pursuit of the minority attack.

Strong chessplayers rely so much on plans and general principles rather than specific-move analysis that they sometimes overlook a simple way of winning because it does not fit into their general strategy. Therefore, an over-reliance on rules or principles can lead to stereotyped play and prove disadvantageous, as many writers (e.g., [60]) have pointed out. The weaknesses of Church's goal-seeking program (see Chapter 6 of this volume) lie primarily in this direction, it seems to me.

The superior player is always on the alert for exceptions to general rules and principles, and supplements his long-range planning with concrete analysis. The ability to effectively balance these two factors seems the hallmark of master play. Botvinnik maintains that the art of playing high-level chess lies in the ability to create positions in which the normal relative values cease to exist. One of Alekhine's particular strengths lay in his ability to create positions that on the surface seemed rather unclear or innocuous, but in fact were deadly. Viennese Grandmaster Rudolf Spielmann complained that he could understand and discover Alekhine's final combinations easily enough ("Give me the positions he obtains, and I would seldom falter"), but that in his own games he was unable to *develop* the kinds of positions which Alekhine concocted. Since computer chess is so much based on "normal relative values" in its evaluation functions, skeptics will wonder with good reason how computers will ever reach expert or master strength.

Another feature of computer play that is related to long-range planning is the computer's comparative inability to isolate, retain, and use information about potentially good moves that do *not* work in a given position but would work beautifully if one or two positional details were to change. The human being would search for some way of rendering the desired move effective, perhaps by means of a forcing sacrifice on his own part or by means of a subtle series of "misleading" moves intended to entice the opponent into a response that permits the maneuver. The latter type of artifice, in particular, would be very hard to program into a computer.

Relatively strict depth limitations versus flexible depth analysis and progressive deepening. Most computer programs are designed to look ahead only 4 or 5 half-moves. Under certain specific conditions, of course, such as when a "quiescent" position is not achieved, the analysis is continued further. Nevertheless, "quiescence" for the computer is based on rather gross factors (check and capture possibilities), so that the computer is rarely likely to look very far ahead. In contrast, the human being may analyze several variations very deeply if the position seems to warrant it.

Hans Berliner [11, 12] has pursued matters of this nature in his discussion of the *horizon effect* in computer chess. As he convincingly demonstrates, opponent's threats already discovered will go "unnoticed" by the computer if analysis is stopped at a certain point; and strong moves of the machine, which would be even more powerful if delayed for a while, are played prematurely. Although Berliner is certainly right that the horizon effect creates real and important problems for chess programmers, I think that he overemphasizes this issue as a weakness of computer chess. Other aspects of computer chess appear more crucial in accounting for its relatively weak play, including some aspects stressed by de Groot [31].

de Groot's human protocols were characterized by a continuous re-evaluation of ideas and specific moves in a given position. Such *progressive deepening*, which de Groot considers very important in the economy and power of human chess thinking, is something that computers cannot yet emulate. It is particularly revealing that de Groot found progressive deepening to be rare in weak players, but characteristic of expert and master play. When a human being analyzes in this manner, he often re-investigates the same moves again and again. A move that was rejected or put aside a few minutes before, because it did not fulfill the specific goals or plans which the player was considering at that time, is reanalyzed—but now more deeply and with a different goal in mind. Usually a computer eliminates a move from consideration once it fails to meet certain pre-determined criteria or is judged much weaker than some other alternatives.

This process of progressive deepening may characterize superior human problem solving in many situations besides chess. For example, some research scientists make a practice of periodically reconsidering specific laboratory results or old hypotheses that initially seemed rather promising but were judged unclear or misleading at that time. The reconsiderations involve attempts to apply new ways of thinking and to take into account additional data accumulated since the last examination of the findings or hypotheses. Novel ideas are not permanently discarded after their first (superficial) examination fails to bear fruit. As he reconsiders the material or hypothesis, the scientist's understanding of the possibilities usually becomes keener. The chessmaster analyzing for hours in his den at home engages in a similar process, and many opening novelties are discovered by means of such a technique. Even under the pressure of tournament play, the chessmaster probably spends an appreciable part of his 2½ hours in similar reappraisals, returning to a move or plan and evaluating it from a somewhat different perspective each time.

Move analysis versus move-and-pattern analysis. As noted earlier, superior chessplayers apparently store old positions and games in their memory, and analyze new positions, in terms of much larger perceptual units or "chunks" than does the computer. Studies of human learning and memory, performed with verbal or pictorial material by experimental psychologists, have similarly revealed that subjects categorize or organize small bits of specific information into larger meaningful units (unless no organizing principle is present, in which case rote learning is the only recourse). Anyone who wants to "develop an exceptional memory"—for example, to remember names of many new acquaintances—usually benefits greatly from training in mnemonic (organizational) devices that have been used by orators and actors for many centuries. The recent nationwide popularity of Lorayne and Lucas' *Memory Book* [70] is a tribute to the utility of such methods.

In view of the importance of "chunking" and patterning in the memory and thought of human chessplayers (see Charness' Chapter 2 in this volume and numerous reports from Simon's group, for example, [23])— and the general absence of such configurational mechanisms in computer-chess programs—attempts would be justified to include pattern analysis along with move analysis in the chess computer's arsenal of weapons. Unfortunately, this goal is much more easily stated than accomplished! The Zobrist–Carlson pattern-recognition approach [101] is the only pro-gram that explicitly defines some important patterns in chess (for example, configurations where a queen and king on the same diagonal are potentially susceptible to a pin by an enemy bishop), which the computer searches for and then takes into account in its analysis of chess positions.

It seems too early to assess the practicality and promise of the Zobrist–Carlson approach, but a program that combines pattern-recogni-tion capacities with the best features of more conventional procedures might be one that would produce chess of a distinctly higher quality than current programs. Quick perception of relevant patterns, plus limited but flexible concrete-move analysis, are characteristic of the thinking of a strong human chessplayer and therefore some combination of the two approaches appears to be a sensible goal for which to strive. As Simon and Chase [84] say, "the patterns that masters perceive will suggest good moves to them." At least, the pattern-recognition notion provides an alternative route for computer chess, and a relatively novel approach which is psychologically appealing has advantages over older, timeworn methods that appear to have reached a dead end.

Explicit instruction versus learning by rules and consequences. There are no current chess-computer programs that improve their play in a manner similar to the way in which a human being develops his chess skill. A program's performance may be changed for the better only by explicit modification of its instructions; the programmer usually makes a rather gross change in the machine's overall evaluation function if, for example, a series of losses indicate that it has a certain weakness. A human being, on the other hand, gains proficiency at chess not only by acquiring knowl-edge of new general principles and specific maneuvers from books or instructors, but also by receiving feedback (often immediate!) about the strength or weakness of particular moves or plans that he adopts in actual games.

The machinery of the human being is arranged so that he can profit directly from the consequences of his actions. Good chess ideas frequently lead to quick victory, bad blunders to rapid defeat. In contrast, unless the programmer can intervene after each game or move to make precise changes in the computer program, the computer will continue to commit the same blunder whenever the identical position or very similar positions arise; the computer does not "learn" from its own experience and practice, but only via mediation of the programming team's experience and practice. Correction of the program so that it will stop making certain major errors is often not a very simple task; and when the mistakes are more subtle, as in high-level chess, "correction" becomes extremely difficult, since the errors are likely to consist of a series of moves (a plan) rather than a single move.

Because the human being's play is constantly being subtly shaped by its consequences, he soon learns which types of positional features, patterns, and tactical devices are likely to be significant in certain types of positions and which are likely to be ineffective or disastrous. He plays thousands of actual games and studies in privacy numerous annotated games of masters and his own past encounters. As a result, the human's ability to vary his plans depending on specific arrangements of the chess pieces often becomes extremely refined—even though he may not be able to verbalize very well the exact reasons for his decisions. Church suggests that this is probably analogous to the problem that excellent speakers and writers of English have in describing grammatical rules. In both English and chess it is much harder to articulate specific rules than to find a reasonable way to deal with a particular situation. By the application of explicit general principles or rules acquired from books and tutors, and by prolonged exposure to the selective effects of his own successes and failures, a human can eventually "learn" to play chess very well. An expert continues to polish his game, not through learning any new rules or principles (all of which he knows by then), but by analyzing his own and other games to determine the contexts in which these general rules can be broken or rearranged in priority.

The general difference between computer and man in "learning capacity" is perhaps the hardest of all for computer programmers to take into account. Conceivably, one or two masters could be more or less permanently assigned to a chess-computer project, to play numerous games against it or watch it play against itself and other programs. They could tell the programmer whenever particularly weak or strong moves occur. The effort involved would probably have to be tremendous, however, since a very large number of games would have to be deeply analyzed for significant progress to occur. Besides, the masters could not easily communicate to the programmer exactly what the nature of certain problems is and what to do about them; and the programmer might not be able to easily implement many suggestions even if he basically understood their nature and potential generality. Then, too, the closer the computer came to playing expert-level chess, the more difficult the interaction among programmers, masters, and the machine would become. Introduction of a subtle change in the program's instructions might produce new weaknesses that would have to be corrected.

Chess programmers have certainly considered the possibility of self-learning or advice-taking machines. A. L. Samuels designed a successful program that improved at checkers (draughts) by playing a large number of games and "learning" from its own mistakes; as a result of positive and negative outcomes, it corrected its own evaluation function. However, when Euwe's Euratom Committee [37] explored the possibility of applying Samuels's techniques and reasoning to chess, they soon came to the sad conclusion that a similar approach to chess "would have to deal not with 31 component numbers but with 31 million or even more," which meant the whole method was impossible to apply to chess.

An expert problem solver must be a very efficient learner and perceiver. He has to detect the important similarities and differences residing in a variety of complex examples and to utilize this information appropriately in his actions. There are no machines currently available that "learn" how to perform subtle and complex tasks; they only follow the explicit instructions of a human being who has already worked out the important factors to be taken into account. The human's ability to learn from experience is so well developed that his best accomplishments on inexact tasks leave a computer far behind. I agree with de Groot's comment that "incorporating experience into the program, in one form or another, is not only indispensable but is the very core of the simulation problem," whether one is involved with expert-level thinking in chess or in some other field.

The "evaluation functions" of man versus machine. Because the weights assigned to various factors in a chess-computer program usually change very little depending on the actual position, the program tends to overvalue certain factors and undervalue others. Consequently, the machine suffers from certain weaknesses in its chessplay. Most of the specific shortcomings listed below seem more "correctable" than the chess computer's overall deficiencies summarized above.

Computer chessplayers are generally *too materialistic*; the game presented in Figure 8.1 is an extreme example of this defect. The weights assigned to "material advantage" are relatively so high that, unless its opening library includes instructions not to do so, a machine will generally accept all gambits (opening sacrifices of a piece or pawn for unclear compensation in the form of time or mobility gain). As chessplayers may say about a greedy opponent, the computer usually "takes everything that isn't nailed down." In contrast, masters often disdain capture of material if they foresee that it will place them on the defensive, or create weaknesses in their position, or cause them to lose time—even if the opponent's compensation for the material loss is not clearcut.

Along the same lines, a machine would not be likely to offer "dynamic" sacrifices of material based on unclear compensation (a possible exception is the knight sacrifice played by CHAOS vs. CHESS 4.0 in the 1974 World Computer Championship; I do not know whether CHAOS' actual analysis has ever been examined in detail to determine why it sacrificed the knight). Sacrifice of a Black rook for White's queen's knight in the Dragon Variation of the Sicilian Defense [68] is a key idea guiding Black's play in that opening, but the sacrifice would not be considered by a computer unless its opening library extended far enough to include such moves (and, if it did, the program would have to "understand" the strategic goals of the sacrifice in order to follow it up correctly when both players were subsequently "out of the book"). Furthermore, a master might pass up an opportunity to regain previously sacrificed material if he thought it would relieve the pressure on his opponent, whereas a chess computer would probably seek to re-establish material balance at its first chance.

Most computer programs consider a fairly limited number of goals and factors in their evaluation functions; they are often *too directed*. Presumably, new factors could easily be added, perhaps in consultation with expert or master players; but the relative weights to be assigned these added factors would be difficult even for a grandmaster to assess. The grandmaster knows that the relative weights of different factors depend on the particular organization of the position, but the nature of these dependencies is hard to communicate to other chessplayers or programmers. Incidentally, masters are almost always excited to discover a move that has several worthwhile functions. You almost "know it's the best move" if it simultaneously performs at least three very valuable functions.

Skilled chessplayers strive to maximize their options, and frequently maintain tension through avoidance of piece exchanges. Computer programs, on the other hand, are *avid exchangers of pieces*, a strategy which often dissipates any existing tension on the board. In its eagerness to exchange pieces, the chess computer often fails to retain valuable opportunities for future action. Furthermore, exchanging pieces when an opponent is cramped may reduce or eliminate any advantage the machine has.

The machine's bias toward exchanging pieces is brought about, at least partially, by the necessary incorporation of steps within the program to prevent a premature evaluation that the position is "quiet." In computer chess, one of the simplest methods of transforming a complex position (with several captures possible) into a quiescent position is by exchanging some or all of the "offending" pieces. However, this course of action may release tension that might be favorable to retain.

It is somewhat paradoxical that computer programs exchange pieces so readily when they are admittedly *weak in the endgame*. Unfortunately, their main competition in recent years has been against fellow computers, in games that are usually decided before the endgame, or that finish with a ridiculously long battle in an endgame that an expert player could win in a few moves by pushing a passed pawn or invading the opponent's position with his king.

Computer chess programs are often *too aggressive*. They tend to make moves that attack their opponent's pieces without much regard for the permanent weaknesses these moves may create in their own positions. In contrast, a master would not make a move merely to threaten an advantageous piece exchange, if the opponent's piece could simply move away and the master's own pawn structure, for example, would be permanently weakened. Like computers, relatively weak human players typically commit this kind of error. An understanding of pawn play is one of the major factors separating master and average players, and unfortunately most computer-chess programmers fail to appreciate the subtleties involved (see, e.g., some of Newborn's naive comments about pawn formations in the opening and pawn play in the endgame in [73]).

Although they will not commit serious blunders, machines *rarely are able to produce constructive moves* in positions in which direct threats and tactical possibilities are absent. In such positions, a strong chessplayer will attempt to reinforce or eliminate his own weak points, and to take aim at his opponent's; long-range planning is the predominant theme, rather than direct attack. The delicate maneuvers that develop—the "tacking" for small advantages—may seem boring to the uninitiated but are a major aspect of competition between strong human chessplayers.

How to beat a chess computer

As a former chess coach, I have a few words of practical advice for below-expert chessplaying readers who may soon have to face a computer program in a regular tournament. The following tips may also serve to summarize the computer's weaknesses.

First of all, there is no reason to be afraid. Even though the computer console may occasionally light up like a Christmas tree and emit some strange sounds, it does not have a brain as good as yours. As long as you have played in a few tournaments and hold at least a Class C rating, you ought to feel very confident. Even if your rating is approximately equal to that of the machine, that is, 1400–1600, do not forget that you can take advantage of the computer's weaknesses once you are aware of them, whereas the machine does not have the advantage of knowing your particular weaknesses beforehand.

Play positionally and avoid tactical scrambles in which you might commit a bad mistake; once considerably behind in material, you will have little chance for a swindle—unlike against human opponents—because the machine will not get overconfident, inattentive, tired, or hungry and make an outright blunder by rushing things. And when ahead it will trade off pieces, in order to increase its relative numerical advantage (a good point to remember, since trades might help you in some losing or cramped positions).

Examine carefully all checks and captures that the machine can conceivably make in the next two or three moves, since the machine will be concentrating on such possibilities. The machine will probably search for ways of attacking your major pieces with its pawns, so consider placing a major piece on a square where the machine's ensuing attacks will only leave it with a weakened pawn structure after you retreat your piece.

"Solid positional play" on your part would be a good policy. This strategy would involve attempts to eliminate weaknesses in your position and to direct your forces toward any weak points in your opponent's pawn structure, particularly near its castled king. Wherever possible, you ought to formulate long-range plans and *gradually* concentrate your pieces toward the achievement of those aims. Take advantage of the horizon effect by developing your threats slowly and making them as subtle as possible. If you see a combination 6 or 7 half-moves (ply) deep, examine it very carefully even if there is a "way out" early in the sequence. The machine may enter the main line and not realize until too late that it's been tricked into the loss of a piece.

Positional sacrifices on your part—for example, offers of a pawn or the exchange to weaken your opponent's kingside, to gain time, or to force your opponent's pieces on to poor squares—are worth strong consideration, even if your opponent's best reply would be to decline them. The machine will almost surely accept the sacrifice and you will be on your way! Conversely, do not worry unduly about speculative sacrifices on your opponent's part; there is little chance the machine will sacrifice a pawn or piece for anything less than a forced checkmate or gain of material.

Play for the endgame. It might be worthwhile for you beforehand to study various types of endings, in order to decide which kind you feel most at home in. Then you could aim for this kind of endgame via appropriate exchanges (as you recall, the machine will readily submit to equal trades of material). Enter the endgame without fear even if you are not a Capablanca, Fischer, or Karpov and even if you have the inferior position. All of today's computer programs are ignorant of niceties concerning the most suitable times and positions to push passed pawns, activate kings, and so forth. In the endgame your chances of outplaying the computer are probably greater than at any other stage of the game.

If you have considerable time to prepare beforehand, and do not care how low you must stoop in order to win a game, inspect standard opening texts like *Modern Chess Openings* for instances of the numerous technical and typographical errors that appear there. Then try to maneuver the machine into one of these unsound variations. The computer's opening library is usually copied from such compendiums and the programmer cannot possibly check every line for accuracy.

For further reassurance you might read Fritz Leiber's story about a computer chessplayer, "The 64-Square Madhouse" [66]. One human grandmaster took direct advantage of the machine's limited horizon to score a victory over it, and another grandmaster found an editorial error in *Modern Chess Openings* that he figured would automatically be placed in the machine's opening library. He was right and he also defeated the computer, which was of master strength (its strength may be the reason why Leiber's story is classified as "science fiction"). At least, unlike the human winners in Lieber's tale, you will not be playing against such a powerful opponent.

Computer chess: Omens, prospects, and values

Chess is often described as the *Drosophila* of the field of artificial intelligence. Use of the *drosophila* (fruit fly) as a model organism enabled geneticists to make important discoveries about the mechanisms of hereditary transmission. By analogy, a number of computer scientists who attempt to model human perception, learning, and problem solving believe that chess is of equivalent importance in their own field.

The theme of this chapter, as well as several other contributions to the present book, is much more conservative. I think that the value of chess as an object for computer simulation of thought processes has not yet been clearly demonstrated. Work on computerized chess has not advanced much in ten years, if we measure its progress in terms of the playing strength of the programs it has created. Hunt's recent comment [56] that an attack on unsolved problems in mathematics, statistics, logic, and psychology "is of more value than studies of the latest robots or machine chessplayers" reflects my own opinion, too.

The field of computer chess continues to be of potential value, however, and therefore it seems to merit moderate support in the future. But I think that its support should be mainly based on evidence of solid achievements and novel implications for our understanding of human memory and thought, or on its contributions to mathematical or computer-programming methodology and theory. If such goals were paramount—instead of annual attempts to win the world computer championship, or at least to do better than last year—then work on the topic would be more likely to proceed in collaboration with logicians, mathematicians, psychologists, and chessmasters, and not be conducted by solitary teams that emphasize the technological and competitive aspects of computer chess. The overall goals would shift from attempts to create a grandmaster computer, and thereby to win a bet with some unimpressed international master, to serious interdisciplinary research aimed at discovering practically and theoretically useful facts about human behavior and other topics that transcend the specific area of chess.

In the event of such a shift in emphases, "secrets" would be minimized, relevant knowledge and experimental results would be more available to all those interested, and progress in designing a strong chess program (as primarily a test of the maturity and power of developing theories) might be much faster than in the past. Furthermore, as noted earlier, the outcomes of such work might have important practical applications in various settings, not only in terms of machines developed to replace human decision makers but, perhaps more important, in terms of new technologies designed to teach human children and adults how to go about solving relatively complex problems.

Therefore, I add a qualified "yes" to the votes of those who think computer simulation of chess, and research related to this topic, are worth investment of some of our time, money, and effort—provided the work is based mainly on cooperative and conservative, rather than competitive, goals. de Groot [31] is apparently of the same opinion: "Creating a master —the original ideal—would in fact require too large a specific investment, if such a creation is possible at all."

Chess competition is fun. I participated in numerous tournaments for more than 20 years and realize that few things are as rewarding as a well-deserved victory against a strong opponent. Nevertheless, I do not believe that governmental and academic departments should support projects that seem to have the winning of computer championships as a major goal. Such projects might be more appropriately sponsored by sports associations or commercial firms. However, if some eccentric billionaire chess fan were to establish a Center for Championship Computer Chess and to supply it with unlimited funds for purchasing the latest and biggest computers and for hiring the most qualified and dedicated personnel, I would be tempted to accept an invitation to join the group—despite my own 10-year absence from the chess wars and my current strong interests in other fields. This confession will probably horrify my professional colleagues and family, but I suppose one never loses the chess "bug." However, after sober reflection, I think I would resist the temptation and continue with my current research on learning processes in pigeons, rats, and humans. Who knows which road will be most profitable in terms of our eventual understanding of human thinking?

Concluding comments

A computer chessmaster or expert is not likely to emerge in the near future.[1] Technological improvements in memory size or speed of calculation of computers probably will not help very much toward achievement of this goal and I have questioned whether such a goal is really a worthy one, anyway. Nevertheless, work will undoubtedly continue on the topic and there are several possible directions that seem potentially more valuable than others. Attempts to introduce structures or patterns into the computer's chess memory and evaluation processes, and attempts to transfer information gained on prior moves for use in subsequent analysis, seem intuitively worthwhile; the thinking of the superior human chessplayer is clearly based on recognition and discrimination of complex patterns and on information and long-range plans evaluated or formulated on previous

---

[1] The five victories scored by CHESS 4.5 against Class B human players at the Paul Masson Tournament in 1976, a year after this chapter was written, are impressive— even though its opponents played poorly and did not follow the strategies recommended above with regard to "How to Beat a Chess Computer"! The machine made no bad mistakes and took advantage of its opponents' many errors; even if we consider this program to have achieved a class B level, it still falls short of expert or master strength.

moves. The assistance of several collaborating chessmasters, to help pinpoint definite weaknesses in a machine's play, would be useful in developing its "self-learning" and "advice-taking" capacities. However, most computer scientists believe that approaches of these kinds are difficult if not impossible to implement effectively with today's computer technology, even though they would probably agree about the desirability of the approaches. But, in view of such pessimism, perhaps these workers ought to lower their sights regarding the playing strength of the chess programs they can produce.

When a laboratory scientist undertakes to study some complex phenomenon or process, he usually begins his research by employing the simplest example of the phenomenon or process that he can find. Those who attempt to develop a computer program that plays entire games of good chess are struggling with an extremely complicated task. An alternative would be first to program a computer that plays simple endgames well and then gradually to work up to more and more complex positions—and not to proceed from one step to a more difficult one until the program can hold its own at the current task with an expert chessplayer. Many experienced chess teachers ask young players to study the endgame first and perhaps we ought to treat the machine more as we do a human. Furthermore, I see few reasons—besides opportunistic, practical ones dictated by the competitive goals of present-day computer chess—to place extensive opening libraries in chess computer programs. A program that could produce decent opening moves "on its own," by following certain general principles of opening play, would be quite an accomplishment—as opposed to current programs that merely regurgitate pages of *Modern Chess Openings.* Lessons learned by programmers in producing a computer chessplayer that could play openings and endings with some proficiency might generate valuable new ideas permitting smoother extension of the program's capacities to the more complex problems posed in the middlegame. In other words, perhaps the time has not yet come to ask a computer to play a full game of good chess. It is not so dramatic to create computers that are mere opening or endgame experts, but in the long run such a course may be more profitable for computer chess than programming a computer to play a complete but poor game.

Despite the past lack of achievement of computer-chess programs, and the reluctance of many overly optimistic workers in the field to accept or confront the problems pointed out in this and other chapters of the present book, a reasonable person would be foolish to state categorically that a computer will *never* compete equally with human masters in chess. Extensions, revisions, or novel additions to current chess programs could conceivably bridge the gap. What would happen to the popularity of the Royal Game if and when computers are able to hold their own with Karpov and Fischer or with the great-grandchildren of these champions? Would chess as a profession be threatened and would masters unite in attempts to vandalize or ban their mechanical counterparts—as certain groups of workers sought to do when they were replaced by machines in the past?

Some writers, perhaps with tongue in cheek, have predicted ugly consequences of this kind if computer chessmasters become a reality. However, I see no reason why the game should ever lose its popularity among human beings. Checkers is still popular today, even though computers play that game very well. Throughout history man has been challenged by difficult intellectual problems even when the solution is available (and can be looked up in the next issue or on the back page). Spectators would still enjoy watching human master tournaments more than computer–master chess events. Human contests would be much more difficult to forecast, and unpredictability generally breeds sporting interest.

Enough of fantasy. If the opinion expressed in this chapter is correct—that the prospects of an expert or master chessplayer are dim unless breakthroughs first occur in our understanding of the operation of the human brain and its relationship to principles of human behavior, and unless we can "train" chessmasters to articulate more explicitly the reasons for their moves—then we are left with a somewhat ironic conclusion. Back in the eighteenth and nineteenth centuries, exhibitions of Kempelen's and Maelzel's chess automata [19] were huge commercial successes and stimulated many authors and technologists to speculate about the relationships between man and machine. Of course, a human being who played expert chess was cleverly concealed inside each of these machines. The automaton's "intelligence" came from its human director; and, similarly, a recent critique [69] of artificial-intelligence research concluded that whatever "intelligence" exists in computer chess is human. Perhaps our chances of success in producing a computer chessmaster in the twentieth or twenty-first century depend on how much more "man" we can put back into the machine—but this time in psychological rather than physical form.

Belle

J. H. Condon and Ken Thompson

Bell Laboratories

9

Introduction

The development of chess programming during the 1970s can be viewed as an intellectual battle between proponents of a highly selective search and advocates of a brute-force, full-width search. The annual ACM tournaments consistently demonstrated that the full-width search not only played better chess, but demonstrated discernible progress from one year to the next. Initially, many observers proposed that these gains were temporary and that this strategy would rapidly approach a ceiling beyond which only minimal improvements could be observed. These predictions have not been substantiated by the course of events. Newborn [155] has even proposed that there is a simple linear relationship between depth of search and USCF rating. He proposes that high level chess can be achieved by making technical refinements which increase the number of positions evaluated per second. Belle plays a pivotal role in this controversy since this program, more than any other, represents the application of the leading edge of computer technology in the service of a brute-force, full-width search.

Background

Belle's historical beginnings date back to 1972. This was a time of importance to serious chess fans. Bobby Fischer's success in the widely publicized world championship candidate's matches had given chess a level of visibility never before achieved in the United States. In addition, the chess program devised by Richard Greenblatt at MIT [48] provided encouragement that machine chess of reasonable caliber was, in fact, feasible. During the summer of 1972, one of us (KT) wrote a chess program for the PDP-11.

This program played in the 1972 New Jersey Open and also in the 1973 ACM Computer Chess Championship. The New Jersey Open was a positive experience because most of the program's opponents were unrated players brought into the chess camp by Fischer's newly found prominence. Belle's performance in the ACM tournament displayed the usual bugs that show up the first time that computer meets computer. Even so, it finished with an even score.

During the next year, Belle was debugged and improved. It played a dozen or so USCF games and earned a rating which wavered about the 1300 mark. It was entered in the 1974 ACM Computer Chess Championships. There it achieved a very lucky 3–1 result.

These early observations of the ACM championships and human tournaments convinced us that a full-width search produced the best chess play, and within this framework, the largest computer will usually win. The all-software version of Belle retired to the ignoble position of /usr/games/chess on distributed UNIX machines.

Chess-specific hardware

In 1976, one of us (JHC) designed and built a small hardware move generator that was attached as a peripheral to a PDP-11. The chess program was completely rewritten in the image of Chess 4.X—the Northwestern program. The key attributes which seem to characterize this Northwestern "clone" are a) a full-width fixed-depth iterative search which incorporates a move-vs-evaluation quiescence search, b) a sophisticated static evaluation function involving a dozen or more positional terms but dominated by material considerations, and c) a large transposition table that discourages reanalysis of the same position. In addition to Belle, Duchess, Cray Blitz, and many of the commercial chess machines have adopted this general strategy.

The evolution of Belle's hardware was based on this first device. Let us take time out to describe this early move generator to help the reader understand the evolution (see Fig. 9.1).

The *from* register is an incrementing 6-bit register. It starts with a value of zero and then increments through the chess board looking for a friendly piece. The Δxy field of the micro-code contains a potential move offset for the friendly piece. For example, Δxy would have 1,1, 2,2, etc., for a bishop ray. The *from* register contents and the Δxy field are two-dimensionally added to yield a 6-bit *to* signal. The *from* and *to* signals addresses the board RAM that holds the individual pieces on the chess board. The chess piece located at *to*, the overflow from the adder, and an *opcode* field from the microcode all go into a test circuit that produces a condition code if the potential move meets the condition desired. If the potential move is pseudo-legal, then *from* and *to* fields are made available to the PDP-11.

micro instruction

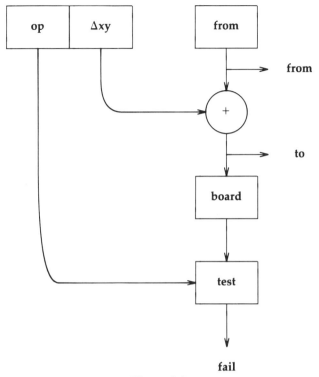

Figure 9.1

Pseudo-legal moves are legal moves if the side moving is not in check. The machine has a special *attack* operation. The position of the attacked square (friendly king) is loaded into the *from* register. The move generator is run as though a *super piece* (union of all pieces) existed on this square. The test circuit is conditioned to match enemy pieces according to the patterns shown in Fig. 9.2.

If the move generator finds no matches, then the pseudo-legal move is in fact legal. The board RAM can be updated and the whole process starts over for the other side.

This first machine left most of the work of the Northwestern clone up to the PDP-11. In fact, the communication between the chess machine and the PDP-11 was so cumbersome that the combination was probably slower than if the PDP-11 had done the whole job.

This hardware/software combination competed in the 1977 World Computer Chess Championships held in Toronto. This tournament was the first of the huge main-frame tournaments. It was estimated that the 16 contestants used computers with a combined cost of $40 million, which would rent for $10 thousand per hour.

Belle fought for last place with Ostrich in computing power and fin-

	QB			QR			QB	
		QB	N	QR	N	QB		
		N	KQBP	KQR	KQBP	N		
	QR	QR	KQR	*from*	KQR	QR	QR	
		N	KQBP	KQR	KQBP	N		
		QB	N	QR	N	QB		
	QB			QR			QB	

Figure 9.2

ished in a tie for fourth place with Chaos. This is attributed more to the cloning than to the hardware. This machine never played in USCF rated events.

Second generation

The deficiencies of the first machine were easy to spot. The machine required too much attention from the PDP-11. It could not perform any evaluation functions, nor did it have a transposition memory. We started work on the next machine which incorporated several important refinements. The move generator stored its moves on an internal stack rather than reporting them to the PDP-11. In addition, two new devices were added which ran in parallel with the move generator. One was a static position evaluator, and the other a transposition memory. The two additional machines followed the changes to the current position produced by the move generator and performed their calculations in parallel on their local copy of the board. The PDP-11 now requested move generation, move making, and move unmaking from the move generator, position evaluation from the evaluator, and position match and store from the transposition device. The PDP-11 was still responsible for the α–β algorithm and the proper coordination of the three devices. The combination could perform searches at the rate of 5000 nodes per second, but the PDP-11 was still a limitation to even faster performance.

The second machine first entered the 1978 ACM Computer Chess Championships. It played and beat all of the strongest competition, winning the tournament 4–0. Moreover, it beat Chess 4.7 1½–½ at speed chess and played "the most beautiful computer chess game yet," mating Blitz in 14 moves.

This performance was mostly lucky. In the next year, this version of Belle played 29 USCF rated games and obtained an official 1884 rating. This was consistently 150 points less than Chess 4.9 during the same period. The day of reckoning came at the 1979 ACM tournament where Belle drew both Chess 4.9 and Chaos to place second. This was a fairer representation of Belle's strength at that time.

The major flaw with the second machine was its inability to order the legal moves. It could only generate moves in *from* square order. This was so intolerably slow for the α–β algorithm that the software generated all of the legal moves five times in each position and selected the moves in five sorted subsets: a) principle variation move, b) favorable captures, c) killer moves, d) unfavorable captures, e) all other moves.

The second machine is now semiretired. It is housed with its own LSI-11 computer and a tuned-coil sensed-response board.

Third generation

Now we come to the current Belle. The authors designed new hardware in the spring of 1980. The goal was a new machine that would execute an order of magnitude faster to be ready for the 1980 World Computer Chess Championship in the fall.

The overall structure would remain. There would be a move generator, an evaluator, a transposition memory, and an α–β search machine, this time in hardware.

The new move generator consists of 64 transmitter circuits and 64 receiver circuits; one each for each chess square (see Fig. 9.3).

The transmitter knows what piece resides on the square and activates its corresponding leads. The receiver sees all attacks on its square. The receiver therefore detects that a pseudo-legal move exists. There is a priority network connected to all receiver circuits which selects the highest valued attacked enemy piece. This is the familiar *to* square, but in this case, it is located in one cycle.

In the next cycle, the *from* square is located analogously to the *attack* function of the first hardware. The transmitter of the *to* cell is energized as though the *super piece* resided there. The receiver circuits then compete

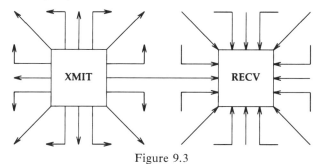

Figure 9.3

205

on the same priority network to yield the *from* location. There is a one-bit disable memory on each square to prevent a move from being found a second time. The move generator also has extra circuitry to detect castling and *en passant*.

The evaluation function is a similar set of 64 circuits. Each circuit is one stage of a finite-state machine. The value passed from stage to stage is a machine state that has the ability to detect pins, discoveries, attacks, defenses, and other things in the general realm of square control. The evaluation machine has a summing tree to report the evaluation into the final accumulator. The accumulation takes 8 cycles. On each cycle the squares of the evaluator are lined up in a different compass direction. After the 8 cycles, all rays in all directions have been evaluated.

A second part of the evaluator machine uses the 8 cycles to scan the pawn structure, 3 files at a time, left to right over the chess board. This section detects passed pawns, blocked pawns, backward pawns, isolated pawns, open files, and half open files.

There is also a static part to the evaluation machine. This machine tracks the board changes and incrementally modifies an evaluation based on these changes. The major evaluation here is material, but other factors such as king safety are also included. This value, since it is immediately available, is used as a fast approximate evaluation for possible quick cut-offs.

The transposition memory consists of 1 megabyte of commercial memory. The memory is organized into 128 K positions of 8 bytes each. The transposition machine maintains incrementally a 48-bit hash code of the current chess position. 16 bits of the hash code plus SIDE-TO-MOVE are used to access an 8-byte position in the memory. The remaining 32 bits of the hash code are stored in 4 bytes of the position to reduce the possibility of collision. False matches are still possible, but have been calculated to occur only every 30 days of computing time. In practice we have detected no anomaly that could be traced to a false match.

The remaining 4 bytes of the position are used to store a value (2 bytes), a flag (1 byte) and a depth (1 byte). There are flags that variously mean a) the value is exact, b) the value is an upper bound, c) the value is a lower bound, d) the position is hierarchally active and should be scored a draw, and e) the position is not applicable.

The memory data path is 16 bits wide. It therefore takes 4 full cycles to store a position. This is one of the major bottlenecks of the whole machine. It only takes 1 cycle to attempt a match since there is usually a failure on the first hash code word.

Lastly, there is the $\alpha-\beta$ machine. This is a 64-bit-wide horizontal micro-code machine. The cycle time is adjustable on a per-cycle basis from 100 to 800 ns. The microcode controls the move generator, evaluator, and transposition machines.

The $\alpha-\beta$ machine is built around a stack pointer that corresponds to the ply depth of search. All data is stored on stacks addressed by the stack pointer. The actual architecture of the machine is not remarkable (Fig. 9.4).

The chess machine is housed in a box containing an LSI-11 general purpose computer and a 30 megabyte Winchester disk. The whole machine executes a tree search at between 100,000 and 200,000 positions per second. The smaller number comes from endgame positions that are dominated by transposition matches. The larger number comes from tactical searches dominated by quiescence search. In middlegame positions, the machine can usually perform 8-ply searches. In the endgame, the depth increases to 10 or 12 ply. Occasionally with locked pawn endgames, the transposition memory allows searches as high as 20 or 30 ply.

Belle executed its first legal move on July 20, 1980. It played its first game (against its predecessor) on August 1. Its fifth game, and first human opponent, was the celebrated "Turing test" in a simultaneous exhibition against the West German Grandmaster Pfleger. Since then, Belle has entered and won the 1980 World Computer Chess Championship and the 1980 and 1981 ACM Computer Chess Championships. It has played 63 rated games. Its performance rating for these games is 2180. Its current official rating is 2168.

Figure 9.4

The book

In the box scores of computer chess programs, there is usually the entry *size of opening book*. Belle stands out by having a book that is approximately two orders of magnitude larger than other programs.

The size of the book (about 360,000 positions and growing) is misleading. It is a comprehensive book containing all openings. Clearly most of the book is not relevant to play. For example, the King's Indian is not important if Belle plays 1 e4 with White and replies to 1. d5 with 1. . . . d4 with Black. Yet the book contains all the latest main variations of the King's Indian defense.

The relationship between useful book to all book is the same relationship as full minimax to best-ordered α–β pruning. Thus Belle's useful book is approximately the square root of the size of its full book.

Why so much book? The answer is not clear. Part of the answer is a desire for Belle to be able to select its own openings from the set of all openings. It is also nice to be able to play an opponent with his favorite opening or to play a simultaneous exhibition with a wide variety of openings. Part of the answer is the busy-work, bug-collecting aspects of compiling and entering the book. In any case, the maintenance of such a data base is a subject in itself.

The book is converted into positions totally independent of moves. Each position is accessed from disk by an extensible hashing scheme. A 32-bit hash code is generated for the position. Just enough of the hash code is revealed (by ANDing with a mask of the form 000 . . . 0011 . . . 111) to allow a single disk access to the block containing the position. The amount of hash code needed is obtained by consulting an in-core tree of bits describing which blocks have been filled and have required splitting, thus revealing one more hash code bit. The chess position, an evaluation, and back references to the book source are stored at the hash address.

The book positions are initialized with evaluations marked "unknown." Some positions (usually at the end of lines) are marked with grandmaster evaluations. The program that maintains the book spans the positions by generating all legal moves from one position and hashing to see if the resulting positions are in the book. This way transpositions are automatically eliminated. Starting at the root the whole book is mini-maxed by spanning moves to the evaluated positions. It takes three weeks of disk seek time to mini-max the entire book.

To add more lines to the book, it is necessary to trace newly added positions back to the root by spanning positions with un-moves and mark these positions "unknown." The normal mini-max then applied to the root will reevaluate all of these positions in light of the newly added lines. This is harder than it sounds because of the complexity of the un-move generator. There are approximately six times as many un-moves in a position as there are moves because of the captures. The real treats are un-promotion, un-castle and un-*en passant*.

Belle does not do well competitively with its huge book. It tends to play everyone's favorite line without ever developing a favorite line of its own. The evaluations in the book are also very hard to verify. Belle has lost about five tournament games by playing into bad openings while it has only won a single game by playing an opening "trap" that it would not have calculated itself.

An experiment

The success of Belle in tournament competition seems to provide evidence that the full-width search strategy produces increasingly better performance as the depth of search increases. We conducted an experiment to examine this idea more systematically.

We define 6 programs named P4, P5, . . . P9. P4 searches the standard (Chess 4.X clone) four plies and then enters a quiescence capture search with full evaluation at the leaves. (Getting out of check does not count as a ply.) P5, P6 . . . are identical programs that search progressively deeper.

The programs were entered into a 20-fold round-robin tournament. Each program played both sides of 10 randomly selected starting opening positions. The positions were chosen by a random number generator selecting positions from *Encyclopedia of Chess Openings* that had 10 moves played by each side and were judged (by mini-max) to be "equal" or "unclear" or "with compensation." Altogether 300 games were played.

The performance rating of each program was determined (on an arbitrary base) by calculating what rating a program needed to expect the performance actually obtained. The performance ratings were then iterated until they converged to one rating point for all programs (Fig. 9.5).

Newborn [155] has suggested that if you double the speed of a brute force program, you will gain 100 rating points. If you assume a 5.5 branching factor, then a ply will yield 250 points. In the linear range of P4–P6 (the range observed by Newborn in existing programs) this relation holds.

In the extended range of this experiment, ratings do not grow as fast as predicted. Any major conclusions about the experiment we leave up to the reader. Here are some of our observations that may be of help.

1. The ratings picked for the basis of the experiment are close to the ratings that Belle obtains against human opponents at the respective

perf	P4	P5	P6	P7	P8	P9
P4 1235	—	5	½	0	0	0
P5 1570	15	—	3½	3	½	0
P6 1826	19½	16½	—	4	1½	1½
P7 2031	20	17	16	—	5	4
P8 2208	20	19½	18½	15	—	5½
P9 2328	20	20	18½	16	14½	—

Figure 9.5

depth settings. This indicates that the standard deviation of human/ computer play is approximately the same as computer/computer play and therefore the results of the experiment are meaningful.

2. The programs do not have a *contempt* factor. This means that if P9 thinks it is down a fraction of a pawn in evaluation, it will attempt to draw with P4. The results show that P9 has a higher rating against P8 than against P7, etc.

3. The evaluation function for each program in the experiment is the same. In the evolution of a program, the evaluation function would evolve to the strength of the program. Belle's evaluation function contains the elements of a 1600 player. It knows much about king safety and pawn formations, while it knows little about weak square complexes and piece cooperation. Clearly, P8 and P9 would benefit from a more sophisticated evaluation function. Such a function would be wasted on P5 and P6.

Conclusion

Belle's very fiber is built around brute force evaluation. Why? Another hard question. Each of us does what he knows how to do. We have made the fastest brute force machine available because we possessed the talent and resources to do so. This is not to say that we are wed to the idea of brute force. We have spent a tremendous amount of time examining alternatives. Every attempt to build a truly selective program fails. Our attempts at selective programs are able to brilliantly solve selected tactical positions, but they are unable to play a game without making horrible mistakes.

In a theoretical sense there is a strong case that brute force programs will keep getting stronger with time. Half of California is trying to generate enough computing power to give brute force programs an extra ply every five years. The extra computing power applied to selective programs will allow them to find tactical solutions to selected problems more quickly, but will it help them to play better chess?

Brute force or selective search? The answer probably lies somewhere between. Most major programs currently do some variable depth searching. Belle and Chess 4.9 do not count getting out of check as a ply. Nuchess does this and more. Yet, with enough extra computing power, these programs will search all positions deeper, no matter how unpromising. This attribute is necessary to guarantee stronger play with more computing power.

Forever is a long time. Brute force programs will surely become world champions. The only question is *when*. Our experiments suggest that it will be quite a long while. Selective search will always loom as a potentially faster road to high-level play. That road, however, requires an intellectual break-through rather than the simple application of known techniques.

Using chess knowledge to reduce search

David Wilkins
SRI International

10

Introduction

The current generation of computer chess programs select a move by exploring huge lookahead trees (millions of positions). Human masters, on the other hand, appear to use a knowledge-intensive approach to chess (see Chapter 2). They seem to have a huge number of stored "patterns," and analyzing a position involves matching these patterns to suggest plans for attack or defense. This analysis is verified and possibly corrected by a small search of the game tree (tens of positions). Since the best humans still play better chess than the best programs, it is reasonable to explore computer programming strategies for using chess knowledge rather than extensive searching. This chapter describes a program named PARADISE (PAttern Recognition Applied to DIrecting SEarch) which uses this approach in an attempt to find the best move in tactically sharp middle game positions from the games of chess masters.

One of the central concerns of the field of artificial intelligence is expressing knowledge and reasoning with it. Chess has been one of the most popular domains for artificial intelligence research, yet programs which emphasize search rather than knowledge play better chess than programs which emphasize chess knowledge. There is still much to be learned about expressing and using the kind of knowledge involved in playing chess. In Chapter 4 the authors of the Northwestern University chess program state that their program is "devoid of chess knowledge" not because they have deliberately traded it for speed of execution, but because "the programming tools we are presently using are not adequate to the task." PARADISE was developed to investigate the issues involved in expressing and using pattern-oriented knowledge to analyze a chess position, to provide direction for the search, and to communicate useful results from the search.

Part of this chapter appeared in *Artificial Intelligence,* 1980, **14,** 165–203, published by North-Holland.

PARADISE encodes a large body of knowledge in the form of production rules, which match patterns in the chess position and post concepts in the data base (this is discussed in more detail later). The program uses the knowledge base to discover plans during the static analysis of a position and to guide a small tree search that confirms that a particular plan is best. The search is "small" in the sense that the size of the search tree is of the same order of magnitude as a human master's search tree. Once a plan is formulated, it guides the tree search (which has no depth limit) for several ply and expensive static analyses are done infrequently.

To reduce the amount of knowledge that must be encapsulated, the domain of the program has been limited to tactically sharp middle game positions. The phrase "tactically sharp" is meant to imply that success can be judged by the gain of a material rather than a positional advantage. The complexity of the middle game requires extensive search, providing a good testing ground for attempts to replace search with knowledge and to use knowledge to guide the search and communicate discoveries from one part of the tree to another.

Because, in our chosen domain, the attacking side can generally win material with correct play, the program uses different models for the offensive and defensive players during its search of the game tree. The offensive player uses a large amount of knowledge, suggests many esoteric attacks, and invests much effort in making sure a plan is likely to work before suggesting it. The defensive player uses much less knowledge and effort, tries any defense that might possibly work, and tries only obvious counterattacks. Trying every reasonable defense enables the offense to satisfy itself that a line really does win. The size of the tree is kept small because the offensive player finds the best move immediately in most cases.

For a knowledge-based program to achieve master level performance, it seems necessary that the knowledge base be amenable to modifications and additions. PARADISE provides for easy modification of and addition to its knowledge base (without adversely affecting program performance), thus allownig the knowledge to be built up incrementally and tuned to eliminate errors. This is accomplished by having the knowledge base composed of largely independent production rules that are written in a straightforward language (Wilkins [171]).

The goal is to build an expert knowledge base and to reason with it to discover plans and verify them with a small tree search. As long as this goal is reached, the amount of execution time used is not important, so PARADISE sacrifices efficient execution in order to use knowledge whenever reasonable. When a desired level of performance is reached, the program could be speeded up considerably by switching to a more efficient representation at the cost of transparency and ease of modification.

Because it grows small trees, PARADISE can find deeper combinations than most chess programs. The position in Figure 10.1 is an example of such a combination from an actual master game. White can mate by sacrificing his queen and playing nine additional moves (against Black's

Figure 10.1 White to move. The deepest combination found by PARADISE.

line of longest resistance), the next to last move not being a check or capture. Thus the search tree must go at least 19 plies deep to find this combination. This is considerably deeper than any other current chess program could probe in a reasonable amount of time, but PARADISE solves this problem after generating a search tree of 109 nodes, in 20 minutes of CPU time on a DEC KL-10. (PARADISE is written in MACLISP.) The fact that PARADISE can accurately analyze all relevant lines in only 109 nodes shows that the program makes good use of its knowledge.

1.	Q–R5ch	N x Q
2.	P x Pch	K–N3
3.	B–B2ch	K–N4
4.	R–B5ch	K–N3
5.	R–B6ch	K–N4
6.	R–N6ch	K–R5
7.	R–K4ch	N–B5
8.	R x Nch	K–R4
9.	P–N3	any
10.	R–R4 mate	

Overview of PARADISE

At the top level, a best-first searching algorithm (which is briefly described later) is used to determine the best move and to control PARA-DISE's knowledge-based analysis (the major component of the program). The system uses a knowledge base consisting of about 200 production rules to find the best move in chess positions. Every production has a pattern (i.e., a complex, interrelated set of features) as its condition. Each production can be viewed as searching for all instances of its condition pattern in the position. For each instance found, the production may, as its action, post zero or more concepts in the data base for use by the system in its reasoning processes. A concept consists of a concept name, instantiations for a number of variables, and a list of reasons why the concept has been posted. The data base can be considered as a global blackboard where productions write information. The productions are built up by levels, with more primitive patterns (e.g., a pattern which matches legal moves) being used as building blocks for more complex patterns. PARADISE's static analysis process controls the use of these productions to suggest plans of action. The searching algorithm (the major component of most chess programs) is used to show that one plan suggested by the pattern-based analysis is in fact the best.

Figure 10.2 shows one of the simplest productions in PARADISE. It attempts to find an offensive plan that attacks a trapped defensive piece. The first three lines in Figure 10.2 constitute the pattern or condition of the production rule while the last two lines constitute the action. The first line specifies one variable that must be instantiated. Because of its name, the variable must be instantiated to a defensive piece that is not a pawn. The next two lines in the production access two more primitive patterns that have already been matched, MOBIL and ENPRIS. The MOBIL pattern matches each legal move that can be made without losing the moving piece. If there are no squares that match MOBIL when DMP1 is the first argument, then DMP1 is trapped. Only in this case will there be any possible instantiations for DMP1 after the second line is matched. The third line prevents the pattern from matching if the trapped piece is already *en prise* (in this case DMP1 should be captured outright rather than attacked).

The action of the production rule posts an ATTACK concept. This concept gives instantiations for two variables and tells the system that the opposite color of DMP1 would do well to attack the square that is DMP1's location. In addition one reason is given for suggesting this concept. This reason consists of attributes describing the threat of the concept and how likely it is to succeed. Concepts are discussed in more detail later. The more primitive patterns (such as MOBIL) and the language in which productions are written are described in detail elsewhere (Wilkins [171]).

To offset the expense of matching patterns, problems must be solved with small search trees. In fact, PARADISE can be viewed as shifting

```
((DMP1)
(NEVER (EXISTS (SQ) (PATTERN MOBIL DMP1 SQ)))
(NEVER (EXISTS (P1) (PATTERN ENPRIS P1 DMP1)))
(ACTION ATTACK ((OTHER-COLOR DMP1) (LOCATION
  (DMP1)) (THREAT (WIN DMP1)) (LIKELY 0))))
```

Figure 10.2   Production rule in PARADISE that recognizes trapped pieces.

some of its search from the usual chess game tree to the problem of matching patterns. PARADISE uses its pattern-oriented knowledge base in a variety of ways to significantly reduce the part of the game tree that needs to be searched. This reduction is large enough that a high level of expertise can be obtained using a large but still reasonable amount of resources. This reduction is also large enough that PARADISE avoids placing a depth limit (or any other artificial effort limit) on its search. The various ways in which the knowledge base is used are briefly mentioned below.

Calculating primitives. PARADISE's knowledge base contains about 20 patterns (productions without actions) that are primitives used to describe a chess position. These patterns are matched once for each position. They range from matching legal moves to matching patterns like MOBIL and ENPRIS. The primitives are relatively complex, and calculating them is expensive (Wilkins [171]).

Static analysis. Given a new position, PARADISE does an expensive in-depth static analysis which uses, on the average, 12 seconds of CPU time on a DEC KL-10. This analysis uses a large number of productions in the knowledge base to look for threats that may win material. It produces plans that should guide the search for several ply and should give information that can be used to stop the search at reasonable points.

Producing plans. The knowledge base is used to produce plans during static analysis and at other times. Through plans, PARADISE uses its knowledge to understand a new position created during the search on the basis of positions previously analyzed along that line of play, thus avoiding a static analysis. Plans guide the search, and a static analysis is only occasionally necessary in positions created during the search. Producing a plan is not as simple as suggesting a move; it involves generating a large amount of useful information to help avoid static analyses along many different lines and to help detect success or failure of the plan as it is executed. (Examples are given later.)

Executing plans. The execution of a plan during the tree search requires using the knowledge base to solve goals specified in the plan. This use of the knowledge base could be viewed as a static analysis where the system's attention is focused on a particular goal or aspect of the position. Such a focused analysis can be done at a fraction of the cost of a full analysis that examines all aspects of the position.

Generating defensive moves. PARADISE does static analyses and executes plans only for the offense (the side for which it is trying to win material). To prove that an offensive plan succeeds, the search must show a winning line for all reasonable (i.e., any move that might be effective) defensive moves. Productions in the knowledge base are used to generate all of the reasonable defenses.

Quiescence searches. When a node is a candidate for termination of the search, PARADISE uses a quiescence search to determine its value. This quiescence search may return information that will cause the termi-

215

nation decision to be revoked. Productions in the knowledge base provide much of the knowledge used in PARADISE's quiescence search. Quiescence searches in PARADISE investigate not only captures but forks, pins, multimove mating sequences, and other threats. Only one move is investigated at each node, except when a defensive move fails.

Analysis of problem upon failure. When either the defense or offense has tried a move that failed, the search analyzes the information backed up with the refutation in an attempt to solve the problem. The knowledge base is used in this analysis to suggest plans that thwart the opponent's refutation. In this way PARADISE constructs new plans using the information gained from searching an unsuccessful plan.

Answering questions. The search often requests certain kinds of information about the current position. The knowledge base is used to provide such information. The most frequent requests ask if the position is quiescent and if there are any obviously winning moves in the position.

The knowledge base performs the eight general functions described above. This paper explains how PARADISE produces plans and uses them to guide the search. The primitives, the production, and the static analysis are described in detail in Wilkins [171]). The tree search and mechanisms for communicating information from one part of the tree to another are discussed in Wilkins [173].

Concepts and knowledge sources

To understand a chess position, a successful line of play must be found. Human masters understand concepts that cover many ply in order to find the best move. A knowledge-based program must also have the ability to reason with concepts that are higher level than the legal moves in a chess position, e.g., the idea that a king position is weakly defended or that a pawn blockade prevents penetration by the opposing king. The system must combine and reason with these concepts in unforeseen ways, discovering an enormous number of lines using a set of productions that is much smaller in size (by an order of magnitude or more) than the number of plans it must recognize.

When a production in PARADISE matches, it may have an action part that posts various concepts in the data base. The program is able to express and use concepts by dividing its knowledge base into various *knowledge sources*. Each knowledge source (KS) provides the knowledge necessary to understand and reason about a certain abstract concept. In its simplest form, a KS is a group of productions that "knows about" some abstract concept, and a list of variables such that an instantiation of the variables represents a specific concept that corresponds to this abstract concept. For example, the production in Figure 10.2 posts an ATTACK concept that corresponds to the ATTACK KS. The ATTACK KS in PARADISE contains productions that know how to attack a particular square SQ for the side COL. With this KS, the system can use the abstract concept of attacking a square in its reasoning, in the expression of plans, and in the communication of discoveries from the tree search.

When a concept in the data base (described below) has a corresponding KS (i.e., they have the same name), it will sometimes be referred to as a *goal*. PARADISE will eventually use the corresponding KS to solve each goal in an attempt to produce a plan to realize that goal. (This may be done by creating other concepts.) There may also be concepts that have no corresponding KS and are not treated as goals. Such concepts are inspected by patterns attempting to match and by the searching routines.

Concepts are posted in the data base by the actions in production rules. KSes then use the information in these concepts as goals to eventually produce a plan of action. These concepts must contain all the information that will be needed to execute other KSes and to guide the search. Each KS expects a certain amount of information in a concept that it executes. (A concept is "executed" when it is used as a goal by its corresponding KS.) At the very least, a KS expects an instantiation of its arguments (such as COL and SQ in the ATTACK KS). The ATTACK KS also expects some information on what the intentions of COL are once SQ is attacked. This information is needed so that the reason for wanting to attack SQ will not be destroyed or negated by an attempt to attack. Among other things, KSes usually expect information on how likely a goal is to succeed and on how threatening a goal is (this is useful in deciding if a sacrifice is warranted).

PARADISE stores information about concepts as a list of attribute-value pairs. A particular concept is expressed by giving its name, an instantiation of its arguments, and a list of attribute-value pairs, called an *attribute list*. If a particular concept is suggested for more than one reason (e.g., if two different productions post an ATTACK concept for white to attack the square Q7), then this concept has a list of attribute lists, one for each reason the concept was suggested. When a production accesses the values of attributes, it may not care which attribute list (within a concept) the values come from, or it may require that the values for each attribute come from the same list, or it may want the "best" (in some sense) value for each attribute whether the different values come from the same list or not, or it may want values for one attribute to come from lists which have some particular value for another attribute. This accessing of the information in a concept is so complex that it can be looked on as pattern matching in itself. Thus the production in a KS can be looked upon as matching patterns in the given chess position and matching patterns in different concepts.

Concepts and their accessing are quite complex. Intuitively, the productions in PARADISE are not making deductions, per se, but coming up with ideas that may or may not be right. Thus there are no "facts" that have certain deduced values with which to reason. The complexity of later analysis requires that a production record "why" it thought of an idea.

In this way, other productions can decide if the idea still looks right in light of what is known at that time.

To summarize, KSes provide abstract concepts that are at a higher level than the productions themselves, and form the language in which PARADISE "thinks." Concepts and KSes are used in the static analysis reasoning process, to formulate plans for communicating knowledge down the tree, to quickly access relevant productions during execution of a plan, and to communicate discoveries made during the search.

Plans

The goal of the static analysis process in PARADISE is to produce plans. Plans seem to play an important role in the problem solving process of move selection for good human chess players. Alexander Kotov in his book *Think Like a Grandmaster* [60, p. 148] writes:

> . . . it is better to follow out a plan consistently even if it isn't the best one than to play without a plan at all. The worst thing is to wander about aimlessly.

Most computer chess programs certainly do not follow Kotov's advice. In a knowledge-based program, the cost of processing the knowledge should be offset by a significantly smaller branching factor in the tree search. Plans help reduce the cost of processing knowledge by immediately focusing the program's attention on the critical part of a new position created during the search, thus avoiding a complete reanalysis of this new position. Having plans also reduces the branching factor in the search by giving direction to the search. Consider, for example, that most programs may try the same poor move at every alternate depth in the tree, always rediscovering the same refutation. PARADISE can detect when a plan has been tried earlier along a line of play and avoid searching it again if nothing has changed to make it more attractive. Most programs also suffer because they intersperse moves that are irrelevant to each other and work towards different goals. PARADISE avoids this by following a single idea (its plan) down the tree.

Like a concept, each plan in PARADISE has a list of attribute lists. Instead of a list of instantiations for a set of variables (as in a concept), a plan has an expression in the *Plan-Language*. The Plan-Language expresses plans of action for the side about to move, called the offense. In general, the offense wants to have a reply ready for every defensive alternative. A plan cannot therefore be a linear sequence of goals or moves but must contain conditional branches depending on the opponent's reply. When the offense is on move, a specific move or goal is provided by the plan. When the defense is on move, a list of alternative subplans for the offense may be given. Each alternative begins with a template for matching the move made by the defense. Only alternatives whose template matches the move just made by the defense are tried in the search. Figure 10.3

(P SQ) matches when the defense has moved the piece P to the square SQ.

(NIL SQ) matches when the defense has moved any piece to SQ.

(P NIL) matches when the defense has moved P (to any square).

(ANYBUT P) matches when the defense has moved some piece other than P.

NIL matches any defensive move.

Figure 10.3   Defensive templates in PARADISE's Plan-Language.

shows the templates PARADISE has for adequately describing defensive moves in terms of their effects on the purpose of the plan being executed. (P and SQ are variables that will be instantiated in an actual plan to particular pieces and squares, respectively.)

The plan for an offensive move can be one of two things: a particular move or a goal. A particular move is simply the name of a piece and a square. Such a plan causes PARADISE to immediately make that move with no analysis of the position other than checking that the move is legal. A goal is simply the name of a KS followed by an instantiation for each argument of the KS. When executing a goal, PARADISE will post a concept corresponding to the KS in the data base by using the given instantiations and the attribute lists of this plan as a whole. The KS will then be executed for this concept. Any plan produced by this execution will replace the goal in the original plan and this modified plan will be used. This process expands and elaborates plans. If executing the KS does not produce a plan then the original plan has failed.

```
(((WN N5)
  (((BN N4) (SAFEMOVE WR Q7)
   (((BK NIL) (SAFECAPTURE WR
      BR))
    ((ANYBUT BK) (SAFECAPTURE
      WR BK))))
   ((BN N4) (CHECKMOVE WR Q7)
      (BK NIL) (SAFECAPTURE WR
      BQ) )))
  ((THREAT (PLUS (EXCHVAL WN
      N5) (FORK WR BK BR)))
      (LIKELY 0))
  ((THREAT (PLUS (EXCHVAL WN
      N5) (EXCH WR BQ)))
      (LIKELY 0)))
```

Figure 10.4 shows a problem and one of the plans PARADISE's static analysis produces for it. (WN means white knight, N5 means square N5, etc.) The internal representation of PARADISE has not been printed unambiguously because the term WR does not specify which White rook. However, it should be obvious to which piece the names refer. The last

Figure 10.4 White to move. An example plan produced by PARA-DISE.

two lines of the plan are attribute lists. The first five lines are the Plan-Language expression for the plan which can be read as follows:

> Play N–N5. If Black captures the knight with his knight, attempt to safely move the rook on Q1 to Q7. Then, if Black moves his king anywhere try to safely capture the Black rook on R7, and if Black moves any piece other than his king, try to safely capture the king with the rook. A second alternative after Black captures the knight is to attempt to safely move the rook on Q1 to Q7 with check. Then, if Black moves his king anywhere try to safely capture the Black queen with the rook.

SAFEMOVE, SAFECAPTURE, and CHECKMOVE are all KSes in PARADISE. After playing N–N5 and NxN for Black in the tree search, PARADISE will execute either the CHECKMOVE goal or the SAFE-MOVE goal. Executing the SAFEMOVE goal executes the SAFEMOVE KS which knows about safely moving a piece to a square. This KS will see that R–Q7 is safe and produce this as the continuation of the original plan, causing the system to play R–Q7 with no further analysis. If for some reason R–Q7 was not safe, then the SAFEMOVE KS would try to make Q7 safe for the rook (by posing a SAFE concept). If some plan is found, the original plan would be "expanded" by replacing the SAFEMOVE goal with the newly found plan. In general, the newly found plan will contain (SAFEMOVE WR Q7) though it may come after a sacrificial decoy or some other tactic. If posting the SAFE concept does not produce a plan, then the SAFEMOVE goal has failed, and the alternative CHECKMOVE goal would be tried. If it also fails, a complete analysis of the position must be done. If Black had answered N–N5 with a king move, it would not match the template (BN N4) and a complete analysis of the position would be undertaken without attempting to make Q7 safe for the rook.

By the use of conditionals, a plan can handle a number of possible situations that may arise. The most important feature of the Plan-Language is that offensive plans are expressed in terms of the KSes. This has many advantages. Relevant productions are immediately and directly accessed when a new position is reached. The system has one set of abstract concepts it understands (the KSes) and does not need to use a different language for plans and static analysis. The system has been designed to make the writing of productions and thus the forming of KSes reasonable to do. Thus the range of plans that can be expressed is not fixed by the Plan-Language. By forming new KSes, the range of expressible plans may be increased without any new coding (in the search routines or anywhere else) to understand the new plans. This is important because the usefulness of the knowledge base is limited by its ability to communicate what it knows (e.g., through plans).

Given a number of plans to execute, the tree search must make decisions about which plan to search first, when to forsake one plan and try another, when to be satisfied with the results of a search, and other such decisions. To make such decisions, it must have information about what a plan expects to gain and why. Such information was available to the productions that matched to produce the plan and must be communicated in the attribute lists of the plan so as to provide many different types of access to this knowledge. Unlike most search-based chess programs, PARADISE must use its information about a plan at other nodes in the tree because it executes a plan without analyzing the newly created positions.

To use the information about plans in an effective manner, PARADISE divides a plan's effects into four different categories which are kept separately (i.e., their values are not combined in any way). These four categories are THREAT, which describes what a plan threatens to actively win; SAVE, which describes counterthreats of the opponent a plan actively prevents; LOSS, which describes both counterthreats of the opponent not defended against and functions the first piece to move in a plan will give up by abandoning its current location (thus providing new threats for the opponent); and LIKELY, which describes the likelihood that a plan will succeed. These four categories have emerged during the development of PARADISE. Experience seems to indicate the system must have at least these four dimensions along which to evaluate plans in order to adequately guide the tree search.

Because the values for these categories must evaluate correctly at different nodes in the tree, they cannot be integers. Instead they (except for LIKELY) are expressions in the *Threat-Language* (Wilkins [171]) which can describe threats in a sophisticated manner. These expressions are evaluated in the context of the current position and may return different values for different positions. The value of LIKELY is an integer. This integer represents the number of unforced moves the defense has before the offense can accomplish its plan. The most likely plans to succeed have a LIKELY of zero (every move is forcing). Both attribute lists in Figure 10.4 have a likelihood of zero.

Creating plans

A detailed description of the static analysis process in PARADISE is given in Wilkins [171]. The concepts and KSes used to produce the plan in Figure 10.4 are briefly described here. The system begins by posting a THREAT concept, the THREAT KS having productions that look for threats. As long as there are concepts present that correspond to KSes, PARADISE will continue to execute KSes. This analysis terminates when only FINALPLAN concepts and other concepts which have no corresponding KS are left. Two different productions in THREAT post MOVE concepts for moving the white rook to Q7. (One recognizes the skewer of the Black king to the rook, and the other recognizes the simultaneous attack on the king and queen where any king moves leaves the queen open to capture with check.) After executing the THREAT and ATTACK KSes, the system executes the MOVE KS on the 50 different MOVE concepts which have been posted by productions. In addition to Q7, there are MOVE goals for moving the rook to QB7, K7, KB8, Q6, QB6, QN6, and QR6, as well as many goals for moving other White pieces. A production in the MOVE KS that recognizes that the proposed move is unsafe matches for the White rook to Q7 MOVE goal. This production posts a SAFE concept for making Q7 safe for the White rook. After the MOVE KS is finished, seven SAFE goals have accumulated. While executing the SAFE KS for the White rook to Q7 goal, one production notices that the Black knight blocks the White queen's protection of Q7. This production posts a DECOY goal in order to decoy the Black knight so that the queen can support the White rook on Q7. The DECOY KS is executed on the seven DECOY goals that have been produced, and one production posts a FORCE goal suggesting N–N5 as a move to decoy Black's knight. It is up to the FORCE KS to decide if N–N5 is forcing enough to provoke a move by the Black knight. There are nine FORCE goals in all, and the production that finds N–N5 forcing posts an INITIAL-PLAN concept which is exactly like the plan shown in Figure 10.4.

After executing the CAPTURE KS, the INITIAL-PLAN KS is executed on the five INITIAL-PLAN goals that have been produced. (Most of the MOVE goals failed without leading to the posting of a plan.) This KS looks for functions given up by a plan or threats not defended against by a plan. Because the plan of Figure 10.4 checks the opposing king, a production posts a FINALPLAN concept for this plan. While executing a different INITIAL-PLAN goal, the INITIAL-PLAN KS notices that the White queen is under attack and is not defended by the plan in question. This causes execution of goals to save the White queen which result in more plans being suggested, and a total of 10 FINALPLAN concepts are eventually posted. The attribute lists of these plans rate only two of them as being likely to win material. These two are the one in Figure 10.4, and a plan starting with R–Q7 immediately. The plan in Figure 10.4 is rated highest and is tried first. This static analysis took more than 24 seconds of CPU time on a DEC KL-10.

The static analysis process is very expensive, and PARADISE uses its plan in the search to avoid doing such analyses. Each static analysis is done entirely by the production rules which can easily be modified to increase or make more precise the knowledge available to the system. The information in concepts allows the system to discard combinations of ideas that are antithetical to each other, so few ridiculous plans are suggested.

How detailed should plans be?

The system must quickly recognize when a plan is not working and abandon it before effort is wasted investigating poor lines. On the other hand, it is expensive to completely analyze a position, so the system wants to use its plan as long as possible. To achieve a balance, plans must adequately express the purpose they intend to achieve. Productions must carefully formulate their Plan-Language expressions at the right level of detail using appropriate goals and descriptions of defensive moves. When executing a plan, the system will retrieve a goal or move from the plan to apply to a new position. Care must be taken to ensure that this move or goal is reasonable in the new position. Plans may become unreasonable when they are too general or too specific. In either case, they have failed to express their purpose.

The example of Figure 10.4 illustrates the issues involved. Consider the first three ply of the plan as ((WN N5) (BN N4) (SAFEMOVE WR Q7)). Suppose this had been expressed as ((WN N5) NIL (WR Q7)). Playing R–Q7 after NxN is reasonable, but if Black moves his king instead, playing R–Q7 will lead the search down a blind alley. Thus (WR Q7) is too specific and does not express White's purpose. This problem can be cured by a more specific description of Black's reply (e.g., (BN N4) instead of NIL) because the template for Black's move will not match if Black moves his king. In fact, PARADISE does not know for sure that R–Q7 will be safe after N–N5 and NxN (although in this particular position it is). To avoid mistakenly playing R–Q7 when it is not safe, PARADISE uses a SAFEMOVE goal to express more accurately the purpose of the plan. For example, the plan could be ((WN N5) NIL (SAFEMOVE WR Q7)). If Black answers N–N5 with NxN then the SAFEMOVE goal is reasonable and quickly produces R–Q7 as the move to play after verifying its safety. If Black answers with a king move, then the SAFEMOVE goal is not what White wants to do, but little is lost because R–Q7 is not safe and the line will be rejected without searching. However, if likely plans had existed for making Q7 safe, the search may still have been led astray. For this reason, PARADISE uses (BN N4) as the template in this plan. The purpose of N–N5 is to decoy the Black knight to his KN4 and this template most accurately expresses this purpose.

Now let us consider the following more general plan: ((WN N5) NIL

(SAFELY-ATTACK BK)). If Black answers with NxN then the SAFELY-ATTACK KS should generate R–Q7 as a safe attack on the Black king. If, instead, Black moves his king then this KS should generate a check by the White queen or knight, which would also be reasonable. Thus this plan produces reasonable moves for every Black reply without ever causing a reanalysis of the new position. This would be a good plan if PARADISE knew (from its patterns) that it could get the Black king in trouble after any reply. However, it only knows of the skewer of the Black king to the rook, the threat of capturing the queen with check, and the fact that the White knight threatens the Black king, rook, and knight from N5. It is accidental that the SAFELY-ATTACK goal works after Black retreats his king. In the general case, such a goal would produce many worthless checks that would mislead the search. Thus this plan is too general to describe White's actual purpose.

It is very important to get the correct level of detail in a plan. The plan should handle as many replies as possible without causing a reanalysis, but it should avoid suggesting poor moves. The templates for describing defensive moves in the Plan-Language and the various KSes have been developed to allow PARADISE's plans to accurately express their purpose. The results have been quite satisfying: the productions in PARADISE now create plans that rarely suggest poor moves but that can still be used for as many plies as a human might use his original idea.

Using plans to guide the search

A brief overview of PARADISE's tree searching algorithm is given here in order to provide background for example problem solutions that follow. A detailed description of the algorithm appears in Wilkins [173]. PARADISE's search tries to prove that one move in the original position is better than any other. This can often be done without knowing the "true" value of each move (something all search-based programs attempt to discover within alpha–beta). For example, suppose that in some position one move will lead to a complicated mate while no other move leads to an advantage. The program does not need to prove that the winning move actually leads to mate (the "true" value). Once it has been shown that none of the other moves forces an advantage, it is only necessary to show that the mating move leads to some advantage (which may be much easier than showing the mate).

When PARADISE uses its search to investigate a plan, it invests some amount of effort to determine a range within which the value of the plan lies. (The idea of having a program use ranges in this way originates in Berliner's B* search, see Berliner [119].) The program uses a threshold of success (usually a small gain over the best result achieved so far), and whenever this threshold is achieved, the current search is terminated. If this threshold success is not enough to prove that one move is best, the same line may be searched again later in an attempt to find a better result.

To show that one move is best in the original position, it is only necessary to show that the lower bound of the range of one plan is better than the upper bound of the range of all other plans. PARADISE continues to initiate searches which narrow the ranges of plans under consideration (possibly until a range converges to a single value). Eventually the ranges are narrowed enough to decide that one move is best. Since a plan is often searched more than once during this process, the search could be described as "progressively deepening" (a term used in DeGroot [31] to describe the chess analysis of human grandmasters).

The program analyzes the situation at the top level after each narrowing of a range to develop a strategy for proving that one plan is best. For example, one strategy might prove that all the moves except the best so far cannot win, while another strategy might prove that the best move so far wins convincingly. By continually reassessing the situation, PARADISE avoids investing a lot of effort in an endeavor which may not be helpful in showing that one move is best.

Each search initiated from the top level is best-first. PARADISE searches down a line, keeping track of unsearched alternatives and their expectations as it goes down. If at some point one of the unsearched alternatives seems better than the current plan, the current line of search is terminated and the search backs up to try the more promising alternative. In this way, PARADISE avoids using unreasonable amounts of resources trying to make a poor line work. Actually, decisions about which alternative is most promising are made only when PARADISE changes plans, and not at every node (as in a classical best-first search). Once a plan is selected for searching, it is used until it is exhausted or until the program determines that it is not working.

The program must make reasonable decisions about which alternative is more promising. The tactical sharpness of PARADISE's domain makes such decisions easier than they would be in positional situations. There is a cost involved in abandoning a line and then later coming back to it, so PARADISE is reluctant to abandon the current line. This reluctance diminishes (and eventually becomes negative) as the current line's depth in the tree becomes larger than the depth of the alternative.

Figure 10.5 shows position 49 from Reinfeld [164]. PARADISE does a static analysis on this position which uses 18 seconds of CPU time and suggests two plans. To show how such plans are used to guide the search, PARADISE's search for this position is sketched below.

```
(PLY 1)
BESTPLAN:
(((WQ R7) (BK R2) (CHECKMOVE
   WR R5) (BK NIL)
   (ATTACKP BK))
 ((HINT 1) (THREAT (PLUS (WIN
   BK) (EXCHVAL WQ R7)))
   (LIKELY 1))))
```

225

Figure 10.5 White to move. A plan produced by PARADISE. (Problem 49 from Reinfeld [164].)

PARADISE begins by doing a best-first search of the above plan. Execution of this plan commences by playing QxPch and producing a new board position. The defense suggests both legal moves, KxQ and K–B1, but tries KxQ first. Because this move matches the (BK R2) template in the plan, PARADISE has ((CHECKMOVE WR R5) (BK NIL) (ATTACKP BK)) as its best plan at ply 3 of the search. Because it is in the middle of executing a plan, PARADISE does not look for better alternatives at this point. The best-first search only looks for better alternatives when a new plan is being selected.

Execution of the CHECKMOVE KS produces ((WR R5) (BK NIL) (ATTACKP BK)) as a plan, which causes R–R5ch to be played. Black plays his only legal move at ply 4, K–N1, which matches the (BK NIL) template in the plan, and leaves (ATTACKP BK) as the current plan. Thus the original plan is still guiding the search at ply 5. Executing the AT-TACKP KS posts many concepts, including MOVE and SAFE concepts, and ((WN N6) ((NIL (SAFEMOVE WR R8)) (NIL (SAFEMOVE WN K7)))) is produced as the best plan in this position. This replaces (ATTACKP BK) in the current plan, thus elaborating it. After playing N–N6, the position in Figure 10.6 is reached.

Figure 10.6 Black to move. Position after N–N6.

Productions that know about defending against R–R8 suggest the six Black moves below. Black plays BxP first in an effort to save the bishop from ensuing skewer. At this point the plan branches. Because both branches begin with a null template, they both match any Black move at ply 6. Thus PARADISE has two plans at ply 7: (SAFEMOVE WR R8) and (SAFEMOVE WN K7). Before executing a plan for the offense, PARADISE executes the QUIESCENCE KS which looks for obviously winning moves. (This was done at ply 3 and ply 5 also, but did not suggest any moves.) Here R–R8 is suggested by the QUIESCENCE KS which causes the (SAFEMOVE WR R8) plan to be executed immediately. PARADISE plays R–R8, finds that Black is mated, and returns to ply 6 knowing that Black's BxP leads to mate. All this has been accomplished without a static analysis; the original plan has guided the search.

```
(PLY 6)
INITIAL DEFENSIVE MOVES:
((BB R6) (BB Q2) (BB N2) (BR
    B4) (BR B3) (BR B1))
```

At ply 6, Black uses KSes to refute the mating line. This involves analysis of the information produced by the previous search. No new moves are found because all reasonable defenses have already been suggested. PARADISE has a *causality facility* that determines the possible effects a move might have on a line of play. Using information generated during the search of the mating line, the causality facility looks for effects a proposed move might have (such as blocking a square that a sliding piece moved over, vacating an escape square for the king, protecting a piece that was attacked, etc.). The causality facility recognizes that neither B–Q2 nor B–N2 can affect the mating line found for BxP so they are rejected without searching.

Black plays R–B4 next, the causality facility having recognized that this move opens a flight square for the Black king. Again PARADISE has both (SAFEMOVE WR R8) and (SAFEMOVE WN K7) as plans at ply 7. Both SAFEMOVE goals would succeed, but R–R8 has a higher recommendation and is played first. Black plays his only legal move at ply 8, K–B2.

The original plan no longer provides suggestions at ply 9. PARADISE must now look for better alternatives or do an expensive static analysis to suggest a new plan. Before trying either of these, the program executes the QUIESCENCE in an attempt to find an obviously winning move. R–KB8 is suggested and PARADISE immediately plays this move without doing a static analysis. This is mate, so PARADISE returns to ply 6 to look for other defenses.

Both R–B3 and R–B1 are tried and both are quickly refuted by playing R–R8 from the SAFEMOVE goal of the original plan, K–B2, and R–KB8 from the QUIESCENCE KS. The search then returns to ply 2 and tries K–B1 in answer to QxPch. The template in the original plan does not match K–B1, so there is no plan at ply 3. However, the QUIESCENCE KS quickly suggests Q–R8, and PARADISE returns from the search convinced that QxPch will mate. This result shows that QxPch is best, so no other best-first searches are initiated.

PARADISE's plans are not always so accurate but space prevents presentation of a longer search. The above analysis uses about 130 seconds of CPU time on a DEC KL-10. It goes to a depth of 9 ply while creating only 21 nodes in the tree. Because of the guidance provided by the original plan, no static analysis was performed except on the original position. By comparison, the TECH2 program (an improved version of TECH [46]) at a depth setting of 6 discovers that it can win material with QxPch, although the horizon effect hides the mate from it. For this analysis, TECH2 uses 210 seconds of CPU time on a KL-10 and creates 439,459 nodes by making legal moves (as well as making 544,768 illegal moves that are retracted). The next section provides an analysis of PARADISE's performance and compares it to that of other programs.

A typical medium-sized search

This section presents the actual protocol produced by PARADISE while solving Problem 82 in Reinfeld [164]. (This program prints squares in algebraic notation to avoid confusion.) This is a typical protocol produced by PARADISE while solving a problem in which the program finds the best line immediately.

PARADISE's initial static analysis on the position of Figure 10.7 uses 20 seconds of CPU time, and produces seven plans. The one beginning with (WB H7) has a LIKELY of 0 and is searched first. The other six plans have a LIKELY of 1 and begin with the following moves: (WQ A3) (WR H7) (WR H8) (WQ F2) (WQ F3) (WQ E1). The protocol that follows was printed by PARADISE as it analyzed this problem. Explanatory comments have been added in lower case.

In the search, the program refuses to search plans that are not likely to succeed when it has already achieved a significant success. This is done because it is not reasonable to invest large amounts of effort trying ideas that don't seem likely to succeed when a winning line has already been found. The validity of this cutoff rests on PARADISE's accurate calcu-

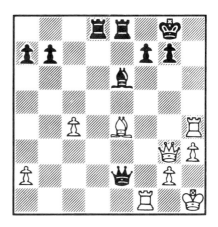

Figure 10.7 White to move. Problem 82 from Reinfeld [164].

lation of LIKELY values (see Wilkins [171]). This could produce errors, though not serious ones because the error would be the selection of a winning move that was not the "best" winning move. No such errors have been made in any position PARADISE has analyzed.

(TOPLEVEL (VALUE . 0))
PLY 1 (EXPECT . 320)
BESTPLAN: ((WB H7) (BK F8) (WQ A3))
NEWBOARD: (E4 WB H7)

 The value of the initial position is 0. (White is trying to achieve a positive score.) The best plan specifies moving the WB to H7, and if Black replies by moving his king to F8, then WQ–A3 is played. The reasoning behind the suggestion of this plan is fairly specific. PARADISE knows that after B–H7, Black must move his king either to H8, where White has a discovered check, or to F8, where White can deliver a second check to which Black's king cannot move in reply. The expectation of this plan (after "EXPECT"), which is calculated from the attribute lists of the plan, is 320 (90 is the value of a queen, so 320 threatens mate). Wherever the word "NEWBOARD" occurs, PARADISE constructs a new board position by playing a legal move.

(PLY: 2) DEFMOVES: ((BK F8) (BK H8))
NEWBOARD: (G8 BK F8)

 The word "DEFMOVES" labels the list of moves under consideration by the defensive search. (Each move is the first part of a plan under consideration.)

TRY CURRENT PLAN
PLY 3 (VALUE . 0) BESTPLAN: ((WQ A3))
NEWBOARD: (G3 WQ A3)

 The phrase "TRY CURRENT PLAN" means that the program is obtaining the next move by executing a plan that was inherited from an earlier analysis. In this example the current plan specifies an actual move rather than a goal, so the move is made immediately without calculating the primitives in this position. Applying the evaluation function to this position yields 0 (given after the word "VALUE").

(PLY: 4) DEFMOVES: ((BR E7))
NEWBOARD: (E8 BR E7)

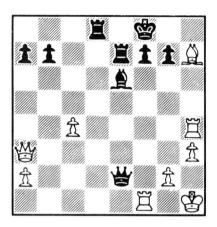

NULL PLAN (VALUE . 0) (STATIC-ANALYSIS 20.4 SECONDS) (4 PLANS)
PLY 5 BESTPLAN: (((WB D3) ((NIL (CHECKMOVE WR H8)) (NIL
   (SAFECAPTURE WB BQ))
(NIL (SAFEMOVE WR H8) (((BK NIL) (SAFECAPTURE WR BR))
   ((ANYBUT BK) (SAFECAPTURE WR BK)))))))
(NEWEXPECT . 90)
NEWBOARD: (H7 WB D3)
   The current plan is finished, so the system does a static analysis that takes 20.4 sec-
onds of CPU time and produces four plans. The best one begins with (WB D3) and
continues with either a rook check on H8 threatening mate, the capture of the Black
queen by the bishop, or the rook move to H8 followed by a skewer of the Black king
to the Black rook. Once again the static analysis accurately recommends the winning
plan. The expectation is now 90, having been recalculated from the new current plan
that only expects to win the black queen.

(PLY: 6) DEFMOVES: ((BR D3) (BR D3) (BQ D3) (BQ F1) (BP G5) (BQ D3)
   (BK G8))
NEWBOARD: (D8 BR D3)
TRY OBVIOUSLY WINNING MOVE
PLY 7 (VALUE . -33) BESTPLAN: ((WR H8))
(NEWEXPECT . 607)
NEWBOARD: (H4 WR H8)
(EXIT OFFENSE (VALUE 1300 . 1300))
   The system finds R–H8 as an obviously winning move. It knows the move will mate
(although it plays it to make sure), so it doesn't check the current plan. If the system
hadn't been sure of the mate, it would have executed the current plan after noticing
that R–H8 duplicates the (CHECKMOVE WR H8) goal in the current plan. A range
is returned as the value, but both the top and bottom of the range are 1300 (the value
for mate) because the value has been determined exactly.

(PLY 6) REFUTE: ((WR H8))
(PLY: 6) DEFMOVES: ((BQ D3) (BQ F1) (BP G5) (BQ D3) (BK G8))
CAUSALITY: (BQ D3) LINE: (D8 BR D3) NO
NEWBOARD: (E2 BQ F1)
   PARADISE backs up to ply 6. A countercausal analysis tries to refute the move
R–H8 by White but no new moves are suggested. The causality facility compares the

proposed Q–D3 move to the tree produced for the R–D3 move and determines that Q–D3 cannot help. Q–D3 is therefore rejected without searching, and Q–F1 is played (the causality facility approves it). The causality facility makes use of considerable information returned by the searching process.

OBVIOUSLY WINNING MOVE DUPLICATED
TRY CURRENT PLAN
PLY 7 (VALUE . -50) BESTPLAN: ((WB F1))
NEWBOARD: (D3 WB F1)

B–F1 is suggested as a winning move, but it duplicates the SAFECAPTURE goal in the current plan (and is not a sure mate) so the current plan is tried.

(PLY: 8) DEFMOVES: ((BR D1))
NEWBOARD: (D8 BR D1)
(VALUE . 49) TRY QUIESCENCE SEARCH
(PLY: 9) NEWBOARD: (H4 WR H8)
(QUIESCENCE VALUE (1300 . 1300))

The current plan is finished, so the offense tries a quiescence search to see if the value holds up. A value of 1300 is returned, so the search backs up with success for White.

(PLY 8) REFUTE: ((WR H8))
(PLY: 8) DEFMOVES: ((BP G5) (BR D2) (BR D7) (BP G6) (BP F5) (BP F6) (BK E8) (BK G8))
NEWBOARD: (G7 BP G5)

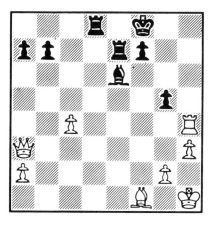

(VALUE . 49) TRY QUIESCENCE SEARCH
(PLY: 9) NEWBOARD: (H4 WR H8)
DEFENDING MOVE SELECTED
(PLY: 10) NEWBOARD: (F8 BK G7)
(PLY: 11) NEWBOARD: (H8 WR D8)
DEFENDING MOVE SELECTED
(PLY: 12) NEWBOARD: (E7 BR D7)
(PLY: 13) NEWBOARD: (D8 WR D7)
(PLY: 14) NEWBOARD: (E6 BB D7)
(PLY: 15) NEWBOARD: (A3 WQ A7)
DEFENDING MOVE SELECTED
(PLY: 16) NEWBOARD: (D7 BB C6)
(QUIESCENCE VALUE (109 . 109))
(EXIT OFFENSE (VALUE 109 . 109))

A quiescence search to a depth of 16 shows that P–G5 fails for Black. The quiescence search knows that White is ahead and that the White rook on H4 is not in danger, yet it plays aggressive moves (at plys 9 through 15) instead of being satisfied. This seems to generate nodes unnecessarily. PARADISE does this because it is a cheap way to get better results. The quiescence search is very inexpensive compared to the regular search. The system thinks it has enough information, yet it may be necessary to search this line again if the "true" value is not found. Because PARADISE sees an inexpensive way (quiescence searching) to improve the result, it risks generating a few unnecessary (though inexpensive) nodes in order to avoid possibly searching this line again later.

(PLY 8) REFUTE: ((WR H8))
(PLY: 8) DEFMOVES: ((BR D2) (BR D7) (BP G6) (BP F5) (BP F6) (BK E8) (BK G8))
CAUSALITY: (BR D2) LINE: (D8 BR D1) NO
CAUSALITY: (BR D7) LINE: (D8 BR D1) NO
CAUSALITY: (BP G6) LINE: (G7 BP G5) NO
NEWBOARD: (F7 BP F5)

Black tries other moves at ply 8. Causality rejects R–D2 and R–D7 on the basis of the tree generated for R–D1, and it rejects P–G6 using the P–G5 tree.

(VALUE . 49) TRY QUIESCENCE SEARCH
(PLY: 9) NEWBOARD: (H4 WR H8)
DEFENDING MOVE SELECTED
(PLY: 10) NEWBOARD: (E6 BB G8)

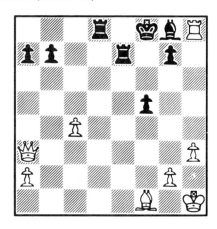

(PLY: 11) NEWBOARD: (A3 WQ A7)
(QUIESCENCE VALUE (59 . 59))
(EXIT OFFENSE (VALUE 59 . 90))

Again the quiescence search confirms the offensive success. This time the value of 59 does not meet the expectation so the offensive search returns a range of 59 to 90 because the expectation of 90 may have been achieved if a static analysis had been done. PARADISE notes in the tree that searching here again may improve the value from 59 to 90. (For example, if the value of 59 is not sufficient to prove that one move is best at the top level, PARADISE may return to this point, do an analysis, and try RxB at ply 11.)

(PLY 8) REFUTE: ((WR H8))
(PLY: 8) DEFMOVES: ((BP F6) (BK E8) (BK G8))
CAUSALITY: (BP F6) LINE: (F7 BP F5) NO

NEWBOARD: (F8 BK E8)
(VALUE . 49) TRY QUIESCENCE SEARCH
(PLY: 9) NEWBOARD: (A3 WQ A7)
(QUIESCENCE VALUE (59 . 59))
(EXIT OFFENSE (VALUE 59 . 90))
(PLY 8) REFUTE: ((WQ A7))
(PLY: 8) DEFMOVES: ((BK G8) (BR A8) (BP A6) (BP A5) (BP B6))
CAUSALITY: (BK G8) LINE: (F8 BK E8) NO
CAUSALITY: (BR A8) LINE: (D8 BR D1) NO
CAUSALITY: (BP A6) LINE: (D8 BR D1) NO
CAUSALITY: (BP A5) LINE: (D8 BR D1) NO
CAUSALITY: (BP B6) LINE: (F8 BK E8) NO
DEFMOVES: ( )
PLY 7 BESTPLAN: ((CHECKMOVE WR H8))
    TERMINATE: PLAN SUCCEEDED
(EXIT OFFENSE (VALUE 59 . 90))

The offensive search terminates because a significant gain has been achieved. PARA-DISE again notes in the tree that searching other plans here may improve the value. The range of 59 to 90 is returned.

(PLY 6) REFUTE: ((WR H8) (WR H8) (WR H8) (WB F1))
(PLY: 6) DEFMOVES: ((BP G5) (BK G8))
NEWBOARD: (G7 BP G5)

OBVIOUSLY WINNING MOVE DUPLICATED
TRY CURRENT PLAN
PLY 7 (VALUE . 0) BESTPLAN: ((WB E2))
NEWBOARD: (D3 WB E2)
(PLY: 8) DEFMOVES: ((BP H4))
NEWBOARD: (G5 BP H4)
(VALUE . 49) TRY QUIESCENCE SEARCH
(PLY: 9) NEWBOARD: (A3 WQ A7)
(QUIESCENCE VALUE (59 . 59))
(EXIT OFFENSE (VALUE 59 . 90))
(PLY: 8) DEFMOVES: ( )
PLY 7 BESTPLAN: ((CHECKMOVE WR H8))
    TERMINATE: ALPHA BETA
(PLY 6) REFUTE: ((WB E2))
(PLY: 6) DEFMOVES: ((BQ E3) (BQ D2) (BQ E5) (BQ G2) (BQ A2) (BK G8))

CAUSALITY: (BQ E3) LINE: (D8 BR D3) NO
CAUSALITY: (BQ D2) LINE: (D8 BR D3) NO
CAUSALITY: (BQ E5) LINE: (D8 BR D3) NO
NEWBOARD: (E2 BQ G2)

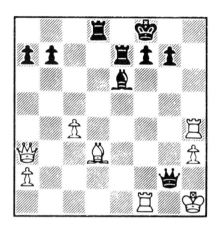

TRY OBVIOUSLY WINNING MOVE
PLY 7 (VALUE . -10) BESTPLAN: ((WK G2))
NEWBOARD: (H1 WK G2)
(PLY: 8) DEFMOVES: ( )

The defensive search now does a null move analysis (see Wilkins [9]). It has no idea what to do so it lets the offense make two moves in a row. However, the offense calls the quiescence search which knows it is the defense's move. It decides the defense can escape from the threat of R–H8, so it calls the position quiescent.

(VALUE . 89) TRY QUIESCENCE SEARCH
ASSUMED ESCAPE FROM (WR H8)
(QUIESCENCE VALUE (89 . 89))
(EXIT OFFENSE (VALUE 89 . 89))
(PLY: 8) DEFMOVES: ( )
(PLY 6) REFUTE: ((WK G2))
(PLY: 6) DEFMOVES: ((BQ A2) (BK G8))
CAUSALITY: (BQ A2) LINE: (D8 BR D3) NO
CAUSALITY: (BK G8) LINE: (G7 BP G5) NO
(PLY: 6) DEFMOVES: ( )
PLY 5 BESTPLAN: ((WQ A5) NIL (CHECKMOVE WQ D8))
NO UNLIKELYS AFTER SUCCESS: QUIT
(EXIT OFFENSE (VALUE 59 . 89))

The search backs up to ply 5 and tries the next plan suggested by the static analysis. This plan has a LIKELY of 1, and the result already achieved is so successful that PARADISE rejects the unlikely plan without searching.

(PLY 4) REFUTE: ((WR H8) (WB D3))
(PLY: 4) DEFMOVES: ( )
PLY 3 LAST PLAN
(EXIT OFFENSE (VALUE 59 . 320))

The search backs up to ply 3. There are no more plans to execute here, but a static analysis has not yet been done so the program makes a note of this. The top of the value range is changed to 320 to reflect the possibility of achieving the original expectation by doing a static analysis to find plans.

(PLY 2) REFUTE: ((WQ A3))
(PLY: 2) DEFMOVES: ((BK H8))
NEWBOARD: (G8 BK H8)

NULL PLAN (VALUE . 0) (STATIC-ANALYSIS 14.2 SECONDS) (2 PLANS)
PLY 3 BESTPLAN: ((WB D3))
(NEWEXPECT . 320)
NEWBOARD: (H7 WB D3)

The defense tries K–H8 at ply 2, and the original plan does not match this move so a static analysis is undertaken. Again PARADISE finds the right idea immediately.

(PLY: 4) DEFMOVES: ((BK G8))
NEWBOARD: (H8 BK G8)
(VALUE . 0) TRY OBVIOUSLY WINNING MOVE
PLY 5 BESTPLAN: ((WB E2))
(NEWEXPECT . 90)
NEWBOARD: (D3 WB E2)
(PLY: 6) DEFMOVES: ( )
(VALUE . 99) TRY QUIESCENCE SEARCH
(QUIESCENCE VALUE (99 . 99))
(EXIT OFFENSE (VALUE 99 . 99))
(PLY: 6) DEFMOVES: ( ) PLY 5 LAST PLAN
(EXIT OFFENSE (VALUE 99 . 320))
(PLY 4) REFUTE: ((WB E2)) (PLY: 4) DEFMOVES: ( )
PLY 3 BESTPLAN: ((WB E4))
(NEWEXPECT . 10)
    TERMINATE: FORWARD PRUNE
(EXIT OFFENSE (VALUE 99 . 320))

The search backs up to ply 3, and the offense tries B–E4 which has been suggested by the static analysis. Its expectation is 10 and B–D3 has already achieved 99 so a forward prune occurs.

(PLY 2) REFUTE: ((WB D3))
(PLY: 2) DEFMOVES: ( )
PLY 1 BESTPLAN: ((WQ A3) NIL (CHECKMOVE WB H7))
NO UNLIKELYS AFTER SUCCESS: QUIT

The search returns to the top level to try the next plan but it is terminated because it has a LIKELY of 1 and the search is over.

BEST MOVE: (E4 WB H7) VALUE: (59 . 320)
PRINCIPAL VARIATION:
1 (E4 WB H7) (G8 BK F8)
2 (G3 WQ A3) (E8 BR E7)
3 (H7 WB D3) (E2 BQ F1)
4 (D3 WB F1) (F7 BP F5)
5 (H4 WR H8) (E6 BB G8)
6 (A3 WQ A7)
TOTAL TIME: 297 SECONDS
NODES CREATED: 36 (22 REGULAR, 14 QUIESCENCE)
STATIC ANALYSES: 2

This example shows how well PARADISE's chess knowledge is employed in the production of plans and in the causality facility. The plans do an excellent job of guiding the search; only two static analyses are done in the entire search. The plans are so accurately specified by the analysis that they never once lead the search off the correct line. White's play in the search is error-free. The causality facility makes good use of information returned from the search; many Black moves that would otherwise have been searched are eliminated in this manner. In addition, the range values accurately express the potential of each node so that the system does not have to waste effort determining the "true" values.

On this problem, CAPS (Berliner [12]) (which has more chess knowledge than any other program that plays a full game of chess) generated a tree of 489 nodes in 115 seconds to obtain a principal variation that was slightly inaccurate but solved the problem. CHESS 4.4 (running on a CDC-6400) produces a tree with 30,246 nodes in 95 seconds of CPU time without finding the solution (which is too deep for it).

Measuring PARADISE's performance

To aid in evaluating performance, PARADISE was tested on positions in the book *Win At Chess* [6]. This book contains tactically sharp positions from master games that are representative of tactical problems of reasonable difficulty. PARADISE's knowledge base was developed by writing productions that would enable the program to solve, in a reasonable manner, 15 chosen positions from among the first 100 in *Win At Chess*. The 85 positions not chosen were not considered during this development. This development process produced one version of the program, called PARADISE-0. Six positions were then picked at random from the remaining 85, and accurate records were kept on the work involved in getting the program to solve these reasonably. The version of the program that solves all 21 positions is called PARADISE.

PARADISE's performance on a problem is classified into one of three categories: (1) problem solved as is (possibly with a minor bug fix), (2) problem not solvable without a change to the program or a major change to the knowledge base, or (3) problem solvable with a small addition to the knowledge base. Category 3 helps measure the modifiability of the knowledge base. It is meant to include solutions that require no changes whatsoever to the program and only a small addition to the knowledge base. "Small" means that it takes less than 20 minutes total of human time to identify the problem and write or modify one production that will enable PARADISE, with no other changes, to solve the problem in a reasonable way (i.e., no ad hoc solutions).

Of the six positions chosen at random, two were in category 1, three were in category 3, and one was in category 2. This latter one inspired the only program changes between PARADISE-0 and PARADISE. These results speak well for the modifiability of the knowledge base, but shed little light on the generality of the program. To better test generality, PARADISE has been tested on the first 100 positions. These positions are divided into five groups of 20, and Reinfeld claims an increase in difficulty with increase in group number. (Eight end-game positions were eliminated, so the groups actually have 18, 19, 18, 20, and 17 positions.) PARADISE is considered to solve only the problems in category 1, while PARADISE-2 solves both category 1 and 3 problems. PARADISE would become PARDISE-2 simply by leaving in the productions written to solve problems in category 3.

Because the 21 developmental problems had not all been solved by one version of the program, these were tried first. Adding new knowledge during program development would (hopefully) not adversely affect performance on earlier problems, but this had to be confirmed. For example, productions added to the knowledge base to solve the last five developmental problems might produce so many suggestions in the first five problems that the search would become untractable in those problems. The testing proved that the new knowledge had no adverse effects. All 21 problems fell into category 1; thus the same version of the program solves them all. In every case, the analysis is either the same as or sharper than that produced by developmental versions of the program. This result provides strong evidence that the knowledge base is easily modifiable. If productions are written carefully and intelligently (a skill the author developed while writing productions for the developmental set), they do not appear to adversely affect the system's performance on positions unrelated to the new productions. This is an essential quality for a modifiable knowledge base.

Table 10.1 shows what percentage of these problems can be solved by PARADISE, PARADISE-2, CAPS, TECH, CHESS 4.4 running on a CDC 6400, and a human player rated as class A (Berliner [12]). PARADISE was limited to 45 minutes of CPU time per problem while the other programs were limited to 5 minutes.

TABLE 10.1   Percentage of problems
solved by chess players

	PARADISE	PARADISE-2	CAPS	TECH	CHESS 4.4	CLASS A HUMAN
Group I	78%	100%	67%	78%	94%	89%
Group II	68%	95%	74%	84%	95%	95%
Group III	94%	100%	61%	61%	78%	94%
Group IV	70%	95%	50%	40%	70%	80%
Group V	65%	94%	41%	47%	76%	53%
All 92	75%	97%	59%	61%	83%	83%

PARADISE already exhibits more generality in this domain than programs like TECH and CAPS. PARADISE-2 outperforms all the programs and the human. This shows that these problems do not push the limits of the expressibility of the production language nor the ability of the program to control the tree search. PARADISE does well on Group III because 7 of those 20 problems are in the 21 problems on which PARADISE was developed.

There are 20 problems solved by PARADISE-2 but not by PARADISE, but only 13 productions were written to solve them. In two instances, an already existing production was modified. In five instances the same production solved two different category 3 problems. This is a strong indication that the productions being written are fairly general and not tailored to the specific problem. These results indicate that the generality of PARADISE is reasonable and that the modifiability of the knowledge base is excellent.

PARADISE uses more CPU time and produces trees with considerably fewer nodes than the other programs. The previous example search is a problem from Group III, and tree sizes of 21 nodes for PARADISE and 439,459 for TECH2 are fairly typical. Table 10.2 compares the average tree size (in number of nodes) for PARADISE-2, CAPS, and CHESS 4.4 on the problems they solved in these 100.

TABLE 10.2   Comparison of average tree size
on first 92 problems (for solved
problems)

	PARADISE-2	CAPS	CHESS 4.4
Group I	19.8	167.8	24,907.3
Group II	28.7	226.4	34,726.0
Group III	35.0	206.1	24,200.1
Group IV	58.4	453.6	31,538.1
Group V	48.4	285.3	25,917.5
All 92	38.1	260.6	28,496.8

PARADISE attempts to use knowledge whenever possible in order to produce trees of the same order of magnitude as those produced by human masters. Table 10.2 shows that this has been accomplished for the most part. CAPS uses a lot of knowledge but invests only about one-fifth of a second per node calculating. CAPS relies on the search to correct mistakes made by inadequate knowledge, and this results in trees one order of magnitude larger than those produced by PARADISE. CHESS 4.4 has little chess knowledge and relies almost entirely on search to discriminate between moves. It generates trees that are three orders of magnitude larger than those generated by PARADISE. The two knowledge-oriented programs (CAPS and PARADISE) grow larger trees for the deeper combinations (groups IV and V), just as most humans would. CHESS 4.4's tree size seems unrelated to the depth of the combination. CHESS 4.4 is of course the best overall chess player of these three programs.

The different CPU time limit given to PARADISE is not as unfair as it seems. PARADISE-2 actually used an average of only 5.5 minutes of CPU time on the 89 problems it solved. Over the whole test set, less than 9% of the nodes generated had static analyses done on them. This shows that the plans do a good job of guiding the search. Because of this, static analyses are not a major overall expense even though an average one takes more than 12 seconds of CPU time. PARADISE could probably be speeded up by a factor of 2 or more with more efficient production matching (for which the program spends 91% of its CPU time).

Summary of long-term prospects

PARADISE discovers and selects moves primarily through analysis with its knowledge base. A small search of the game tree is done, primarily to verify the results of the knowledge-based analysis. In the best performance programs, on the other hand, there is almost no knowledge used in the initial analysis of a position. Instead of using the search to verify reasonably selected moves, these programs use the search to discover the reasonable moves.

PARADISE exhibits expert performance on positions it has the knowledge to understand, showing that a knowledge-based approach can solve some problems that the best search-based programs cannot solve because the solutions are too deep. (Of course, by the time you read this, the best search programs may be able to solve every problem PARADISE could.) PARADISE has the advantage of using higher level concepts (provided by the KSes) in its reasoning. This would hopefully make it easier for a human chess master (perhaps together with a programmer) to understand the program and improve it.

By using the knowledge base, the program selects only a few moves for searching and conducts a goal-oriented search (using its plans). The concepts in PARADISE communicate enough information to keep antithetical ideas from being combined to produce ridiculous plans. By communicating plans down the tree, PARADISE can understand new positions on the basis of its analysis of previous positions. By having particular goals in mind when looking at a new position, the system quickly focuses on the relevant part of the knowledge base. Plans in PARADISE express their purpose fairly well, without being too general or too specific. They contain enough additional information to enable the system to decide when a line has succeeded or failed, so the search can be controlled without a depth limit.

The advantages mentioned above must be weighed against the disadvantages of the approach used in PARADISE. The program cannot play a whole game of chess, and extending it requires considerable human effort. Furthermore, gaps in knowledge can catastrophically affect its performance.

Search-based programs play the whole game of chess, while PARADISE can only handle tactically sharp middle game positions. It would seem that the approach used in PARADISE would work very well for endgames also. Endgame knowledge could be encoded in production rules; this would require some new concepts, both primitive and higher level (e.g., pawn blockades). The search algorithm also appears appropriate for the endgame; following a single plan to its conclusion is a good tactic in the endgame. It may be harder to extend PARADISE to handle nontactical situations in the middle game. The search algorithm would not work as well in this situation since no single line of play is clearly best. A depth limit would be necessary and PARADISE's evaluation procedure would have to be modified to consider strategic factors. Perhaps the knowledge base could be used to improve the evaluation process. It should be possible to represent strategic knowledge in PARADISE-like production rules, although the language may have to be extended to express strategic ideas properly. A major problem in this is that it requires a large amount of human effort to develop a good knowledge base and to make sure the program uses it properly.

Like all knowledge-based programs, the strength of PARADISE depends on the completeness of the knowledge base. If a piece of knowledge is missing, the program may make a terrible blunder; something a full-width searching program would never do. PARADISE uses a mix of search and knowledge that involves more knowledge and less search than previous programs that include chess middle games in their domain. Because of this, one might expect PARADISE to miss combinations more often than programs that do more searching, but this has not been the case in the comparison on the test positions. PARADISE recognizes mating attacks that the other programs miss. PARADISE-2's knowledge base appears complete enough to outperform the programs with which it was compared on the first 100 positions in Reinfeld [164], even on positions within their depth limit.

Since gaps in knowledge are so harmful, it is necessary to be able to add new knowledge easily. The biggest advantage of the approach used in PARADISE (and the primary justification for the CPU time used) is the extendibility of the knowledge base. The testing of the program indicates that PARADISE's knowledge base is amenable to modification. Production rules (and therefore KSes) can be written quickly and inserted in the knowledge base to improve system performance without adverse affects. This means that gaps in knowledge can be easily filled. The play of most serious programs cannot be improved as easily. (An extra few milliseconds in the evaluation function of a search-based program drastically increases the time required to complete the search.)

For PARADISE's knowledge base to achieve the completeness needed to rival the best search-based programs (in middle game tactics), many productions would have to be added. There is no evidence that suggests large numbers of productions will harm PARADISE's performance (although problems may arise). New productions do not seem to increase significantly the branching factor when the added productions are at the right level of specificity (see Wilkins [171]). New productions do not increase significantly the analysis effort largely because plans guide PARADISE's search so well that a static analysis is done at less than 9% of the nodes generated. Thus most new productions will rarely be executed. Even when executed, productions usually do not match, and the system can often determine this with little effort. Even when matched, well-written productions take only a few milliseconds to a few hundred milliseconds to match. Compared to the 12 seconds of CPU time PARADISE spends on a typical analysis, this is not significant. The limiting factor in PARADISE's incremental improvement appears to be the ability to recognize more complex tactics at the correct level of specificity.

Weighing the above tradeoffs in order to judge which approach is best depends on the current technology. With developments such as faster machines, parallelism, better searching algorithms, or better hashing techniques, programs that rely on search can search deeper and perform better. Those who predicted in the early 1970s that adding two or three ply to the search would not significantly improve play were wrong. But it is hard to judge how much another few ply will help. It may turn out that deeper insight gained from the use of knowledge is necessary.

The development of better pattern recognizers or better knowledge representation techniques might increase the power of PARADISE's production language, allowing PARADISE to perform better. It is almost certain that more knowledge, properly incorporated, will improve play. There is little doubt that with current machines and our current understanding of how to use knowledge, good search-based programs solve a larger class of problems with less expense than do the best knowledge-based programs. However, techniques for using knowledge are only beginning to be developed and understood. This research shows ways to effectively use a large knowledge base that can be extended easily. However, this is only a start, and there is still much progress to be made in representing and using knowledge. As progress is made, a large effort to develop an extensive chess knowledge base and a search which uses the knowledge may result in a knowledge-based program which can approach and even surpass the performance of the best human chess masters.

Appendix
CHESS 4.5:
Competition in 1976

Peter W. Frey
Northwestern University

The Northwestern chess program entered two tournaments in 1976. The first was the Fourth Annual Paul Masson American Chess Championships held in California on July 24 and 25. The second was the Seventh Annual ACM Computer Chess Championship held at Houston on October 19–21. The same version of the program which had competed in the 1975 National Computer Chess Championship at Minneapolis (see Chapter 1) was entered in both tournaments. In 1976, however, the program was run on a more powerful computer, a large scale Control Data Cyber 170 system.

These tournament games are of interest for two reasons. First, it is worthwhile to determine if the quality of play improves by a significant amount when a chess program is run on a more powerful machine. Second, both tournaments involved competition against human opponents. The only previous games for CHESS 4.5 against a human opponent were those against David Levy at Minneapolis (see Chapter 1).

The Paul Masson American Chess Championships

CHESS 4.5 was entered in the B section of the California tournament. It played against 5 human opponents with USCF ratings ranging between 1693 and 1784. The program had a perfect 5–0 score. Nobody was more surprised at this outcome than the authors, David Slate and Larry Atkin. They have consistently maintained that the program is about C class in strength. One of the human opponents at the Paul Masson tournament remarked that the program was the "strongest 1572 player that he had ever seen." Three of the games from the California tournament are presented.

Paul Masson, Round 1

WHITE CHESS 4.5		BLACK Neil Regan (1693)	
1. P–K4	P–QB4	2. N–KB3	N–QB3
3. P–Q4	PxP	4. NxP	P–KN3
5. N–QB3	B–N2	6. B–K3	N–B3
7. B–QB4	Q–R4	8. O–O	O–O
9. N–N3	Q–B2	10. P–B3	P–Q3
11. N–N5	Q–N1	12. Q–K2	P–QR3
13. N–B3	B–Q2	14. P–QR4	N–QN5
15. B–N6	Q–B1	16. N–R5	N–B3
17. NxN	QxN	18. P–R5	R/R–B1
19. B–Q5	NxB	20. PxN	Q–B5
21. QxP/K7	B–N4	22. QxP/Q6	B–Q5+
23. BxB	QxB+	24. R–B2	R–B3
25. Q–R3	R–B5	26. R–Q1	R–K1
27. RxQ	R–K8+	28. R–B1	RxR+
29. KxR	RxN+	30. K–B2	RxQ
31. PxR	Resigns		

Paul Masson, Round 4

WHITE Wesley White (1742)		BLACK CHESS 4.5	
1. P–K4	N–QB3	2. P–Q4	P–Q4
3. P–K5	P–B3	4. P–KB4	B–B4
5. N–KB3	P–K3	6. P–QR3	N–R3
7. B–Q3	PxP	8. P/BxP	B–K5
9. O–O	BxN	10. RxB	NxP/Q5
11. B–N6+	PxB	12. QxN	P–B3
13. Q–Q3	N–B4	14. P–KN4	B–B4+
15. K–B1	N–R5	16. P–N4	NxR
17. QxP/N6+	K–Q2	18. PxB	Q–KB1
19. B–B4	RxP	20. N–B3	NxP/K4
21. Q–N5	N–B2	22. Q–N6	R–R8+
23. K–N2	RxR	24. N–K2	RxP/R6
25. N–Q4	R–K1	26. P–N5	N–R1
27. NxP/K6	RxN	28. Q–R7	QxB
29. QxP+	R–K2	30. QxN	R–K7+
31. K–R1	Q–KB8 Mate		

Paul Masson, Round 5

WHITE CHESS 4.5		BLACK Herbert Chu (1784)	
1. P–K4	P–K3	2. P–Q4	P–QN3
3. N–KB3	B–N2	4. N–B3	B–N5
5. B–Q3	N–KB3	6. B–KN5	P–KR3
7. BxN	QxB	8. O–O	P–KN4

9. Q–Q2	N–B3	10. P–QR3	B–K2
11. N–N5	B–Q1	12. P–K5	Q–N2
13. Q–K3	P–R3	14. N–B3	P–N5
15. N–K1	B–N4	16. P–B4	B–K2
17. P–B5	PxP	18. BxP/B5	NxP/Q5
19. BxP/Q7+	KxB	20. QxN+	K–B1
21. N–Q3	K–N1	22. Q–Q7	Q–N4
23. RxP/B7	Q–K6+	24. K–R1	B–Q1
25. QxP/N4	K–R2	26. P–K6	B–N4
27. R–K1	R/KR–KN1	28. RxQ	BxR
29. R–N7	R/R–KB1	30. P–KR4	Resigns

ACM Computer Chess Championship, 1976

At Houston, the annual battle between computer programs followed a familiar script. At the end of the first three rounds, two programs had a perfect 3–0 record. One was CHESS 4.5 and the other was CHAOS. Both programs were running on powerful machines: CHESS 4.5 on an advanced CDC Cyber 170 system at Minneapolis and CHAOS on an Amdahl computer at the University of Michigan.

ACM, 1976, Round 4

WHITE   CHESS 4.5   **BLACK   CHAOS**

1. P–K4	P–QB4	2. N–KB3	N–QB3
3. P–Q4	PxP	4. NxP	N–B3
5. N–QB3	P–K3	6. NxN	P/NxN
7. P–K5	N–Q4	8. NxN	P/BxN
9. B–Q3	P–N3	10. O–O	B–KN2
11. Q–K2	B–N2	12. P–QN3	Q–K2
13. P–QR4	Q–N5	14. B–R3	Q–B6
15. P–B4	P–B3	16. B–Q6	P–B4
17. P–R5	K–B2	18. Q–B2	B–KB1
19. BxB	R/KRxB	20. Q–R4	Q–B4+
21. K–R1	K–N2	22. P–QN4	QxP/N5
23. R/R–N1	QxP/R4	24. RxB	Q–R5
25. B–N5	Time Forfeit		

During the tournament, CHESS 4.5 played several "blitz" games against interested spectators. Special rules were adopted. The human player had 5 minutes of clock time for the entire game. The machine was set to average 5 seconds of computation time for each move. In tournament play, the machine usually averages about 80 seconds per move. If the human player had not exhausted his 5 minutes by the 60th move, he automatically won. Two of these "blitz" games are presented below.

ACM, 1976, Demonstration

WHITE	Englebretson (2039)		BLACK	CHESS 4.5
1. N–QB3	N–QB3		2. P–K4	P–K3
3. P–Q4	P–Q4		4. P–K5	P–B3
5. P–B4	Q–Q2		6. N–B3	Q–B2
7. B–N5	P–QR3		8. BxN+	PxB
9. O–O	R–N1		10. Q–K2	N–R3
11. K–R1	B–K2		12. PxP	QxP
13. N–K5	R–N3		14. Q–R5+	N–B2
15. B–K3	RxP/N7		16. NxP/B6	RxP/B7
17. NxB	KxN		18. N–R4	N–Q3
19. N–B5	N–B4		20. B–N1	NxP
21. BxN	QxB		22. N–N3	Q–B3
23. R/B–K1	QxP		24. R–KB1	R–KB7
25. RxR	QxR		26. Q–N5+	Q–B3
27. Q–N3	P–K4		28. R–QB1	P–B3
29. P–KR3	R–B1		30. N–R5	B–Q2
31. Q–R3+	Q–Q3		32. Q–KN3	K–B2
33. N–N7	Q–K2		34. N–B5	P–K5
35. NxP/R6	K–N1		36. R–K1	P–B4
37. N–B7	P–Q5		38. N–Q5	Q–K3
39. N–B4	Q–QB3		40. N–R5	Q–KN3
41. QxQ	PxQ		42. N–N3	P–K6
43. K–N1	R–K1		44. K–B1	P–Q6
45. K–N1	P–Q7		46. R–Q1	B–R5
47. R–N1	P–B5		48. N–K2	B–B7
49. R–R1	P–Q8=Q+		50. RxQ	BxR
51. N–B3	P–K7		52. NxP	RxN
53. P–QR4	P–B6		54. P–R5	P–B7
55. P–R6	P–B8=Q		56. P–R7	Q–B3
57. P–R8=Q+	QxQ		58. Resigns	

ACM, 1976, Demonstration

WHITE	Brieger (2131)		BLACK	CHESS 4.5
1. P–K4	N–QB3		2. P–Q4	P–Q4
3. P–K5	P–B3		4. P–KB4	B–B4
5. P–KN4	B–K5		6. N–KB3	NxP/Q5
7. NxN	BxR		8. P–K6	P–QR3
9. B–Q3	P–QB4		10. P–N5	Q–Q3
11. Q–R5+	K–Q1		12. Q–B7	K–B2
13. N–B5	Q–N3		14. N–N3	B–B6
15. N–B3	PxP/N4		16. PxP/N5	P–Q5

17. B–KB4+	K–B3	18. B–K5	B–Q4
19. NxB	QxP	20. R–Q1	KxN
21. Q–B5	K–B3	22. Q–K4+	K–N3
23. Q–Q5	Q–N5+	24. K–K2	P–R3
25. Q–Q7	PxP	26. Time Forfeit	

Peter W. Frey
Northwestern University

Early in 1976, there were very few knowledgeable individuals who would have wagered that a computer chess program could hold it own against a strong human player (USCF rating above 2000). Slate and Atkin, in particular, estimated the strength of their program at this time to be about 1800 on the USCF scale. Although it is no small achievement to develop a program which can play at this level, a rating of 1800 is not particularly impressive in world-class chess. This level of skill is clearly inconsistent with the claim that a machine will soon be the world champion.

In the last two years, improvements in the program and the availibility of more powerful computing equipment have led to a reassessment of machine chess ability. After a period of high expectations and relatively little progress in the early 1970s, these recent developments are quite encouraging. The first signal came in July, 1976 when CHESS 4.5 won the Class B section of the Paul Masson American Chess Championship in California. The message became louder in February, 1977 when CHESS 4.5 won the 84th Minnesota Open Tournament against expert and high Class A players. One of the games in particular demonstrated that CHESS 4.5 could play an entire game of reasonably good chess. The game with Charles Fenner, in fact, was one of the best games ever played by a computer.

84th Minnesota Open, Round 2
February 19, 1977

WHITE CHESS 4.5, CYBER 176	BLACK Charles Fenner (2016)	Computing Time
1. P–K4	P–QB4	Book
2. N–KB3	P–K3	Book

3. P–Q4	PxP	Book
4. NxP	P–QR3	Book
5. P–QB4	N–KB3	Book
6. B–Q3	Q–B2	Book
7. O–O	B–B4	110
8. N–N3	B–R2	67
9. N–B3	N–B3	64
10. B–N5	N–K4	83
11. BxN	PxB	128
12. Q–K2	P–Q3	59
13. K–R1	B–Q2	47
14. P–B4	NxB	59
15. QxN	O–O–O	345
16. R/R–Q1	B–B3	99
17. P–KB5	B–N1	95
18. P–N3	P–KR4	99
19. PxP	P–R5	62
20 RxP	PxP/6	71
21. QxP/3	R/Q–N1	88
22. PxP	QxP	67
23. RxQ	RxQ	161
24. N–Q5		197

Fenner offers a draw, 4.5 declines

24.	B–K1	
25. N–N6+	K–Q1	67
26. RxP/7	B–B3	266
27. RxB+	K–B2	67
28. R–QB8+	RxR	1
29. PxR	BxP+	102
30. K–N1	R–KR1	269
31. N–Q5+	K–B3	173
32. N–R5+	Resigns	204

96 seconds per move average

In March, 1977, Donald Michie attempted to set up an official match between CHESS 4.5 and David Levy to determine if a computer was capable of defeating the International Master. If Levy lost, Kozdrowicki, Michie, McCarthy, and Papert would be able to collect on their famous wager. If no program beats Levy by September, 1978, then Levy will collect. Although Slate and Atkin were not optimistic about their program's chances, they consented to the match and David Cahlander arranged for the CYBER 176 to be available at Control Data headquarters in Minneapolis. The match was held on April 1, 1977 at Carnegie-Mellon University in Pittsburgh.

Levy Challenge Game
April 1, 1977

WHITE CHESS 4.5, CYBER 176	BLACK David Levy	Computing Time
1. P–K4	P–QB4	Book
2. N–KB3	P–Q3	Book
3. P–Q4	PxP	Book
4. NxP	N–KB3	Book
5. N–QB3	P–KN3	Book
6. P–B3	B–N2	Book
7. B–K3	O–O	Book
8. Q–Q2	N–B3	Book
9. B–QB4	P–QR3	Book
10. NxN	PxN	70
11. O–O	N–Q2	209
12. P–B4	N–N3	193
13. B–K2	B–K3	80
14. P–QN3	N–B1	59
15. P–QR3	Q–R4	163
16. P–QN4	Q–B2	93
17. P–B5	B–Q2	121
18. B–R6	Q–N3+	644
19. K–R1	Q–Q5	115
20. QxQ	BxQ	75
21. R–B3	B–N2	118
22. BxB	KxB	143
23. R–QN1	N–N3	107
24. R/3–B1	R/B–QN1	153
25. R/N–Q1	P–B3	46
26. P–QR4	P–QR4	129
27. P–N5	PxP/N	68
28. PxP/5	R–QB1	134
29. R–Q3	R–B4	143
30. R–N3	R/1–QB1	243
31. R/1–B3	P–R5	118
32. P–R4	P–R6	64
33. PxP	PxP	391
34. R–K3	B–K3	249
35. P–R5	P–N4	245
36. N–Q5	P–R7	75
37. R–QR3	BxN	142
38. PxB	RxP/7	148
39. B–Q1	R–Q7	318
40. K–R2	R–B8	137
41. B–N3	P–R8=Q	118
42. RxQ	RxR	63
43. R–K3 and resigns		

122 seconds per move average

This convincing win gave notice that Levy is not planning to lose his wager. It would appear that Levy's considerable experience with computer chess is an important asset when he competes against a machine. His playing style in this game clearly took advantage of the machine's inability to make long-range plans.

During the spring and summer of 1977, several changes were made in the Northwestern chess program in preparation for the Second World Computer Chess Championship to be held in August in Toronto, Canada. As a reflection of these changes, the program's name was altered from CHESS 4.5 to CHESS 4.6. One of the modifications was the capacity to "think" on the opponent's time. While the opponent is thinking or calculating, CHESS 4.6 works on a reply to the move which seems most likely. If the opponent subsequently makes this move, the machine is prepared to make a quick reply. If not, then CHESS 4.6 starts afresh and calculates a reply in the normal fashion.

In addition, several coefficients in the evaluation function were changed (the primary change involved a heavier weighting for King safety), the quiescence search was expanded to include additional checking moves, and the efficiency of the transposition table was enhanced. A new option was also introduced which permits moves to be entered in algebraic notation.

CHESS 4.6 had a successful tournament at Toronto, winning all 4 of its matches. The major event of the tournament was expected to be the game between CHESS 4.6 and the Russian program, KAISSA. Unfortunately, the tragedy of Stockholm reoccurred, except this time in reverse. KAISSA was unexpectedly beaten in the first round by DUCHESS, an American program written at Duke University. Because of this loss, KAISSA never had enough points to be paired with CHESS 4.6. In a replay of Stockholm, a demonstration match between KAISSA and CHESS 4.6 was arranged after the regular tournament.

Demonstration Game, Second World Computer Championship
August 8, 1977

WHITE—KAISSA (USSR)	BLACK CHESS 4.6 (USA)	Computing Time
1. P–K4	N–QB3	Book
2. N–KB3	P–K3	Book
3. P–Q4	P–Q4	Book
4. B–Q3	PxP	222
5. BxP	B–Q2	288
6. O–O	N–B3	65
7. R–K1	NxB	78
8. RxN	B–K2	84
9. P–B4	P–B4	67
10. R–K1	O–O	77
11. N–B3	P–B5	74
12. Q–Q3	Q–K1	196

13. P–KN3	PxP	135
14. P/RxP	Q–B2	215
15. B–B4	P–KN4	84
16. P–Q5	PxP	329
17. NxP/Q	PxB	61
18. NxB+	NxN	343
19. QxB	N–N3	300
20. QxQ+	RxQ	286
21. P–KN4	R–Q2	349
22. R/R–Q1	R/1–Q1	84
23. RxR	RxR	242
24. K–N2	K–N2	70
25. N–N5	R–Q7	75
26. R–QN1	R–B7	118
27. P–N3	N–K4	216
28. R–KR1	RxP/R	221
29. R–R4	N–Q6	77
30. N–R3	R–N7	413
31. P–N5	K–N1	233
32. NxP	RxP/7+	411
33. K–N3	RxN	216
34. RxR	NxR	83
35. KxN	K–B2	148
36. P–N4	K–K3	161
37. K–K4	P–QR3	185
38. K–B4	K–Q3	158
39. K–K4	P–B4	179
40. PxP+	KxP	143
41. K–Q3	P–QR4	174
42. K–B3	P–R5	135
43. K–Q3	K–N5	137
44. K–B2	KxP	115
45. Resigns		

163 seconds per move average

On the basis of the tournament results, Levy concluded that "American computer programs dominate the world scene even more than Eastern European chess players dominate the human circuit" (*Chess Life and Review,* Jan., 1978, p. 33).

One of the surprising discoveries in computer chess is that a full-width program can compete effectively at speed chess. In fact, the evidence suggests that these programs may be better at speed chess (relative to humans) than at regular tournament chess. Because the machine cannot manipulate the chess pieces,[1] special rules are employed for speed chess. The human player has 5 minutes total time as usual. The machine is set to average 5 seconds per move. If the machine has not given mate or announced mate

[1] Slate and Atkin are working on a robot arm which may correct this limitation.

by move 60, it loses on time.

An interesting example of blitz chess played under these special rules occurred in September, 1977 in London at the Aaronson chess tournament. The opponent was Michael Stean, a grandmaster with a rating of 2485. David Levy moved the pieces for the program.

Blitz Chess against Michael Stean in London
September 18, 1977

WHITE CHESS 4.6, CYBER 176	BLACK Michael Stean (2485)	Computing Time
1. P–K4	P–QN3	Book
2. P–Q4	B–N2	2
3. N–QB3	P–QB4	10
4. PxP	PxP	3
5. B–K3	P–Q3	6
6. B–QN5+	N–Q2	6
7. N–B3	P–K3	3
8. O–O	P–QR3	2
9. BxN+	QxB	6
10. Q–Q3	N–K2	8
11. R/R–Q1		

Stean: The damned computer has one of my pawns.

	R–Q1	
12. Q–B4	N–N3	14
13. R/B–K1	B–K2	3
14. Q–N3	Q–B3	3
15. K–R1	O–O	9
16. B–N5	B–R1	6
17. BxB	NxB	5
18. P–QR4	R–N1	8
19. Q–R2	R–N5	3
20. P–QN3	P–B4	5
21. N–KN5	PxP	8
22. N/3xP	RxP/7	14
23. RxP	QxR	6
24. NxQ	RxP/N7	4
25. N/5–K4	R–N5	17
26. P–B4	N–B4	3
27. P–R3		3

Stean: This computer is a genius.

	N–N6+	
28. K–R2		4

Stean: Help.

	RxN	
29. Q–KB2	P–R3	20
30. NxR	NxN	5
31. Q–B3	R–N1	10
32. RxN	R–KB1	6
33. Q–N4	BxR	6

34. QxP/6+	K–R1	10
35. QxB	R–B3	4
36. Q–K5	R–QN3	5
37. QxP/5	RxP	9
38. Q–QB8+	K–R2	7
39. QxP	Resigns	3

7 seconds per move average

Sometimes the computer makes moves which have a mechanical appearance. An observer might comment that only a dumb machine would play like that. There are other times, however, when the program makes moves which are quite creative and seem to be alarmingly human. In the following match, which has been dubbed the "game of symmetry," the machine seems to be hiding an impish smile.

The Twin-Cities Open
April 29, 1978

WHITE Bill Elger (1668)	BLACK CHESS 4.6, CYBER 176	Computing Time
1. P–QB4	N–KB3	Book
2. N–QB3	P–Q4	Book
3. PxP	NxP	Book
4. P–K4	N–N5	Book
5. P–Q4	QxP	55
6. QxQ	N–B7+	145
7. K–Q1	NxQ	51
8. B–KB4	P–QB3	74
9. B–K5	N–K3	66
10. N–B3	N–Q2	52
11. B–N3	P–QN4	77
12. P–QR3	P–N4	104
13. B–Q3	N/2–B4	379
14. B–B2	B–KN2	292
15. P–R3	B–N2	65
16. R–K1	R–Q1+	64
17. K–K2	B–QR3	80
18. K-K3	B–R3	200
19. N–K5	P–KN5+	121
20. P–B4	PxP e.p.+	100
21. K–B2	R–Q7+	165
22. Resigns		

100 seconds per move average

In May, 1978, CHESS 4.6 entered a simultaneous exhibition sponsored by the Minnesota Chess Association. Walter Browne, current United States champion, took on 44 different opponents at one time. In a simultaneous exhibition, the grandmaster proceeds from one board to the next in steady procession and each opponent is required to move when the grandmaster reaches his table. In this environment, successive moves may be separated by rather long breaks, especially during the middle-game. Because of this arrangement, CHESS 4.6 had more time to calculate each move than normally would be the case in a regular tournament. Walter Browne also had the considerable handicap of playing 43 other opponents at the same time. Despite this, Browne indicated before the exhibition that he fully expected to beat the machine. The result did not fulfill this expectation; in fact, CHESS 4.6 played a remarkably solid game.

Walter Browne Simultaneous Exhibition
May 6, 1978

WHITE Walter Browne (2547)	BLACK CHESS 4.6, CYBER 176	Computing Time
1. P–Q4	N–KB3	Book
2. P–QB4	P–B4	Book
3. N–KB3	PxP	Book
4. NxP	P–K4	Book
5. N–N5	B–B4	Book
6. N/1–B3	O–O	162
7. P–K3	P–Q3	142
8. B–K2	P–QR3	158
9. N–R3	N–B3	248
10. N–B2	B–B4	241
11. O–O	Q–Q2	255
12. P–QN3	K–R1	395
13. B–N2	R–KN1	356
14. N–R4	B–R2	458
15. B–R3	P–R3	272
16. R–B1	R/R–Q1	503
17. N–N4	NxN	254
18. BxN	Q–B2	70
19. Q–K1	B–B4	527
20. B–KB3	B–Q6	395
21. BxB	PxB	410
22. B–K2	B–B4	426
23. P–B3	P–K5	535
24. P–B4	B–Q2	468
25. N–B3	Q–R4	364
26. Q–R4	B–B3	349
27. R–QB2	P–QN4	285
28. P–KN4	P–N5	387
29. N–Q1	R–Q3	517
30. N–B2	R/1–Q1	302
31. R–Q1	RxR+	295
32. BxR	R–Q3	357
33. Q–N3	Q–Q1	511
34. R–B1	R–Q7	255

35. P–N5	PxP	460
36. PxP	N–R2	560
37. P–N6	PxP	486
38. QxP	Q–R5	226
39. Q–B5	B–Q2	330
40. Q–B4	QxQ	292
41. PxQ	P–K6	319
42. N–K4	P–K7	248
43. BxP	RxB	203
44. NxP	B–B1	176
45. R–Q1	R–K1	139
46. P–QR3	PxP	116
47. R–R1	P–N4	176
48. PxP	R–K4	85
49. P–N4	P–R4	92
50. N–Q3	RxP+	69
51. K–B2	PxP	61
52. NxP	R–QR4	115
53. K–K3	B–K3	72
54. K–Q4	N–N4	81
55. N–B2	P–R7	79
56. N–N4	R–R5	45
57. K–B5	N–K5+	118
58. K–N5	B–Q2+	90
59. N–B6	N–B6+	67
60. K–B5	BxN	48
61. KxB	RxP+	90
62. K–Q6	R–Q5+	52
63. K–K5	R–Q8	31
64. Resigns		

Many observers (including Levy) have remarked that computer programs are especially weak in the endgame. The play of CHESS 4.6 in the last 15 or so moves of this match is anything but weak. It may be that this game is an exception to the rule or it may be that the endgame weakness theme has been overplayed.

At the present time (July, 1978), David Slate is working on a new version of the Northwestern program, CHESS 5.0. The new program is written entirely in Fortran and can be easily converted to run on other machines. In addition, the new program has a cleaner structure than its assembly-language predecessor and can be modified more easily. If completed by the end of August, this program is destined to compete with David Levy to conclude the famous wager. If present plans are fulfilled, CHESS 5.0 will run on one of the most powerful computers, the Cray-1. The match late this summer may be interesting.

Appendix to the second edition

David J. Slate and Peter W. Frey
Northwestern University

A great deal has transpired in the world of computer chess since 1978 when the first edition of this book was published. The technical aspects of chess programming have not changed very much and thus the information provided in the original chapters is still current. Despite the lack of progress in theory, hardware modifications and software finesse have definitely produced a noticeable improvement in across-the-board play.

Here we present a selection of games played by computers in organized competition since the publication of the first edition. Some of these games were chosen because they represent exciting chess and are enjoyable for that reason alone. Others illustrate trends that have developed over the last few years, such as the ascendance of super-brute-force chess computers using custom-made chess-specific hardware, and the proliferation and marked improvement of microprocessor-based programs. In addition, a few games were selected because they demonstrate problems in chess programming or problems with the way that computer chess tournaments are currently run.

It was very difficult to make this selection. There have been many tournaments and many interesting games. A comprehensive record of computer chess play is available through the newsletter published by the International Computer Chess Association (ICCA). The interested reader can receive additional information by writing directly to the ICCA at Vogelback Computing Center, Northwestern University, Evanston, Illinois, 60201, USA.

Game 1: 1978 North American Computer Chess Championship Round 2, December 3, 1978, Washington, D.C.

Belle (White) vs. Chess 4.7 (Black)

Belle consists of specially constructed computer-chess hardware driven by a DEC PDP-11 computer. It was designed, built, and programmed by Ken Thompson and Joe Condon of Bell Telephone Laboratories in Murray Hill, New Jersey. Ken is an officer and active participant in the ICCA. A description of the most recent version of Belle appears as one of the two new chapters that were prepared for the second edition of this book.

Chess 4.7, by David Slate of Northwestern University and Larry Atkin, formerly of Northwestern, was the reigning world champion at the time this game was played. Chess 4.7 had developed a reputation as the most successful example of the "brute-force" tree-searching techniques, examining an average of 3600 positions per second on the Control Data Cyber 176. In this game, it became a victim of brute force, losing a tense tactical battle to Belle, who at this time weighed in at about 5000 positions per second.

Notes accompanying the game score are by Hans Berliner (HB) of Carnegie-Mellon University, and by David Slate (DS). David's remarks include information from the machine records which were printed at the tournament site by Belle and Chess 4.7.

White	Black
Belle	**Chess 4.7**
1. e2–e4	Nb8–c6
2. d2–d4	d7–d5
3. Nb1–c3	

HB: This is undoubtedly the best move against this frequently essayed opening of Chess 4.7. Black is forced to play 3. . . . e7–e6, after which he gets a cramped French Defense position because c7–c5 cannot be played immediately. If instead Black played 3. . . . d5xe4, White would reply d4–d5 with an advantage.

3.	e7–e6
4. Ng1–f3	Bf8–b4
5. e4–e5	Ng8–e7
6. Bc1–d2	Ne7–f5
7. Nc3–e2	Bb4–e7
8. c2–c3	O–O
9. Ne2–f4	f7–f6

HB: White has achieved a slight space superiority and Black must now break here in order to alleviate the pressure since the usual c7–c5 requires too much preparation.

10. Bf1–d3	f6xe5
11. d4xe5	

HB: After 11. Nf3xe5 Black can play Be7–f6 with a satisfactory game.

11.	g7–g5!

HB: A fine, though antipositional idea. Black must create some room for himself on the K-side before White gets too strong there. The weakening of the K-side is two sided as White must also weaken himself or submit to the loss of a pawn.

12. g2–g4!

HB: Best. After 12. Nf4–h5, g5–g4 followed by Nc6xe5 Black will gain enough time and space to be able to overcome any adverse effects due to his open king's position.

DS: Belle's 12. g2–g4 was predicted by Chess 4.7.

12.	Nf5–g7!
13. Nf4–g2	b7–b6?

HB: Here I suspect most Masters would play the "automatic" 13. ... Rf8xNf3, 14. Qd1xRf3, Nc6xe5, 15. Qf3–e2, Ne5xBd3, 16. Qe2xNd3, e3–e4. This results in settling upon White a very inferior pawn position and inactive minor pieces against Black's fine center and active minor pieces; cetrainly worth half a pawn. In view of what transpires, Black's play must be judged inferior. In any case, White is not interested in preventing this line.

14. Qd1–e2	Bc8–b7
15. Rh1–g1	

HB: Probably White does not play the beckoning 15. h2–h4 because of Rf8xNf3, 16. Qe2xRf3, Nc6xe5, 17. Qf3–e2, Ne5xBd3+, 18. Qe2xNd3, g5xh4, which gives Black two pawns for the exchange; however, it would be appropriate for White to prepare for this thrust along the rook file by 15. O–O–O. If above, 17. Bd3xh7+, Kg8xBh7, 18. h4xg5+, Kh7–g8, 19. Qf3–h3, with a wild position that White need not let himself in for. The text is weak.

15.	a7–a5

HB: Both sides are hard put for a good idea. On this and the next moves, Rf8xNf3 is stronger than ever before, and White should castle on the queen's side.

16.	a2–a4	Kg8–h8
17.	h2–h3	Kh8–g8
18.	Rg1–h1	h7–h6
19.	h3–h4	d5–d4

HB: Why has Black not tried this obvious move before? The answer is that it leads to a ferocious attack for White. White should now play 20. Qe2–e4!, Rf8xNf3, 21. Qe4–h7+ (not Qe4xRf3, Nc6xe5 with a good game for Black), Kg8–f8, 22. Bd3–g6!, Be7–f6!, 23. e5xBf6, Qd8xf6, 24. h4xg5, h6xg5, 25. Bg6–e4, Rf3xf2, 26. Bd2xg5 with a winning position for White. Black, seeing much danger, but not being able to see to the end of all this, considers this to be his best chance. He would have been better advised to have played 19. . . . . Rf8xNf3 (better late than never), 20. Qe2xRf3, Nc6xe5, 21. Qf3–e2, Ne5xBd3+, 22. Qe2xNd3, e6–e5, 23. Qd3–g6, Qd8–d6, 24. Qg6xQd6, c7xd6, with Black having somewhat the worst of it.

DS: Here Chess 4.7 did predict 20. Qe2–e4, Rf8xNf3 as Hans suggests, but then predicted the inferior continuation 21. Qe4xRf3, Nc6xe5, with slight advantage to Black.

20. h4xg5?   Nc6–b4!!

HB: A tremendous move which now makes White play correctly to save himself. After the correct 21. c3xNb4, Bb7xNf3, 22. Bd3–h7+, Kg8–h8! (not Kg8xBh7, 23. Rh1xh6+, Kh7–g8, 24. Qe2–d3, Bf3xNg2, 25. Qd3–h7+ leading to mate), 23. Rh1xh6! (not 23. Qe2–d3, Be7xg5, 24. Qd3–g6!, Bf3xNg2, 25. Bd2xBg5, Qd8xBg5 and Black has a decent position), Bf3xQe2, 24. Bh7–b1+, leading to a draw by repetition. Less exact would be 21. Rh1xh6?!, Rf8xNf3!, 22. c3xNb4, Be7xg5, 23. Rh6–h2, a5xb4, with a wild position which appears to favor Black.

DS: Here Chess 4.7 did a six-ply search and predicted an eight-ply (remember the quiescence search) principal variation which exactly matched the moves actually played through 24. Nf3xd2. This included the blunders by both sides: 21. g5xh6??, Nb4xBd3+??. Unfortunately, Chess 4.7 scored this line as only a small advantage for White, not realizing the power of White's resulting attack, and not seeing the strength of the alternative 21. . . . . d4xc3.

21. g5xh6??

HB: A blunder that should lose because now the attack on the rook file is gone.

DS: Belle predicted 21. . . . . Nb4xBd3+, 22. Qe2xNd3, Rf8xNf3, 23. h6–h7+, Kg8–f7, 24. Qd3xd4, with a small advantage for Black.

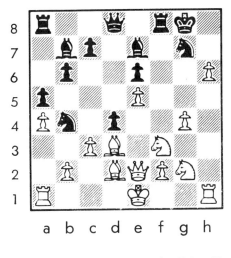

21. . . . . .   Nb4xBd3+??

HB: Black returns the compliment and lands in an irrevocable loss. From the theoretical point of view this must be the worst move ever made by any version of the Northwestern program; it turns a sure win into a sure loss. From a practical point of view the situation is anything but easy. 21. . . . d4xc3 wins by force as White then has three pieces *en prise* and cannot begin to save all of them. If 22. B–h7+, Kg8xBh7, 23. h6xNg7+, Kh7xg7, 24. Bd2–h6+, Kg7–g8, 25. Ra1–d1 (Bh6xRf8, Qd8xBf8 leaves Black in complete control), Bb7xNf3!!, 26. Rd1xQd8, Ra8xRd8, 27. Bh6xRf8, Bf3xQe2 and Black wins. Less precise is 21. . . . . Bb7xNf3, 22. h6xNg7!, Bf3xQe2, 23. g7xRf8=Q+, Be7xQf8, 24. Bd3–h7+ and White still has many chances. After the text move, NxB, however, Black is hopelessly lost.

DS: Chess 4.7 changed its predicted line, but still saw only a small advantage for White, and, of course, missed 21. . . . . d4xc3. It thought for 888 seconds, and had to terminate its eight-ply search before completing it. The principal variation it found was 22. Qe2xNd3, d4xc3, 23. Qd3xc3, Rf8xNf3, 24. h6–h7+, Kg8–h8.

22. Qe2xNd3

DS: Belle predicted 22. . . . . d4xc3, 23. Qd3–g6, c3xBd2+, 24. Nf3xd2, Rf8–f7, 25. h6–h7+, Kg6–h8, 26. Qg6xRf7 with slightly more than a pawn advantage for White.

22. . . . . .   d4xc3

DS: Now Chess 4.7 calculated an advantage of nearly two pawns for White.

23. Qd3–g6!

HB: This must be what was not appreciated by Chess 4.7. White's attack is now overwhelming and Black dare not capture any more material.

23. . . . . .   c3xBd2+

DS: Chess 4.7 now sees White's advantage at three and one-half pawns. Its view of the impending disaster was 24. Nf3xd2, Rf8–f7, 25. h6xNg7, Rf7xg7, 26. Qg6xe6+, Rg7–f7.

24.	Nf3xd2	Rf8–f7
25.	h6xNg7	Rf7xg7
26.	Qg6xe6+	Rg7–f7
27.	Qe6–h6!	Rf7–g7
28.	Qh6–h8+	Kg8–f7
29.	e5–e6+	

HB: Winning the exchange and more; in effect, ending the game.

29.	. . . . .	Kf7xe6
30.	Qh8xRg7	Bb7xNg2
31.	Rh1–h6+	Ke6–d7
32.	O–O–O	

HB: After all these hours of indecision about where to take up a royal residence! The rest is silence. It is interesting that two such search-oriented programs whose strong suit is obviously tactics should make so many tactical errors. The answer is in the fact that the outcomes of the various tactical forays were far from easy to evaluate insofar as mating and material threats abounded even after a quiet move terminated the quiescence search. Thus even Chess 4.7, with its excellent judgment of positions, was fooled.

32.	. . . . .	Bg2–d5
33.	Nd2–e4	Kd7–c8
34.	Rh6–h8	Bd5xNe4
35.	Rd1xQd8	Be7xRd8
36.	Qg7–e7	Kc8–b7
37.	Qe7xBe4+	Kb7–a7
38.	Rh8–g8	Ra8–b8
39.	g4–g5	Bd8–e7
40.	Rg8xRb8	Be7xg5+
41.	f2–f4	Bg5xf4+
42.	Qe4xBf4	Ka7xRb8
43.	Kc1–d2	Kb8–b7
44.	Kd2–d3	Kb7–c8
45.	b2–b4	a5xb4
46.	Qf4xb4	Kc8–d7
47.	Qb4–b5+	Kd7–d8
48.	Kd3–d4	Resigns

(1–0)

This win for Belle was a portent of things to come. Chess 4.7 reflected a decade of progress for a particular philosophy of chess programming and had reached somewhat of an asymptote for this strategy as implemented on a conventional supercomputer. Belle incorporated this same philosophy but in a more powerful hybrid machine. In succeeding years, Ken Thompson and Joe Condon increased their speed advantage and the authors of Chess 4.7 quietly readied their creation for the museum. David Slate had already begun to work on a new program, Nuchess, which placed more emphasis on chess knowledge while still maintaining a powerful search component.

Game 2: North American Computer Chess Championship
Round 4, December 5, 1978, Washington, D.C.

Blitz (White) vs Belle (Black)

This short game was a lovely display of the tactical power of Belle. The win gave Belle a spotless 4–0 record for the tournament and first place. Ken Thompson was very pleased with this game and he appeared at the following year's tournament in a custom designed tee shirt with the final position printed on the front and the game score emblazoned on the back.

Blitz, authored by Robert Hyatt of the University of Southern Mississippi, is also a search-oriented, brute force chess program. Although it fared poorly in this game, it was reincarnated two years later on a CRAY-1 to do some tactical crunching of its own.

The commentary for this game is provided by Hans Berliner of Carnegie-Mellon University, the former World Champion of Correspondence Chess. Hans described this game at the time it was played as "undoubtedly the most brilliant game of chess yet played by a computer." He added that "if Mikhail Tahl or Bobby Fischer had played it, the game record would undoubtedly be making the rounds of the chess journals."

White	Black
Blitz	Belle
1. e2–e4	e7–e5
2. Ng1–f3	Nb8–c6
3. Nb1–c3	Ng8–f6
4. Bf1–b5	Nc6–d4
5. Bb5–c4	

HB: White is best advised to head for the draw with 5. Nf3xNd4, e5xNd4, 6. e4–e5, d4xNc3, 7. e5xNf6, Qd8xf6 (not c3xd2+ because after Bc1xd2 White has an advantage), 8. d2xc3 with a known drawn position. This is why White seldom plays 4. Bf1–b5 in this opening. As the game shows, Black is prepared for this variation in its opening book and White is not. White can also play 5. Bb5–a4, but this cedes Black the initiative for a pawn.

$$5. \ldots \ldots \quad Bf8–c5$$
$$6 \ Nf3xe5?$$

HB: Not advisable. This pawn cannot be held and the capture by White only furthers Black's development. White is under the illusion that he is winning something.

$$6. \ldots \ldots \quad Qd8–e7$$

DS: So far, all of Belle's moves have been made from its predigested library of opening moves.

$$7. \ Bb5xf7+??$$

HB: This is already ruinous; the "attack upon" and "win" of pawns only loses pieces. However, after any knight retreat Black rapidly gains the upper hand with d7–d5 (a move that would not be possible if White had played 5. Bb5–a4). From now on it is all Black's show.

$$7. \ldots \ldots \quad Ke8–f8$$

DS: At this point in the game, Belle predicted 8. d2–d3, Qe7xe5, 9. f2–f4, Qe5–e7, 10. Bf7–c4, d7–d6 with about a pawn advantage for Black.

$$8. \ Ne5–g6+?$$

HB: White probably thinks that after 8. . . . h7xNg6, 9. Bf7xg6, he will have three pawns for the knight. If he had looked a little farther, he would discover, however, that Rh8–h6 for Black snares the bishop. This probably accounts for his change of heart on the next move.

$$8. \ldots \ldots \quad h7xNg6$$
$$9. \ Bf7–c4 \quad Nf6xe4$$
$$10. \ O–O$$

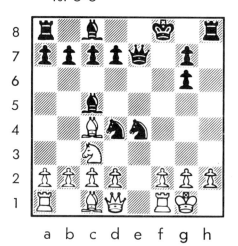

10. . . . . .   Rh8xh2!!

HB: A "stock" sacrifice which in this case has some beautiful points. Black must have been able to see 7 ply ahead (including detecting mate on the last ply) in order to make this move. Not bad for a machine!

DS: Belle predicted 11. Nc3xNe4, Qe7–h4, 12. Ne4–g3, Qh4xNg3, 13. Bc4–d5 with an advantage of 3.38 pawns for Black.

11. Kg1xRh2

HB: If 11. Nc3xNe4 then Qe7–h4, 12. Ne4–g3, Qh4xNg3!!, 13. f2xQg3+, Nd4–f3 mate, with an even more beautiful ending.

11. . . . . .   Qe7–h4+

DS: Belle saw the mate here but did not predict that White would delay it as long as possible. Belle's principal variation was 12. Kh2–g1, Ne4–g3, 13. Nc3–e4, Qh4–h1 mate.

12. Kh2–g1   Ne4–g3!!

HB: The *coup de gras!* Now White can capture a piece giving check and threatening the queen, only to be mated on the next move. Very appealing to human eyes, but just good old search for Belle. Now, White delays the immediate mate one move. The two main lines are indeed very appealing.

13. Qd1–h5   g6xQh5
14. f2xNg3+   Nd4–f3!! mate

(0–1)

This game demonstrates the power of combining a comprehensive opening library with a competent search mechanism which sees far enough ahead to take advantage of tactical opportunities. Belle's developing moves in the opening in response to Blitz's pawn hunger probably reflect that Belle was still in its opening library. The beautiful mop-up at the end demonstrates the merciless precision of a full-width search mechanism when the opponent gets into serious trouble. The power of this exhaustive lookahead search becomes much more impressive as depth increases. The move 10. . . . Rh8xh2 was possible because Belle could see far enough ahead to appreciate its devastating impact. Programs which lack goal-directed search mechanisms or the ability to see as far ahead as Belle would probably not have initiated this continuation.

Game 3: 1979 North American Computer Chess Championship
Round 3, October 29, 1979, Detroit, Michigan

Chess 4.9 (White) vs Duchess (Black)

Duchess, by Tom Truscott, Bruce Wright, and Eric Jensen of Duke University has been one of the stronger chess programs in tournament play since it first entered the competition in 1974. In 1977, Duchess tied for first place in the North American Championship.

The 1979 tournament was the last hurrah for Chess 4.X. It temporarily snatched the title back from Belle but in subsequent years could not match the additional depth that Belle achieved through hardware improvements. In this game with Duchess, Chess 4.9 played a nice combination to get a winning advantage.

The annotation for this game is provided by Mike Valvo, an International Master and David Levy's replacement as the tournament director in the recent major computer chess competitions. Mike's comments reflect his conversations with his technical consultant, Ken Thompson. Information from the machine record is also provided by David Slate.

White	Black
Chess 4.9	Duchess
1. e2–e4	d7–d5
2. e4xd5	Qd8xd5
3. Nb1–c3	Qd5–d6

MV: The center counter defense is not played very often by Black in tournament competition and this last move, Qd6, is so rare that theory only mentions one game in which it was tried. Its sole benefit seems to be that Chess 4.9 is now out of its extensive book on this line of play.

4. d2–d4	Bc8–f5
5. Ng1–f3	Nb8–c6?!

MV: Rather provocative; 5. . . . c7–c6 is more sensible.

6. Nc3–b5	Qd6–d7
7. Bc1–f4	Ra8–c8
8. Nf3–e5!	

MV: Tempting is 8. d4–d5 but White has no reply after 8. . . . Nc6–b4. For example, 9. Nf3–e5, Qd7xd5!, 10. Qd1xQd5, Nb4xQd5, 11. O–O–O, e7–e6!

8.	Nc6xNe5
9. d4xNe5!	

MV: The natural 9. Bf4xe5 allows Black to regroup. The point of 9. d4xNe5 is that the d4 square becomes available for the White knight.

DS: Chess 4.9 predicted 9. . . . a7–a6, 10. Qd1xQd7, Bf5xQd7, 11. Nb5–c3, g7–g6, 12. Bf4–e3, Bf8–h6, with about one-third pawn advantage for White. Chess 4.9 had previously predicted correctly Black's 6th, 7th, and 8th moves.

9. . . . . .   Qd7–c6

MV: Black is in severe difficulties, but alternatives offer little; for example, 9. . . . Qd7xQd1+, 10. Ra1xQd1, a7–a6, 11. Nb5–d4, Bf5–d7, 12. e5–e6!

10. Qd1–f3!?

MV: Not 10. Nb5xa7 because of Black's reply, 10. . . . Qc6–e4+, 11. Bf4–e3, Rc8–d8 and Black slips away. However, 10. Qd1–e2 seems best here: 10. . . . Qc6xc2, 11. Qe2xQc2, Bf5xQc2, 12. Ra1–c1, Bc2–e4, 13. Nb5xc7+, Ke8–d8, 14. e5–e6.

10.	Qc6xQf3
11. g2xQf3	a7–a6
12. Nb5–d4	Bf5–d7
13. O–O–O	g7–g6
14. Nd4–b3	Rc8–d8
15. Nb3–a5	Bd7–c8
16. Rd1xRd8+	Ke8xRd8
17. Bf1–c4	Kd8–e8
18. Rh1–d1	Bf8–h6
19. Bf4–d2	Bh6–g7?

MV: Black has defended well, but now lets the entire game slip. It is necessary to play 19. . . . Bh6xBd2+ and after 20. Rd1xBd2, e7–e6 Blacks stands well.

20. Bd2–c3   c7–c6

MV: Black should have played 20. e7–e6.

21. e5–e6   Bg7–h6+
22. Kc1–b1   f7–f6

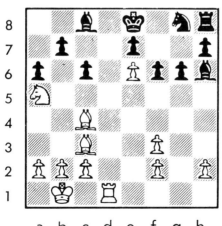

23. Na5xb7!

MV: An elegant temporary sacrifice.

DS: In computing its previous move, 22. Kc1–b1, Chess 4.9 thought for ten minutes and foresaw the upcoming sacrifice, rating this line of play as 2.5 pawns in White's favor. The principal variation it saw at that time was 22. . . . . f7–f6, 23. Na5xb7, Bc8xNb7, 24. Bc3–a5, Ke8–f8, 25. Rd1–d7, Bb7–a8, 26. Rd7–d8+, Kf8–g7, 27. Rd8xBa8. A terse message appeared on Chess 4.9's hardcopy at this time, "Be Careful."

23.	. . . . .	Bc8xNb7
24.	Bc3–a5	Ke8–f8
25.	Rd1–d7	

MV: The point of the "sacrifice." In order to avoid an immediate mate, Black must lose the bishop. The remainder requires no comment.

25.	. . . . .	Bh6–f4
26.	h2–h3	Bf4–e5
27.	Rd7xBb7	g6–g5
28.	Bc4xa6	h7–h5
29.	a2–a4	Rh8–h6
30.	Ba6–c4	f6–f5
31.	Ba5–d2	Rh6–g6
32.	a4–a5	Be5–d4
33.	a5–a6	Bd4xf2
34.	a6–a7	Bf2xa7
35.	Rb7xBa7	g5–g4
36.	Bd2–c3	Ng8–f6
37.	Bc3–b4	Nf6–g8
38.	Ra7–a8+	Kf8–g7
39.	Bb4–c3+	Kg7–h6
40.	Bc3–d2+	Kh6–g7
41.	f3xg4	h5xg4
42.	h3xg4	Rg6xg4
43.	Bc4–d3	f5–f4
44.	Bd2–c3+	Kg7–h6
45.	Ra8–f8	c6–c5
46.	Bc3–e5	f4–f3
47.	Rf8xf3	c5–c4
48.	Rf3–f4	Rg4–g1+
49.	Bd3–f1	Kh6–g5
50.	Rf4–f7	Kg5–h6
51.	Kb1–a2	Rg1–h1
52.	Bf1xc4	Rh1–e1
53.	Be5–g7+	Kh6–g5
54.	Bg7–f8	Re1–e4
55.	Rf7–g7+	Kg5–f6
56.	Bc4–d3	Re4–a4+
57.	Ka2–b3	Ra4–a7
58.	Rg7xNg8	Kf6xe6

59. Bd3–c4+	Ke6–e5
60. Rg8–g7	Ra7–b7+
61. Kb3–c3	Resigns

(1–0)

The mop-up by White is slow and methodical, with Chess 4.9 taking awhile to hit upon an effective plan. Despite this, the outcome is not seriously in doubt after the midgame foray in which White forced the win of Black's bishop. Down by two pieces and a pawn and facing a futile battle, Black properly resigned after White's 61st move.

Game 4: 1979 North American Computer Chess Championship Round 4, October 30, 1979, Detroit, Michigan

Duchess (White) vs Chaos (Black)

Chaos, a strong contender since 1973, currently hails from the University of Michigan. It is the work of Fred Swartz, Mike Alexander, Jack O'Keefe, and Victor Berman. In the 1979 tournament, Chaos ran on the powerful Amdahl V/6. The program has a more selective search and a more complex evaluation function than the "brute force" programs. Consequently, it searches many fewer nodes per second than most of the competition. The program is also characterized by its sheer size, taking up as much memory as half a dozen of its opponents.

This game is interesting because of its wild start and the tenacity that Chaos displayed fighting back from an early disadvantage. As a result of opening exchanges, Duchess (White) was up the exchange and two pawns. But then Duchess failed to find a winning idea, Chaos fought back, and finally an opposite-color-bishops endgame was reached in which, although still ahead by two pawns, Duchess could not find a way to make progress. Normally this type of game is adjudicated by the tournament director to reduce expenses and to prepare for the next round. In this case, the game was in the final round, and since both teams had continued access to their computers, the game was allowed to continue.

For the next 60 moves (about six hours), the two players shuffled pieces back and forth, a pawn was occasionally moved, and Duchess even succeeded in winning another pawn. In the end, the game was adjudicated as a win for Duchess even though there was little indication that she had found a winning plan. After 110 moves the patience of the spectators, the participants, and presumably even the programs, had been exhausted. The tournament director, David Levy, had already left to keep a London appointment. He had deputized two chess players to be awakened, if necessary, to adjudicate the game. Endgames which go on interminably have been a frustrating problem at many of the computer tournaments. A similar difficulty occurred at the 1981 Philidor vs L'excentrique game which also appears in this Appendix. Comments are by Peter Frey.

White Duchess	Black Chaos
1. e2–e4	c7–c5
2. Nb1–c3	Nb8–c6
3. g2–g3	e7–e6
4. Ng1–f3	d7–d5
5. e4xd5	e6xd5
6. d2–d4	Bc8–g4
7. Bf1–e2	Ng8–f6
8. Bc1–g5	Bg4xNf3
9. Be2xBf3	Qd8–e7+
10. Ke1–f1	c5xd4
11. Nc3xd5	Qe7–d8
12. Qd1–e2+	Ke8–d7
13. Qe2–b5	Ra8–b8
14. Nd5xNf6+	g7xNf6
15. Qb5–f5+	Kd7–c7
16. Bg5xf6	Bf8–e7
17. Bf6xRh8	Qd8xBh8
18. Qf5xf7	

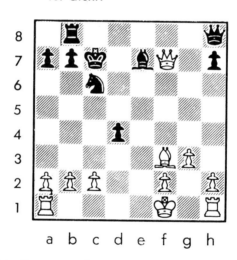

At this point in the game, the contest seems to be all but over. White has treated Black's Sicilian opening with very little respect. Black has two fewer pawns than White and is down the exchange with little compensation. Given this miserable start, the Chaos programming team was all but ready to pack up and get an early start for home. After her powerful beginning, Duchess continued to make progress for the next few moves but in the long run, failed to seize upon a winning plan.

18.	Qh8–g8
19. Qf7xQg8	Rb8xQg8
20. Bf3–e4	Rg8–h8

21. f2–f4	Nc6–a5
22. Kf1–e2	Na5–c4
23. Rh1–b1	Be7–f6
24. Ke2–d3	Nc4–b6
25. Rb1–e1	Kc7–b8
26. Ra1–b1	Nb6–a4
27. Be4–f5	h7–h5
28. Bf5–g6	Na4–c5+
29. Kd3–c4	Nc5–d7
30. Re1–e8+	Rh8xRe8
31. Bg6xRe8	Nd7–b6+
32. Kc4–c5	h5–h4

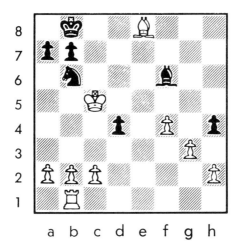

Computer chess is often viewed as a research paradigm for machine intelligence, especially for investigations of long-range planning. In this particular game, Duchess seems determined to demonstrate that machines have no facility for planning ahead. In this position, almost any chess amateur would proceed to activate White's pawn majority on the king side and march on bravely until Black had to sacrifice material to prevent an aspiring pawn from being promoted. After 32. . . . h5–h4, Black gives White the opportunity to create adjacent passed pawns, a truly formidable advantage in a situation like this. Instead, White chooses the immediate gain of a pawn at the expense of preserving its powerful pawn formation on the king side. In pawn and minor piece endings, many of the strong chess programs are unaware of simple strategic ideas that most class D human players have mastered.

33. g3xh4	Kb8–c8
34. h4–h5	Kc8–d8
35. Be8–b5	Kd8–c7
36. h5–h6	a7–a6
37. Bb5–d3	Bf6–h8

38.	Bd3–f5	Nb6–a4+
39.	Kc5–b4	b7–b5
40.	Kb4–a5	Kc7–b7
41.	Bf5–e4+	Kb7–a7
42.	h6–h7	Na4–b6
43.	h2–h4	Nb6–c4+
44.	Ka5–b4	Ka7–b6
45.	c2–c3	a6–a5+

With three pawns, a knight, and a bishop, Black is launching a fierce attack. With six pawns, a rook, and a bishop, White is running for cover. What is going on here?

46.	Kb4–b3	d4xc3
47.	Rb1–d1	Nc4–d2+
48.	Rd1xNd2	c3xRd2
49.	Kb3–c2	b5–b4
50.	h4–h5	Kb6–c5
51.	Kc2xd2	Bh8xb2
52.	h5–h6	Bb2–h8

Black's attack on the queen side has netted two pawns and a rook at the cost of one pawn and a knight. Black has also generated a promotion threat and White must now play carefully.

53.	Kd2–e3	Kc5–c4
54.	Be4–c2	Kc4–d5
55.	Bc2–b3+	Kd5–c5
56.	Ke3–e4	Kc5–d6
57.	Ke4–f5	Kd6–d7
58.	Kf5–g6	Kd7–e7
59.	f4–f5	Bh8–e5
60.	Bb3–c2	Be5–f6
61.	Bc2–e4	Bf6–h8
62.	Be4–f3	Bh8–e5
63.	Bf3–c6	Be5–f6
64.	Bc6–e8	Bf6–e5
65.	Be8–b5	Be5–h8
66.	Bb5–c4	a5–a4
67.	Bc4–g8	Bh8–f6
68.	Bg8–d5	Bf6–e5

The kings have moved to the king side and White is attempting to advance his pawns. The Black king is aiding his bishop in a blocking action while the White bishop waltzes gaily about to a tune that only he seems to hear. If White has a plan here it is far too sophisticated for flesh and blood players to understand.

69.	Kg6–g5	Be5–f6+
70.	Kg5–f4	Ke7–f8
71.	Kf4–e4	Kf8–e7

```
72. Bd5–e6        a4–a3
73. Ke4–d3        Bf6–h8
74. Kd3–c4        Bh8–c3
75. Kc4–c5        Ke7–d8
76. Kc5–d6        Kd8–e8
77. Be6–b3        Bc3–b2
78. Kd6–e6        Bb2–h8
79. Bb3–a4+       Ke8–f8
80. Ba4–d1        Kf8–e8
81. f5–f6         Ke8–f8
82. Bd1–b3
```

After the White king probes Black's defense on the queen side he returns to the king side for another round there. Finally, White activates its pawn on the *f*-file and places its bishop to defend the a2–g8 diagonal. White now appears to have a simple win: f6–f7 followed by a march by the White king to devour Black's remaining two pawns in exchange for White's two pawns on the *h*-file. After this exchange, White can advance its pawn on the *a*-file and Black can only defend by sacking its bishop for the pawn. White should then be able to promote its remaining pawn with little difficulty. Unfortunately, this plan requires a lookahead search which is considerably deeper than any current computer program can see.

```
82. . . . . .     Kf8–e8
83. Bb3–a4+       Ke8–f8
84. Ba4–d1        Kf8–e8
85. Bd1–b3        Ke8–f8
86. Bb3–c4        Kf8–e8
87. Bc4–b5+       Ke8–f8
88. Bb5–a4        b4–b3
89. Ba4xb3
```

White has won another pawn and is in even better shape to initiate the plan mentioned above. With the current position, this plan forces Black to trade its last pawn for one of White's pawns on the *h*-file. With passed pawns on both side of the board, White should win easily.

```
89. . . . . .     Kf8–e8
90. Bb3–c2        Ke8–f8
91. Bc2–d3        Kf8–e8
92. Bd3–b5+       Ke8–f8
93. Bb5–a6
```

If the White bishop remains on the a4–e8 diagonal, the Black bishop can capture the pawn at f6 with impunity. The White king dare not recapture since this will produce a stalemate.

```
93. . . . . .     Kf8–e8
94. Ba6–d3        Ke8–f8
95. Bd3–e2        Kf8–e8
```

96. Be2–h5+	Ke8–f8
97. Bh5–g4	Kf8–e8
98. Bg4–f3	Ke8–f8
99. Bf3–e4	Kf8–e8
100. Be4–g6+	Ke8–f8
101. Bg6–f5	Kf8–e8
102. Bf5–e4	Ke8–f8
103. Be4–b1	Kf8–e8
104. Bb1–f5	Ke8–f8
105. Bf5–c2	Kf8–e8
106. Bc2–a4+	Ke8–f8
107. Ba4–d1	Kf8–e8
108. Bd1–e2	Ke8–f8
109. Be2–f3	Kf8–e8
110. Bf3–c6+	Ke8–f8
111. Bc6–d5	

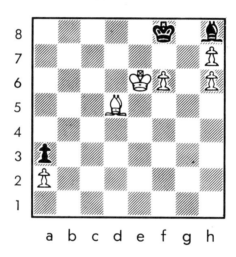

With the White bishop wandering about aimlessly, the participants and observers finally gave up. The game was concluded with the result to be determined by best play adjudication. This gave a win to White since a win clearly is present. The fact that White seems totally incapable of finding the win in no way influences this decision. This would appear to be a questionable rule. If White cannot find a win on its own, why should the tournament rules specify that White be given the win?

Game 5: Chessmates Grand Prix
Round 1, June 7, 1980, Evanston, Illinois

Ken Mohr (White) vs Bebe (Black)

Many people have wondered if a programmer has to be a very good chess player himself in order to create a strong chess program. No one has a definitive answer to this question and there are reasonable arguments for both sides of the question. The performance of Bebe, a newcomer to the computer chess scene, indicates however that a person unfamiliar with chess can produce a very formidable program. Bebe is the creation of Tony Scherzer of SYS-10, Inc., a small computer company in Hoffman Estates, Illinois. Tony, who has both software and hardware experience, decided one day a few years ago that it would be fun to build a chess playing machine. His lack of either chess or computer-chess experience did not concern him and he proceeded, in the spirit of Belle, to design and build a special chess-playing machine. He started by designing a 16-bit computer with a microprogrammed, pipelined, bit-slice architecture which executed instructions at 6 million per second. He then wrote a program of the brute-force variety in the general purpose set of instructions for this machine. In order to increase execution speed, he recoded time-critical functions in machine microcode. Eventually he built special hardware to do move generation and position evaluation. The result of this effort was a new machine which was similar in many ways to Belle. It was somewhat slower (about 22,000 positions per second) but also less costly.

The name Bebe is short for "black box," a colloquial term for a machine whose internal workings are mysterious and hidden from inspection. This was appropriate for Tony and his assistants because very early in its development the machine surpassed them in chess-playing ability and they no longer felt competent to evaluate the results of their further modifications of Bebe. To demonstrate the flavor of this interesting creation, we have selected one of Bebe's earliest tournament efforts. The opponent was a human player with a USCF rating of 2086. The game is very typical of the wild tactical battles that a computer can generate when its opponent attacks aggressively.

Early in the game, White gives up two pawns in an attempt to catch Black with a piece pinned to its king. Black successfully defends its material so White tries a new idea, attacking the vulnerable king position. True to computer form, Black cooperates by ignoring the threat and showing more interest in capturing pawns than defending its king. White, unable to find a clear win, makes a rook sacrifice to force the Black king into the open. With his queen and rook, White chases Black's king merrily about the board but fails to deliver a fatal blow. Finally White forces Black to trade its queen for a rook but this is too little, too late. Black's king evades White's remaining checks and escorts a pawn to the eight rank and to victory.

Shortly after this game, David Levy visited the Chicago area and paid a visit to Tony Scherzer. He was so impressed by Bebe's performance that he immediately invited Bebe to the World Championship in Linz, Austria. In this European tournament, Bebe distinguished itself in a very unusual way; it managed to draw all four of its games. Comments on this game are by Peter Frey.

White	Black
Ken Mohr	**Bebe**
1. e2–e4	e7–e5
2. Ng1–f3	Nb8–c6
3. Bf1–b5	a7–a6
4. Bb5–a4	b7–b5
5. Ba4–b3	Ng8–f6
6. O–O	Bc8–b7
7. d2–d4	e5xd4
8. e4–e5	Nf6–e4
9. Bb3–d5	Ne4–c5
10. Nf3–g5	Nc6xe5
11. Bd5xBb7	Nc5xBb7
12. Rf1–e1	

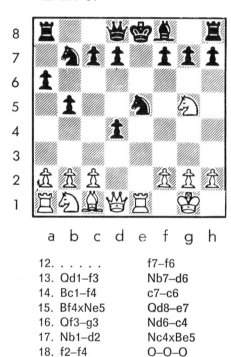

12.	f7–f6
13. Qd1–f3	Nb7–d6
14. Bc1–f4	c7–c6
15. Bf4xNe5	Qd8–e7
16. Qf3–g3	Nd6–c4
17. Nb1–d2	Nc4xBe5
18. f2–f4	O–O–O
19. Ng5–h3	Qe7–b4

Black is putting up a spirited defense. At times it is unclear who is attacking and who is defending. White is hard pressed to find a way of turning his positional pressure into a clear advantage.

20. f4xNe5	Qb4xNd2
21. a2–a4	b5xa4
22. Ra1xa4	Qd2xc2
23. Ra4xa6	Kc8–b7

Black's amazing courage indicates that he is clearly not your standard flesh and blood chess player. After giving up most of his pawn cover, the

Black king boldly sallies forth to attack the offending White rook. To paraphrase a familiar line, the computer enters where angels fear to tread.

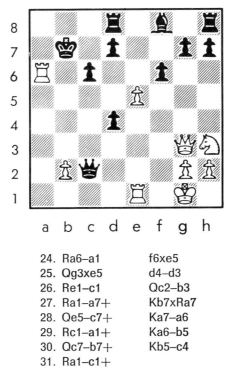

24.	Ra6–a1	f6xe5
25.	Qg3xe5	d4–d3
26.	Re1–c1	Qc2–b3
27.	Ra1–a7+	Kb7xRa7
28.	Qe5–c7+	Ka7–a6
29.	Rc1–a1+	Ka6–b5
30.	Qc7–b7+	Kb5–c4
31.	Ra1–c1+	

White has launched a blistering attack on the Black king. Black currently enjoys a material advantage, but it is not clear whether the Black king will live long enough to benefit from these extra troops. Even if the Black king can avoid being mated, his escape may come at the expense of several major pieces.

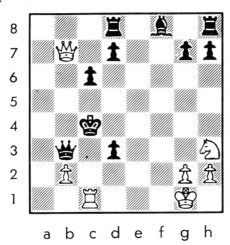

31.	. . . . .	Qb3–c2
32.	Qb7–a6+	Kc4–b3
33.	Qa6–b6+	Bf8–b4
34.	Rc1xQc2	d3xRc2
35.	Qb6–e3+	Kb3xb2
36.	Qe3–d4+	Bb4–c3
37.	Qd4–b6+	Kb2–a2
38.	Qb6–a6+	Ka2–b1
39.	Qa6–d3	Kb1–b2
40.	Qd3–e2	Rd8–e8
41.	Resigns	

The White queen has run out of checks and the Black pawn at c2 has become an unstoppable threat. With the Black rooks coming into play, all hope for White has evaporated. After observing the tactical resourcefulness of the computer in this game and the weak long-range planning of Duchess in the previous game, why should a human player try to shoot it out with any of the stronger chess programs? A quiet positional battle is much better fighting turf for humans.

Game 6: Third World Computer Chess Championship
Round 2, September 26, 1980, Linz, Austria

Nuchess (White) vs Belle (Black)

This tournament marked the official debut of Nuchess, by David Slate and William Blanchard. Nuchess is a completely new program which aspires to combine chess knowledge with the strength of a powerful search mechanism. To make programming easier, it is written in FORTRAN rather than assembler as the previous Northwestern University chess programs. By using FORTRAN, Slate and Blanchard hoped to be able to add a more sophisticated evaluation function and quiescence search without the tedious effort that assembly language would require. A style of coding was selected which made it easier to add chess-specific knowledge without sacrificing too much of the efficiency which had become a trademark of the earlier Chess 4 series. At this early stage of its development, Nuchess differed from Chess 4.9 in being slower (2000 positions per second vs 3600) and having a slightly better understanding of threatened pieces and passed pawns in its quiescence analysis.

Belle had also been completely redesigned for this tournament. At the end of 1979, Ken Thompson announced that he was going to build an incredibly fast machine with a speed approximating a million nodes per second! Belle did not achieve this goal for the tournament at Linz, but did come in at an impressive 160,000 positions per second. Note that this is an 80 to 1 advantage over Nuchess.

This game, a king's gambit accepted by transposition, soon lands in murky waters. White wins back his pawn and another to boot, but Black works against White's pinned *d*-pawn and awkwardly placed pieces forcing White to lose the exchange. White has aspirations of winning another pawn as compensation but has not looked deep enough. In trying to hold onto its material, White allows Black's rook to penetrate to the eight rank and attack the king. In an apparent attempt to intensify its attack, Black gives back the exchange for a pawn. Black's aggressive behavior causes little trouble for the White king but does succeed in winning another White pawn, evening up the material and producing a sharp position in which both sides have active pieces and passed pawns. After considerable maneuvering in an attempt to win, White is forced by Black's dangerous passed *a*-pawn to settle for a draw by perpetual check. Notes are by David Slate based on Nuchess' hardcopy.

White	Black
Nuchess	**Belle**
1. f2–f4	e7–e5
2. e2–e4	e5xf4
3. Ng1–f3	d7–d5
4. e4xd5	Ng8–f6
5. Bf1–b5+	c7–c6
6. d5xc6	Nb8xc6
7. d2–d4	

This is the first move out of book for Nuchess. Its 5-ply search predicted 7. . . . Qd8–a5+, 8. Nb1–c3, Bf8–b4, 9. Qd1–d3, Bc8–f5, 10. Qd3xBf5, Bb4xNc3, 11. Nf3–d2, and scored the final position as a quarter pawn advantage for White.

7.	Bf8–d6
8. O–O	O–O
9. Nb1–c3	Bc8–g4
10. Bb5–c4	Bd6–b4
11. Nc3–e2	Bb4–d6
12. Ne2xf4	

A 4-ply search evaluated this position as a 0.38 pawn edge for White and predicted a series of captures: 12. . . . Bd6xNf4, 13. Bc1xBf4, Bg4xNf3, 14. Rf1xBf3, Qd8xd4, 15. Qd1xQd4, Nc6xQd4. The exchange which followed, however, was not quite as bloody.

12.	Bg4xNf3
13. Rf1xBf3	

Nuchess did a 6-ply search before making this move and foresaw giving up the exchange on f3 as well as the capture of Black's pawn at b7. Its principal variation matched what actually happened except for 16. . . . Bc5–d6.

13.	Bd6–c5
14. c2–c3	

At this point in the game, Nuchess' evaluation reached its most optimistic value, over one pawn ahead. Its principal variation matched the moves actually played through 17. . . . Ra8–b8.

14.	Nc6–e5

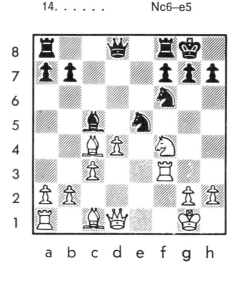

15. Bc4–e2	Ne5xRf3
16. Be2xNf3	

The evaluation dropped to +0.54 pawns as Nuchess began to see the problems posed by 17. Ra8–b8.

16.	Bc5–d6
17. Bf3xb7	

The score continued to drop, this time to −0.35 pawns, as Nuchess predicted having to give up its own pawn at b2.

17.	Ra8–b8
18. Qd1–f3	

Nuchess improved its outlook to a little better than even, predicting that it would hold its pawn at b2 while allowing Black's rook to check on e1.

18.	Rf8–e8
19. Bb7–c6	Re8–e1+
20. Kg1–f2	

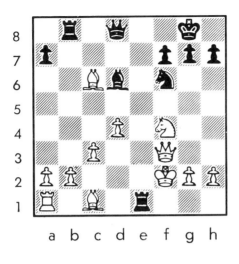

20.	Re1xBc1
21. Ra1xRc1	

Nuchess had not predicted that Black would give back the exchange. In calculating for 21. Ra1xRc1, White scored the position as a 0.29 pawns in its favor and foresaw all the moves that were subsequently played through 24. . . . Rb2xa2.

21.	Rb8xb2+
22. Kf2–g1	Qd8–c7
23. g2–g3	Bd6xNf4
24. g3xBf4	

At this point, Nuchess thought that Black would play g7–g5, since White's *f*-pawn is pinned to the pawn at h2. Despite this potential tactical shot by Black, Nuchess was still happy about the position.

24.	Rb2xa2
25. Rc1–b1	Qc7–d6
26. Bc6–b5	Qd6–b8
27. Bb5–d3	Qb8–e8
28. Kg1–h1	a7–a5
29. Bd3–b5	Qe8–d8
30. Bb5–c4	

Nuchess' evaluation had been rising for the last several moves and now reached a value of +0.84 pawns. After this, however, it started to drop again.

30.	. . . . .	Ra2–c2
31.	Rb1–b7	Qd8–a8
32.	Bc4xf7+	Kg8–h8
33.	Bf7–d5	Qa8–e8
34.	Rb7–b1	Nf6xBd5
35.	Qf3xNd5	Rc2xc3

The Black rook has won White's valuable passed pawn. The White queen dare not capture Black's passed rook pawn because of 36. . . . Qe8–e4+ forking the White king and rook. This tactical shot by Black improves its position considerably. Without the adjacent passed pawns, White no longer has a clear advantage.

36.	Qd5–e5	Qe8–a8+
37.	d4–d5	Rc3–c8
38.	Rb1–g1	

A 7-ply search by Nuchess evaluated the position at +0.18 pawns with a principal variation of 38. . . . Qa8–b7, 39. f4–f5, Qb7–f7, 40. Qe5–e6, Rc8–f8, 41. Rg1–f1.

38.	. . . . .	Qa8–b7
39.	f4–f5	Qb7–f7
40.	Rg1–b1	

A more aggressive alternative at this juncture for White would be 40. Qe5–e6.

40.	. . . . .	a5–a4
41.	Rb1–b8	Rc8xRb8
42.	Qe5xRb8+	Qf7–g8
43.	Qb8–e5	a4–a3
44.	f5–f6	

An 8-ply search by Nuchess evaluated the position as 0.19 pawns in White's favor with the following lengthy prediction: 44. . . . h7–h6, 45. f6xg7+, Qg8xg7, 46. Qe5–e8+, Kh8–h7, 47. Qe8–e4+, Qg7–g6, 48. Qe4–e7+, Kh7–g8, 49. d5–d6, a3–a2, 50. Qe7–d8+, Kg8–h7, 51. Qd8–c7+. Note that Nuchess did not anticipate that Black would steer toward a draw by repetition with, for example, 47. . . . Kh7–h8, as Black actually played. The reason for this is that Nuchess has a "weariness" factor, which causes the program to become more and more willing to draw as the game "drags" on longer and longer. This "weariness" factor depends on the move number and the number of consecutive "reversible" moves made up to the current position. It is a dynamic factor in the draw score as opposed to a static rule such as the "contempt" factor discussed in connection with Game 7 in this series. By move 44, the weariness factor had reached a third of a pawn, which was more than Nuchess thought its advantage was. Nuchess, however, does not attribute, "weariness" to its opponent and so while it steered toward the draw, it did not assume that Belle would try for the draw also.

44.	h7–h6
45. f6xg7+	Qg8xg7
46. Qe5–e8+	Kh8–h7
47. Qe8–e4+	Kh7–h8
48. Qe4–e8+	Kh8–h7
49. Qe8–e4+	Kh7–h8
50. Qe4–e8+	

drawn by repetition
(1/2–1/2)

This game is interesting in that it could easily have been played by two strong amateur human chess players. There were no obvious "computer blunders." The two programs played quite similar games. Nuchess, in fact, did a fairly good job of anticipating Belle's moves. Belle made 43 moves after Nuchess departed from its opening library. Of these 43, Nuchess anticipated 26. With this tendency to "think" alike, it is not surprising that each program tends to correctly anticipate the other's potential threats.

Game 7: 1980 North American Computer Chess Championship
Round 4, October 28, 1980, Nashville, Tennessee

Challenger X (White) vs Belle (Black)

Challenger X was an experimental chess computer from Fidelity Electronics. A similar machine was eventually sold commercially as the "Champion Sensory Challenger." Its authors are Dan and Kathe Spracklen, who previously developed the Sargon chess program which runs on several popular microcomputers. For this tournament, the Challenger program was loaded on special equipment which ran the 6502 processor at 4 megahertz (as compared to 1 megahertz on the Apple computer). Even at this faster speed, the Challenger only has a small fraction of the computing power of Belle. Despite this, the Challenger had Belle in serious trouble and nearly drew the game. Challenger finished the tournament with a very respectable 2.5–1.5 record.

In addition to demonstrating the improvements in microprocessor-based chess programs, this game illustrates an interesting problem in games between computers and humans and between two computers: how to evaluate a chance to draw. Most modern chess programs are able to recognize situations in which one or both players may claim a draw. In addition, many programs detect such conditions during their lookahead search which enables them to play towards or away from a draw depending on how they evaluate the alternatives. The easiest solution is to count a draw as equivalent to an "even" position, so the computer will play for one if it thinks it is otherwise behind and avoid one if it thinks it is ahead. But there are other possibilities. For example, one might, in advance of a game, inform the program that its opponent is weaker (or stronger) than it is. This can be done by defining a "contempt" factor which biases a stronger program to avoid a draw even when the current score shows it to be behind, or vice versa for a weaker program. This strategy is discussed in Chapter 4 of this book.

In this game with Belle, Challenger would have been well advised to set a negative contempt factor, i.e., play for a draw even when slightly ahead, indicating proper respect for Belle's considerable crunching power. For this tournament, Challenger X was hardwired into a memory module which allowed no possibility of changing this factor which was set so that the program would refuse to seek a draw unless it were at least a half pawn behind. In fact, Challenger had an opportunity to draw by repetition in the game; it declined that opportunity and then went on to lose.

There are at least two interesting lessons in this game. First, even a microprocessor-based program can sometimes outplay a powerhouse like Belle and reach an advantageous position. Second, although a lowly micro may on occasion outplay Belle, it is ill-advised to treat such a beast with contempt. For this arrogance, Belle deals out swift and certain punishment.

The commentary on this game is by David Levy, a long-time devotee of computer chess, an International Master, and the tournament director for all the major computer chess tournaments during the first decade of this new pastime. Additional notes are provided by David Slate from the printed record that Belle produced at the tournament.

White	Black
Challenger	**Belle**
1. e2–e4	e7–e5
2. Ng1–f3	Nb8–c6
3. Bf1–b5	a7–a6
4. Bb5–a4	Ng8–f6
5. O–O	Nf6xe4

DL: The Open Variation, which leads to very lively play, has long been a favorite of Viktor Korchnoi, and was used by him several times during his 1978 World Championship match against Karpov.

6. d2–d4	b7–b5
7. Ba4–b3	d7–d5
8. d4xe5	Bc8–e6
9. c2–c3	Bf8–c5

DL: Up to now both programs have been following well-known opening theory, taken directly from their opening books. Now, however, Challenger is out of book and at once makes a serious strategic mistake.

10. Bc1–e3?

DL: This allows Black to saddle its opponent with doubled, isolated pawns. Normal here is 10. Nb1–d2.

10.	Bc5xBe3
11. f2xBe3	Ra8–b8
12. Nb1–d2	Ne4–c5

DL: Threatening 13. . . . Nc5–d3, forking the pawns on e5 and b2, as well as the slower plan of 13. . . . O–O, followed by . . . Nc5–d7, . . . Rf8–e8, . . . Nd7–f8, and . . . Nf8–g6, when the White pawn at e5 would soon be lost.

13. Qd1–e1	Nc5–d3
14. Qe1–g3	O–O
15. Ra1–b1?	

DL: Perhaps it is a little unfair to give this move a question mark, since the correct continuation requires a depth of analysis well beyond the scope of Chess Challenger, but from the pure chess point of view, White should be criticized. The correct move was 15. Bb3–c2, when Black would almost certainly have played 15. . . . Nd3xb2, allowing the combination 16. Bc2xh7+, Kg8xBh7, 17. Nf3–g5, Kh7–g8, 18. Qg3–h4, Rf8–e8, 19. Qh4–h7+, Kg8–f8, 20. Ng5xf7, Be6xNf7, 21. Rf1xBf7+, Kf8xRf7, 22. Ra1–f1+, Qd8–f6 (not 22. . . . Kf7–e6 because 23. Qh7–f5+, Ke6–e7, 24. Qf5–f7 mate), 23. e5xQf6 and White will win.

DS: In its calculations for its 14th move, Belle, with an 8-ply search, anticipated that White would respond with Ra1–b1.

15.	Qd8–e7?
16. Bb3–c2	Qe7–c5

DL: Belle had pinned all of its hopes on this move when making the previous one, but a better plan would have been 15. . . . h7–h6. Now

White cannot capture on d3 because of . . . Qc5xe3+, but there is something better for White.

DS: Belle predicted 17. Nf3–g5 with an 8-ply search and scored the position as equal. Up to this point it had evaluated the game as a little in its favor.

17. Nf3–g5

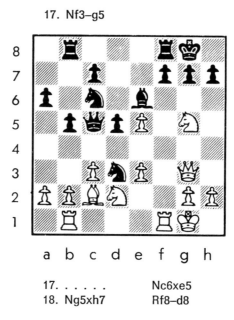

| 17. . . . . . | Nc6xe5 |
| 18. Ng5xh7 | Rf8–d8 |

DL: Not 18. . . . Kg8xh7, 19. Qg3xNe5, winning both of Black's knights.

DS: Belle anticipated 19. Nh7–f6+ and rated the position as 0.4 pawns advantage to White. This was based on an 8-ply search.

19. Nh7–f6+	Kg8–f8
20. Bc2xNd3	Ne5xBd3
21. Nf6–h5	g7–g6
22. Nh5–f6	Be6–f5?

DL: This move soon lands Black in trouble. There were numerous alternatives, such as 22. . . . b5–b4.

DS: Belle did a 7-ply search here, predicted 23. Qg3–g5, and judged the position as 0.2 pawns in White's favor.

23. Qg3–g5	b5–b4
24. Nf6–h7+	Kf8–e8
25. Nh7–f6+	Ke8–f8

DL: Here, and for the next few moves, White could force a draw.

DS: Belle saw no way to prevent the draw but thought that White should try to do better. It predicted 25. Nd2–b3 instead of Nh7–f6+.

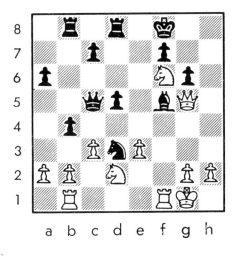

26. Nd2–b3	Qc5–c4

DS: Belle predicted 27. Nb3–d4 with an evaluation of 0.38 pawns advantage for White.

27. Nf6–h7+	Kf8–e8
28. c3xb4	Rb8xb4

DS: Belle did an 8-ply search on this move, predicting 29. Nb3–d4 with an advantage for White of 1.12 pawns.

29. Nh7–f6+	Ke8–f8
30. Nf6–g4	Rd8–d6
31. Ng4–h6	Qc4–e4!

DL: A dual purpose move, putting pressure on g2 (see later) and supporting the king side.

DS: Belle's 8-ply search predicted 32. Nh6xBf5 and judged that White had an advantage of about one pawn.

32. Rf1xBf5!?

DL: An interesting sacrifice that gives up the exchange and, unfortunately for White, simply fails. If White had vacillated, however, Black could have played . . . Bf5–e6 or . . . Nd3–e5 followed by . . . Ne5–g4, when Black has the more active game.

32.	g6xRf5
33. Qg5–g8+	Kf8–e7
34. Qg8xf7+	Ke7–d8
35. Nh6xf5	Rd6–c6
36. h2–h4	

DL: A typical computer move, and not a bad try. In many variations White only just fails to promote this pawn.

DS: Belle did not expect this move. It had been expecting 36. Nb3–d4 or 36. Qf7–g8+. After the pawn move, Black's evaluation improved to an even game.

36. . . . . .   Rc6–c2!

PWF: The Black king is fearless. He has dismissed his defending troops from the royal chamber and apparently plans to deal with the wrath of White's attack on his own.

37. Qf7–f8+   Kd8–d7
38. Qf8–f7+   Kd7–c8

DS: Belle's 7-ply search predicted 39. Qf7–g6 and now judged the position to be a one pawn advantage for Black.

39. Qf7–g6   Kc8–b7
40. Nb3–a5+

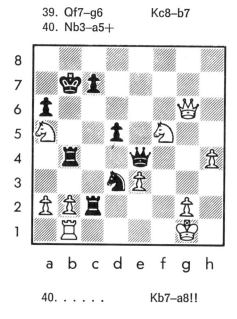

40. . . . . .   Kb7–a8!!

DL: A very profound move. Black gives up a pawn with check in order to cause its opponent to lose a tempo (a move). White then finds its queen on the wrong flank, and in bringing it back to the K-side White hands over the initiative for just long enough.

DS: Belle searched 7-plies, predicted 41. Qg6xa6+, and judged the position as advantageous to Black by 1.1 pawns.

41. Qg6xa6+   Ka8–b8
42. Qa6–g6

DL: This move is forced. White has to prevent mate on g2.

42. . . . . .   Nd3–e5!

DL: A deadly blow. Threatening the queen as well as . . . Rc2xg2+.

DS: Belle did an 8-ply search before selecting this move and judged the position as a three pawn advantage for Black.

43. Qg6–g8+	Kb8–a7
44. Rb1–f1	Rb4xb2

DS: At this point, Belle saw an overwhelming edge for Black. After failing to make its brave attack stick, White is in very serious trouble.

DL: White could well resign here, to save further embarrassment.

45. Kg1–h1	Rc2xg2
46. Na5–c6+	Ne5xNc6
47. Qg8–a8+	Ka7xQa8
48. a2–a4	

DL: Having delayed mate for as long as possible, White finally runs out of checks and can find no further defense. With victory at hand, Belle surprisingly displays a bug.

48.	Ka8–b8?
49. a4–a5	Kb8–a8?
50. a5–a6	Ka8–a7?
51. h4–h5	Ka7–b6?
52. a6–a7	Rg2–g1+

DL: At last!

53. Kh1xRg1	Qe4–g2 mate

(0–1)

DL: This has to be one of the most exciting games in the history of the ACM tournaments.

Game 8: Fredkin Prize Incentive Match
November 14, 1980, Carnegie-Mellon University

Belle (White) vs Gibson (Black)

This was the second Fredkin Prize Incentive Match. The first had been held a few months earlier between Chess 4.9 and a human player with a USCF rating of 2050. That had ended in a tie with each player winning a game. In this match, Belle was paired against a human player with a rating of 2132. The first game of the match ended in a draw. We present here the second game, which gave Belle a 1½ to ½ victory and offered further evidence that Belle was nearing master strength.

Belle's win in this game did not result from an obvious blunder by its opponent or from a single devastating tactical shot. Instead, Belle used tactical threats to skillfully immobilize the opponent's pieces and then steadily increased the pressure until Black could no longer hold the position. Hans Berliner was especially impressed by Belle's ability in this game to maintain control of the dark squares in such a way that Black's lone bishop was much less useful than White's knight. This type of play by Belle is significant since it is a side effect of the search process rather than being produced by special knowledge which might have been programmed into the evaluation function.

White	Black
Belle	Gibson

1. e2–e4	e7–e5
2. Ng1–f3	Nb8–c6
3. Bf1–b5	a7–a6
4. Bb5–a4	Ng8–f6
5. O–O	d7–d6
6. Ba4xNc6+	b7xBc6
7. d2–d4	Nf6xe4
8. d4xe5	d6–d5
9. Nb1–d2	Bc8–g4
10. c2–c3	Ne4xNd2
11. Bc1xd2	Bf8–e7
12. Qd1–a4	Qd8–d7
13. e5–e6	

DS: This move was selected by the 8-ply search but none of the shallower searches. Belle predicted 13. . . . . Bg4xe6 and scored the position as 0.1 pawns advantage for White.

13.	Bg4xe6
14. Nf3–e5	Qd7–d6
15. Bd2–f4	Qd6–c5
16. Qa4xc6+	Qc5xQc6
17. Nd4xQc6	

DS: Predicting 17. . . . . Be7–c5 and judging the position as slightly advantageous to Black. Belle's evaluation reached its lowest point in the game with this move.

17.	Be7–f6

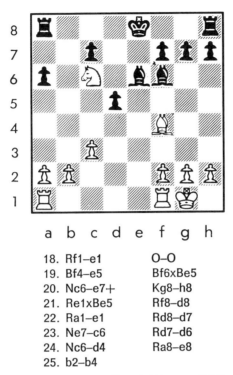

18. Rf1–e1	O–O
19. Bf4–e5	Bf6xBe5
20. Nc6–e7+	Kg8–h8
21. Re1xBe5	Rf8–d8
22. Ra1–e1	Rd8–d7
23. Ne7–c6	Rd7–d6
24. Nc6–d4	Ra8–e8
25. b2–b4	

DS: Belle's 8-ply search predicted 25. . . . Kh8–g8 and scored an advantage to White of 0.28 pawns.

25.	g7–g6
26. f2–f4	Kh8–g8
27. f4–f5	g6xf5
28. Nd4xf5	Rd6–c6

29. Re1–e3	Kg8–f8
30. Nf5–d4	Rc6–d6

31.	Re5–h5	Kf8–g8
32.	Re3–e5	c7–c6
33.	Re5–g5+	

DS: Belle's 8-ply search predicted 33. . . . . Kg8–f8 and judged the position as 1.2 pawns in White's favor. This is the first point at which Belle thought it was winning material. The 2- and 3-ply iterations wanted to play Re5–g5+ but did not realize that it would win material. The 4-ply search selected Rh5–h6 because it did appear to win a pawn. The selection of Re5–g5+ by the 8-ply search occurred because Belle foresaw the pawn capture and judged the resulting position as better than that resulting after 33. Rh5–h6.

33.	. . . . .	Kg8–h8
34.	Rh5–h6	Re8–g8
35.	Rg5–h5	

DS: Now Belle sees winning two pawns. It is interesting that all the iterations wanted to play 35. Rg5–h5 but not for the same reasons. The 2-ply search thought it was good positionally. Iterations 3 through 6 thought it would win one pawn. Iterations 7 through 9 saw it winning two pawns.

35.	. . . . .	Rg8–g6
36.	Rh6xh7+	Kh8–g8
37.	Rh7–h8+	Kg8–g7
38.	Rh5–h7+	Kg7–f6
39.	Rh8–a8	Kf6–e5
40.	Ra8xa6	

DS: At this point, Belle realized that she would soon safely acquire a third pawn.

40.	. . . . .	Ke5–e4
41.	Ra6xc6	Rd6xRc6
42.	Nd4xRc6	Be6–d7
43.	Rh7–h4+	Rg6–g4

PWF: Not Ke4–d3 because Nc6–e5+ and Black loses his bishop.

44.	Rh4xRg4+	Bd7xRg4
45.	h2–h4	f7–f6
46.	b4–b5	Ke4–d3
47.	Nc6–e7	Kd3xc3
48.	b5–b6	d5–d4
49.	b6–b7	d4–d3
50.	b7–b8=Q	d3–d2
51.	Qb8–b3+	Resigns

(1–0)

DS: In this game, Belle correctly anticipated its opponent's move 22 times. Discounting the moves from the opening library when no prediction is made, this approximates 50%.

Game 9: Fredkin Prize Incentive Match
Second game, August 26, 1981, Vancouver, B.C.

Belle (White) vs Storey (Black)

Carl Storey, a Canadian with a USCF rating of 2206, defended the honor of human masters everywhere against the upstart computers by winning both games against Belle and a $2500 prize. He may have read a book or two on computer chess before the match. His playing style could be called "textbook" anticomputer technique: Play careful, quiet, positional chess, and wait for an opportunity to lure the machine into an endgame it doesn't understand. Probe the machine's defenses until it makes a strategic error and then infiltrate and mop up.

The commentary for this game is based on comments by Hans Berliner published in the ACM Sigart Newsletter, April, 1982, and from Belle's printed record as analyzed by David Slate.

White Belle	Black Storey
1. e2–e4	g7–g6
2. d2–d4	Bf8–g7
3. Ng1–f3	d7–d6
4. Nb1–c3	Ng8–f6
5. Bf1–e2	O–O
6. O–O	c7–c6
7. a2–a4	Qd8–c7
8. h2–h3	e7–e5
9. Rf1–e1	Nb8–d7
10. Be2–f1	Rf8–e8

HB: Both sides have followed standard book openings so far.

11. d4–d5	a7–a6
12. Bc1–g5	

HB: This is an unusual move for White.

12.	h7–h6
13. Bg5–e3	c6xd5
14. Nc3xd5	Nf6xNd5
15. Qd1xNd5	Nd7–f6
16. Qd5–c4	Qc7xQc4
17. Bf1xQc4	Nf6xe4

HB: The position already favors Black somewhat; however, 17. . . . Bc8–d7 would have been even stronger for Black.

18.	Be3xh6	Bg7xBh6
19.	Re1xNe4	Bc8–f5
20.	Re4–h4	Bh6–g7

HB: Belle's best chance here is 21. Nf3–g5, Re8–e7, 22. Ng5–e4, with tactical chances.

21.	Bc4–d5	Re8–e7
22.	c2–c3	e5–e4
23.	Nf3–d4	Bg7xNd4
24.	c3xBd4	Kg8–g7

PWF: The game to this point is very instructive. Storey selected a quiet opening and has managed to trade pieces and pawns without entering into any wild tactical battles. The material is equal and Black seems to have a slight positional advantage. Compare this middle game to the shoot-out in Game 5 where the human opponent lost to Bebe.

25.	Rh4–f4	Ra8–e8
26.	b2–b4	Bf5–c8
27.	Ra1–a3	f7–f5
28.	Ra3–g3	e4–e3?

HB: A better move for Black would have been 28. . . . Kg7–f6.

29.	f2xe3	Re7xe3
30.	Kg1–h2	Re3xRg3
31.	Kh2xRg3	Re8–e1
32.	Bd5–b3	b7–b6
33.	Rf4–f3	Re1–e4
34.	Rf3–d3	Bc8–b7
35.	Bb3–d1	Re4–e1
36.	Kg3–f2	Re1–e7

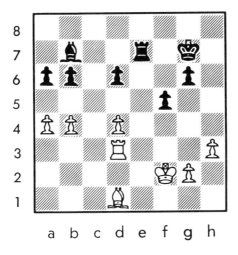

PWF: Who is winning here? Certainly an amateur chess player would not know. What should White do? Not an easy question at all. Belle's problem is that there are no obvious short-range goals and therefore even a relatively deep lookahead does not find anything useful to do. To play this position properly, the program has to possess special knowledge about this type of endgame position. Computer chess programs currently do not have such knowledge.

37. Bd1–f3?

HB: This move is suicidal; after this move the only hope for White is 38. g2xBf3. Even then it is doubtful that the position could be saved.

DS: All iterations chose this move, but only the last one (9-ply) correctly anticipated that Black would trade the bishops. Belle saw only a small (0.13 pawns) advantage for Black at this point.

37.	Bb7xBf3
38. Kf2xBf3	Re7–c7
39. Rd3–b3	Rc7–c4
40. a4–a5	b6–b5
41. Kf3–e3	

DS: After a 10-ply search, Belle concluded that it was a pawn down. But this score oscillated over the next few moves between about minus one pawn and minus one-half pawn.

41.	g6–g5
42. Ke3–d3	Kg7–f6
43. Rb3–c3	Rc4xRc3+
44. Kd3xRc3	

DS: All of the iterations chose this move, but the deeper Belle looked, the worse its evaluation became. The 3-ply search scored it as −0.09 pawns. The 13-ply search scored it as −1.38 pawns. It is clear that Belle's static evaluation function was unable to see the hopelessness of its situation, but the deep lookahead search began to get the idea.

44.	f5–f4
45. Kc3–d3	Kf6–f5
46. d4–d5	Kf5–e5
47. Kd3–e2	Ke5xd5
48. Resigns	

(0–1)

HB: This game provides an apt demonstration for the computer chess community that going 11 plies deep in an endgame is not enough for Master play unless the terminal nodes are evaluated with a lot of knowledge.

Game 10: 1981 Mississippi State Championship
Round 4, September, 1981, Hattiesburg, Mississippi

Joseph Sentef (White) vs Cray Blitz (Black)

Cray Blitz was developed at the University of Southern Mississippi by Robert Hyatt and Albert Gower. Previously known as Blitz (see Game 2), the program was modified in 1980 to run on the CRAY-1, one of the most powerful computers ever built, and has been a formidable brute-force chess player ever since. In September, 1981, Cray Blitz became the first computer to win a State championship in the United States. It went 5–0 in the Mississippi State Championship tournament but was ineligible to accept the title.

The game presented here was against Joseph Sentef, a master and former State champion with a USCF rating of 2262. The game is another example of the wild, hair-raising tactical battles that often result when human players try an aggressive approach against one of the stronger computer chess programs. The computer miraculously survives an attack on its king and then wins quickly when its opponent blunders under time pressure after the long tense struggle.

The commentary on this game is based on an annotation by Robert Hyatt. He provides interesting technical data on the program's performance, including the number of nodes examined, the machine's evaluation, and the reply it anticipates. Hyatt also includes occasional remarks as the game progresses.

White	Black
Sentef	Cray Blitz

1. c2–c4	Ng8–f6
2. Nb1–c3	c7–c6
3. Ng1–f3	d7–d5
4. c4xd5	c6xd5
5. d2–d4	Nb8–c6
6. g2–g3	Nf6–e4

Cray Blitz has a limited opening library on the English opening. In selecting this move, it examined 384,000 nodes, expected White to reply with Bf1–g2, and evaluated the position as 0.18 pawns in Black's favor.

7. Bf1–g2	Ne4xNc3
8. b2xNc3	e7–e6
9. O–O	Bf8–d6
10. Qd1–c2	O–O

The machine's deliberation included 508,000 nodes and produced an expectation of Ra1–b1 with an evaluation of 0.12 pawns for Black.

11. Nf3–g5	f7–f5
12. f2–f4	Nc6–a5
13. Qc2–d3	Qd8–d7
14. Bc1–d2	Na5–c4
15. Bd2–c1	Qd7–a4

This move was selected after considering 356,000 nodes. The machine expected a reply of e2–e3 and judged the position to be 0.22 pawns in Black's favor.

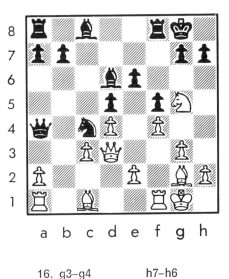

16. g3–g4	h7–h6

White pondered for 30 minutes before launching his attack on the king side. Cray Blitz was totally unaware of what was to come. It examined 378,000 nodes, thought it was winning a pawn (1.24 pawns in Black's favor), and expected g4xf5.

17. g4xf5	h6xNg5	
18. f4xg5	Bd6–a3	
19. g5–g6	Ba3xBc1	
20. Ra1xBc1	Nc4–d6	

Cray Blitz is starting to perceive the danger and recalls its knight for defensive work close to home. The evaluation dropped to 0.89 pawns and the 11-ply principal variation anticipated that the game would continue 21. Qd3–h3, Rf8xf5, 22. Qh3–h7+, Kg8–f8, 23. Qh7–h8+, Kf8–e7, 24. Qh8xg7+, Ke7–d8, 25. Rf1xRf5, Nd6xRf5. This is exactly what happened.

21. Qd3–h3	Rf8xf5
22. Qh3–h7+	Kg8–f8
23. Qh7–h8+	Kf8–e7
24. Qh8xg7+	Ke7–d8

At this point, the machine senses the potential trouble which is ahead. After examining 359,000 nodes, it judges the position as being in White's favor for the first time (−0.43 pawns). It predicts 25. Qg7–h8+, Kd8–e7, 26. g6–g7, Nd6–f7, 27. Rf1xRf5, e6xf5, 28. Bg2xd5.

25. Rf1xRf5	Nd6xRf5

White is under time pressure and decides to capture immediately at f5. Cray Blitz recaptures with his knight and now judges the position as favorable (+0.41 pawns). The White pawn at g6 now looks less dangerous.

26. Qg7–f6+	Nf5–e7
27. g6–g7	Qa4–e8
28. Bg2–f3	Kd8–d7
29. Rc1–f1	Ne7–g8

The machine believes it will be able to hold the position. It judges that it is still slightly ahead (0.31 pawns) and anticipates 30. Qf6–g5 followed shortly by a queen exchange.

30. Qf6–g5	Qe8–e7
31. Qg5–g6	Kd7–d6
32. e2–e4	d5xe4

White took ten minutes before making the pawn advance to e4. He is now in serious time trouble. Black did not expect this move. It now judges the position as favorable to White (−0.22 pawns) and anticipates 33. Qg6–g3+.

33. Bf3xe4   Qe7–h4

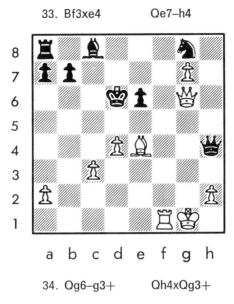

34. Qg6–g3+   Qh4xQg3+

Cray Blitz examined 610,000 nodes before capturing at g3. It now judged the position as clearly in White's favor (−1.46 pawns) and anticipates 35. h2xQg3, Bc8–d7, 36. Rf1–f8, Ra8–c8, 37. Rf8xRc8, Bd7xRc8, 38. Be4–h7, Ng8–e7, 39. g7–g8==Q, Ne7xQg8, 40. Bh7xNg8.

35. h2xQg3   Bc8–d7
36. Rf1–f8   Ra8–c8

The machine looked at 1,395,000 nodes and judges the position as −1.31 pawns. It anticipates 37. Rf8xRc8. White has less than 8 minutes to make his next 14 moves.

37. Be4–h7   Rc8xc3

Blitz's outlook suddenly improves. It now judges the game as dead even.

38. Rf8xNg8   Rc3xg3+
39. Kg1–f2   Rg3–g5
40. Bh7–e4   b7–b6
41. Kf2–e3   e6–e5
42. Rg8–a8   Rg5–g3+

White now has one minute to make his next eight moves. Cray Blitz judges the position in its favor (+0.64 pawns) and anticipates 43. Be4–f3.

43. Ke3–f2   Rg3xg7
44. d4xe5+   Kd6xe5
45. Be4–f3   Bd7–e6

The smoke has cleared and Black has an extra pawn. The machine now evaluates the position in its favor by 0.76 pawns and predicts Ra8–e8.

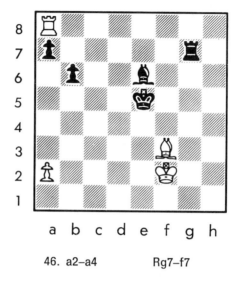

46. a2–a4	Rg7–f7

Cray Blitz's evaluation improves by almost a pawn. It now judges the position at +1.66 after examining 733,000 positions. The principal variation was 47. Ra8–e8, Rf7–f4, 48. a4–a5, b6xa5, 49. Kf2–e3, Kf4–f7, 50. Bf3–e4.

47. Kf2–e3?	Rf7xBf3+

White's mistake under time pressure ends the battle. The machine now evaluates the position as +4.09 pawns. White is down a bishop and a pawn no matter what he does.

48. Ke3xRf3	Be6–d5+
49. Kf3–e3	Bd5xRa8
50. a4–a5	Ba8–e4
51. Ke3–d2	Ke5–d4

The machine now perceives the pawn promotion. Its evaluation jumps to +10.87 pawns.

52. Kd2–c1	b6–b5
53. Kc1–b2	Kd4–c4
54. a5–a6	b5–b4
55. Kb2–a2	Kc4–c3
Resigns	

(0–1)

After 55. . . . Kc4–c3, Blitz announced mate in 6.

Game 11: Second World Microcomputer Chess Championship
Round 2, September, 1981, Travemunde, West Germany

Fidelity X (White) vs Princhess 2.9 (Black)

Microcomputers that play chess, unheard of only a few years ago, now have their own tournaments. The better programs even give the mainframes a tough battle. The surprising ability of current microcomputer programs seems to indicate that in a few years just about anyone will be able to afford a chess computer which plays at a very respectable level.

The game presented here is between two of the better programs. Fidelity X, the eventual winner of the tournament, is a more recent version of Challenger X which participated in Game 7. It is a small unit designed specifically for chess. The program was produced by Dan and Kathe Spracklen. Princhess 2.9 is the creation of Ulf Rathsman of Sparga, Sweden. It finished second in the tournament with a 5–2 score.

Fidelity X won a pawn early in the game with a simple tactical shot. Princhess fought back, however, and finally evened the material in the endgame. But then, apparently underestimating the importance of a passed pawn, Princhess let Fidelity X push its pawns while ignoring its own. This finally led to its downfall. Commentary by Peter Frey.

White Fidelity X	Black Princhess 2.9
1. e2–e4	e7–e5
2. Ng1–f3	Nb8–c6
3. Bf1–b5	Nc6–d4
4. Nf3xNd4	e5xNd4
5. O–O	Bf8–c5
6. d2–d3	Ng8–e7
7. Bc1–g5	c7–c6
8. Bb5–c4	f7–f6?

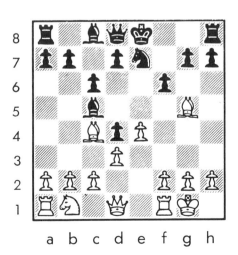

Black's opening moves are notably weak. Its attempt to dislodge the White bishop at g5 by 8. . . . f7–f6 is bad for two reasons. It weakens the king's position and at the same time opens the door to a simple tactical shot for White.

9.	Bg5xf6	g7xBf6
10.	Qd1–h5+	Ne7–g6
11.	Qh5xBc5	Qd8–b6
12.	Qc5xQb6	

With the Black king trapped without pawn cover, White should keep its queen in order to mount an attack on the vulnerable Black monarch. Trading queens at this juncture is very beneficial for Black. A stronger move for White would have been 12. Qc5–d6.

12.	. . . . .	a7xQb6
13.	Nb1–d2	d7–d6
14.	Nd2–f3	b6–b5
15.	Bc4–b3	c6–c5
16.	Bb3–d5	Ng6–f4
17.	Bd5–b3	Bc8–g4
18.	Nf3–d2	Bg4–e2
19.	Rf1–e1	Ra8–c8

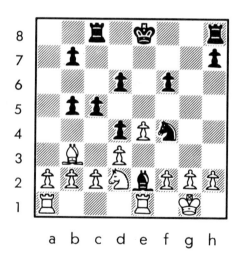

White has been playing passively and now finds itself short of space. Careful play is now required or Black's aggressiveness may begin to pay dividends.

20. g2–g3	Nf4–h3+
21. Kg1–g2	Be2–g4
22. f2–f3	Bg4–d7
23. Bb3–d5	Rc8–c7
24. a2–a4	b5xa4
25. Nd2–c4	Ke8–e7
26. Nc4–b6	Nh3–g5
27. Nb6xBd7	Rc7xNd7
28. f3–f4	Ng5–f7
29. Bd5–c4	Rh8–a8
30. Bc4–b5	Rd7–d8
31. Ra1xa4	Ra8xRa4
32. Bb5xRa4	

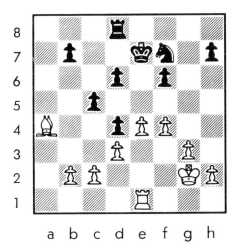

32.	b7–b5
33. Ba4–b3	Nf7–h6
34. e4–e5	f6xe5
35. f4xe5	Nh6–f5
36. Re1–e4	Nf5–e3+
37. Kg2–h3	d6xe5
38. Re4xe5+	Ke7–d6
39. Re5–e6+	Kd6–c7
40. c2–c3	Rd8–d6
41. Re6–e7+	Kc7–c6
42. Re7xh7	d4xc3
43. b2xc3	Rd6xd3
44. Rh7–h6+	Kc6–c7
45. Rh6–h7+	Kc7–b6
46. Rh7–h6+	Kb6–a5
47. Bb3–e6	Rd3xc3
48. Be6–c8	

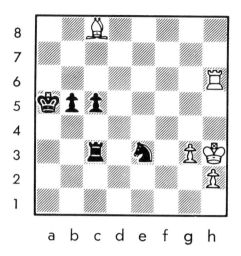

After an interesting battle, the material is equal. The game has become a contest to see who can promote a pawn first. Although both sides have opportunities, Black has the more favorable position.

48.	. . . . .	Ne3–d5
49.	Rh6–a6+	Ka5–b4
50.	Kh3–g4	Rc3–c4+
51.	Kg4–g5	Rc4–e4
52.	h2–h4	Re4–e5+
53.	Bc8–f5	Nd5–e3
54.	g3–g4	Ne3xBf5
55.	g4xNf5	

The White pawns are on the move. The Black pawns are passive spectators.

55.	. . . . .	Re5–e4
56.	f5–f6	Re4–e5+
57.	Kg5–g6	Re5–e3
58.	f6–f7	Re3–g3+
59.	Kg6–f6	Rg3–f3+
60.	Kf6–g7	Rf3xf7+
61.	Kg7xRf7	Kb4–c3
62.	h4–h5	Resigns

(1–0)

This game between two of the strongest microcomputer programs indicates that there is still a significant difference between microcomputer chess and mainframe chess. Fidelity X played a steady if not spectacular game. Princhess was notably weak in the opening, aggressively strong in the middle game, and woefully uninformed about what is required in the endgame. With the rapid advances in computer miniaturization and with small-system programmers gaining chess experience, one can be optimistic about future improvements in this area.

Game 12: 1981 North American Computer Chess Championship
Round 3, November 9, 1981, Los Angeles, California

Philidor (White) vs L'excentrique (Black)

Philidor, running on an Osborne-1 microcomputer, is the creation of David Broughton, Mark Taylor, David Levy, Mike Johnson, and Kevin O'Connell, and was represented at the tournament by David Levy. This marked a major change of roles for the British master. In the past, Levy had been the director of almost all of the major computer chess tournaments and had gained considerable publicity by betting that no computer could beat him in a tournament-style match. Perhaps Levy is hedging his bets on the philosophy that if "you cannot beat them, you might as well join them." At ACM 81, Philidor did very well for a micro, scoring 2.5–1.5.

L'excentrique, by Claude Jarry of McGill University in Montreal, is an efficient implementation of the brute force strategy, searching 20,000 nodes per second on an Amdahl V7. The program is almost devoid of chess knowledge and emphasizes deep search with minimal time spent evaluating terminal nodes. Monty Newborn, who was Jarry's advisor at McGill, says that L'excentrique is compact, clean, and simple. This approach appears to have some merit because the program has performed well in tournament competition, including a win over Chess 4.9 at the world championship in 1980.

The game came down to a king and pawn ending in which, despite its two-pawn advantage, Philidor could find no way to make progress. Both sides began to make aimless king moves. At the prearranged adjournment time, the tournament director assessed the situation and determined that White had a won position and awarded the game to Philidor. Commentary on this game is by Mike Valvo.

White	Black
Philidor	L'excentrique
1. e2–e4	c7–c6
2. d2–d4	d7–d5
3. e4–e5	Bc8–f5
4. Ng1–e2	e7–e6
5. Ne2–g3	Bf5–g6
6. Bf1–d3	h7–h5?

In this variation of the Caro Kann opening, either 6. . . . Bg6xBd3 or 6. . . . c6–c5 are to be preferred.

7. O–O

White could have gained a positional advantage by 7. Bd3xBg6.

7.	. . . . .	h5–h4
8.	Ng3–e2	Bg6xBd3
9.	Qd1xBd3	Nb8–d7
10.	Nb1–d2	Bf8–e7
11.	c2–c3	Qd8–c7
12.	Nd2–f3	

The thematic break initiated by 12. f2–f4 is more than adequately met by 12. . . . g7–g6.

12.	. . . . .	O–O–O
13.	Bc1–f4	b7–b5?

"Beauty is skin deep, but ugly goes clean to the bone." After this, Black's game is technically lost.

14.	a2–a4	Qc7–b7
15.	b2–b4	

15. a4xb5, c6xb5, 16. Ra1–a5, a7–a6, 17. Rf1–a1, Nd7–b8, 18. b2–b3! and White has excellent attacking prospects.

15.	. . . . .	b5xa4

15. . . . a7–a6 offers better defensive prospects. White can, however, triple on the *a*-file and coupled with knight maneuvers to c5, force Black to concede.

16.	Ra1xa4	f7–f5
17.	Bf4–e3	

Pointless. 17. Rf1–a1 wins material.

17.	. . . . .	Nd7–b6
18.	Ra4–a2	Nb6–c4

18. . . . Kc8–d7 offers prospects of defending the *a*-pawn.

19.	Be3–f4	

It is still not too late for Rf1–a1 with ideas similar to those mentioned earlier.

19.	. . . . .	Kc8–d7
20.	Ra2–a4	

White seems to have no idea about what's going on.

20.	. . . . .	a7–a6
21.	g2–g3	h4–h3
22.	Ra4–a2	Rh8–h5
23.	Rf1–e1	

Why?

23.	Rd8–f8
24. Bf4–c1	g7–g5
25. Nf3–d2	Nc4xNd2
26. Bc1xNd2	Rf8–a8

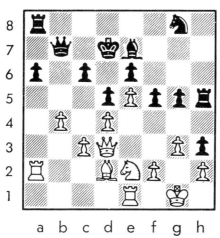

Black is in trouble. 26. . . . Qb7–b5 is no better; 27. Qd3xQb5, a6xQb5, 28. Ra2–a7+, Kd7–c8, 29. Re1–a1 and White can then position his knight on a5.

27. Re1–a1

Finally!

27.	Qb7–b5
28. Qd3xQb5	c6xQb5
29. f2–f4	g5–g4
30. Ra2xa6	Ra8xRa6
31. Ra1xRa6	Be7–d8
32. Ra6–d6+	Kd7–e7
33. Bd2–e1	

The obvious move for a human here would be 33. Ne2–c1. Note that 33. Rd6–c6, Ke7–d7, 34. Rc6–c5, Bb6 does not win a pawn for White.

33.	Bd8–c7
34. Rd6–a6	Ng8–h6
35. Be1–d2	

The obvious move here is still Ne2–c1.

35.	Nh6–f7
36. Ra6–c6	Ke7–d7
37. Rc6–a6	

White realizes that Rc6–c5 fails as described before.

37.	Nf7–d8
38. Ne2–c1	

Finally!

38.	Rh5–h7
39. Nc1–d3	Kd7–c8
40. Nd3–c5	Bc7–b8?

Black overlooks 40. . . . Rh7–e7, 41. Ra6–a8+, Bc7–b8, 42. Ra8–a5, Re7–a7!

41. Nc5xe6	Rh7–h6!
42. Ne6–c7	Rh6xRa6
43. Nc7xRa6	Nd8–e6
44. Bd2–e3	Bb8–c7
45. Kg1–f1	Kc8–d7

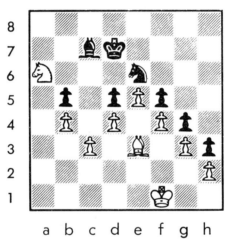

46. Na6xBc7

After this, the game is a draw. The only winning chance was 46. Na6–c5+.

46.	Ne6xNc7
47. Kf1–e2	Nc7–a8

Humans would abandon this position as a draw. But Black has a losing plan beginning with this move.

48. Ke2–d3	Na8–b6
49. Be3–d2	Nb6–c4
50. Bd2–c1	

White avoids the exchange, preventing Black's attempt at hari-kari.

50.	Kd7–e7
51. Bc1–d2	Nc4xBd2??

The purpose of the knight's migration and the only way to lose.

52.	Kd3xNd2	Ke7–f7
53.	Kd2–e3	Kf7–e7
54.	Ke3–f2	Kf7–d7
55.	Kf2–e3	Kd7–c7
56.	Ke3–d3	Kc7–d7
57.	Kd3–d2	Kd7–e7
58.	Kd2–e3	Ke7–d7
59.	Ke3–d3	Kd7–e7
60.	Kd3–d2	Ke7–d7

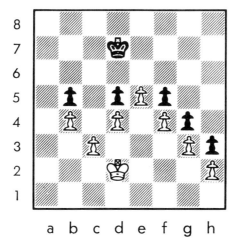

By prior arrangement, the game was adjudicated at midnight. Mike Valvo determined that best play for both sides would produce a win for White. It is extremely doubtful, however, that Philidor could find the winning sacrifice. This raises the question of adjudication by best play without regard to level of the players.

The uncomfortable outcome of this match is quite similar to that in the Duchess-Chaos match in Game 4. Adjudication by best play not only can give a win to a program which, in all likelihood, would never find it on its own, but also can lead to subjective decisions. Recent analysis questions whether the position above is a win for White. Black, with proper play, may be able to hold the position.

One of us (PWF) would like to see the tournament rules modified to hasten the rate of play and remove the need for matches to be adjudicated by the tournament director. One possible way to do this would be to set a 1 minute per move time control for the entire match and declare any game which is not decided in 100 moves a draw. The 1 minute time limit would decrease the depth of search by slightly more than one-half ply. This would decrease the level of performance slightly but the benefits of the change outweigh this negative factor. Against human opponents, the machines could adopt whatever time limit had been established for that particular tournament. The 100-move rule would make it necessary for the programs to deal effectively with endgame play. The current rules allow some of the programs to essentially avoid dealing with this important aspect of the game. The 100-move rule would penalize programs very heavily for not being able to play efficiently in the endgame. This is desirable and fair.

With both of these rules in effect, the computer chess tournaments would not drag on late into the night for four consecutive days. The maximum length of time for any one game would be 3 hours and 20 minutes. It would be possible to play two games a day and finish a four-round tournament in a weekend. The telephone expense of the tournament would be reduced considerably and many teams would be able to maintain time on the mainframe of their preference if weeknight games were not required. From the point of view of the spectators, the matches would be more exciting with moves coming every minute or less in each game. With all games completed in less than 4 hours and with no problems over adjudication, the pairings for the next round could be done before the programmers started to make preparations for the next match. These benefits seem to outweigh the fact that the level of play would be reduced slightly.

Game 13: 1981 North American Computer Chess Championship
Round 4, November 10, 1981, Los Angeles, California
Cray Blitz (White) vs Belle (Black)

This brute-force battle, which decided the 1981 championship, is both exciting and instructive. In spite of rumors to the contrary, even the strongest programs make tactical mistakes. The nature of an exhaustive, full-width search is such that brute-force programs tend to "see" all of the short-range (a few moves deep) exchanges, some of the middle-range tactics, but very little of the long-range (ten moves deep or more) tactical threats. Thus the computer has a definite horizon which is much sharper than that of the human player. Humans sometimes fall prey to a short-range shot but at the same time can apprehend some very deep tactical threats. When a computer wins by making a nice tactical combination, it is often because the relevant exchanges just happened to lie within its search boundary. The machine's horizon depends not only on the nominal depth of its full-width search but also on the nature of the quiescence analysis done at the terminal nodes. Programs typically search sequences of captures at the end nodes of the full-width tree and sometimes also extend the lookahead for certain kinds of checks and other threats. Also, some of the programs do not search all lines full-width to the same fixed depth. For example, Belle and Nuchess do not count checks as plies, so even a "5-ply" search may examine five checking moves by one side and the responses to them by the opponent. All of these factors influence a program's ability to calculate tactical variations accurately.

310

In this game, a crucial position arose after Belle's 27th move. Belle had calculated on its 26th move that Cray Blitz would play 28. Qe6xNb6 and Belle would then have mating threats that would force Blitz to sacrifice a queen for a rook. Belle expected to be slightly ahead after its 31st move. Belle completely missed the effectiveness for Blitz of 28. Bc1xh6. On the other side of the board, Cray Blitz also missed 28. Bc1xh6 and thought it was winning a whole piece after Qe6xNb6, failing to see Belle's threat. The game then went exactly as Belle had predicted through move 31 and both sides (especially Blitz) were surprised to find that Belle easily won the resulting queen vs rook and bishop ending. The reason that Cray Blitz did not perceive what was about to happen when it played 28. Qe6xNb6 is that it did "only" a 6-ply search and fell prey to the "horizon effect" produced by its own checks on moves 29 and 30 which delayed Black's mating threat and effectively pushed it past the 6-ply limit.

These two delaying moves, while not likely to confuse a human master, add 4 plies to the crucial variation and thus invalidated the accuracy of Blitz's 6-ply search. Belle, which does not count a checking move as a ply, suffered only a 2-ply delay in its search and was not so easily fooled. The importance of adding sophistication to the quiescence search is emphasized by submitting this position to Nuchess which has special heuristics for this aspect of the search. With a nominal 4-ply search which examined 29,411 nodes, Nuchess saw at move 28 what Blitz failed to see after processing 183,992 nodes. Nuchess, however, missed Bc1xh6 just like the other programs and evaluated the position after 31. . . . . Qd3xRf1 as a close game just as Belle had done.

The evaluative commentary for this game is provided by Mike Valvo. The notes by David Slate are based on information from the machines' records.

White Cray Blitz	Black Belle
1. e2–e4	e7–e5
2. Ng1–f3	Nb8–c6
3. Bf1–c4	Ng8–f6
4. Nf3–g5	d7–d5
5. e4xd5	Nc6–a5
6. Bc4–b5+	c7–c6
7. d5xc6	b7xc6
8. Qd1–f3	Ra8–b8
9. Bb5xc6+	Na5xBc6
10. Qf3xNc6+	Nf6–d7
11. d2–d3	Bf8–e7
12. Ng5–e4	

DS: Until now both machines were playing from their opening book. After 12. Ng5–e4, Black is out of its book and has to calculate on its own for the first time.

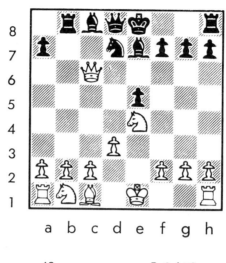

| 12. . . . . . | Bc8–b7? |

MV: This is the wrong move for Black. Instead, Belle should have played 12. . . . Rb8–b6!? and then 13. Qc6–a4, f7–f5, 14. Ne4–g3, O–O and Black has adequate compensation for the pawns with moves like Bc8–b7, Rb6–b4, and Be7–c5.

DS: After Black's unexpected move, White is now out of book also.

13. Qc6–a4	Qd8–c7
14. Nb1–c3	Bb7–c6
15. Qa4–c4	Qc7–c8
16. Nc3–d5	Bc6xNd5
17. Qc4xBd5	Qc8xc2
18. O–O	

MV: At this point, Black is simply a pawn down without any immediate prospects to win it back. Any attempt to play positionally on the weak white pawns is dealt with by either d3–d4 or f2–f4.

| 18. . . . . . | f7–f6? |

MV: Now Black cannot castle. Black would have done better to play a pawn down with 18. . . . Qc2–c8 and 19. . . . O–O.

DS: Belle's computations for this move took 9 minutes and involved a complete 7-ply search and the first move of the 8-ply search. It judged the situation as a 1.05 pawn advantage for Blitz and expected 19. . . . Ne4–c3.

19. f2–f4?

MV: White would be better to consolidate with 19. Bc1–e3. The text allows Black to castle.

DS: Blitz completed a 5-ply search and the first move of the 6-ply search. Its calculations took just 1 minute and produced an evaluation of 1.24 pawns in its favor with the expectation of 19. . . . Be7–c5+ leading to massive bloodshed on c5 and elsewhere.

19. . . . . .   Nd7–b6

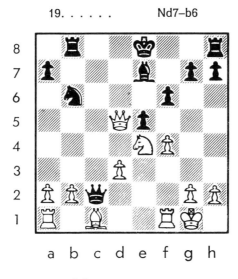

20. Qd5–a5

MV: The win has already slipped away. If 20. Qd5–b5+, then Nb6–d7, 21. Qb5–c4, Rb8–c8 and Black has some compensation.

20.	Qc2xd3
21. Qa5xa7	O–O
22. Qa7xBe7	

MV: If Ne4–g3 or Ne4–c3 instead, Black has winning chances: 22. . . . Be7–c5+, 23. Kg1–h1, e5–e4.

22.	Qd3xNe4
23. Qe7–e6+	Kg8–h8
24. f4xe5	f6xe5
25. Rf1xRf8+	

MV: White is already in trouble. Probably better to play 25. Bc1–g5, Qe4–d4+, 26. Kg1–h1, Qd4xb2 and White should survive.

25.	Rb8xRf8
26. h2–h3	Qe4–e1+

DS: Belle did an 8-ply search in 3½ minutes, judged the position as 0.21 pawns in its own favor, and predicted 27. Kg1–h2, h7–h6, 28. Qe6xNb6, Rf8–f1, 29. Qb6–d8+, Kh8–h7, 30. Qd8–d3+, e5–e4, 31. Qd3xRf1, Qe1xQf1.

27. Kg1–h2	h7–h6

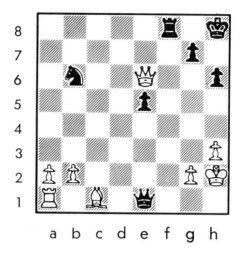

28. Qe6xNb6??

MV: White is totally lost after this move. Instead, 28. Bc1xh6!! forces at least a draw. For example, 28. . . . Qe1xRa1, 29. Qe6–g6, Rf8–g8, 30. Bh6–f4, Rg8–d8, 31. Bf4xe5, Rd8–d7 and White can draw with 32. Qg6–e8+ or attempt to win with 32. Qg6xNb6.

DS: In selecting this move, Blitz did a complete 5-ply search and the first move at the 6th ply. It evaluated the position as 4.11 pawns in its own favor and predicted 28. . . . Rf8–f2, 29. a2–a3, Qe1–f1, 30. Qb6–g6, Kh8–g8.

28.	Rf8–f1
29. Qb6–d8+	Kh8–h7
30. Qd8–d3+	e5–e4
31. Qd3xRf1	Qe1xQf1
32. a2–a3	e4–e3
33. Bc1xe3	

DS: Blitz perceives that the Bishop has to capture the pawn or the pawn will reach the eighth rank.

33.	Qf1xRa1
34. Be3–d4	h6–h5
35. Bd4–c3	g7–g5
36. Bc3–e5	Qa1–e1
37. Be5–c3	Qe1–f2
38. Kh2–h1	g5–g4
39. h3xg4	h5xg4
40. Kh1–h2	Qf2–h4+
41. Kh2–g1	g4–g3
42. Kg1–f1	Kh7–g6
43. Resigns	

(0–1)

References
and
bibliography

1. Abrahams, G. *Not Only Chess*. London: Allen & Unwin, 1974.

2. Adelson-Velskiy, G. M., Arlazarov, V. L., Bitman, A. R., Zhivotovskiy, A. A., and Uskov, A. V. Programming a computer to play chess. *Russian Math. Surveys*, 1970, **25,** 221–262.

3. Adelson-Zelskiy, G. M., Arlazarov, V. L., and Donskoy, M. V. Some methods of controlling the tree search in chess programs. *Artificial Intelligence*, 1975, **6,** 327–360.

4. Andric, D. Blitz blitz. *Chess Life & Review*, 1970, **25,** 308.

5. Atkin, L. R. CHESS 3.6: A chess-playing computer program. Master's thesis, Northwestern University, Evanston, Illinois, June, 1975.

6. Atkin, R. Multidimensional structure in the game of chess. *Int. J. Man-Machine Studies*, 1972, **4,** 341–362.

7. Baylor, G. W. A computer model of checkmating behaviour in chess. *Heuristic Processes in Thinking* (de Groot and Reitman, eds.), Moscow: Nauka, 1966.

8. Baylor, G. W. and Simon, H. A. A chess mating combinations program. *Proc. Spring Joint Computer Conference*, April, 1966, 431–447.

9. Bell, A. G. *Game Playing with Computers*. London: Allen & Unwin, 1972.

10. Berliner, H. J. A comment on improvement of chess-playing programs. *SIGART Newsletter*, 1974, **48,** 16.

11. Berliner, H. Some necessary conditions for a master chess program. *Proc. Third Intern. Joint Conference on Artificial Intelligence*, 1973, 77–85.

12. Berliner, H. Chess as problem solving: The development of a tactics analyzer. Unpublished doctoral thesis, Carnegie-Mellon University, 1974.

13. Bernstein, A. and Roberts, M. de V. Computer vs. chessplayer. *Scientific American*, 1958, **198,** 96–105.

14. Bernstein, A., Roberts, M. de V., Arbuckle, T., and Belsky, M. A chess-

playing program for the IBM 704 computer. *Proc. Western Joint Computer Conference*, 1958, **13,** 157–159.

15. Binet, A. *Psychologie des grands calculateurs et joueurs d'Echecs.* Paris: Hachette, 1894.

16. Binet, A. Mnemonic virtuosity: A study of chessplayers. *Genetic Psychology Monographs*, 1966, **74,** 127–162. [Translated by M. L. Simmell and S. B. Barren from *Revue des Deux Mondes*, 1893, **117,** 826–859.]

17. Botvinnik, M. Will computers get self-respect? *Sovietsky Sport*, 1975 (June 15).

18. Botvinnik, M. M. *Computers, Chess, and Long-range Planning.* New York: Springer-Verlag, 1970. [Translated by A. Brown.]

19. Carroll, C. M. *The Great Chess Automation.* New York: Dover, 1975.

20. Charness, Neil. Memory for chess positions: The effects of interference and input modality. Unpublished doctoral dissertation, Carnegie-Mellon University, May 1974.

21. Chase, W. G., and Clark, H. H. Mental operations in the comparison of sentences and pictures. *Cognition in Learning and Memory* (L. G. Gregg, ed.). New York: John Wiley, 1972.

22. Chase, W. G. and Simon, H. A. The mind's eye in chess. *Visual Information Processing* (W. G. Chase, ed.). New York: Academic Press, 1973.

23. Chase, W. G. and Simon, H. A. Perception in chess. *Cognitive Psychology*, 1973, **4,** 55–81.

24. *Chess Informant*, Vol. 15. Belgrade: FIDE, 1973, p. 50.

25. *Chess Life & Review*, 1975, **30,** 506, 652.

26. Church, R. M. Strategies of pattern transformation. Paper presented at the annual meeting of the Psychonomics Society. Boston, 1974.

27. Clarke, M. Some ideas for a chess compiler. *Artificial and Human Thinking* (Elithorn and Jones, eds.). Amsterdam: Elsevier, 1973.

28. Cleveland, A. A. The psychology of chess and of learning to play it. *American Journal of Psychology*, 1907, **18,** 269–308.

29. Collins, J. W. *My Seven Chess Prodigies.* New York: Simon and Schuster, 1974.

30. de Groot, A. D. Perception and memory versus thought: Some old ideas and recent findings. *Problem Solving: Research, Method, and Theory* (B. Kleinmuntz, ed.). New York: John Wiley, 1966.

31. de Groot, A. D. *Thought and Choice in Chess.* The Hague: Mouton, 1965.

32. de Groot, A. D. and Jongman, R. W. Heuristics in perceptual processes. International Congress of Psychology, Moscow, August 1966.

33. Djakow, I. N., Petrowski, N. W., and Rudik, P. A. *Psychologie des Schachspiels.* Berlin: Walter de Gruyter, 1927.

34. Edwards, D. J. and Hart, T. P. The α-β heuristic. *Artificial Intelligence Memo No. 30* (Revised), MIT Research Laboratory of Electronics and Computation Center, Cambridge, Massachusetts, 1963.

35. Elithorn, A. and Telford, A. Game and problem structure in relation to the study of human and artificial intelligence. *Nature*, 1970, **227,** 1205–1210.

36. Elo, A. E. *The USCF Rating System.* U.S. Chess Federation Publication,

1966. Described also in: Harkness, K. *Official Chess Handbook*, New York: David McKay, 1967, 183–205.

37. Euwe, M. Computers and chess. *The Encyclopedia of Chess* (A. Sunnucks, ed.). New York: St. Martin's Press, 1970.

38. Evans, L., Gligoric, S., Hort, V., Keres, P., Larsen, B., Petrosian, T., and Portisch, L. *How to Open a Chess Game*. New York: RHM Press, 1974.

39. Evans, L., and Korn, W. *Modern Chess Openings*, 10th Ed. New York: Pitman, 1965.

40. Feigenbaum, E. and Feldman, J. (eds.), *Computers and Thought*. New York: McGraw-Hill, 1967.

41. Fine, R. *The Ideas Behind the Chess Openings*. New York: David McKay, 1943.

42. Fine, R. *The Psychology of the Chessplayer*. New York: Dover, 1967.

43. Fine, R. The psychology of blindfold chess: An introspective account. *Acta Psychologica*, 1965, **24**, 352–370.

44. Fine, R. *Basic Chess Endings*. Philadelphia: David McKay, 1941.

45. Fuller, S., Gaschnig, T., and Gillogly, J. *Analysis of the Alpha-Beta Pruning Algorithm*, Technical report, Department of Computer Science, Carnegie-Mellon University, July, 1973, 51pp.

46. Gillogly, J. J. The technology chess program. *Artificial Intelligence*, 1972, **3**, 145–163.

47. Good, I. J. A five year plan for automatic chess. *Machine Intelligence II*, (Meltzer and Michie, eds.). Edinburgh: University of Edinburgh Press, 1966.

48. Greenblatt, R. D., Eastlake III, D. E., and Crocker, S. D. The Greenblatt chess program. *Proc. AFIPS Fall Joint Computer Conference*, 1967, **31**, 801–810.

49. Hammond, K. R. Computer graphics as an aid to learning. *Science*, 1971, **172**, 903–908.

50. Harkness, K. and Batell, J. S. This made chess history. *Chess Review*, 1947 Feb.–Nov. (monthly column).

51. Harris, L. R. The heuristic search under conditions of error. *Artificial Intelligence*, 1974, **5**, 217.

52. Harris, L. R. The heuristic search and the game of chess. *Proc. Fourth Intern. Joint Conference on Artificial Intelligence*, 1975.

53. Hart, P., Nilsson, N., and Raphael, B. A formal basis for the heuristic determination of minimum cost paths. *IEEE*, 1968, **4**, 100–107.

54. Hearst, E. Psychology across the chessboard. *Psychology Today*, 1967 (June), 28–37.

55. Hubermann, B. J. A program to play chess end games. *Stanford Technical Memo CS 106*, 1968, Computer Science Department, Stanford University.

56. Hunt, E. B. *Artificial Intelligence*. New York: Academic Press, 1975.

57. James, W. *The Principles of Psychology*, Vol. 2. New York: Henry Holt & Co., 1890. (Republished by Dover Publications, 1950.)

58. Kister, J., Stein, P., Ulam, S., Walden, W., and Wells, M. Experiments in chess. *Journal of the Association for Computing Machinery*, 1957, **4**, 174–177.

59. Knuth, D. E. and Moore, R. An analysis of alpha-beta pruning. *Artificial Intelligence*, 1975, **6,** 293–326.

60. Kotov, A. *Think Like a Grandmaster*. Dallas: Chess Digest, 1971. [Translated by B. Cafferty.]

61. Kozdrowicki, E. W. and Cooper, D. W. Coko III: The Cooper–Koz chess program. *Communications of the ACM*, 1973, **16,** 411–427.

62. Kozdrowicki, E. W. and Cooper, D. W. When will a computer be world chess champion? *Computer Decisions*, 1974 (Aug.), 28–32.

63. Kozdrowicki, E., Licwinko, J. S., and Cooper, D. W. Algorithms for a minimal chessplayer: A blitz player. *Inter. J. Man–Machine Studies*, 1971, 141–165.

64. Krogius, N. V. *Chess Psychology*. Chicago: Alfred Kalnajs, 1972.

65. Leedy, C. and Dubeck, L. Physiological changes during tournament chess. *Chess Life and Review*, 1971, **26,** 708.

66. Leiber, F. The 64-square madhouse. In *The if Reader of Science Fiction*. New York: Doubleday, 1966.

67. Levy, D. Computer chess—past, present and future. *Chess Life & Review*, 1973, **28,** 723–726.

68. Levy, D. *Sacrifices in the Sicilian*. New York: David McKay, 1974.

69. Lighthill, J. *Artificial Intelligence: A General Survey*. London, England: Science Research Council, 1972.

70. Lorayne, H. and Lucas, J. *The Memory Book*. New York: Ballantine Books, 1975.

71. Luce, R. D. and Raiffa, H. *Games and Decisions*. New York: Wiley, 1957.

72. Miller, G. A. The magical number seven, plus or minus two. *Psychological Review*, 1956, **63,** 81–97.

73. Newborn, M. *Computer Chess*. New York: Academic Press, 1975.

74. Newell, A., Shaw, J., and Simon, H. Chess-playing programs and the problem of complexity. *IBM J. Res. Develop.*, 1958, **2,** 320–335.

75. Newell, A., and Simon, H. A. *Human Problem Solving*. Englewood Cliffs, N.J.: Prentice-Hall, 1972.

76. Newell, A. and Simon, H. An example of human chess play in the light of chess-playing programs. *Progress in Biocybernetics* (Weiner and Schade, eds.). Amsterdam: Elsevier, 1965.

77. Nilsson, N. *Problem Solving Methods in Artificial Intelligence*. New York: McGraw-Hill, 1971.

78. Polya, G. *How to Solve It*. Princeton: Princeton University Press, 1945.

79. Scott, J. J. A chess playing program *Machine Intelligence IV* (Meltzer and Michie, eds.). Edinburgh: University of Edinburgh Press, 1969.

80. Scurrah, M. and Wagner, D. A. Cognitive model of problem solving in chess. *Science*, 1970, **169,** 290–291.

81. Shannon, C. E. Programming a computer for playing chess *Philosophical Magazine*, 1950, **41,** 256–275.

82. Shannon, C. E. Programming a computer to play chess. *Scientific American*, February, 1950, 48–51.

83. Simon, H. A. How big is a chunk? *Science*, 1974, **183,** 482–488.

84. Simon, H. A. and Chase, W. G. Skill in chess. *American Scientist*, 1973, **61**, 394–403.

85. Simon, H. A. and Gilmartin, K. A simulation of memory for chess positions. *Cognitive Psychology*, 1973, **5**, 29–46.

86. Simon, H. A. and Newell, A. Heuristic problem solving: The next advance in operations research. *Operations Research*, 1958, **6**, 1–10.

87. Simon, H. and Simon, P. Trial and error search in solving difficult problems: Evidence from the game of chess. *Behavioral Science*, 1972, **2**, 425–429.

88. Slagle, J. R. *Artificial Intelligence: The Heuristic Programming Approach*. New York: McGraw-Hill, 1971.

89. Slagle, J. and Dixon, J. Experiments with some programs which search game trees. *Journal of the Association for Computing Machinery*, 1969, **16**, 189–207.

90. Sternberg, S. High-speed scanning in human memory. *Science*, 1966, **153**, 652–654.

91. Tan, S. T. Representation of knowledge for very simple pawn endings in chess. Unpublished doctoral thesis, Department of Machine Intelligence, University of Edinburgh, 1972.

92. Tikhomirov, O. K. and Poznyanskaya, E. D. An investigation of visual search as a means of analyzing heuristics. *Soviet Psychology*, 1966, **5**, 2–15. [Translated from *Voprosy Psikhologii*, **2**, 39–53.]

93. Tikhomirov, O. K. and Vinogradov, Yu. E. Emotions in the heuristic function. *Soviet Psychology*, 1970, **8**, 198–223.

94. Tiller, T. (ed.) *Chess Treasury of the Air*. Baltimore, Maryland: Penguin Books, 1966.

95. Turing, A. M. Computing machinery and intelligence. *Mind*, 1950, **59**, 433–460.

96. Turing, A. Digital computers applied to games. *Faster than Thought: A Symposium on Digital Computing Machines* (B. V. Bowden, ed.). London: Pitman, 1953.

97. von Neuman, J. and Morgenstern, O. *Theory of Games and Economic Behavior*. Princeton, N.J.: Princeton University Press, 1944.

98. Wagner, D. A. and Scurrah, M. J. *Cognitive Psychology*, 1971, **2**, 454–478.

99. Wickelgren, W. *How to Solve Problems*. San Francisco: W. H. Freeman, 1974.

100. Winograd, T. Understanding natural language. *Cognitive Psychology*, 1972, **3**, 1–191.

101. Zobrist, A. L. and Carlson, F. R., Jr. An advice-taking chess computer. *Scientific American*, 1973, **228**, 92–105.

102. Zweig, S. *The Royal Game*. New York: Viking Press, 1944.

103. Averbakh, Y. and Maizelis, I. *Pawn Endings*. London: B. T. Batsford, 1974. [First published in Russian.]

104. Michie, D. A theory of evaluative comments in chess. Technical report, CS74015-R, Virginia Polytechnic Institute and State University, Blacksburg, Virginia, 1974.

105. Adelson-Velskiy, G. M., Arlazarov, V. L., and Donskoy, M. V. Algorithms of adaptive search. In Elcock, E. W., and Michie, D. (Eds.), *Machine Intelligence 9*. New York: Wiley, 1979, 373–384.

106. Arlazarov, V. L. and Futer, A. L. Computer analysis of a Rook end-game. In Elcock, E. W. and Michie, D. (Eds.), *Machine Intelligence 9*. New York: Wiley, 1979, 361–371.

107. Ashby, W. R. Can a mechanical chess player outplay its designer? *British Journal of Philosophy of Science*, 1952, **3**, 44–57.

108. Atkin, R. H. and Witten, I. H. A multidimensional approach to positional chess. *International Journal of Man-Machine Studies*, 1975, **7**, 727–750.

109. Atkin, R. H., Hartston, W., and Witten, I. H. Fred CHAMP, positional-chess analyst. *International Journal of Man-Machine Studies*, 1976, **8**, 517–529.

110. Atkin, R. H. Positional play in chess by computer. In Clarke, M. R. B. (Ed.), *Advances in Computer Chess 1*. Edinburgh: Edinburgh University Press, 1977, 60–73.

111. Baudet, G. M. On the branching factor of the alpha–beta pruning algorithm. *Artificial Intelligence*, 1978, **10**, 173–199.

112. Baudet, G. M. The design and analysis of algorithms for asynchronous multiprocessors. Ph.D. Thesis, Computer Science Dept., Carnegie Mellon University, 1978.

113. Bellman, R. Stratification and control of large systems with applications to chess and checkers. *Information Sciences*, 1968, **1**, 7–21.

114. Bell, A. G. and Jacobi, N. How to read, make, and store chess moves. *Computer Journal*, 1979, **22**, 71–75.

115. Berliner, H. J. A representation and some mechanisms for a problem solving chess program. In Clarke, M. R. B. (Ed.), *Advances in Computer Chess 1*. Edinburgh: Edinburgh University Press, 1977, 7–29.

116. Berliner, H. J. On the use of domain-independent description in tree searching. In Jones (Ed.), *Perspectives in Computer Science*. New York: Academic Press, 1977.

117. Berliner, H. J. A chronology of computer chess and its literature. *Artificial Intelligence*, 1978, **10**, 201–204.

118. Berliner, H. J. Computer Chess. *Nature*, 1978, **274**, 745–748.

119. Berliner, H. J. The B* tree search algorithm: A best-first proof procedure. *Artificial Intelligence*, 1979, **12**, 23–40.

120. Birmingham, J. A. and Kent, P. Tree-searching and tree-pruning techniques. In Clarke, M. R. B. (Ed.), *Advances in Computer Chess 1*. Edinburgh: Edinburgh University Press, 1977, 89–107.

121. Bramer, M. A. Representation of knowledge for chess endgames: towards a self-improving system. Ph.D. Thesis, Open University, Milton Keynes, 1977.

122. Bramer, M. A. Representing pattern-knowledge for chess endgames: an optimal algorithm for King and Pawn against King. In Clarke, M. R. B. (Ed.), *Advances in Computer Chess 2*. Edinburgh: Edinburgh University Press, 1980.

123. Bramer, M. A. and Clarke, M. R. B. A model for the representation of pattern-knowledge for the endgame in chess. *International Journal of Man-Machine Studies*, 1979, **11**, 635–649.

124. Bratko, I. and Michie, D. A representation for pattern-knowledge in chess endgames. In Clarke, M. R. B. (Ed.), *Advances in Computer Chess 2*. Edinburgh: Edinburgh University Press, 1980.

125. Bratko, I., Kopec, D., and Michie, D. Pattern-based representation of chess end-game knowledge. *Computer Journal*, 1978, **21,** 149–153.

126. Bratko, I. and Niblett, T. Conjectures and refutations in a framework for chess endgame knowledge. In Michie, D. (Ed.), *Expert Systems in the Micro-electronic Age*. Edinburgh: Edinburgh University Press, 1979, 83–101.

127. Clarke, M. R. B. A quantitative study of King and Pawn against King. In Clarke, M. R. B. (Ed.), *Advances in Computer Chess 1*. Edinburgh: Edinburgh University Press, 1977, 108–118.

128. Clarke, M. R. B. (Ed.) *Advances in Computer Chess 1*. Edinburgh: Edinburgh University Press, 1977.

129. Clarke, M. R. B. (Ed.) *Advances in Computer Chess 2*. Edinburgh: Edinburgh University Press, 1980.

130. Ewart, B. *Chess: Man vs. Machine*. A. S. Barnes, 1980.

131. Fishburn, J. and Finkel, R. Parallel alpha–beta search on Arachne. Technical Report 394, University of Wisconsin–Madison, 1980.

132. Frey, P. W. and Atkin, L. R. Creating a Chess Player, *Byte*, Oct. 1978, 182–191, Nov. 1978, 162–181, Dec. 1978, 140–157, Jan. 1979, 126–145.

133. Gillogly, J. J. Games. *Encyclopedia of Computer Science and Technology*, 1977, **8,** 392–408.

134. Haldane, J. B. S. The mechanical chess-player. *British Journal of the Philosophy of Science*, 1952, **3,** 189–191.

135. Harding, T. D. *The Chess Computer Book*. New York: Pergamon Press, 1982.

136. Hayes, J. E. and Levy, D. N. L. *The World Computer Chess Championship*. Edinburgh: Edinburgh University Press, 1976.

137. Horowitz, I. A. and Mott-Smith, G. *Point Count Chess*. Allen and Unwin, 1973.

138. Jones, R. D. The design and implementation of a chess playing program for the IBM 360. M.Sc. Thesis, University of Toronto, 1971.

139. Jones, M. Parallel search of chess game trees. M.Sc. Thesis, School of Computer Science, McGill University, 1978.

140. Kopec, D. and Niblet, T. How hard is the play of the King-Rook-King-Knight ending? In Clarke, M. R. B. (Ed.), *Advances in Computer Chess 2*. Edinburgh: Edinburgh University Press, 1980, 57–81.

141. Levy, D. N. L. *Computer Chess 1977: World Computer Chess Championship, US Computer Chess Championship*. Rockville, MD: Computer Science Press, 1978.

142. Levy, D. N. L. *1975 U.S. Computer Chess Championship*. Rockville, MD: Computer Science Press, 1976.

143. Levy D. N. L. *1976 U.S. Computer Chess Championship*. Rockville, MD: Computer Science Press, 1977.

144. Levy, D. N. L. The robots are coming: Or are they? *Chess Life and Review*, May 1976, 250–260.

145. Levy, D. N. L. *Chess and Computers*. Batsford Press, 1976.

146. Levy, D. and Newborn, M. *More Chess and Computers*. Rockville, MD: Computer Science Press, 1981.

147. Marsland, T. A., Campbell, M. S., and Rivera, A. L. Parallel search of game trees. Technical Report TR80-7, Department of Computing Science, University of Alberta, 1980.

148. Messerschmidt, H. J. Parallel programming for a chess endgame database. *Software—Practice and Experience*, 1980, **10**, 475–487.

149. Michalski, R. and Negri, P. An experiment on inductive learning in chess and games. In Elcock and Michie (Eds.), *Machine Intelligence 8*. Edinburgh: Edinburgh University Press, 1977, 175–192.

150. Michie, D. King and Rook against King: Historical background and a problem on the infinite board. In Clarke, M. (Ed.), *Advances in Computer Chess 1*. Edinburgh: Edinburgh University Press, 1977, 30–59.

151. Michie, D. A theory of advice. In Elcock and Michie (Eds.), *Machine Intelligence 8*. Edinburgh: Edinburgh University Press, 1977, 151–168.

152. Michie, D. A prototype knowledge refinery. In Clarke, M. (Ed.), *Advances in Computer Chess 2*. Edinburgh: Edinburgh University Press, 1980.

153. Moussouris, J., Holloway, J., and Greenblatt, R. CHEOPS: A chess-oriented processing system. In Elcock and Michie (Eds.), *Machine Intelligence 9*. New York: Wiley, 1979, 351–360.

154. Negri, P. Inductive learning in a hierarchical model for representing knowledge in chess end games. In Elcock and Michie (Eds.), *Machine Intelligence 8*. Edinburgh: Edinburgh University Press, 1977, 193–204.

155. Newborn, M. M. Computer chess: recent progress and future expectations. In Moneta, J. (Ed.), *Information Technology*. Amsterdam: North Holland, 1978.

156. Newborn, M. M. The efficiency of the alpha–beta search on trees with branch-dependent terminal node scores. *Artificial Intelligence*, 1977, **8**, 137–153.

157. Newborn, M. M. Recent progress in computer chess. In Yovits, M. (Ed.), *Advances in Computers, Vol. 18*. New York: Academic Press, 1979, 59–117.

158. Pearl, J. Asymptotic properties of minimax trees and game searching procedures. *Artificial Intelligence*, 1980, **14**, 113–138.

159. Piasetski, L. An evaluation function for simple King and Pawn endings. M.Sc. Thesis, McGill University, 1976.

160. Pitrat, J. A program for learning to play chess. In Chen, C. H. (Ed.), *Pattern Recognition and Artificial Intelligence*. New York: Academic Press, 1976, 399–419.

161. Pitrat, J. A chess combination program which uses plans. *Artificial Intelligence*, 1977, **8**, 275–321.

162. Pitrat, J. The behaviour of a chess combination program using plans. In Clarke, M. (Ed.), *Advances in Computer Chess 2*. Edinburgh: Edinburgh University Press, 1980, 110–121.

163. Proskurowski, W. Ordering method to accelerate the solution of mate-in-two chess problems by computer. *Computer Journal*, 1974, **17**, 80–81.

164. Reinfeld, F. *Win At Chess*. New York: Dover Books, 1958.

165. Soule, S. and Marsland, T. A. Canadian computer-chess tournament. *SIGART*, 1975, **54**, 12–13.

166. Spracklen, D. and Spracklen, K. SARGON: A Computer chess program. Rochelle Park, NJ: Hayden Book Co., 1978.

167. Spracklen, K. and Spracklen, D. First steps in computer chess programming. *Byte*, Oct. 1978, 86–98.

168. Spracklen, D. and Spracklen, K. An exchange evaluator for computer chess. *Byte*, Nov. 1978, 16–28.

169. Tan, S. T. Describing pawn structures. In Clarke, M. (Ed.), *Advances in Computer Chess 1*. New York: Edinburgh University Press, 1977, 74–88.

170. Waterman, D. A. Generalization learning techniques for automating the learning of heuristics. *Artificial Intelligence*, 1970, **1,** 121–170.

171. Wilkins, D. E. Using patterns and plans to solve problems and control search. AIM-329, Computer Science Dept., Stanford University, 1979.

172. Wilkins, D. E. Using patterns and plans in chess. *Artificial Intelligence,* 1980, **14,** 165–203.

173. Wilkins, D. E. Using knowledge to control tree searching. *Artificial Intelligence*, 1982, **18,** 1–51.

174. Zobrist, A. L. A hashing method with applications for game playing. Technical Report 88, Computer Science Dept., University of Wisconsin–Madison, 1970.

Subject index

Texts and Monographs in Computer Science

Springer Books on Professional Computing

Computer Confidence: A Human Approach to Computers
Bruce D. Sanders. viii, 90 pages. 23 figures. 1984. ISBN 0-387-90917-6

The Unix System Guidebook: An Introductory Guide for Serious Users
Peter P. Sylvester. xi, 207 pages. 6 figures. 1984. ISBN 0-387-90906-0

The American Pascal Standard: With Annotations
Henry Ledgard. vii, 97 pages. 1984. ISBN 0-387-91248-7